FINDING MYSELF:

ESSAYS ON

RACE, POLITICS AND CULTURE

Also by Clem Seecharan

Indo-West Indian Cricket (with Frank Birbalsingh)
India and the Shaping of the Indo-Guyanese Imagination 1890s-1920s
'Tiger in the Stars': The Anatomy of Indian Achievement in British Guiana 1919-1929
Bechu: 'Bound Coolie' Radical in British Guiana 1894-1901
Joseph Ruhomon's India: The Progress of her People at Home and Abroad and how those in British Guiana may Improve Themselves
Sweetening 'Bitter Sugar': Jock Campbell, the Booker Reformer in British Guiana 1934-1966
Muscular Learning: Cricket and Education in the Making of the British West Indies at the End of the 19th Century
From Ranji to Rohan: Cricket and Indian Identity in Colonial Guyana 1890s-1960s
Mother India's Shadow over El Dorado: Indo-Guyanese Politics and Identity 1890s-1930s

CLEM SEECHARAN

FINDING MYSELF:

ESSAYS ON

RACE, POLITICS AND CULTURE

PEEPAL TREE

First published in Great Britain in 2015
Peepal Tree Press Ltd
17 King's Avenue
Leeds LS6 1QS
England

ISBN13: 9781845232247 4

Supported using public funding by
ARTS COUNCIL
ENGLAND

To my friend, David de Caires (1937-2008)
thinker and publisher
for whom defending the life of the mind and
the 'open word' was worth any personal sacrifice

Me (left) and my brother Ken, 1957

CONTENTS

Part I: Introduction

"Tiger in the Stars": Ian McDonald and my Retrieval of Self-Belief 11

Part II: In Search of Me

1. Indians in Guyana: An Overview 59

2. India's Awakening and the Imagining of the 'East Indian Nation' in British Guiana 87

3. Sugar in my Blood 102

4. *Girmitiyas* and my Discovery of India 114

5. In Sir Vidia's Shadow, Out of Historical Darkness 140

Part III: Locating Cheddi Jagan

6. The Shape of the Passion: The Historical Context of Martin Carter's Poetry of Protest, 1951-64 163

7. Balram Singh Rai's Anticommunism and Cultural Idealism 189

8. Whose Freedom at Midnight? Machinations towards Guyana's Independence, May 1966 204

9. The Anatomy of Cheddi Jagan's Marxism 225

Part IV: Miscellaneous Pieces: Rodney, James and Madray

10. Culture and Ethnicity in Post-Emancipation Guyana 253

11. 'Helping Lions Learn to Paint': Walter Rodney (1942-80) 263

12. Empire and Family in the Shaping of a West Indian Intellectual: The Young C.L.R. James, a Preliminary Assessment 271

13. Interview with Ivan Madray, the Forgotten Cricketer: 'Da Coolie Ga Mek Abi Hunt Ledda' 284

Index 326

ACKNOWLEDGEMENTS

Versions of these revised essays first appeared in the following places:

'Indians in Guyana: An Overview' in *The Encyclopedia of the Indian Diaspora* (Singapore: National University of Singapore, 2006); 'India's Awakening' in Rita Christian and Judith Misrahi-Barak (eds), *India and the Diasporic Imagination* (Les Carnets du Cerpac: Presses Universitaires de la Mediterranee, 2011); 'Sugar in my Blood' was drawn from *Sweetening 'Bitter Sugar': Jock Campbell, the Booker Reformer in British Guiana 1934-1966* (Jamaica: Ian Randle Publishers, 2005); 'Girmitiyas and my Discovery of India' from the introductory essay to the second edition of Brij Lal's, *Girmitiyas: The Origins of the Fiji Indians*, (Suva, Fiji: Fiji Institute of Applied Studies, 2004); 'In Sir Vidia's Shadow: Out of Historical Darkness', from *The Arts Journal* (Guyana), Vol. 1, No. 1, 2004; 'The Shape of the Passion: The Historical Context of Martin Carter's Poetry of Protest', from *All Are Involved: The Art of Martin Carter*, Ed. Stewart Brown (Leeds: Peepal Tree Press, 2000); 'Balram Singh Rai's Anticommunism' was drawn from the introductory chapter of Baytoram Ramharack's *Against the Grain: Balram Singh Rai and the Politics of Guyana* (Trinidad: Chakra, 2005); 'Whose Freedom at Midnight?' appeared in *The Round Table*, Vol. 97, Issue 398 (October, 2008), and was republished in R. Holland, S. Williams and T. Barringer (eds.), *The Iconography of Independence: 'Freedoms at Midnight'* (London: Routledge, 2009); 'The Anatomy of Cheddi Jagan's Marxism' appeared in John La Guerre and Anne-Marie Bissessar (eds), *From Calcutta to Caroni: The Indian Diaspora* (St Augustine, Trinidad: School of Continuing Studies, University of the West Indies, 2006); 'Culture and Ethnicity in Post-Emancipation Guyana' in *Slavery & Abolition*, Vol 18, No. 2, Aug. 1977; 'Helping Lions Learn to Paint' is from the introductory essay to Eusi Kwayana, *Walter Rodney: His Last Days and Campaigns* (Birmingham: R. Ferdinand-Lalljie, 2010); 'Empire and Family in the Shaping of a West Indian Intellectual' from *Moving Worlds*, Vol. 11, No. 1 (2011); 'Interview with Ivan Madray, the Forgotten Cricketer' from Frank Birbalsingh and Clem Seecharan, *Indo-West Indian Cricket* (London: Hansib, 1988).

I am grateful I am grateful to Jeremy Poynting for publishing this book and for his compilation of a comprehensive index; Hannah Bannister for the cover design; and my wife Chris and my Aunt Sheila for their tireless support over many decades. To four of my great friends and mentors I wish to express my thanks for their inspiration and magnanimity: Ambassador David Dabydeen, Professor Denis Judd, Dr Ian McDonald and Dr Tulsi Singh. Finally, I must acknowledge the immense pleasure a few other friends have given me: Rita Christian, Peter Fraser, Phyllis Knight (1929-2014), Jonathan Moore and Andrew Wright. I argue with them, sometimes raucously (fortified by the red nectar), as we endeavour to comprehend the enigma that is humankind.

PART I: INTRODUCTION

Ian and Mary McDonald, c. 1984, shortly before I began corresponding with him.

'TIGER IN THE STARS': IAN MCDONALD AND MY RETRIEVAL OF SELF-BELIEF

I: A STAR BY WHICH TO STEER

This is the right time to assess what Ian McDonald, the Guyanese poet, writer, broadcaster and business executive means to me. This collection of essays, like much of what I have written over the last twenty-five years, owes much to his example and inspiration. Born in Trinidad in 1933, he moved to British Guiana in 1955, after graduating from Cambridge. So Ian had been living there for thirty years when, in early 1985, I felt impelled to write to him. I have, over many years, read scores of his pieces on history, poetry, literature, philosophy, economics, sugar, biography, love and falling in love, reading, the legacy of great writing (the magic of words in shaping thought), and the beauty of being alive. I realised, gradually, that I had encountered a remarkably subtle and discerning mind – one of the foremost intellectuals of our region. It wasn't just the diversity and richness of the content or the facility for deploying authoritative quotes to enhance a vital point or clinch an argument by which I was impressed; I was also drawn to the compelling, elegant poetry of the prose, the fresh clarity of the style – so easy on the mind but profound in what it conveys. Here is an example taken from one of the more than a thousand pieces he wrote, over twenty years, for the *Stabroek News* (founded by his friend, David de Caires [1937-2008] in 1986, to whom this book is dedicated): 'Walking in our garden until night finally obscured the glorious setting of the sun, my wife showed me through the branches the crescent of the moon riding in the black velvet of the night with a star close by like a spark from a silver fire. There are such times when life is so inexpressibly beautiful that tears come to the eyes before you can help yourself'.

But intimations of an underlying darkness, stunting body and mind in our shared Guyana were also present in the writing. There was the humanity that allowed one to empathise with the creeping diminution of spirit that could claim the most resilient and seemingly unconquerable, a recognition of how impotent we were to elude the sticky web of received dogmas and certainties, without which millennial visions wither fast. But McDonald's pieces were also crafted from an amazing optimism that seemed to mock the futility of the derelict Guyana of the early 1980s. He saw the trajectory of decline early, in his poem, 'State of the Nation', written, I believe, in the early to mid-1970s:

Affairs in the young Republic do not go well.
Problems weigh like stones on every man.
In everyone's heart there is growing doubt.
The most placid have begun to grumble:
The playing children notice the unusual scowls.
In the rumshops there is moody silence with bursts of anger,
And the churches are filled with arid sermons.
The nation seems to trudge a weary road:
On all sides ardour is withdrawn.
......
The people are a flame, not easily put out,
Unless you raze wide swathes around their rights.
What has happened? Why are knives pulled in the streets?
There is not much time, that is generally recognised.[1]

He was right. The regime would continually subtract from the democratic legacy that we had all struggled for (so-called bourgeois democracy), and tenaciously sought to protect, in the former British West Indies. The worst years of Forbes Burnham's Guyana were still to come, in the early 1980s. The maximum leader had embarked on a grand experiment from around 1970, pontificating grandiloquently on his vision of creating the world's first Co-operative Socialist Republic – a narcissistic dream that became a nightmare. Like his arch-enemy, Cheddi Jagan, and several Guyanese politicians and intellectuals, Forbes was a fantasist. He was bent on promoting his own vision of Utopia: a version of El Dorado that required negating colonial achievements, even the best of them, and remaking history as a narrative that was destined to culminate in his messianic journey to nowhere. By the early 1980s, Burnham's world had degenerated into squalor and massive deprivation: shortages of virtually every food item, including wheaten flour and dal (indispensable to Indian cuisine), which he banned, deeming them superfluous to indigenous tastes – they were extravagant indulgences: a colonial hangover.[2] The mind, too, was denuded of nutriment in a land where three or four daily newspapers had been the norm during the colonial period, for the great leader had severely restricted access to newsprint. Opposition parties or unyielding religious organisations could ventilate their anger at the consuming nullity only through single-page or stapled stencilled newssheets. Very few books of worth were imported; hardly any were published locally. I recalled buying, from a Government store, a copy of Gaddafi's *Green Book*, which I never did read but have kept until today – a testament to the times, I suppose. Burnham's failed experiment, which had been partially supported by Jagan, disciple of the Russian vision of the promised-land, had yielded a wasteland, the best educated, most skilled, or simply those with relatives in North America having fled overseas: whole villages, in some cases.

I returned to Guyana briefly in mid-1982 to do research, but involuntarily spent four years. I felt trapped. I had lost my way. Having started a PhD at the University of the West Indies in Trinidad, I was forced to drop out when they informed me belatedly that, as a Guyanese (a pariah at the time throughout the region), I was not entitled to the concessionary fees paid by students from Anglophone Caribbean countries, such as Jamaica and Barbados, or even Canada or Australia, which provided grants to the institution. Guyana, with its own impoverished university was not contributing to the running of UWI. I endeavoured to pursue some research in Georgetown on aspects of Indo-Guyanese history, but my focus and will had deserted me. The abrupt severing of all institutional connections, with its framework for academic guidance and periodic monitoring, affected me badly. I began drinking in rumshops with all manner of people (very enriching, in retrospect), frequenting whore houses (not primarily for sex), and, when I felt like it, assisting my father minding his cattle. I was really living off him (of which I was ashamed), although I did work for a short time, in a fashion, at the University of Guyana. Still, with a strange intensity, I was deeply immersed in my reading – just about any old book I could get my hands on, for new books were impossible to access: history, literature, cricket, politics and philosophy. I asked around and borrowed books from everybody, for I had exhausted the sad, derelict library in New Amsterdam. Yet I was drifting. Politics had become boring, as every political group, in this land of El Dorado, imagined that it possessed the genuine Marxist legacy that was the key to the real utopia: 'history and time are on our side!' (Cheddi Jagan). It had also become dangerous. Most were afraid to speak, to challenge the ruling dogmas that crippled the intellect. This had bred a national paralysis. Here is another of McDonald's poems from the 1980s, appropriately titled: 'Caged'.

> The stroke stuns him into just a stare:
> Mouth screams without a scream being there.
> Neck-muscles tighten, throat-apple thrums.
> Plucks with fingers at his lips and tongue
> To rip out songs or words or anything,
> He strains and sweats to say a single word.
> Paradise would be to let out half a cry:
> Nothing comes; his eyes rage.
> Think of birds that can no longer fly:
> His skull is like a bolted cage,
> No opening anywhere.
> The slightest motion, a shivering in the cheek
> Like wings in flutter before flight.
> No further movement comes:

> Inside there alone, alone, alone, alone,
> Wings nailed right through to bone.[3]

'Think of birds that can no longer fly… Wings nailed right through to bone'! That's how I felt. Then, one morning in early 1985, I tuned in to 'Viewpoint', a five-minute commentary on the Government-owned radio (GBC), generally closed to any views that challenged the 'paramountcy' of the ruling party, which had shamelessly rigged several so-called general elections in Guyana. The speaker's voice was beautifully modulated, in a refined accent I could not place; it was made for radio – in the vigorously smooth and seductive manner of Tony Cozier (the great Barbadian cricket commentator) – easy on the ear and enthralling to the mind. It was Ian McDonald. I was so moved by what he had said in those five minutes that I spent several hours meditating on the gist of it – for it stayed with me. His talk had to do with the sustaining vision of Indians in Guyana, of specific relevance to my PhD thesis that had run aground. I decided to write to him. Exhilaration, passion, anger, frustration, an impotent rage, and perhaps a redeeming intellectual grasp that could not be put out all melded somehow in articulating my gratitude for his sagacious comments (sadly the letter is lost). I felt an immediate kinship with this man, whom I had never seen (Guyana had no television). I thought he had peered into my soul and found an essence that was floundering yet eminently deserving of some kind of resuscitation.

I don't know how often in the transformation of people who lose their way and somehow manage to step back from the void – retrieving ambition and self-belief – a timely, possibly dramatic, flash of illumination is essential. How much is owed to a triggering by someone's inadvertent, empathetic words that opened sealed doors to self-discovery: the resurrection of hope and a sense of possibilities? I speak only for myself: Ian McDonald was that man. And while I will cite several excerpts from his writing and lines from his poems that inspired me, I must call up that seminal 'Viewpoint' of early 1985, which I requested of him and received a few days later, delivered in an official manner by a messenger (I had to sign for it) from Plantation Rose Hall, a few miles away from my village, Palmyra, in the county of Berbice. At that time, famished for some trace of recognition, the promptness and manner of McDonald's response, in a society where common courtesies had long dried up, was – to me – recognition of a high order. It has stayed with me. Ian's talk was captioned 'Tiger in the Stars'. It was, indeed, the star that rekindled my interest in my research and gave me the will to turn my life around. It is the foundation, the inviolable prompting, of much of my work; and the essays collected here owe their primal inspiration to the man I consider my principal mentor, friend and a great man of letters. Ian McDonald was one of the few intellectuals who sustained a life of the mind in derelict Guyana, when the utopian dogmas of Burnham and Jagan were rapidly exhausting the rich legacy of our colonial education, rendering philistinism the norm. It was not surprising to learn, therefore, that one of Ian's great friends was Guyana's finest poet, Martin Carter (1927-97); others of no less erudition were: Arthur Goodland, Bill Carr, David de Caires, Miles Fitzpatrick and Lloyd Searwar – men whose intellect, imagination and independence of thought would yield to no mould.

But before I quote from 'Tiger in the Stars', I wish to locate something elemental to Ian McDonald's mental universe: his impeccable facility for discerning redeeming shafts of light in areas of darkness, however impenetrable. Despair could never conquer. 'Candle-Light' is a poem from the early 1980s, when daily power-cuts and myriad privations had to be endured as standards evaporated and the infrastructure collapsed in Guyana. The elusive socialist utopia notwithstanding, many kept their resolve, carrying on, never losing their basic humanity – satisfying simple needs: a chat, a drink, a laugh – above all, self-deprecating humour that mocked the idiocy of our rulers. The stark, economic lines of the poem resonate with the redeeming pursuit of simple pleasures and the will to survive:

No beauty
Is here
It is stark.
But one night
Light failed
Over half the town;
The old generator
Took its time to start.
In that instant
Candle-flies in season,
Brightening and fading,
Were hundreds in the room
As if girls
Had flung them
At a wedding.

That once,
Such beauty
In this sad place,
The glimmering
Of candle-flies.[4]

Hope kindled! The glimmering of candle-flies! McDonald's 'Tiger in the Stars', as will be seen, made me appreciate how important it was to document the achievements of the 'bound coolies', the indentured labourers from India (my ancestors included), who found hope amidst the hard toil in the sugar-cane fields of British Guiana. They had escaped the remorseless poverty and hunger of their homeland and the tyranny of caste, but were resolved to shape a new world in their new land. I believe Ian's narrative helped me to transcend the meanness and misery of mere existence in a place where words had lost their original meaning and were corrupted in defence of grandiose dreams that sought to distort the country's history of struggle and achievement in the colonial period. McDonald's 'Tiger in the Stars' gave me the strength to pull back from the edge; to chart a new course that had as its destination redemption in the eyes of my ancestors, who had made immense sacrifices to give us a better life. I felt that I could no longer squander that legacy.

This is an excerpt from 'Tiger in the Stars' that is now central to my intellectual vision:

> What would Guyana be without those thousands of Indians who have played outstanding roles in politics, the professions, the public service, the trade unions and business, the arts and culture, the intellectual development and the religion of the country?... In every walk of life, there have been more than one equivalent to what Rohan Kanhai is to cricket. But it is not only the personalities. It is also the richly variegated culture which has helped to form the fabric of the nation and enhanced our lives, whether we are Indian or not. What would Guyana be without Indian customs, Indian religion and its age-old practices and philosophy, Indian festivals and holy days, Indian clothes and jewellery, Indian food and spices, Indian dance and song and music, Indian architecture, Indian learning, Indian attitudes to life and death inherited from centuries ago? Without this myriad of legacies, contributed out of a great culture, it would simply not be Guyana at all...
>
> Thirty years ago, a few months after I first arrived in Guyana [1955], I met an impressive Indian man during a visit to the Corentyne. He was a senior civil servant. One of his brothers was a doctor, another was a famous lawyer, and the youngest sister was away at university. But their father had started in the fields of Port Mourant long ago cutting cane. This distinguished civil servant recounted a story I have always remembered as fresh as if told this morning. When he was a little boy an old man, it may be his grandfather, used to tell him about the time he came over the 'black water' from India. It seems like months, if not years the voyage lasted. And the one clear memory the old man had was that each night on deck he looked at the stars blazing in the sky and gradually, as night succeeded night, his eyes, coached by the imagination, gradually picked out the shape of a tiger leaping in the sky amidst the constellations. This is what he recalled in the hardship and the monotony and the homesickness of the journey – a tiger leaping amid the stars. And he told it to his grandson and his grandson told it to me and during that Corentyne weekend traced himself for me that tiger-shape still blazing in the sky. And now at nights, at certain times of the year, I still look up and I think of the old man on his long voyage, and the generations who have done well after him, and it seems to me the tiger leaping in the stars must have become for him a sort of symbol of pride and strength and beauty which he could not then hope to possess but which perhaps

> he could yearn for in his new land one day. And it seems to me, also, that the generations have not misplaced the symbol or the old man's yearning.[5]

The story had such a profound impact on McDonald that he wrote a poem in the 1980s to immortalise this symbol of pride, of effort and achievement, for Indians in Guyana: 'A Leopard in the Sky'.

> In October
> On pure moonless nights
> There is a leopard in the sky.
>
> Above the black outline of trees
> Amidst the thousand glittering stars
> I trace the daring of its leap.
>
> Night after night
> At sea in the terrible boat
> He saw the leopard burning in the stars.
>
> Bound from Calcutta
> To the sweet green plantations
> Gopaul Singh, grown old, remembers only this.
>
> He died here yesterday.
> Forever he has made me see
> A leopard burn and leap among October stars.[6]

So that tiger or leopard leaping amidst the stars was not only a 'star by which to steer' for the Indians of Guyana, it was also Ian McDonald's inviolable source of inspiration for nearly sixty years: 'On pure moonless nights…I trace the daring of its leap'.

Energised and metamorphosed by McDonald's tiger leaping in the sky, I went to the National Archives in Georgetown, to the ship's registers, to ascertain precisely where some of my ancestors originated in India. I discovered much, including caste background, which revealed to me why we had been so obsessed with cattle-rearing, yet I had just scratched the surface. I had learnt nothing, for instance, on why my maternal great-grandmother travelled alone to British Guiana (aged twenty), as a 'bound coolie' indentured to Rose Hall sugar-estate (through which Ian had sent me 'Tiger in the Stars'). I had learnt nothing about their reasons for leaving everything and venturing to a strange land, so far away; nothing, too, about the skills and attitudes that were crucial to their adaptation to that distant land and the means and measure of prosperity they acquired in a few years. I was induced to conceive now, in 1985 – given their remarkable achievement – that many of them probably did catch a glimpse of a tiger or a leopard 'leaping in the sky', on their voyage to Demerara. And did this become 'a sort of symbol of pride and strength' – the source of their irrepressible endeavour to succeed? McDonald concluded that 'the generations had not misplaced that symbol', the yearning to achieve. That did it for me. I was a part of this narrative of effort and achievement; I must help to tell it; I could not continue to let the side down. The PhD, on hold for nearly four years, must be resurrected. How? Where? When?

I got to know Ian McDonald well, during 1985 and 1986, when I taught at the University of Guyana. I would visit him in his office in Georgetown a couple times a month. The man was his words. I was touched by a ready magnanimity that made me think I was still somebody; that I did have something to contribute; that there was really a huge, untouched swathe of academic research awaiting my effort. Moreover, he made me feel that it could start with me, moving from the promptings of autobiography – finding myself – and pursuing the wider framework: toiling in the vineyard to find the wider historical context. One of the things I recall him saying to me, on several occasions, was that I must also write about the work of Jock Campbell, the great reformer in the sugar industry of Guyana. I noted this, but didn't think I would get around to such a project any time soon. I had to finish my thesis. I had found a kind of mission.

Imbued now with a renewed sense of purpose, miraculously, things started to fall into place. I was allowed to leave Guyana with US $12 in October 1986. Young, intrepid David Dabydeen had won the Commonwealth Poetry Prize in 1984 and I read a piece that said he was teaching at the Centre for Caribbean Studies, University of Warwick, England. I had no idea where that was. I wrote to David from 'the heart of darkness', as I put it to him. He told me later that he rather liked that, and he prevailed upon his superiors to accept me for a PhD as I was marooned in derelict Guyana, languishing in the rumshops and whore houses and subsisting as a cattle-herder. He is a writer and poet and is brilliant at crafting an elegant, persuasive tale. It made an impact: exotic, sad and irresistibly moving.

I was, therefore, going to complete my abandoned PhD – in England. I arrived at bleak, wet Heathrow in mid-October 1986 – penniless, apart from the US $12, courtesy of my Guyanese rulers. David Dabydeen quickly persuaded the university to break all the rules – only he could have done that – admitting me as a part-time student to do graduate work although I was on a student visa. This lessened my annual fees significantly. Meanwhile, I had barefacedly turned up at my aunt's home in Golders Green, London, telling her that I had come to complete my PhD. I was ashamed but she gave me a room, fed and clothed me, and provided the funds for me to survive, at no time reproving me in any way; she never asked me where the funds would come from. Extraordinary! Dabydeen got a part-time engagement for me in early 1987, teaching an evening course in Caribbean history to his literature students. This was the context in which I met Chris Vaughan, my wife of nearly 25 years. Strangely, she took to me; and for the next several years she provided the funds for me to complete my doctorate and subsist, until I found employment. I was still able to stay at my aunt rent-free, as the bulk of the research had to be done in London. Such brazenness! Such luck! Chris often says that I was one of the few 'investments' she made that have paid off. She adds, laughing out loud: 'There was no rational reason at the time, mind you, for such an investment; and my friends cautioned me against it'. I often add: 'You followed your heart, not your mind'. 'Don't you flatter yourself', she responds. It has been a totally fulfilling relationship that, I hope, will last to the end of my innings.

But I kept in touch with Ian McDonald through all the years that I laboured on the PhD, ever seeking his inspiration and reassurance, continually asking for myriad favours. He continued to send me the pieces he delivered on 'Viewpoint' or, from around 1987, those he wrote weekly for the *Stabroek News*. The astounding diversity of topics and the depth of the knowledge-base that fed such beautifully crafted and learned writing energised me to pursue my research with a passion. I could not afford to let him down, as I could not those who had given me what I knew was the last chance: Chris, Saba (my aunt), and David Dabydeen. Professor Alistair Hennessy (1926-2013) had founded the Centre for Caribbean Studies at the University of Warwick in 1984, thus providing David and me with a unique framework to follow our intellectual interests. I worked tirelessly, daily, at the Public Record Office at Kew (now The National Archives), the Newspaper Library (Colindale), the British Museum (The British Library), the Colonial Office Library and the Royal Commonwealth Society Library. I was a resurrected man and I was not returning to my cross, squandering the miracle that had presented itself to me.

I recall clearly that the typescript of 'Tiger in the Stars' Ian sent me in early 1985 was accompanied by a few earlier 'Viewpoints'. I was drawn instinctively to one titled, 'Rohan Kanhai: Batsman Extraordinary', broadcast on the GBC on 5 February 1983. Kanhai, from Plantation Port Mourant, about 9 or 10 miles from my village, was a boyhood hero to me and my best friend, Tulsi Singh (from around 1958), as he was to virtually everyone in my district. Kanhai's plantation was also where the 'bound coolie' from India who had seen the tiger leaping in the stars was dispatched as a cane-cutter. So I was immediately lured by a parallel between his astounding achievements and the 'batsman extraordinary', Rohan Kanhai. I was deeply moved not only by the poetic celebration of Kanhai's genius as a West Indies cricketer, but also Ian's rare power in capturing the emotions that Rohan released among those who had the privilege of watching him at his best. He wrote:

> [In Kanhai]...all the ingredients of greatness were there like no other batsman. And mixed into that mixture already so supremely rich there was one final ingredient, a flair and a touch, that no one can define and

> no one can wholly grasp but which one knew was there and felt it as the man took the field and made his walk to the wicket – something uniquely his own, a quality that made excitement grow in the air as he came in, a feeling that here was something to see that made the game of cricket more than a sport and a contest, made it also an art and an encounter with the truth and the joy that lies in all supreme human achievement.[7]

McDonald was seeking to grasp 'the power of being properly affected': the intricate web of emotions generated between the gifted actor and the crowd. As the ever-wise William Hazlitt wrote in an essay, 'On Taste', in 1819: 'Genius is the power of producing excellence: taste is the power of perceiving the excellence thus produced in several sorts and degrees, with all their force, refinement, distinctions, and connections. In other words, taste (as it relates to the productions of art) is strictly the power of being properly affected by works of genius'.[8] It is noteworthy that Ian played tennis at the highest level (captaining Cambridge and Guyana as well as the West Indies in the Davis Cup), so as a sportsman, poet and intellectual he brought vast powers of discernment in sculpting Kanhai's unique stature as a batsman, and he saw it as a work of genius and an art form. And as Hazlitt saw it, without the nobility of taste to apprehend and appreciate, the work of genius is not complete: '[Taste] is entire sympathy with the finest impulses of the imagination...The eye of taste may be said to reflect the impressions of real genius, as the even mirror reflects the objects of Nature in all their clearness and lustre, instead of distorting or diminishing them'.[9] The cricketer of genius needs the taste, 'the entire sympathy', of the observer/spectator for the work to be rendered complete. This is what McDonald brought to the extraordinary skills of Rohan Kanhai.

In early 1987 David Dabydeen persuaded the Guyanese publisher, Arif Ali, to do a series of books the following year, to mark the 150th anniversary of the Indian presence in the Caribbean. And David implored me to take a bit of time off from my thesis to do a little one, in collaboration with Frank Birbalsingh of York University, Toronto: *Indo-West Indian Cricket* (1988). While researching for it, I went back to Ian's article on Kanhai, but I also found something that threw up a challenge I found irresistible. It was a piece he had done for the Souvenir Programme to mark the tour of India to Guyana, in March-April 1983: 'Five Great Berbician Cricketers'. Of these, four were from Plantation Port Mourant (also the birth place of Cheddi Jagan): Rohan Kanhai, Basil Butcher, Joe Solomon and Alvin Kallicharran (he was younger: born 1949). This is what Ian had written:

> It is the fact that three of the best and most famous players in the history of cricket were born almost next door to each other in a small village [Port Mourant] in a distant county [Berbice] in a country [British Guiana] far from the mainstream of the world. Can you imagine the chances

> against any three famous artists, scientists, businessmen, saints or sportsmen having exactly the same remote birthplace? The odds are astronomical… I speak, of course, of Rohan Kanhai [born 1935], Joe Solomon [born 1930] and Basil Butcher [born 1933]. All three Guyanese, all three Port Mourantians – perhaps, indeed, all three learnt their cricket in the same backyard. *There must be something special in the Berbice air, some special mixture in the soil of Port Mourant, to have grown such a crop of cricketing genius* [emphasis added].
>
> I have seen hundreds of Test cricketers in scores of marvellous matches over the past 35 years. And, so far, I have not yet seen any cricketer, any sportsman, so touched by the Gods with genius as Rohan Kanhai. Every time he went to bat you could hear him whisper to himself: 'Can I work miracles?' And he himself would give the answer: 'Of course I can.' And Kanhai could. He is to cricket what Mozart is to European music, what Bob Marley is to reggae, what Sparrow is to calypso – simply the best there has ever been. He leads them all in glory.

Although Kanhai was my boyhood hero, I did not agree totally with Ian's verdict, but it had moved me to do a long article, for the little book, on the great cricketer; and what he had said about the air and the soil of Port Mourant impelled me to fathom the peculiar qualities of the place – and the time – that had also given Guyana its premier Indo-Guyanese leader, Cheddi Jagan (1918-97). In the process, I discovered a forgotten Test cricketer from Port Mourant, who played only two Test matches for the West Indies, against Pakistan in 1958, when he migrated permanently to England to play professionally in the leagues: Ivan Samuel Madray (1934-2009). My interview with Madray, who became a good friend over two decades, took place in London in November 1987 and is reproduced in this collection. It helps us to comprehend something of what Ian was after: why such world-class cricketing gifts emerged, in the 1950s, from a small sugar plantation in a colonial backwater.

Still enthralled by this enigma, I returned to the exceptional cricketing phenomenon that was Port Mourant, in a book of 2009: *From Ranji to Rohan: Cricket and Indian Identity in Colonial Guyana, 1890s-1960s* (dedicated to my boyhood friend, Tulsi Singh). Here again, my inspiration was another very fine piece on Rohan Kanhai by Ian McDonald, which appeared in the *Stabroek News* of 26 November 2006. He is absorbed by the source and composition of what he calls the 'compelling genius' of Kanhai; and one feels the mental strain, the agony, as he grapples with elusive psychological strands, in his effort to comprehend it:

> …When Rohan Kanhai came out to bat there was at once that expectant, almost fearful, silence that tells you are in the presence of some extraordinary phenomenon. Of course, you could look forward to his technical brilliance. Was there ever a more perfect square cover drive? And has anyone in the history of the game made a thing of such great technical beauty out of a simple forward defensive stroke?
>
> And, more than just technical accomplishment, there was the craft

and art of Kanhai's batting – no mighty hammer blows or crude destruction of a bowler, simply the sweetest exercise of the art of batting in the world.

But in the end I am not even talking about these things, important though they are. There was something much more about Kanhai's batting. It was, quite simply, a special gift from the Gods. You could feel it charge the air around him as he walked to the wicket. I do not know quite how to describe it. It was something that kept the heart beating hard with a special sort of excited fear all through a Kanhai innings as if something marvellous or terrible or even sacred was about to happen. I have thought a lot about it. I think it is something to do with the vulnerability, the near madness, there is in all real genius.

It comes from the fact that such men – the most inspired poets, composers, artists, scientists, saints as well as the greatest sportsmen – are much more open than ordinary men to the mysterious current that powers the human imagination. In other words, their psyches are extraordinarily exposed to that tremendous, elemental force which nobody has yet properly defined. This gives them access to a wholly different dimension of performance. It also makes them much more vulnerable than other men to extravagant temptations. The Gods challenge them to try the impossible and they cannot resist. This explains the waywardness and strange unorthodoxies that always accompany great genius.

When Kanhai was batting every stroke he played one felt as one feels reading the best poetry of John Donne or W.B. Yeats or Derek Walcott or listening to Mozart or contemplating a painting by Turner or Van Gogh or trying to follow Einstein's theory of relativity – one felt that somehow what you are experiencing is coming from 'out there': a gift, infinitely valuable and infinitely dangerous, a gift given to only the chosen few in all creation.

II: 'DEAR IAN': LETTERS FROM ENGLAND, 1986-90

When I was in Guyana in February 2014, I spent an evening with Ian and his beautiful wife, Mary, an accomplished cook, very fine gardener and generous host. Ian told me that he was donating his massive, priceless papers to the University of the West Indies (St Augustine); and that he had unearthed some of the correspondence between us, from 1986 to 1990, when I first went to England, researching for my doctorate. A few of my handwritten letters are now only partially legible because some of his papers were badly damaged a few years ago, when the raging Atlantic jumped over the sea-wall, sped across the public road and swamped Mary's garden and penetrated Ian's study on the ground floor. Unfortunately, he could find none of the early letters I wrote to him in Guyana, during my lost years, and I have kept no copies. However, he decided to lend me his file that contained our letters between 1986 and 1990. I had no record of these either, so it was a most unexpected fortune to access these letters after 25 years or so because they tell the story of my resurgence as I researched in London; they also demonstrate powerfully and accurately Ian McDonald's place in my intellectual resurrection.

I propose, therefore, as a tribute to Ian's contribution to my restored self-belief and scholarship, nearly 30 years after our initial contact, to reproduce, as I see fit, excerpts from our correspondence, for he has had no input into what I have selected. I have changed little, apart from the odd word or expression in pursuit of clarity, because I wish to convey the precise emotions, often permeated by a sense of wonder and the imperative of a mission (a virtual cause), which possessed me in my early years of researching in London. This is palpable not only in my letters, but also in those that I received from Ian. What is evident is that he, too, was possessed by immense joy that I had got going, that I was enjoying my work. The excerpts are cited chronologically, but they are sometimes interspersed with my comments and supplementary pieces by Ian, in order to explain the context or sketch the wider implications.

My first letter is dated 23 November 1986, written from Golders Green, London, and addressed to 'Dear Mr McDonald'; all the others are to 'Dear Ian'. In this letter, written about one month after my arrival, my optimism and resolve are eloquent, but the residual anger bred by Burnham's tragic political experiment in Guyana still festered; it was perpetuated by memories of the recent, blatant rigging of the elections in December 1985, by his successor, Desmond Hoyte. I had voted in a Guyana elections for the first time, for a very small party, yet that party was deemed to have polled no votes in my district. I am sure I did not spoil my vote:

> Dear Mr McDonald,
>
> ...It's already terribly cold, perpetually damp, and an eternal bleakness hangs mysteriously, yet already familiarly, over the old town. But my spirits will not be dampened: I am possessed by a strange, somewhat uncomfortable but exciting, sense of wonderment – an ineffable spirit of renewal and a vision of distinct possibilities. The intellectual landscape of London, the pursuit of knowledge as a legitimate, worthwhile exercise, a reverence for the past, and striving to commune with that past – these things have set me alight. I hope this magical glow within me will not fade. But the backdrop to all this, I suspect, is your own unbridled enthusiasm and infectious optimism which, somehow, have rubbed off on me.
>
> ...I hope our rulers recognise now that the crude carnival of words and the paramountcy of Moloch have no place in a modern nation state. The messianic promptings of the late one [Forbes Burnham had died in 1985] can no longer be sustained (thank God!); and the massive, daunting task of recreating a liveable environment cannot be achieved by regimentation and the emasculation of individual instincts, desires, etc. It is a real tragedy that a man of your stature is marooned on the fantasies of these savage surrealists, these brutal re-makers of history. I hope something does change...

My research is really absorbing. I regret I didn't get to London earlier. The British have kept everything, and have kept it well. There is a reverence here for these documents. And thousands, every day, make use of them: an old man working on the history of his ancestral village; a woman consulting the *Southampton Times* (I think), preparing a talk on early women's groups in her area; the ubiquitous doctoral students from everywhere. What a joy to be here!

I am working at the Public Record Office at Kew, consulting the massive Colonial Office files. My pace is slow, but the work is very rewarding; and I am starting to commune with the British Guiana of the 1920s. Fortunately, the old issues of the *Argosy* and the *Chronicle* are available at the Newspaper Library at Colindale. They are a mine: long, informative articles, and well-written too. The editorials are a model of top-class journalism. However, the Library is weak on small, obscure newspapers. Could you please find out for me, from the Newspaper Archives (across the road from your office), what minor newspapers they have for the 1920-50 period? ...

I go up to the University of Warwick once a month to meet with David Dabydeen. He is really kind and very helpful...

Thanks very much for the deep interest you show in my work. I admire you very much, and your support and encouragement bring much joy and satisfaction.

Your friend,
Clem Seecharran

Ian wrote promptly to Joel Benjamin, the Librarian of the University of Guyana, a very thorough professional, who soon sent a list of the newspapers held at the National Archives, from the 'Long Notebooks', adding that it was the 'most comprehensive' one available. Joel added that he was told by Tommy Payne, the archivist, that they had a complete set of *Indian Opinion*, organ of the British Guiana East Indian Association. That proved to be incorrect: apart from a few issues in the 1940s and a photocopy of a volume (from 1937-8) I bought from Paul O'Hara many years later, I have not been able to access this rare newspaper. It is noteworthy that Ian was more optimistic than me with regard to small changes made by the Government since the rigged elections of 1985.

He responded to my latter on 10 December 1986. He said in part:

Dear Clem,
It... was especially good to learn that already you are absorbed in your research, delighting in your work, and stimulated by London and its perennial, never-fading attractions. The reverence for the past and the safeguarding of documents is such a precious thing. 'The old man working on a history of his ancestral village' is something infinitely valuable in any society...

Wife [Mary], small son [Jamie], and self are all well and happy. Life is very full. There are good signs of changes in the right direction – corporation executives allowed more scope to get on with the job, the bringing back of flour which has had a great impact for good, the reversal

of the decision to preserve the late President's body, permission given for a new weekly newspaper which has now started to come out [*Stabroek News*, founded by David de Caires] and which is very promising, the crackdown and the jailing of the Rabbi [Washington, a black American leader of a sect that used to beat up Burnham's enemies], etc. There is a more relaxed and optimistic feeling around, though the economic problems remain desperate.
All best wishes,
Ian

I wrote to Ian again on 21 December 1986. He was a friend and admirer of Jock Campbell (Chairman of Booker, 1952-67), who had taken him to work for the company in British Guiana in 1955, after he graduated from Cambridge. He felt that Jock was one of the great reformers in the social history of the region, and had suggested to me on several occasions that I should do a study on him. I never forgot that, although I was, understandably, obsessed that I did not falter again, in pursuit of the doctorate on Indians in Guyana after the end of indentureship in 1917.

Dear Ian,

...It's always a great pleasure to hear from people that one respects...I am pleased to know that you, your lady [Mary] and your little boy [Jamie] are well and happy. As you say, 'Life is very full'. I know what you mean. It always pains me to spend Christmas away from my ancestral village. The simple pleasures among a people I have never lost touch with – my travels notwithstanding – must rank with the most meaningful experiences that have contributed to the construction I am.

The research gives me tremendous satisfaction, and I am trying to get as much done... so that I may travel to Guyana... Now that I am immersed in the work, I can see more clearly a few cardinal gaps, hitherto blurred, which can only be properly filled through interviews with old folks in the villages...

I have not written to Lord Campbell [Jock] as yet. Of course, I am anxious to meet with the great man, but I feel the meeting will be infinitely more productive after I will have completed a bit more of the research. Meanwhile, Rhodes House, Oxford, has the private papers (including diaries) of Governors Denham and Lethem [former Governors of British Guiana]. This news comes to me like the fresh sea-wall breeze on a moonlight night [Ian's house is a stone's throw from the famous sea-wall in Guyana]. I am now pursuing other possible repositories for similar papers. This exploratory work is fun in itself, and it gives me a feeling of nervous joy and adventure.

Thanks very much for your 'Viewpoints'. 'The Experience of a White West Indian' was especially pleasing to read. It has a universal message – even bigotry must, eventually, be moderated by universal standards of excellence. And you manifest that universal standard of excellence in everything you do. This is why life is so full for you. It pains me to hear some black people complaining about racism all the time. It's an obsession, and it becomes the guarantee for the perpetuation of mediocrity, even failure. I go out, do the best I can, and let others judge...

Whenever it's convenient, please do get the information on the minor newspapers, 1920-50, for me. Colindale is very poor on this. I suspect this area will cause me the biggest problem. I know you are always busy; you don't have to reply promptly; but whenever you do, I'll appreciate it.

Cheers!

Clem

Ian replied on 8 January 1987. I had told him that David Dabydeen was looking at possibilities of funding, primarily from wealthy Indians in the UK, for the establishment of a Centre for the Study of Indians in the Diaspora. He was excited by this. Such a centre was opened in 1991 by David (called Centre for Research in Asian Migration), but it was discontinued after two years for lack of funding. I was attached to it as a research fellow.

Dear Clem,

It is always good to hear from you and it is a great pleasure to know that your own work is going well and that prospects seem extremely promising.

The possibility of a Centre for the Study of Indians in the Diaspora is great news. It would surely be a truly worthwhile project. And surely you will find a good place in it if/when it is established. I imagine a man like Jeremy Poynting might also benefit – I much admire his outstanding work in the study of Indo-Caribbean literature.

...I hope you received my letter dated 30 December sending Joel's information about the availability of newspapers in the Archives here.

Please keep in touch. It is always stimulating to hear from you.

Yours,

Ian

My response was dated 19 January 1987. Ian had taken the initiative in reviving the country's oldest literary journal, *Kyk-Over-Al* (founded by A.J. Seymour [1914-89] in 1945); and I was recalling the tradition of writing in British Guiana, in the late 19th century, epitomised by that masterly classic, still a peerless mine of information on everything in the colony, *Timehri*. I was also bemoaning the tragedy precipitated when societies experience fundamental change, too quickly, throwing up unbridgeable chasms between political/ethnic groups, and falling apart completely. This breeds unassuageable hatred and the flight of old, established groups who, whatever their historical wrongs, helped to create a tradition of educational excellence and a standard of professionalism that the new society diminishes or discards at its peril. I was really alluding to the demise of our sound, enviable educational heritage (highly respected in the region and at the University of the West Indies) and our public service traditions, mortally wounded by the carnival of dogmas in Guyana, nepotism and the consequent flight of most of the best Guyanese professionals. The rigged elections, too, had had their personal effect: a residual anger lodged in me. Fortunately, it did not consume me; it was transformed into an instrument of resolve – to pursue my research relentlessly; to strive for thoroughness and scholarly integrity, even if excellence were unattainable.

Dear Ian,

Greetings from a Siberian London! They say it's been the coldest winter in nearly half a century; and I was hardly equipped for it. But I have survived, and the weather is improving – it got up to 1 degree Celsius yesterday...

I was delighted to receive *Kyk*, no. 35, and I was equally pleased to get the catalogue of newspapers at the Archives from Joel Benjamin. You can always depend on him to get things done: a most un-Guyanese Guyanese man. Do thank him for me, please.

The catalogue shows tremendous strength in 19th century holdings, but it begins to taper off at the turn of the century. I suspect this is related to a significant change in the character of the sugar industry after the great depression of the late 1890s. As small English and Scottish planters were superseded by larger, impersonal, joint-stock ventures, there was a diminution in the resident white population. A great loss to the colony were, of course, the few remarkable planters/writers – like William Russell, Beckett, etc, – who sought to recreate, on this philistine wild coast, the rudiments of an intellectual life. The highest manifestations of this effort survive in some of the editorials in late 19th century newspapers and, even more impressively, in that peerless jewel of Caribbean scholarship, the Rolls-Royce of intellectual endeavour, *Timehri*, the journal of the Royal Agricultural and Commercial Society from the early 1880s.

Unfortunately, my period of study, 1917-39 [changed to 1919-29], seems to be a time of less literary exuberance, though, I am pleased to note, it did produce a veritable Kaieteur of official reports: sessional papers, administration reports, petitions by various interest groups – words cascading upon words; but a mine of information on just about everything. However, the voice of the peasant/worker is obscured. That is why it is so urgent that I should embark on a programme designed to record the rich experiences of the less articulate folks. I hope that things work out at Warwick and the funding comes through. [It never did and I did not embark on this project. Not the only one that never got off the ground!]

I've come across some interestingly provocative documents on J.A. Luckhoo, redeeming in some ways, in view of the infamy the family acquired among Indians in Guyana... following the rise of Cheddi Jagan in the 1950s.

I've enjoyed reading *Kyk*. Jeremy Poynting's article is a pathfinder. He is a very nice man: learned and energetic. We have been corresponding recently. Thanks for your piece that reveals so much about Donald McDonald. As I read it, I thought it is time you start working on your autobiography. As I said to Jeff Stollmeyer a few years ago in Trinidad [1982], the story of your life is necessarily an important part of the social history of the region. There are so many white people who endeavoured to make a contribution towards erasing some of the terrible legacies of slavery and indentureship, and this also should be recorded and appreciated as integral to the history of the region. The Rev J.B. Cropper and the

Canadian Mission, for example, made it possible for the hitherto neglected East Indians to make massive strides in the educational sphere. In the county of Berbice, the Berbice High School (founded in 1916), accelerated this process, thus enabling them to catch up with all the frontrunners in a relatively short time. Cropper was also a respected adviser to the early British Guiana East Indian Association.

I was saddened to learn of the death of Phyllis Allfrey [1908-86; writer, editor, socialist activist and politician from Dominica]. I had hoped to see her some time. What a pity she didn't write her autobiography!... Your obituary piece was most welcome; and, of course, that on Arthur Goodland. What a fascinating human being! You must tell me more about him.

And Christopher Nicole [born in British Guiana in 1930; author of at least 200 novels and a history of West Indies cricket]! His autobiographical novel, *White Boy*, a neglected if not unknown work, gives a most intimate peek into the world of the overseer/manager on the plantation. It is terrifyingly enmeshed in, yet strangely aloof from, the turbulences of the late 1930-40s. The 'terrified consciousness', of which Ken Ramchand speaks, underpins the whole work. In a way, it's an epitaph on Empire, and an ambivalent assessment of the dawning, complex uncertainties as things begin to fall apart [for the colonial elite]. But the initial euphoria, the brief sustaining of grandiose possibilities for change, interlaced with the utopian rhetoric, is also there. Then the Naipaulian gloom descends! Do you know Nicole? How could I get in touch with him? I have not met Sir Jock [Campbell] as yet, but I hope to see him in the summer. I am preparing myself for this meeting. [In fact, I did not see Jock until May 1990, after I had completed my thesis.]

To you, your lady, and your young son, a special thought from the other side of the Atlantic!

Cheers,
Clem

Ian received this letter on 29 January 1987, and replied on 3 February 1987. He reminded me, as he did periodically over the next few years, that the story of Jock Campbell should be told.

Dear Clem,

...I remember cold such as you experienced once when I was at Cambridge [early 1950s] and the Cam froze for weeks on end and the skaters were out on the river surface. The days were lovely – cold with sun, cloudless blue sky, thick snow, hard glassy ice. I liked it much better than the dull, dripping, shivery days.

I enjoyed your comments on the planters/writers, men like Russell (is there a monograph on him?); that jewel of Caribbean scholarship, *Timehri*... J.B. Cropper and the Canadian Mission...

If ever there was a life-story of a white man involved in the West Indies/Guyana that needs telling, it is the story of Sir Jock Campbell. He was thinking of writing his memoirs but made no headway. You should discuss it with him [emphasis added].

My grandmother, Hilda McDonald, a very remarkable woman herself, knew Phyllis Allfrey. I wish I had got to know more about her.

It would take me a long time to tell you about Arthur Goodland. It will have to wait until we can talk. He was certainly one of the most remarkable and likeable men I have ever met. He too deserves a memoir…

Continue to make the most of your time and keep well and creative.

Yours,

Ian

My next letter to Ian is dated 15 February 1987. I speak here about integrity as a historian, not pandering to anyone's political agenda – not having to look over one's shoulder fearful of letting the 'comrades' down – but assessing people, whatever their ethnic background or political outlook, with magnanimity (in most cases) and in the context of their time. One's conception of contemporary priorities or political predilection, therefore, should not be instrumental in judging people's attitudes and responses several decades before. I had been reflecting on the shaping of peoples, the whole question of identity and community, so I think I wanted to underline that civilisations, ultimately, are a consequence of contact and exchange between diverse peoples, however oppressive or destructive encounters often are between them; that evolutionary change was potentially the more enduring, if less glamorous, than revolutionary change. Growth and advancement come out of exposure to new ideas, new challenges, over time; those who have no such encounters or learn nothing from them atrophy. Their creative potential is lessened; their civilisation may become moribund and wither away. Slavery and indentureship were oppressive, but there is much in the history of colonial Guyana that has shaped the present for the good. This should be recognised, celebrated, not expunged from the collective memory. Much of what I was trying to articulate was prompted by ideas that were germinating about the epistemology of the thesis.

Dear Ian,

…Thank you for E.V. Luckhoo's address. I shall write to him… I suspect he is somewhat of a patriarch to the family and he is old enough to remember and, therefore, should be able to capture the spirit of the old days with a measure of informed intimacy. Most of the middle class Indian personalities were probably known to him personally. Besides, the Ruhomons (Joseph and Peter) were E.V.'s father's first cousins. E.A. Luckhoo, E.V.'s father, was the Mayor of New Amsterdam for many years, the first Indian to be so honoured. Unfortunately, there is a tendency to minimise, if not trivialise, the contribution of these early participants in the social and political life of British Guiana. They are seen as a privileged, insular group, pursuing their own parochial interests. This, I feel, is inadequate and incorrect. Their role needs to be examined in the context as well as the limitations of their time: what was realistically possible. One also needs to address the limitations of their own sense of the possible – by-and-large, a people just out of the plantations in a creole environment; yet the extent to which their tentative, faltering steps conveyed to all Indians, unobtrusively and gradually, a sense of self-worth and self-confidence. The Jaganite euphoria of the 1950s cannot be comprehended in isolation from the seemingly parochial and pedestrian efforts of these earlier years and the seminal achievements...

No one has written much, if anything, of note on William Russell, James Rodway (the first historian of Guyana), J.G. Cruickshank, Walter Roth (the eminent anthropologist), J.A. Luckhoo, Ayube Edun, A.A. Thorne, etc. The Marxist perspective tends to see even accomplished individuals as essentially superfluous to the historical narrative; obsession with the class struggle as the 'motor of history' tends to force such actors (often of remarkable achievement) back into conceptual categories defined as organically antagonistic to the working class, while dismissing their contribution as being motivated by the agenda of colonialism. This approach cannot recognise excellence because judgement on the basis of intrinsic merit is not ideologically tenable. This is flawed because it misses so much and impoverishes the intellectual legacy. In Guyana, in particular, Marxism provided intellectual comfort of sorts: one could legitimately marginalise the gnawing, perennial agony of race, save for the white exploiter, of course. So that even the positive contribution of a man such as Russell goes unacknowledged in any academic discourse, informed by a somewhat crusading zeal to right historical wrongs. I am very uncomfortable with this.

It was a most rewarding experience re-reading your novel, *The Humming Bird Tree* (1969), after a decade or more. It was also a special challenge grappling with Gordon Rohlehr's critical introduction to the Heinemann edition (1974). Now Rohlehr is a very brilliant man, and like Rodney, his friend and contemporary, comes from that group of fine scholars spawned by the exciting social experience of the early 1950s in British Guiana. I like the manner in which he blends historical/social antecedents in seeking to deconstruct the architecture of a work à la F.R. Leavis. He has done an excellent job with your book. However, a major, possibly unconscious, flaw in Rohlehr's critique is the seepage of something of the artistic engineering of 'socialist realism' into his assessment. He sees your response as 'colourless' and insipid – devoid of militancy, I suppose. You have let the side down by not allowing the protagonist to make a clean break with the stifling, colourless world of the white planter: forget Cambridge; play cricket with Kaiser and the boys; rescue Jaillin from the cheap perversions of the Syrian; and 'put down your bucket' in the village. Great! But would this not vitiate the historical realities and the literary plausibilities of the elemental construction that is Allan [the young, white protagonist]?

Distorting history and twisting artistic possibilities for what is seen as a moral, cultural and political imperative is untenable. It produces the wasteland that is the Soviet reality. All art is inevitably corrupted by this kind of social engineering. Art is dead; it's propaganda! Art, for me, is about individual pursuit of truth and freedom, largely unfettered by the most altruistic conceptions of social purpose.

I have found *The Humming Bird Tree* to be a work most faithful to what I see as this sacred, universal intellectual responsibility. I am using your novel, along with Nicole's *White Boy*, in a course I teach at Warwick University. The response from my students, all whites, has been most interesting. They are drawn to the moral dilemmas of Allan, and most of them feel that a more tendentious, radical construction of him would have been unconvincing, a vitiation of artistic integrity, however politically appealing... They are using the Heinemann paperback edition with Rohlehr's introduction.

The writing of history, too, must not be shackled by the imperatives of any cause. The historian should not have to look over his shoulder, and must feel free to slaughter sacred cows, if necessary...

Cheers,
Clem

Ian's reply was dated 20 March 1987, and he informed me that President Hoyte had announced the establishment of the Guyana Prize for Literature.

Dear Clem,

...I absolutely agree with you that more should be done to recognise, record, reveal (and even revere) the lives and contributions of the early pioneers. They have been given very short shrift. They deserve much better. In my opinion they faced infinitely more difficult circumstances than their highly publicised successors. Their achievements need recognition, as you say, 'in terms of the limitations of their times'.

Thank you for your generous and, I thought, perceptive comments about *The Humming Bird Tree*. I am pleased that you are using it. The responses from your students seem most interesting...

Yours,
Ian

As almost always with Ian, the conversation could not elude references to cricket, cricket personalities or a cricket book. On 3 July 1987 he wrote asking that I get him a paperback on Rohan Kanhai that he was certain had been published. I had no idea of such a book, and I am still not aware of the existence of any such work. But the exchange is interesting:

Dear Clem,

I wonder if I could ask you for some help. I have been asked to do an article on Rohan Kanhai for the series of profiles in East Indians in Guyana which is to be collected in a volume as part of the effort to mark the 150th anniversary in 1988 of East Indians in Guyana. I am sure that your article, 'The Tiger of Port Mourant', will be of help in doing such an article, and I would love to have a sight of it if I can.

Could you also possibly look for the paperback book on Rohan which I know has been produced, and if you can find a copy send it to me when you can? I haven't been able to put my hand on a copy here.

All the best,
Ian

Apparently, I did not reply promptly to Ian's last two letters because I had been spending some time with my girlfriend, Chris, in the beautiful Lake District (Cumbria), which has over the last 27 years become our spiritual home. But my search for the book on Kanhai that Ian had requested proved fruitless. I think we concluded eventually that no such book existed. I replied on 2 August 1987:

Dear Ian,

...I have been away in the Lake District for a few weeks. It has been a life-enhancing experience. I was privileged, indeed, to share this with my girlfriend, Chris, an intelligent, articulate and loving woman, who has brought much joy and sharpened enthusiasm to my life...

I have asked David Dabydeen to send you a typed copy of 'The Tiger of Port Mourant: R.B. Kanhai'. I don't have a copy other than a hand-written final draft. David has assured me you will receive it shortly...May I remind you that you have been an inspiration to me over the last couple of years; and I hope you will recognise something of your peculiar way of seeing in my essay on Rohan Kanhai...

I regret very much that I have been unable to locate any other work on Kanhai. I checked with Souvenir Press, the publisher of Kanhai's *Blasting for Runs* (1966). They are aware of no other book on Kanhai. Foyles, also, could not help. Do you know the name of the book or the publisher? I recall asking Kanhai in 1982 about a paperback book on him; and he said that a pirated edition of his book of 1966 had been published in India. I have heard of no other book on Kanhai. If you have more information, I will try again.

I am pressing on with my research at the PRO. I hope to complete the research by December. I will start to write the thesis in January. If it's good enough, I think I could get Macmillan to publish it in the Warwick University Series on the Caribbean, edited by Alistair Hennessy...

All the best with your very fine work. You are always present in my thoughts, and I speak of you often...

Your friend,

Clem

On 18 September 1987, Ian wrote to say that he had just returned from a vacation in Canada and Antigua; he was refreshed and in a very productive frame of mind. He had given up on the elusive paperback book on Kanhai and was now after a copy of Kanhai's *Blasting for Runs*:

Dear Clem,

...Immediately...one dives again into the hurly-burly of life here which, to tell the truth, I find very invigorating. But I must say it was refreshing to have a break and I wrote 15 poems during the time which pleased me greatly.

I am afraid I have not yet received the copy of 'The Tiger of Port Mourant' from David Dabydeen. Perhaps you could remind him about this. I look forward to seeing the book in which your essay appears.

Could I possibly ask you to try and get hold of a copy of Rohan's *Blasting for Runs*? My copy has disappeared from my library and I am really anxious to have a copy if you can get hold of one.

...The last time I saw E.V. Luckhoo he promised me that he would write to you and I have no idea why he has not. If and when I see him again I will remind him, but at the moment he is out of the country. At the age of 75 or more, he may be getting a little slow in keeping up with correspondence.

I am glad your research is going well and I really look forward to seeing your thesis: 'The Advancement of the East Indian Community in British Guiana, 1915-28'. [In fact, by the time I had completed it in April 1990, the title was: 'Indians in British Guiana, 1919-29: A Study in Effort and Achievement'.]

...I also look forward to seeing you and your girlfriend in December/ January [1988] when you come out. I enclose a couple of 'Viewpoints'. [Chris and I did not get to Guyana until June 1997, although we got married on 25 May 1990. The witnesses at our wedding were my friend, Alvin Kallicharran, and his ex-wife, Nazli. By the time Chris and I got to Guyana, both my parents had died: my mom in October 1995, my dad in April 1997.]

All the best,
Ian

On 28 February 1988 *Indo-West Indian Cricket* was published by Hansib in London. I sent a copy to Ian, but I was also informing him that I had been unable to find a copy of Kanhai's book, *Blasting for Runs*. I also told him that Chris and I were making regular pilgrimages to a little village in Powys, Wales: Hay-on-Wye, famed for its second-hand bookshops. I was making progress with the thesis, and I was requesting that he procure some documents from Indranie Luckhoo, daughter of the first Indian legislator in Guyana, J.A. Luckhoo, who met Gandhi on several occasions in 1919-20 and 1923-4 in India, in connection with the aborted Colonisation Scheme, which aimed at getting free Indians to go to Guyana with the end of indentureship in 1917.

Dear Ian,

...I've tried really hard, without success, to get a copy of Kanhai's book for you. Souvenir Press (London) printed 2,000 copies in 1966, and it has never been reprinted [apart from the pirated edition in India, Kanhai mentioned to me]. J.W. McKenzie, the largest cricket bookshop in England, is still trying to get a copy for me. Let's hope it turns up.

Meanwhile, I've made several trips to Hay-on-Wye in Powys, Wale. This little village has some 9 or 10 really good second-hand bookshops, yet no trace of Kanhai's book. Rewarding in other ways, though! I've picked up several books by Mittelholzer; Chris and I are trying to get the whole lot: we reckon 25 in all. It's fun.

...Thanks very much for the 'Viewpoints' that you send from time to time. It's very interesting to watch your mind at work; it has become a passion watching you: the way you see; and the joy you unfailingly bring to your observations and analyses. [I think I was referring specifically to a couple of pieces Ian had done on two poets... I believe, Robinson Jeffers and Gerald Manley Hopkins.] Chris is impressed with your writings and looks forward to meeting you...

Do you know Indranie Luckhoo, the daughter of J.A. Luckhoo (JAL)? I met her some years ago [1983], a very nice, elegant lady. It was very sad to learn from her that she disposed of all of her father's papers; she burnt them, I believe, because she was moving into a substantially smaller place. I'm very absorbed by my research at the moment and I would like to have any information on JAL's two visits (with J.J. Nunan, Attorney-

> General of British Guiana) to India in 1919/20 and 1923/4 re the Colonisation Scheme. Please ask her for me if she has got anything left. She had promised me that she would let me have a look at the diary JAL kept in India, which she has retained. But I did not get in touch with her again. Anything relating to his Indian missions would be gold. You may photocopy a few bits if there's anything left. I have been unable to locate a single copy of *Indian Opinion* [organ of the British Guiana East Indian Association]. Otherwise, the research and the writing, though demanding, have been most productive. I hope to complete the thesis by early 1989 [I did not do so until a year later, early 1990].
>
> At last, a copy of Indo-West Indian Cricket! Please note that the official spelling of my name is different [Shiwcharan], but I pronounce it the same way [SEECHARRAN]. I hope you like the book. I enclose a few order forms. Please pass them around for me.

In all my letters to Ian McDonald I spelled my name: CLEM SEECHARRAN. The spelling of my name has been rendered in several versions, some of which I did not like – in fact, detested. When I had to bear those particular versions I felt as if I were a different person and, at times, was not at ease with myself. The vagaries in spelling were a consequence of the colonial bureaucracy's difficulty in recording Indian names presented to or pronounced for them by Indians in the Caribbean, who were often illiterate in English and Hindi. I will attempt to navigate my way through the vagaries of the spelling of my name. This is no simple matter!

I was born at Palmyra Village, East Canje, Berbice, on Thursday, 13 April 1950; my registered name was TOOLSIE: nothing more; my father's name was given as SHIWCHARAN. However, I knew him as SYDNEY SEECHARRAN, both of which are his own names; his surname is not included; if it were, he should have been called SYDNEY SEECHARRAN JAGMOHAN or SHIWCHARAN JAGMOHAN. At times he called himself SYDNEY HARRIPAUL. No wonder I was mired in the same mess! My official name was really TOOLSIE SHIWCHARAN, but I never used it and was not made aware of it until I was about 15. When I was in primary school I was known as CLEMENT SEECHARRAN. I was comfortable with this, so when I moved to secondary school in New Amsterdam, Berbice, I continued to use this version, although, occasionally, for show, I recall resorting to a stylised version: C. TULSI SEECHARRAN, possibly because I was drawn to the name of a big company in British Guiana: T. GEDDES GRANT.

But in 1965, as I was about to go to school in Georgetown, I was told that my name was not CLEMENT SEECHARRAN; it was TOOLSIE SHIWCHARAN – I hated that. So I was taken to a lawyer's clerk to get a deed poll. I wouldn't have minded CLEMENT TOOLSIE SEECHARRAN; but I was informed that it had to be CLEMENT TOOLSIE SHIWCHARAN, as SHIWCHARAN was my father's official name. He, too, would have had to get a deed poll if I were to retain SEECHARRAN. He was not keen to do so. Therefore, between 1966 and 1968, when I was at school in Georgetown, CLEMENT TOOLSIE SHIWCHARAN I was. This was not me. I felt this name had been thrust upon me. I was not fully at ease with myself for those two years. When I had a chance to spell it otherwise, I would revert to CLEMENT SEECHARRAN, especially when I was in Berbice on vacation. Therefore, on my return to Berbice to work, teaching at my old high school, between 1968 and 1970, I was CLEMENT SEECHARRAN. I was myself again.

In 1970 I went to study in Canada; I was there for 7 years: I was CLEMENT TOOLSIE SHIWCHARAN – I hated it. I returned to Guyana for two years, 1977-9, when I reverted to my more comfortable mode: CLEMENT SEECHARRAN. I went back to Canada for a couple of years, 1979-81: it was CLEMENT TOOLSIE SHIWCHARAN all over again, the version I used for the year I spent in Trinidad, in 1981-2, on the aborted PhD.

Now, to my lost years in Guyana: officially I was CLEMENT TOOLSIE SHIWCHARAN, but my informal daily version was CLEMENT SEECHARRAN. Yet, when I taught at the University of Guyana, in 1985-6, for the first time I became CLEMENT SHIVCHARRAN. I don't know why, but I didn't bother to challenge it because I was not comfortable with my official name, so I must have thought anything would suffice.

I came to England in 1986; I studied at the University of Warwick between then and 1990: I was CLEMENT TOOLSIE SHIWCHARAN. I did not like it, but I was so exhilarated by my research and recovery of self-belief that I ignored it. My name on the book, *Indo-WestIndian Cricket* (1988), of which I was co-author, is CLEM SHIWCHARAN. However, when I got the job at the University of North London, in 1993, I decided I would use the version of my name I was most comfortable with. It was not official, but no one challenged me. I was now CLEM SEECHARAN. I got a deed poll and changed it to this version in 1999, shortly before I applied for British citizenship, which I got.

CLEM SEECHARAN I am now and CLEM SEECHARAN I will be until they plant me! These have been the happiest and most productive years in my life. And don't call me CLEMENT, as old acquaintances do from time to time! What's in a name?

Enough!

In a letter dated 8 March 1988, Ian acknowledged receipt of *Indo-West Indian Cricket*, greeting it most generously; but he was clearly overly optimistic about its financial prospects. He indicated that he was contemplating approach Indranie Luckhoo, whom he had never met, about the documents I had mentioned.

> Dear Clem,
>
> Thanks very much indeed for the copy of *Indo-West Indian Cricket*. I have just this minute received your letter and the book and already I have leafed through the book with delight. Already I can see it as a wonderful

achievement and you are to be congratulated. If handled right, it should obviously sell thousands of copies in Guyana and Trinidad particularly, not to mention North America. This is really just a rushed note to catch the mail and I will follow it up with a longer letter...

I will see what I can do about getting in touch with Indranie Luckhoo.

In the meanwhile all best wishes and very many congratulations on your book.

Yours,
Ian

Before I could reply to Ian's letter, he wrote on 24 March 1988 to say that he had met Indranie Luckhoo and she allowed him to photocopy the few of her father's documents that she had kept. He was still pursuing *Indian Opinion* but had had no luck.

Dear Clem,

...I have been in touch with Indranie Luckhoo. She is a pleasant, old-school lady, but extremely frail looking; I understand she is suffering from some debilitating illness the doctors can do little about. She lives at 150 Church St, Georgetown, in case you want to write to her any time.

I have been able to get a few things from her and enclose photocopies of all that I have found, including what is left of J.A. Luckhoo's diary. I have not read this right through myself, but it looks fascinating and includes his visit to Britain and India in 1919-20. I hope this material turns out to be of some help to you. Let me know if you receive these copies safely. And if in exchange you could send £15 for *Kyk-over-Al* it would be much appreciated...

Indian Opinion seems to be very rare, if not completely unavailable. Joel Benjamin [the Librarian] tells me they have one single copy at the University of Guyana, but all their efforts to obtain copies of other issues have failed.

...A group of us have started a company, Demerara Publishers, to reprint old Guyanese titles and publish new books in Guyana. The worthwhile material is endless and the prospects are exciting.

Peterloo Poets are publishing my collection of poems, *Mercy Ward*, in May/June so please look out for it.

I have distributed the order forms which you sent for *Indo-West Indian Cricket*. I hope you get a good response. What really should happen is that all the bookstores here should have numerous copies, but I am afraid that the foreign exchange problem will forestall that.

Yours,
Ian

I responded to Ian's letters of 8 and 24 March 1988 on 30 March, thanking him for the documents he had obtained from Indranie Luckhoo. I was also worried about a poem he had published in *Kyk-over-Al,* no. 37, and requested reassurance about its prompting. Meanwhile, my fruitless search for Kanhai's *Blasting for Runs* [long before Amazon or Abebooks] continued. The search for *Indian Opinion* was equally unproductive.

Dear Ian,

...I am grateful and indeed deeply indebted to you for the J.A. Luckhoo material: the diary entries are precious; I already recognise a few gems that will strengthen and enrich this massive effort [the thesis] which possesses me completely. I have unearthed a great deal of information from the Public Record Office, the India Office Library, and the Newspaper Library, Colindale. I will drop Indranie a line this weekend. When I met her briefly, one evening in 1983, she already looked pretty frail. It's sad to hear that her condition cannot be improved. I will write her a nice letter. [I recall writing Indranie to thank her, but did not get a reply. I believe she was, indeed, terminally ill and died shortly after Ian met her.]

Thanks very much for *Kyk*, no. 37, which I enjoyed immensely. Your sad poem moved me very deeply. Chris and I read it several times aloud. You will tell me more about its prompting. Chris has also read *The Humming Bird Tree* and has recommended it to several of her friends. Congratulations on *Mercy Ward*. You are a very fine poet and deserve a lot of credit... Your achievement in the midst of the local dereliction is extraordinary – a major source of inspiration for what I am doing.

The idea of Demerara Publishers is a fantastic one. I would love to make a contribution. I think Peter Ruhomon's *Centenary History of the East Indians in British Guiana* should be republished. I could do an introduction for it. It's a classic and rare.

I've had no news yet from J.W. McKenzie re Rohan's book. I've travelled to many parts of this country but have had no luck as yet. I used the British Museum's copy when I was working on *Indo-West Indian Cricket*. My copy, too, seems to have gone missing: it was autographed by Rohan [I did locate it eventually at my family home in Guyana].

...The disappearance of *Indian Opinion* is a great loss indeed. Could you please ask old Jai, Jainarine Singh, if he has any idea what became of the British Guiana East Indian Association's documents? He was the editor of *Indian Opinion* in the 1940s, when the paper was a weekly.

Thanks for your help and encouragement. It's special when it comes from you.

Thanks again, for everything.

Best wishes,

Clem

Ian responded on 26 April 1988. As usual, he was punctilious in pursuing another request from me about missing BGEIA documents, noting definitively that they were 'dispersed out of existence'. He explained the prompting of his sad poem; and expressed grave reservations about the future of West Indies cricket, Test cricket in general.

Dear Clem,

Thanks for your letter dated 30 March... which I saw on my return from my visit to Barbados where I attended the wedding of my eldest son. It was a very good occasion and afterwards my wife and small son went on to Antigua, where my parents live...

I am glad you found the Luckhoo material useful and that your research is making good progress. It must all be very exciting.

I have been in touch with Jainarine Singh and unfortunately he has none of the old papers left. The BGEIA's collection seems to have been dispersed out of existence and/or destroyed by fire. He has no copies of *Indian Opinion* but remembers having sent two copies of each issue to the Colonial Secretary [Secretary of State for the Colonies in Whitehall] at the time and wonders what happened to those copies. It continues to amaze me how much essential archival material has gone missing.

I am pleased that you enjoyed *Kyk*, no. 37 and that my poem moved you. It seems to have struck a chord in many people. Jamie, our little son of five, was very sick last year – terribly high fever which was desperately worrying for a while. He has since recovered and is right now enjoying bursting good health, so don't worry. The poem grew starkly in a rush – written in about ten minutes – out of the experience of him being so ill one particular night.

The poem is titled: 'That my Son be Kept Safe'. It is a long poem but I reproduce it in its entirety because most people can empathise with the poet's experience and the range of emotions that possess him on the edge of a potentially monumental personal tragedy:

My small son burns with fever,
his whole body is furnace hot,
burning to death he seems.
'I'm so sick, Dad,' he'd said,
his eyes beseeching me to help.
Now his eyes are closed,
his dark lashes long like mine they say.
His breath rasps hard and dry;
it is agony to hear it.
To touch his brow stops the heart.
The doctor, stone-faced, stern-browed –
though we try to catch a saving glance –
will not look us in the eyes.
My wife, smoothing the bed, doing anything,
anything to help, to keep busy,
trembles with fear. I tremble equally.
It is the worst fear in the world,
fear of a sadness beyond all sadness:
God forbid this should befall.
All the years that pass
would not cancel out the hour.
Why are we constructed so?
Were it not better to be a stone?

I remember times we watched him,
coming to his bed because we could not hear his breathing,
bending low and lower to catch the breath
just raising the small chest.
The slightest twitch of coverlet or ribbon
showing he was safe among the smothering pillows
was most sweet, most easing

of this fear we all have always
that they will die and leave us
No hope at all, the rest of life made senseless,
No ransom can ever meet this threat.

He burns to death
and my whole self cries to heaven.
For him to keep safe I would vow it now
to be good in God's sight always, always:
good father, good husband, good man,
Christ's good soldier even.
Though rum's still sweet
and friendship's fine, and laughter,
and a girl's walk catches the groin
and the world is so beautiful
and the wonder of every minute never ceases
I would give it all away forever
to let his eyes not close, my God,
that my son be kept safe.
And if God will not listen,
if God stops his ears,
so that my small son be saved,
I would make a pact
with the hobgoblin in Hell
who loves sudden misery,
who strikes when life is most fit,
to give all my gold
give blood-health, body-tune, eyesight,
the touch of wind and water that I love,
memories I have of tenderest hours,
reason that controls all things
the life God gave me,
the immortal soul,
I would give all away
should my son be safe now:
safe now, my God, my God![11]

When Ian was nearing 80, in 2012, he wrote a powerful piece, 'Grief', in which he revisited the most unbearable form of grief imaginable, a life-changing terror – the death of a child:

> Grief, true grief, grief in all its unalterable, life-changing terror… such grief is another story entirely. For real grief there is no consolation. A beloved dies and no words of sympathy make any difference…
>
> In the end, it is the death of children before your own death that freezes you in eternal, inconsolable grief until the end of your time, heaven's time, any time. The inescapable Buddhist truth, 'From all that he loves, man must part', is meant to make Stoics of us all. Such a death 'has no lessons worth learning', as the writer Aleksandar Hemon [a Bosnian] wrote in his absolutely harrowing account of his baby's death entitled, 'Aquarium'… with devastating precision: his child's death had become '…an organ in our bodies whose sole function is a continuous secretion

of sorrow'. Time does not diminish that organ or limit its function or reduce the awful distress it causes. The loss of the life of a child is something parents may gradually mention less and less to themselves even, but he or she never gets over it. The never-healing wound. The deepest, most heartfelt prayer ever uttered is: 'Please God, do not thus afflict me'.[12]]

Returning to Ian's letter of 23 April 1988:

> You will be glad to hear that the reprint of Peter Ruhomon's book [*Centenary History of the East Indians in British Guiana*] is now at the printers and should be out by the end of May. [This book was 'specially reprinted by the 150th Anniversary Committee of the Arrival of Indians in Guyana, May 5, 1838', the Chairman of which was Yesu Persaud.]
>
> ...I very much enjoyed *Indo-West Indian Cricket* and thought you did a really excellent job. There are a lot of things to discuss but again time is limited at the moment. Many thanks for making generous mention of me in the book.
>
> I have found the Test series against Pakistan disappointing – especially the match at Bourda [from 2-6 April 1988: Pakistan won by 9 wickets]. It is not so much that the West Indies played so badly at Bourda but much more that I found the cricket, especially the West Indian cricket, of such poor quality. I enclose copy of a piece I wrote at the time, 'The Last days of Test Cricket'...
>
> All best wishes,
> Ian

On 5 April 1988 Ian sent me three photographs of J.A. Luckhoo while he was a law student in London, just before the First World War. They were given to him by Indranie Luckhoo. The Luckhoo documents had arrived at the right time, as I was writing a chapter of the thesis on his and Attorney-General Nunan's work on the British Guiana Colonisation Scheme. His diary entries, in India, when he met Gandhi several times, made me feel that my hands were really touching history: a strong emotion. I responded to Ian on 2 May 1988. I was excited about a conference to mark the 150th anniversary of the Indian presence in the Caribbean, to be held at the Centre for Caribbean Studies, University of Warwick, in May 1988. The architect of it was David Dabydeen, and he had asked me to give a paper on J.A. Luckhoo.

> Dear Ian,
>
> ...Thanks very much for the photographs of J.A. Luckhoo. I have completed a long essay on him and J.J. Nunan, the architects of the British Guiana Colonisation Scheme. Do you know where I could get a picture of Nunan? He was Attorney-General of British Guiana from 1906 to 1924, an inordinately long time for colonial officials. He was an articulate, learned, stubborn and irrepressible man. This essay is a chapter of my thesis; I'm presenting it at a conference at the University of Warwick next week. It should be an exciting event: Cheddi Jagan, Clive Thomas [who gave the Walter Rodney Lecture], Ken Ramchand, Frank Birbalsingh, Hugh Tinker and many others will be participating.

I have asked David Dabydeen to send you a few small publications on aspects of West Indian literature. They were published by the Centre for Caribbean Studies at Warwick...One of them is by an Englishwoman, Karina Williamson, who makes several references to *The Humming Bird Tree*, in assessing the literary achievement of those two Dominicans: Jean Rhys and Phyllis Allfrey. I think, at last, scholars are beginning to recognise your literary contribution. Your new collection of poems, *Mercy Ward*, is coming out at the right time. [Ian sent me a copy in September 1988, while wishing me 'success in your excellent work'.]

Unfortunately, *Indo-West Indian Cricket* will not be available in Guyana. The publishers seem to have written Guyana off...

Congratulations on your son's marriage! It's good to hear that Jamie is in fine form again...

I am hoping to finish the thesis by December. [This was clearly unrealistic and showed my inexperience as a researcher and writer: I kept setting myself targets that were unattainable. I did not really get into the writing until 1989. I wrote for most of that year and had the final version ready around February 1990.]

It is very painful to learn of the dispersal/destruction of the BGEIA records. *Indian Opinion*, too, seems to have encountered the same fate. I have seen no trace of the early issues, in the 1920s, in the Colonial Office files. I think it was published monthly then, though somewhat irregularly. The first editor was Joseph Ruhomon. Re: the issues from the 1940s, when Jainarine Singh edited it, I'll check at the PRO (Kew), as Colindale does not have a single copy.

...Keep up your excellent work. You have been a great example – hard to follow, but I'm trying. I hope I don't disappoint you.

Cheers,
Clem

Ian's reply was dated 26 May 1988. He remarked on the many events in Guyana to mark the 150th anniversary of the Indian presence in the country, and the impending publication of an anthology of writings to celebrate the occasion.

Dear Clem,

...David Dabydeen has sent the Warwick Centre Occasional Papers for which many thanks. They are well worth having. I was interested to see the comments that Karina Williamson made on *The Humming Bird Tree*.

...The celebrations that marked the 150th anniversary here were a great success and there was an outstanding programme of exhibitions and cultural events as well as an excellent film festival (not to mention a succulent food festival also). There were a number of good papers at the conference and during the week: both Hoyte [the President of Guyana, 1985-92] and Ramphal [Secretary-General of the Commonwealth, 1975-90] gave extremely good addresses. All in all it was a week full of good things and indeed the programme was so packed that one had to miss quite a few things.

I will send you a copy of the Indo-Guyanese anthology which I helped to compile and which is due out in late 1988.

I am not sure when the Ruhomon book will be available from the printers, but I have made a note to send you a copy when it is.

Thank you for your generous comments. It has been a great thing how you have taken hold of your life and begun to prepare and produce such valuable work. May you go from strength to strength!

All best wishes,

Ian

The anthology was edited by Joel Benjamin, Laxmi Kallicharan, Ian McDonald and Lloyd Searwar. It was titled: *They Came in Ships: An Anthology of Indo-Guyanese Prose and Poetry*. It is highly significant, and an eternal joy to me, that it concludes with an Afterword: 'Tiger in the Stars' by Ian McDonald. However, because of the collapse of Demerara Publishers, the book was not published until 10 years later, considerably enlarged with more recent Indo-Guyanese writing and section introductions, in 1998, by Jeremy Poynting, at Peepal Tree Press.

Ian sent the Peter Ruhomon book on 12 September 1988, with a note that read, in part:

'We had the launch of the reprint of Ruhomon's *Centenary History of the East Indians in British Guiana* – exactly the same place (then the East Indian Cricket Club) where the original book was launched 50 years ago. There was even one person present who had been there 50 years ago!

The price of the book is US $10.

I had written to Ian around 6 February 1989 to enquire if any relatives of Joseph and Peter Ruhomon were still alive in Guyana because I was writing a bit on both of them in my thesis. He replied on 10 March:

As far as I can discover none of Joseph and Peter Ruhomon's relatives live in Guyana. When the reprinting of Ruhomon's *History of the East Indians* was done and a launching ceremony was being planned, I understand various efforts were made to unearth any relatives in Guyana (not the best use of words but you will know what I mean), but none could be found. However, Lloyd Searwar... is distantly connected to the Ruhomons and he tells me that he has some memories of conversations with Peter. Perhaps you might write to Lloyd Searwar or visit him when you are next in Guyana...

I responded on 29 March 1989:

Thanks for the information on Peter Ruhomon's relatives. You are correct: to find a relative, you will have to 'unearth' one from Le Repentir Cemetery. This is a poignant commentary on the state of the land – a total break in that elemental, genealogical spine around which history, effort and achievement, are contextualised and celebrated; the essence of continuity is irreparably ruptured. The Ruhomon brothers were pioneers, writing and speaking on diverse subjects – dedicated to a life of the mind: the first Indian intellectuals in the colony. Peter was, for nearly two decades,

> Secretary of the Wesleyan East Indian Young Men's Society; and the lectures delivered to that body by Indians and non-Indians represent something entirely civilised and civilising: Joseph Ruhomon on Rabindranath Tagore; James Rodway on aspects of the history of British Guiana in the 19th century; Peter Ruhomon on Wordsworth; A.P. Sherlock on 'The Plodder and the Genius'; A.R.F. Webber on journalism and politics. The list is endless. Yet how many people in Guyana know of this?

In the letter of 10 March 1989 (cited above), Ian responded to some positive comments I made about his new book of poems, *Mercy Ward*, as well as to similar complimentary remarks on the poems, by David Dabydeen and Ken Ramchand.

He said:

> I was extremely pleased to hear that Ken Ramchand had nice things to say about *Mercy Ward*. I always thought very highly indeed about Ken's work but have had little or no contact with him over the years. It is good to know that he has read the poems. And thank you for your generous remarks which, I can assure you, are a great encouragement. One writes in some isolation here, as you know, and it is good to get words of appreciation and understanding from 'outside'.

Earlier, on 9 January 1989, Ian sent me wonderful news:

> We are all very well here. Mary had a baby boy just before Christmas, Darren Christopher. Both he and Mary are fine and it is a great relief and joy that all has turned out well.
>
> ...Thank you and Chris for tracking down a copy of *Hope against Hope* [by Nadezhda Mandelstam; Chris had found a copy at Blackwells in Oxford]. By coincidence I have just borrowed a copy from Martin Carter and I am reading it right now. It is one of the great books. I will be very pleased to get my own copy.

On 18 January 1989, the book had arrived. Ian was overjoyed:

> I want to thank you right away for *Hope against Hope* which has just arrived. I am most grateful to you and Chris for this lovely book which I will treasure. In fact, I had just finished reading Martin Carter's well-thumbed copy; it is undoubtedly one of the great books – essential reading for anyone who wants to understand the 20th century. Thanks very much again and I send all best wishes.

On 29 March 1989 I wrote to Ian that my progress with the thesis was most encouraging; I had completed four chapters, with possibly two more to be done. On 5 May he commented on my progress, and he also revealed a potentially exciting development:

> I am really delighted how well your work on the thesis is going. In a letter David Dabydeen told me that you were doing superb work and this is extremely exciting news. I am looking forward very much to seeing it in due course.

David Dabydeen and Ken Ramchand both mentioned to me the possibility of an Honorary Doctorate at UWI. I was utterly dumbfounded to be told this. I know that such things often do not come off or, if they do, take a very long time, but just the fact that people are thinking of it is honour enough.

On 29 May 1989 I sent Ian a letter from the village of Fillongley in Warwickshire. I had moved in with Chris the previous month. I was working 10 or 12 hours a day on the thesis, so the tranquillity of the village was ideal for my concentration on the demanding daily exercise of writing. I was in good spirits:

Dear Ian,

Greetings from this nice, little village outside of Coventry!... I now live most of the time with Chris. It's very quiet here, and I have been able to do a great deal of writing. I have completed the final draft of the thesis... It has been very hard work, but I'm pleased that I'm coming to the end. I look forward to your reading it later.

Thanks very much for your excellent pieces. I treasure them. They already constitute a remarkable chronicle/analysis of the consuming tragedy. I shared them with Chris (she is a keen student of your literary and other pieces) and she recognises, for the first time, an element of despair in your perspective. She appreciates your clinical observations, the retention of your humanity, and your civilised touch amidst the darkness. I'll be reading excerpts from some of your recent pieces at a talk I'm giving in London shortly.

David Dabydeen, Ken Ramchand and I have talked at great length about the diversity, depth and immensity of your contribution to the region over several decades. You deserve an Honorary Doctorate. You have earned it. David has discussed *Mercy Ward* on BBC Radio 4. I was very pleased with some of his observations. I am enclosing a tape of the conversation....

We had a very good conference on the three Guianas at the Centre for Caribbean Studies (Warwick) this month. I also enjoyed the social side of it immensely. Chris and I try often to get interesting people over. Cheddi [Jagan], Basdeo [Panday], Alvin Kallicharran and Professor Singaravelou (University of Bordeaux) came to supper and we talked late into the night. Singaravelou is from Pondicherry, South India: a social geographer; a charming man of great learning. He is author of a three-volume study of Indians in the Caribbean. Unfortunately, it's in French. But I learnt much from him about French Guiana in three or four days. A totally rewarding encounter!

...I agree with your remarks on Tony Cozier in its entirety. After Arlott, the poet, give me Tony! He knows the game thoroughly and all the players, past and present. He is precise. His English is pleasantly neutral. And, as you say: no jingoism. An unsung West Indian!

...Many thanks for getting the books to my dad [sent through Rose Hall Sugar Estate]; my people, at Palmyra, follow your 'Viewpoints' closely...

Your friend,
Clem

I did not hear from Ian again until I got his letter of 27 September 1989: he was away on holiday. It speaks of deep satisfaction; literary recognition; engagement with and publishing of Martin Carter's poems; enjoying his baby son, Darren; but there is also a touch of despair about life for many in Guyana. Ian writes:

> Dear Clem,
>
> We returned from leave at the end of August and have settled in again. There is a huge amount to do and life is very full. The systematic problems continue. More and more people seem to be leaving or planning to leave. It is very 'sadful', as an old lady said to me.
>
> ...*Mercy Ward* has been getting some good reviews, including one in the Times Literary Supplement and, of course, David Dabydeen's excellent piece in *Poetry Review*. Harry Chambers at Peterloo Poets seems to be pleased and wants to bring out a second volume of my poems – so I am happy about that. I also greatly appreciated David's comments in the BBC interview – and thank you very much for the tape which I got safely. No doubt because of that I was asked by the BBC to do an interview when I arrived in London and ended up giving three of them for various programmes. I enjoyed the experience.
>
> When I got back there was one more book from you for your family and I passed this on to your father.
>
> ...I enclose a copy of Martin Carter's *Selected Poems* which has imperfections in the production but, importantly, gives the accurate and authentic text of all the poems which in many cases has been missing in the past.
>
> Martin is certainly one of the great West Indian poets and deserves a major publisher and wider audience. I am trying to see what can be done through Wilson Harris and Fred D'Aguiar to get Faber or Chatto to publish it, but if this fails we are thinking in terms of a UK edition by Jeremy Poynting at Peepal Tree Press.
>
> I also enclose a few recent 'Viewpoints' for interest.
>
> We are all very well. Darren is now nine months old and a great delight. Last week we spent an anxious time, with Hurricane Hugo sweeping through the Eastern Caribbean causing great havoc. My old parents and my sister and family live in Antigua so we were very concerned. However, all is well with them though my parents' house was somewhat damaged.
>
> All the best to yourself and Chris.
>
> Yours,
>
> Ian

My letter to Ian, dated 15 October 1989, was badly affected by the water from the Atlantic that invaded Ian's study: parts of it are indecipherable. I was nearing the end of the thesis that had already taken me three years, so I was expressing anxieties not only about the completion of the work but I was nervous about possibilities of employment. I had no faith that the Centre for Caribbean Studies at Warwick was going anywhere; I could see no scope for expansion; and although I would soon be its first PhD graduate, my future there was not promising. I was not blaming David Dabydeen; he was always trying to help me, but the options were very thin. It must have been extremely difficult for Chris, who was funding me day after day (she had virtually exhausted her funds on me), with no guarantee that, at nearly 40, I was employable. Therefore, I could not let her or my aunt down; neither could I let Ian down because he had resurrected me and his hopes in me never withered. I could not countenance dropping out again. The thesis had to be done. Yet I was saying to Ian (this part of the letter is barely legible) that whatever the difficulties, I am continually renewed by the peculiar beauty of the Lake District in England: the solitude of the sculpted hills; the wide valleys with their busy becks tirelessly renewing and replenishing the lakes with the water saturating the high fells; the dry stone walls of this remarkable place, constructed stone by stone long ago, to keep the sheep in. I am ever energised by its natural gifts, its beauty reaching me, even from afar as I approach it, no matter how often I visit – this place where mind and world are melded. I can decipher tantalising bits from one half of the page, then this line which I can read almost completely: 'I wish I knew who sculpted these wonderful hills and decorated the valleys with the pretty lakes, each one with a personality of its own, each one evoking in me peculiar responses... renewing my hopes and rekindling my love of life'. I recall the first time Chris took me to the Lake District, in July 1987; she pricked my poetic pretentions autographing a book she had bought for me in Ambleside thus: 'A place where poetry is only a shadow of the beautiful reality'. We were at Glenridding (Patterdale), by Ulleswater.

Dear Ian,

...Chris and I were away in the Lake District for a week. It was a necessary visit to that noble region, our spiritual home. I needed to recharge my batteries before, what I hope will be, my final bit of hard, sustained toil on the thesis. I am looking now at completing by the end of the year [1989]. It is difficult work, rendered harder by the fact that I get no financial assistance from the University of Warwick. Without Chris's massive financial sacrifice and encouragement and my aunt's amazing magnanimity in London, I definitely would have packed it in a while back. I must add that your expectations of and confidence in me have also given me the strength to persist. What the future holds beyond here, I do not know. The Centre for Caribbean Studies is run by Professor Hennessy, a fine scholar, but not an imaginative man in terms of the growth and innovation of the Centre. David Dabydeen tries all the time to help me, even wangling a few pounds out of Hennessy from time to time (he thinks we are two Guyanese crooks: he may have a point!), but David's hands are tied: there are very few options. So I must finish the thesis and try to find employment elsewhere.

I cannot return to Guyana, yet there is a lot of research I wish to do on Guyana; so I must find employment in the UK to be able to achieve my goals. I hope to do a book on Jock Campbell after I finish the thesis, you will be pleased to know.

Many thanks for the Martin Carter anthology [*Selected Poems*, Demerara Publishers, 1989]. It's an excellent selection from the rich work of the great man. Congratulations! Your foreword is brilliant: it places the poems in the wider social and political context as well as within the shifting intellectual promptings of Carter...

I like your quote from Randall Jarrell [(1914-65); American poet and essayist]: good writing has to be struggled at; worked and reworked tirelessly; it just does not fall into one's lap.

[Ian had noted the virtual impossibility of creating a great poem, quoting from a letter by Randall Jarrell:

...how is a great poem created? One thing can be said for sure: infinitesimally few great poems are ever created. Randall Jarrell in a letter to a fellow poet spelt it out about right: 'How hard it is to write a great poem! How few good poems there are! What strange things you and I are, if we are! To have written one good poem – good used seriously – is an unlikely and marvellous thing that a couple of hundred writers in English, at most, have done – it's like sitting in the yard in the evening and having a meteorite fall in one's lap'.

Ian concluded: 'And if you or I, think or hoping ourselves poets, can ever write one small fiery scrap to flare one moment across the sky, that would be a marvel and enough for one life'.]

This is exactly how V.S. Naipaul sees his craft: 'The actual words, the neatness that comes out in the words, is arrived at after a lot of hard work. Writing is always a discovery and the discovery occurs at the moment of writing... The incubation actually occurs subconsciously during the first year of doing nothing, of playing, of writing rubbish, writing 20,000 words then throwing them away as I did for my last novel [*The Mimic Men* (1967)]. I think there are few people who feel so worthless and so useless as the novelist, who'll spend several weeks, several months, trying to write something and nothing is happening. I really go down sometimes feeling that I don't deserve my meal, you know. The terrible thing is that one day I know that I'll spend a couple of years and there'll be nothing at the end to show. But that's the sick period. The actual writing, when it's going well, when you know what you are doing, that is very good, that is very nice (*The Listener*, 23 May 1968)'.

Cheers,
Clem

I did not hear from Ian until 4 January 1990. He was delighted that the thesis was nearing completion; and was enquiring about my options. But he was pained by the passing of his close friend, the poet, A.J. Seymour (1914-89).

Dear Clem,

...I note in your letter of 15 October that you hope to have your thesis finished by the end of 1989. I was delighted to read this and hope that you will indeed have been able to put the finishing touches to it by now. What are your plans for your thesis? Could you not earn a research fellowship somewhere with it? I hope very much that you are able to continue your research work and find a suitable and secure position from which you can continue your studies.

You will be pleased to know that Martin Carter's *Selected Poems* won the 1989 Guyana Prize for Poetry. This was worth US $5,000 to Martin and is some small recognition of his stature as a poet. What Martin really needs is a Metropolitan publisher.

I like your quote from V.S. Naipaul writing in *The Listener* in 1968. I see by the way that he has been honoured with a knighthood, a honour he deserves, but which may be sneered at I suppose by some West Indians.

The saddest news is that Arthur Seymour died on Christmas Day [1989]. The great old man was a dear friend of mine. I enclose copy of an article I did for *Stabroek News* and also copy of my Eulogy at the funeral. [AJS was founder editor of *Kyk-over-Al*, the literary journal that Ian was instrumental in resurrecting and which he edited for many years.]

I also enclose copy of *Kyk*, no 40, which came out a few days before Arthur died so I was able to put it in his hands at the hospital. It is the last issue in which his name will appear. I feel a great sadness at this. The next issue of *Kyk* (a joint issue with *BIM* [Barbados]), planned for June 1990, will serve as a memorial to AJS.

All the best to yourself and Chris for 1990.

Yours,

Ian

In *Kyk-Over-Al*, no. 39, to mark Seymour's 75th birthday, Ian had written generously of AJS's many-faceted achievements: 'His overall contribution to the cultural tradition of Guyana and the Caribbean is truly astonishing. I do not think the younger writers and academics grasp it fully. The AJS bibliography compiled by the National Library in 1974 was already 100 pages long and since then must have doubled in length. This amazing man's work contains poems, historical publications, reviews, broadcasts, essays, addresses, entries in anthologies, forewords, lectures, talks, pamphlets, memoirs, sermons, eulogies, magazine work, and books in such profusion that one would be excused for thinking this was the record of a school, not one man alone.' For the man's poetry, see *A.J. Seymour: Collected Poems, 1937-1989* (edited by Ian McDonald and J. de Weever, with an introduction by Ian McDonald, New York: Blue Parrot Press, 1990.)

I did not reply to Ian until 26 February 1990. I was putting the finishing touches to the thesis, so I was proud to tell him that, after nearly three-and-a half years, the thesis was virtually done and I was about to submit it. I went back to my ritual query about the infamously irretrievable *Indian Opinion*, organ of the British Guiana East Indian Association. I wrote of my sadness to learn of A.J. Seymour's death; through Ian, I had been able to meet with him on 6 November 1985, at his home in Georgetown, when he autographed a copy of *Kyk-over-Al* (July 1981) for me. He had edited the magazine from 1945 to 1961; I think this issue was the first in 20 years, a collection of pieces from several back issues.

Dear Ian,

...It was sad to hear of AJ's passing. Your eulogy captures brilliantly the man's immense contribution to West Indian literature; his abundant humility comes over well also. Painful though it was, it seems appropriate that his last public appearance was shared with you. Your labour of love on *Kyk* is a wonderful tribute to this accomplished, decent, gentle man – an oasis of integrity in an area of darkness.

It was disturbing to read an article in yesterday's *Observer* that claims the population of Guyana has declined to what is was in 1960. And no hopes for change: more rigged elections and Cheddi's rhetorical nullity! Is there any truth to the rumour that Booker is returning?

Ian, I am, indeed, happy to say that I have completed the thesis; just a few mechanical bits to do: bibliography and acknowledgements. My supervisor (Professor Alistair Hennessy) is very pleased with it. The title of the thesis is: 'Indians in British Guiana, 1919-29: A Study in Effort and Achievement.' I had to drop two chapters because it was too long. However, the material will go into volume two of this study of Indians in Guyana, covering Indo-Guyanese politics, 1916-45. [In fact, the material excluded was used in my book of 2011: *Mother India's Shadow over El Dorado: Indo-Guyanese Politics and Identity, 1890s-1930s* (Ian Randle Publishers).

Do you know if any issues of *Indian Opinion*, organ of the British Guiana East Indian Association (BGEIA), have survived? My failure to access it leaves a gaping void in my research, not for the 1920s, but for the late 1930s-early 1940s.

I have done a section on Indian cricket in British Guiana for the thesis, including the seminal role of J.A. Veerasawmy (the first Indian to represent the colony in inter-colonial cricket, 1910), and the pre-eminent part played by the British Guiana East Indian Cricket Club (founded in 1914). I saw a reference to a book by Veerasawmy: *How to Become a Great Batsman and a Great Bowler* (1936).

Many thanks, Ian, for your encouragement over the years. I hope I don't disappoint you. You are, indeed, a good friend. Do give my regards to Mary and the boys...

Cheers,

Clem

The saga over my pursuit of the elusive *Indian Opinion* deserves a little book in itself. In a letter of 25 April 1990, Ian had another tale to tell of this little organ of the BGEIA. Whatever the problems, however, his optimism was unconquerable. This was always important to me: it continually enhanced my effort: hanging in; never yielding to despair; seeking and finding a silver lining.

Dear Clem,

It must give you a feeling of great personal and professional satisfaction that you have completed your thesis. I hope indeed that you do get it published by Macmillan.

I have heard of J.A. Veerasawmy but I have not heard of his book on cricket. I would love to get hold of a copy.

Mary and the two boys and myself are very well and, despite all the

> difficulties and nonsenses in Guyana, life is full and interesting and there are a multitude of stimulating challenges. I have now got together all the material for *Kyk*, no. 41, which is to be a joint issue with the Barbadian magazine, Bim, and is due to come out in June. There are a number of exciting projects which we are developing at Demerara Publishers, including a children's magazine and a revival of the scholarly journal, *Timehri*.
>
> I am also doing a good deal of writing and enclose some recent pieces which may be of interest.
>
> ...Regarding your inquiry about *Indian Opinion* I have a sad tale to tell. There is, I believe, at the University of Guyana an issue of *Indian Opinion* marking the centenary of the arrival of Indians in Guyana. But no copies of any other issue seem to have survived – except that last year a bound volume of *Indian Opinion* [a complete collection of the monthly magazine of 1937 and 1938] turned up in the house of Paul O'Hara (Paul Persaud). Paul lent it to me and I lent it to Joel Benjamin [Librarian of the University of Guyana] who was overjoyed to see it. After Joel's tragic death [in 1989 at the age of 45], his widow Anna mentioned to me that Joel had returned the bound volume to Paul at his home. Unfortunately, Paul cannot remember this and says he does not have the volume any longer. The sad upshot is that the precious, apparently unique, volume of old *Indian Opinion* has gone missing. If I am ever able to track it down, I will let you know.
>
> Yours,
> Ian

On 13 May 1990 I responded thus to Ian:

> What a pity the volume of *Indian Opinion* has vanished. It is so crucial to my work that it is painful to think it may be irretrievable. I do have a photocopy of the Centenary Number of 1938. Judging by this single issue, I can envisage what a mine it must have been. Thanks a lot for taking valuable time in your effort to help me. I am pleased to tell you that, in my thesis, I acknowledge the great contribution that you have made to my self-belief in recent years. I must say how grateful I am for your encouragement and help as I struggled with this massive project. You are a real friend.

On 14 June 1990 Ian wrote again about the missing volume of *Indian Opinion*: 'I have not given up hope of retrieving the lost volume of Indian Opinion and will, of course, let you know if it is ever found.'

The volume was soon ascertained to be in the safe keeping of Mr Paul O'Hara; so I went to see him around 2005 to ask if he would allow me to photocopy excerpts from his precious possession. No luck! The nonagenarian would allow no one to take the volume out of his house again. However, he seemed amenable to the idea of the whole volume being photocopied and sold to anyone who was prepared to pay a fairly heavy sum. I left Mr O'Hara and informed Ian that I would ponder on the matter. A couple of years later I asked Ian to negotiate a price with Mr O'Hara; this he did and I was soon able to have a photocopy of the entire volume of *Indian Opinion*. It was a crucial document in the composition of my book of 2011: *Mother India's Shadow over El Dorado: Indo-Guyanese Politics and Identity, 1890s-1930s.* My debt to Ian, as usual, cannot be repaid.

Apart from doing outstanding literary work, as poet, prolific columnist and editor of *Kyk-over-Al*, Ian was a very busy senior executive of the Guyana Sugar Corporation. So the fact that he also found time to keep up with a vast correspondence, while pursuing the myriad tasks I set him from time to time, is truly extraordinary. Besides he and Mary had two very young sons. Such diverse achievement could not have been possible without Mary's selfless commitment to Ian and their family. She, too, is a remarkable person.

Enclosed with Ian's letter of 25 April 1990 was a piece he had written captioned the 'Death of Communism'. I had liked that and I wished to draw a parallel with the Guyanese political wasteland. In my letter of 13 May 1990 I spoke of the 'inviolable truth' of his conclusion while quoting from his piece: '…those regimes [in Eastern Europe] that crumbled were the victims of language suddenly made free. They lived by the corrupted word and they perished by the word made free…' I added: 'Your exposition gains poignancy in the context of your own environment'. Indeed, it was the collapse of the Soviet system that finally made it possible for the United States to turn against the PNC, the party of Burnham and Hoyte, thus belatedly, after 28 years, accommodating Cheddi Jagan, whom they had ejected from power in 1964, before Guyana's independence, for fear of his pro-Soviet communist predilection.

I continued on the issue of the word made free, pointing to an excellent journal of the colonial period, *Timehri*: 'What a joy to learn that *Timehri*, that jewel, will be resurrected! A few days ago, at a conference at Warwick, I spoke of this masterpiece of colonial scholarship, in underlining the folly – I must have said 'thuggery' – of denigrating every aspect of the colonial experience. As an intellectual site, for advancing diverse spheres of knowledge relevant to the colonial environment, *Timehri* is peerless in the English-speaking Caribbean. Such treasure!'

Ian wrote continually about the use of language, the power of words, to enhance the human condition, on one hand, or strengthen the chains that imprison the human spirit, on the other, redounding to the death of creativity and the atrophy of the capacity of societies to renew themselves. He was referring specifically to the collapse of Soviet totalitarianism in the late 1980s, but he was also reflecting on to the tragedy that was Burnham's Guyana. The following is an excerpt from his piece, 'The Tongue Set Free', in *A Love of Poetry* (2013):

> When the language used by those in power deteriorates to the point where it bears no relation to reality, no relation to truth, society simply cannot function properly. Laws become meaningless, rules need not be

obeyed, political exhortations are ignored, all functions of the state are undermined, and men seek their own solutions outside the charade of official promulgations... a society, through language's debasement, inexorably sink beneath a mass of lies, evasions, unspoken fears and hatreds and public/private schizophrenia.

...when one thinks back with a shudder to the days when Guyana sunk to the lowest point , late 1970s to 1985, it seems so clear now that what was being said and written at the highest level of Government was language contrived to defend the indefensible – the need to mobilize the people as grounds for party paramountcy, the goals of proud self-sufficiency and self-reliance to explain the ban on flour and the empty shelves, the need to focus and advance the development effort to excuse stifling freedom of the media.

Indeed, I have no doubt at all that the political and economic decay which overtook Guyana at the time was accompanied by a parallel decay in the arts of expressing ourselves clearly, concisely, properly, truthfully. An effect can become a cause, reinforcing the original cause and producing the same effect in intensified form. Thus the decay in Guyana caused deterioration in the teaching and the use of language and that deterioration intensified the decay of the state.[12]

The thesis – completed in April 1990, about three and a half years after I had started – was, as I have remarked, profoundly inspired by Ian McDonald's piece, 'Tiger in the Stars'. It was as if that image had, indeed, become the spur to effort and achievement to the generations since the 'bound coolie' at Plantation Port Mourant had told his story about his magical sighting on the boat from India to Guyana. So when the thesis was published in 1997 in the Warwick University Macmillan Series, I chose as the title: *'Tiger in the Stars': The Anatomy of Indian Achievement in British Guiana, 1919-29*. The book was launched at London Metropolitan University in June 1997, with Professor Hennessy introducing it.

It was only after this task, which had cast a shadow over me for more than ten years, was done, that I considered Ian's perennial suggestion that I undertake a major study of Jock Campbell. I met Jock for the first time at his home in Nettlebed, Oxfordshire, on Wednesday, 9 May 1990. He was 78, physically frail, but mentally sharp; intellectually, he was as captivating as Ian had told me over many years. It took a little while before he agreed to co-operate with me (I think at Ian's prodding), facilitating over 20 interviews that marked a virtual ten-year project before the book was published in 2004: *Sweetening 'Bitter Sugar': Jock Campbell, the Booker Reformer in British Guiana, 1934-66*.

On 14 June 1990, Ian wrote about the Jock Campbell project:

I was delighted to learn that you met Jock Campbell and that you are contemplating a study of his work in British Guiana. The book you have in mind, as outlined, I think would provide a most interesting work. Jock has mentioned the project to me and I will be sending him various speeches of his in my possession which I am sure will be useful in the project.

The problem was funding; no one would fund it, including Booker. In fact, I had written to Michael Caine, the Chairman of Booker, after I met Jock Campbell, enquiring whether they could provide some funding. I wrote to Ian on 28 June 1990:

> Booker are unable to provide any funds. Michael Caine says: 'our priorities do not allow such expenditure'. It was a cold response but I am determined to proceed. I have no idea if anyone will provide funds for this project… But I usually achieve whatever I really want to do – eventually. Anyway Jock seems keen on the project. Let's hope for the best.

On 7 September 1990 Ian responded:

> I hope your work continues to go well and that you continue to establish yourself in the UK so that your productive work can go on. I hope in particular that you find the time, opportunity and money to do the book on Jock Campbell. It deserves to be done and you are an excellent man to do it. I am disappointed that Booker did not agree to making a grant to do the work. I hope some other source of funds materialises. In the course of your work if you think I can do anything to help, please let me know because the project is near to my heart.

I got a demanding full-time job in 1993; I now had the money, but little time. I had to wait the granting of sabbaticals to do the monumental research required. Even so, I did travel from London to Nettlebed (Oxfordshire) whenever I could to interview Jock; I did interview others as well; I did archival work; I was exhilarated by the project – and the man. Jock, sadly, died on 26 December 1994 (aged 82), two weeks after London Metropolitan University had conferred an honorary doctorate on him. The book was not published until 2005; but through it all, Ian never lost faith in me. I dedicated the book to him in appreciation of his friendship and inspiration over many years. Although it was awarded the Elsa Goveia Prize, 2005, by the Association of Caribbean Historians, I was still anxious about Ian's response. So when he offered the following verdict on the book, I knew, finally, I had not let him down. I had, indeed, contributed something to the legacy of 'Tiger in the Stars':

> I find Professor Clem Seecharan's book on Jock Campbell magnificent. Because I held Jock in such esteem, and still hold his memory in high honour, if this book had fallen short in telling his story I think I would have been the first to be critical. But it measures up exceedingly well to the man and what he tried to do and what he achieved. It is a book of immense significance in telling the story of Guyana at a particularly important juncture in its history – the era just prior to independence. But for me it is also a book which tells the story, and fills in countless interesting details, about the life of an extraordinary man who was my friend and mentor in an unforgettable period of my life… [This] is a big book in every sense – well over 600 pages in length, brimmingly rich in original research, scholarly detail and precious interview material,

above all large in purpose and achievement. I am sure it will be considered an absolutely essential text in understanding a crucial era in Guyana's history, and as time goes on I believe it will be regarded as a classic in the nation's intellectual journey.

It was, soon after, a great honour, on 2 June 2005, for me to invite Ian McDonald to deliver the inaugural Sir Frank Worrell Lecture at London Metropolitan University. As usual, he brought his perspicacity, his poetic imagination and elegant prose to his lecture: 'Cricket: A Hunger in the West Indian Soul'. For me that was a great day: we had come a very long way since I wrote Ian that first letter, in early 1985, from Palmyra Village in Berbice. It was an outstanding address, but one particular thought lodged with me: the unique role that cricket has played in these West Indian islands, scattered in the Caribbean Sea, with little that binds them apart from cricket. Ian observed:

> In the writings of W.B. Yeats there is a wonderfully eloquent phrase; he speaks of 'a community bound together by imaginative possessions'. Yeats used this phrase in the context of discussing the importance of the National Theatre of his beloved Ireland...And he wrote that it is impossible for a nation to exist if there were 'no national institutions to revere, no national success to admire without a model of it in the minds of the people'.
>
> When I think of cricket and the hope of West Indian nationhood the words Yeats spoke so eloquently strike me with a chord that sings. Economically, we are much divided and sometimes seem tempted to go our separate ways. Politically, we remain suspicious of each other and therefore cannot so far summon the will to come together in the many ways we must know are necessary for practical nationhood. But cricket, there I have always hoped we are different and better and more confident and more together. Truly cricket is supremely an imaginative possession which binds our Caribbean together. If it is no longer to be so we have lost something of infinite value.[13]

The essays included in this book all owe something to the faith and inspiration that Ian McDonald has reposed in me over the last 30 years. I hope they are imbued with the spirit and magnanimity he would like to see in a modern, tolerant Guyana, where he migrated to nearly 60 years ago, the place he has helped to shape for the good, against unimaginable odds, by his magnanimous prose and poetry – by his inviolable intellectual integrity.

May all Guyana be influenced in the years ahead by 'The Tiger in the Stars' – daring to leap among the stars: going beyond all boundaries – a symbol of effort and achievement; tolerance and magnanimity!

Therefore it is entirely apt that I conclude with an excerpt from Ian McDonald's piece, 'Magnanimity', from a collection of his essays published in 2012 as *A Cloud of Witnesses*. I commend it to my fellow Guyanese, as we approach our 50th anniversary of independence. It is one of the most profound – probably the wisest – reflections on our national malaise I have encountered. It is the most illuminating intellectual signpost we could possibly plant, on our long, winding road, from our stubborn ethnic bigotry towards the building of a nation:

> In a democracy what is needed above all to avoid a state of continuous civil strife, and the consequential displacement of interest in the needs of the community at large, is magnanimity – magnanimity on all sides: magnanimity of the minority which recognises that those who win cannot be expected to observe a saint-like self-denying ordinance when favours for loyalty are being handed out; but, above all, the magnanimity of the majority who must try their utmost to play the essential role of evenhandedly arbiter, keep the settlement of old scores to a minimum and, overcoming every temptation offered by power, keep reminding themselves that winner must not take all – must indeed bend backwards to give up considerably more than the more fanatic players on their side think justified...
>
> It isn't easy – it is indeed very hard – but democracy without a ruling magnanimity at its heart will never work at all well. You could call it the Mandela Lesson in honour of that very great man. It is a lesson which needs to sink more deeply into our body politic than it ever has done since we became a nation.

I can't improve on this, can you?

Notes

1. 'State of the Nation', *Jaffo the Calypsonian* (Leeds: Peepal Tree Press, 1994), p. 54.
2. We knew, however, of the extravagance of tastes of the great leader: Chivas Regal, truly a colonial hangover.
3. 'Caged', *Selected Poems*, Edward Baugh (ed), (Oxford: MacMillan, 2008), p. 51
4. 'Candle-Light', *Selected Poems*, p. 43
5. 'Tiger in the Stars', in Joel Benjamin, Lakshmi Kallicharan, Ian McDonald and Lloyd Searwar (eds), *They Came in Ships: An Anthology of Indo-Guyanese Prose and Poetry* (Leeds: Peepal Tree Press, 1998).
6. 'A Leopard in the Sky', *Selected Poems*, p. 56.
7. 'Kanhai: Batsman Extraordinary', Viewpoint broadcast on GBC, 5 February, 1983, mimeo.
8. William Hazlitt, 'On Taste', *Sketches and Essays* (Worlds Classics,OUP, 1903), p. 153.
9. Ibid., p. 154.
10. 'Five Great Berbician Cricketers', *International Cricket Souvenir Programme: West Indies v. India, 1983,* Susil Dharry, editor.
11. 'That My Son be Kept Safe', *Between Silence and Silence* (Leeds: Peepal Tree Press, 2003), pp. 19-20.

12. 'Grief', *A Love of Poetry* (Guyana: Caribbean Press, 2013), p. 93-95.
13. 'Cricket: A Hunger in the West Indian Soul', *The Bowling Was Superfine*, Eds. Stewart Brown and Ian McDonald (Leeds: Peepal Tree Press, 2012), p. 17.

Books by Ian McDonald

Fiction
The Humming Bird Tree (London: Heinemann, 1974 [1969]).

Poetry
Mercy Ward (Cornwall: Peterloo Poets, 1992)
Essequibo (Cornwall: Peterloo Poets, 1992)
Jaffo the Calypsonian (Leeds: Peepal Tree Press, 1994).
Between Silence and Silence (Leeds: Peepal Tree Press, 2003).
Ian McDonald Selected Poems, edited by Edward Baugh (Oxford, Macmillan Caribbean, 2008).

Essays
A Cloud of Witnesses (The Caribbean Press, 2012).
A Love of Poetry (The Caribbean Press, 2013).
'Five Great Berbician Cricketers', in *International Cricket Souvenir Programme: West Indies v. India, 1983*, Susil Dharry, editor.
'Tiger in the Stars' in Joel Benjamin, Laxmi Kallicharan, Ian McDonald and Lloyd Searwar (eds), *They Came in Ships: An Anthology of Indo-Guyanese Prose and Poetry* (Leeds: Peepal Tree Press, 1998).

PART II: IN SEARCH OF ME

Indentured Indians in British Guiana

Primitive beginnings: Indians threshing *padi* (unhusked rice) in British Guiana

INDIANS IN GUYANA: AN OVERVIEW

> In February, 1594, Sir Robert Dudley made inquiries about the rumoured Empire of Guiana... He sent a small boat to investigate and its crew returned, after great hardships, to say that the natives had told them of goldmines so rich that the people of the country powdered themselves with gold-dust.[1]
>
> – Michael Swan (1957)

> Guyana has always been a land of fantasy. It was the land of El Dorado...[2]
>
> – V.S. Naipaul (1991)

> I am a revolutionary and I have... revolutionary confidence in the future, because what I stand for [the Soviet system] is winning...I am not only fighting for the people of Guyana. I am fighting for the people of the world.[3]
>
> – Cheddi Jagan (1984)

The Historical Origins of the Community:

Guyana (British Guiana until 26 May 1966) is on the 'southern frontier' of the Caribbean. Although it is situated on the north-eastern shoulder of South America, it is considered a part of the Caribbean because of stronger historical links with the archipelago of islands to the north. Occupied by the Dutch in the late 16th/early 17th centuries, it required monumental effort to colonize it. They had tried to circumvent the necessity for onerous hydraulic works by establishing the early settlements upriver, away from the flat coastland, the mangrove swamps below sea-level. That proved futile: the fertility of the soil diminishes rapidly away from the coast, in the hilly sand and clay belt. Only the Dutch, with their peerless mastery of 'empoldering' – the reclaiming of land through a complex drainage and irrigation system – and access to enslaved African labour, could have constructed and maintained the astounding labyrinthine system of dams, embankments, canals, drains, ditches, 'kokers' or sluices, without which the coastland is uninhabitable. Because of this inauspicious beginning, Guyana never became a mature slave society, like Jamaica, Barbados and the Leeward Islands. Yet it engendered a rebellious spirit among the enslaved.

Because of Guyana's relative underdevelopment when emancipation came in the 1830s, freed Africans were able to buy land, away from the sugar plantations, to create their own villages. This was the source of the militancy of the African people in the 1840s, as they sought to enhance their bargaining position with the planters. In 1842, in the counties of Demerara and Essequibo, they went on strike when the planters reduced wages unilaterally. There was division in the ranks of the latter; the labour supply was eclectic; many plantations could not weather a free labour environment. The workers were therefore able to force a reversal of the wage-slash. In 1848, however, when African workers took similar action against another wage-slash, the planters successfully resisted their demands. They had been fortifying themselves since 1845, having introduced over 11,000 indentured labourers from India and more than 10,000 from Madeira. The plantocracy were resolved to halt the demonstrated capacity of Africans to negotiate wage rates on their terms.

Indian indentureship, therefore, was introduced specifically to enable sugar plantations to retain a body of contract labour ('bound coolies'), in a colony where the freed African people were erroneously perceived to have abundant options for independent livelihood. Moreover, the fact that one-third of the funding of indentureship originated from general revenue, to which Africans contributed inordinately through high indirect taxation on foodstuffs, meant that they were, in reality, subsidizing a system designed to curb their fledgling assertion of rights. This was the context of African perception of Indian indentureship as irreconcilably subversive of their welfare. It was aggravated by the perennial hydrological hazards on the coastland of Guyana. Floods, alternating droughts, chronic malaria, in an environment dominated by the order, size and power of the drained and irrigated sugar plantations, nullified agricultural initiative and embedded in the African inconsolable hurts – colonial oppression, then 'Indian racism'.

Immeasurably more than in environmentally gentler Trinidad, every perceptible advance by Indians would evoke and reinforce those sentiments. The sense of being a victim was magnified and perpetuated by this hard land. In the graphic imagery of the historian, James Rodway (1848-1927):

> Every acre at present in cultivation has been the scene of the struggle with the sea in front and the flood behind. As a result of this arduous labour [African] during two centuries, a narrow strip of land along the coast has been rescued from the mangrove swamp and kept under cultivation by an elaborate system of dams and dykes. Scattered along the rivers and creeks lie a thousand abandoned plantations, most of them indistinguishable from the surrounding forest; these represent the failures of the early settlers [Dutch]. At first sight the narrow line of sugar estates seems but a very poor show for such a long struggle with nature, but when all the circumstances are taken into consideration it is almost a wonder that ...[British Guiana] has not been abandoned altogether. [4]

This evocative assessment remains inviolable.

In 1943 Dr F.C. Benham calculated that the cost of maintaining the hydraulic systems on the plantations that year alone was $459,000 or $2.79 per ton of sugar produced. He conveyed in bewildering detail the Byzantine geometric patterns etched on this reclaimed land:

> Each square mile of cane cultivation involves the provision of 49 miles of drainage canals and ditches and 16 miles of high level waterways. If these figures are raised to cover the whole area under cane the sum total approaches 5,000 miles. Some estates do, in fact, have more than 300 miles of waterways to maintain.[5]

This is incomprehensible to outsiders; Guyanese still take it for granted at their peril. Walter Rodney dramatized the Herculean effort expended in the making of this unlikely colony, on the periphery of the Amazon basin: 'This meant that slaves moved 100 million tons of heavy waterlogged clay with shovel in hand, while enduring conditions of perpetual mud and water.'[6]

It required coerced labour to sustain effort; but it was also necessary to create El Dorado here. Guyana needed (still needs) myth to provoke effort. Fantasy is endemic to its psyche. It breeds inexhaustible visions of riches in the bush – a place so fecund its forests and magnificent rivers must reach the end of the earth; its mountains of gold and diamonds touching the moon. The inaccessibility of the interior of the colony, to most, deepened the myth and lent plausibility to its most surreal representations. Ever since Sir Walter Raleigh's delusional quest for El Dorado, in the late 16th century, Guyana's 'maidenhead' has been on the verge of being penetrated.[7]

Fantasy found a hospitable space in the imagination of the colony's indentured labourers from India; it would vacillate between the exuberant and the melancholy. Because of African repugnance to indentureship, it was difficult for Indians to abjure the stubborn lore that they 'took bread out of the mouths' of Africans. Therefore they would continually deny agency for their migration to the colony; they would attribute it to kidnapping, to trickery, to being duped into going to distant lands. The blame would fall on the evil *arkati*, the recruiter who allegedly stole them all from their villages. They would seek double-billing in the historiography of oppression. They would cultivate the myth that indentureship was a 'new system of slavery'.[8]

The Conditions and Specific Features of the Migration Process:

Of the 238,909 Indian labourers taken to British Guiana between 1838 and 1917, 193,154 or 81% arrived between 1851 and 1900; 75,808 or 31.7% were repatriated between 1843 and 1955. Only 9,668 or 12.7% returned after 1917, when the last batch of indentureds left India; about 85% of the immigrants to Guyana originated in the same region – eastern United Provinces (contemporary Uttar Pradesh [UP]) and western Bihar. The impoverished eastern districts of UP alone contributed 70.3%;

while 15.3% were from the contiguous western districts of Bihar; only 5 or 6% were south Indians, from Madras Presidency (primarily contemporary Tamil Nadu). Most Madrasis had arrived before 1863, when attitudes rooted in slavery still lingered.

However, it is wrong to label indentureship as 'new slavery', however oppressive the conditions in the aftermath of emancipation in 1838. A definitive instrument for rejecting this common characterization was the contract, the 'conditions of service and terms of agreement' all indentured labourers were required to sign in India, before embarkation for the plantation colonies. It is arguable that those terms were often more honoured in the breach and that it took decades for the contract, in its most benign form, to evolve. However, implicit in the signing of a contract was the notion of Indian indentured labourers as free agents with rights. Enslaved Africans had no such concession to their humanity: they were property – deprived of the fruits of labour and their autonomy as individuals, for life, with no recourse to law or any statutory 'protector'. It is therefore erroneous to equate Indian indentureship with African slavery.

The indentureship contract evolved over time, but the basic terms were established by the 1870s. After completing five years of indentureship with a registered employer, and a total of ten years of continuous residence in the colony, and having procured a 'certificate of exemption from labour', Indians were entitled to a 'free return passage'. The immigrant had to work every day except Sundays or authorised holidays: seven hours in the field and 10 hours in the factory. Able-bodied males, sixteen years and over, were paid 1/- per day; adult males not able-bodied, minors of and above ten years of age but under sixteen and female adults were paid 8 pence per day, but were entitled to extra pay when working beyond the stipulated hours. The contract legitimized child labour. Indentured labourers also had the option of task-work, with ostensibly higher remuneration computed on the basis of wage rates obtained by unindentured workers. This, as will be seen later, was one of the most contentious issues, as workers continually contested the basis on which earnings from task-work were calculated. The alleged grievance was that the vagaries of differing tasks were often not given due recognition. But, unlike enslaved Africans, Indians had recourse to the Immigration Agent General or his district agents – 'protectors' – authorized to visit plantations to investigate specific complaints. Indentured labourers were allowed to visit the office of the 'protector' to seek redress of grievances. This, however, often resulted in labourers being prosecuted for breach of contract. In fact, in comparison with the rights of employers, those of Indian labourers were breached consistently, even within the judicial system. Between 1874 and 1895, only 208 employers were prosecuted successfully; on the other hand, 65,084 indentured labourers were convicted of breaches of labour laws.

Indentureship was not a just system, but assertions that it was a continuation of slavery were fundamentally flawed. African resentment that 'coolies' were pampered usurpers of material benefits which were rightfully theirs was not assuaged by claims of common oppression.

Indian indentureship to Guyana lasted over 75 years. Genuine social and economic reasons impelled a minority of enterprising men and women to flee their desert of hope in eastern Uttar Pradesh and western Bihar: land-hunger, chronic debts, famine, cholera and small pox epidemics, young girls widowed in their early teens, etc. Most were not kidnapped or tricked by the infamous recruiters, the *arkatis*, into bondage. But these were desperate people; they must have been seduced by the blandishments of recruiters: an element of deception cannot be discounted. Young men seeking escape from the perennial yoke of acquired family debts, or the macabre spectre of an early grave, because of famine and disease, were especially vulnerable. Many must have left wives and children behind whom they would never see again. Many girls and young women were in the same boat. About 82% of the women taken to Guyana were between 10 and 30 years, with 30% between 10 and 20 and 52.6% between 20 and 30. Of the male immigrants 85.6% were in the 10-30 age-group. This is entirely corroborative of what Brij Lal unearthed on Fiji;[9] therefore, his findings with regard to the marital status of the indentureds are arguably applicable to Guyana. He found that 86.8% of the adult male immigrants to Fiji were reportedly single; and, surprisingly, 63.9% of the adult females were reportedly single. Moreover, of the 36.1% of the women *not* reportedly single, only 73% were accompanied by their husbands. These were people on the move, largely unencumbered by spouses, siblings or children. They were, indeed, seeking a new beginning.

Because 90% of girls were married between 10 and 14, according to the UP census of 1891, it is probable that most of the indentured women who declared themselves 'single' were, in fact, widowed because of the high mortality of child-husbands in the late 19th century. Some may have been deserted by husbands who found migratory employment in Assam and Bengal and never kept in touch. Some women, driven by penury, may have succumbed to sexual advances by villagers or sought refuge in prostitution in provincial towns. There was no future for such women in India. Even in her parents' village, a widowed girl was socially dead. Many women succumbed to despair. A minority did not – flight resurrected hope; women endowed with abundant imagination, courage and drive. But both men and women often had a lot to hide. The guilt festered. Because the recent past evoked pain and concealed much that would necessarily have jeopardized the assumption of a new persona, collective amnesia cohered quickly – a watertight instinct to forget. People have a remarkable capacity to unlearn. The past in India had to be re-imagined in Guyana.

The Historical Experience in the Country:
V.S. Naipaul (born 1932) recalls of his Trinidadian boyhood:

> To me India seemed very far away, mythical, but we were at that time, in all the branches of our extended family, only about forty or fifty years out of India...The *Ramayana* was the essential Hindu story...[I]t lived among us the way epics lived. It had a strong and fast and rich narrative and, even with the divine machinery, the matter was very human. The characters and their motives could always be discussed; the epic was like a moral education for us all.[10]

It was easier to appropriate an imagined India from this great Hindu classic rather than Uttar Pradesh and Bihar. The latter have no resonance whatsoever in the lands where Indian indentured labourers settled.

The Indo-Guyanese universe would be permeated by the mythical. The India of the *Ramayana*, reinforced by *Ram Lila* festivals, the dramatization of the text, fed the imagination – it was the real homeland. It spoke of a golden age. It helped them to forget the recent past. It absorbed pain and loss – the gnawing guilt. Like the images of Bollywood, from the 1930s onwards, it was escapism, fantasy. The real India was too evocative of recent traumas: for most, a terminal break with all relatives; the abdication of communal responsibilities; the consuming poverty that killed young husbands, wives and children – the widowing of young child-brides and the implacable stigma; the pervasive servitude of spirit. The appeal of the *Ramayana* is rooted in its narrative of exile, redemption, triumphal return and the arrival of an age of splendour, the rule of Lord Rama. The loyalty, self-abnegation, the utter selflessness of his wife, Sita, the quintessence of Indian womanhood, also, enthrals. The tale is the antithesis of the impoverished, caste-ridden districts of eastern UP and western Bihar, in the late 19th and early 20th centuries. Poignantly, the theme of exile and return fed the illusion of impermanence on the Guyanese plantation, while the myth of *Ram Rajya,* the benevolent rule of Lord Rama, offered redemption from the perceived 'new slavery' in the new land. The *Ramayana* offered a sustaining vision.[11]

Indians on the plantations resisted and often encountered brutal reprisals. They combined passive forms of resistance with active ones. Because of poor wages and a perception that their contracts were not being honoured, desertions were common: between 1876 and 1910, there were 20,058. But in July 1869, at Plantation Leonora, a tradition of militancy was born. Basdeo Mangru observes:

> At Leonora about forty workers of the shovel gang complained that their wages were withheld for non-completion of an assigned task on water-logged soil. They became violent, assaulted the deputy manager and confronted the police, who were armed with Enfield Rifles, with their long, knotted *hackia* sticks. As was the fashion of the time those who articulated workers' grievances were arrested, convicted and incarcerated.[12]

The next year violence was more widespread, enveloping Plantations Hague, Uitvlugt, Mon Repos, Non Pareil, Zeelugt, Vergenoegen and Success.

A strike at Devonshire Castle (Essequibo), in October 1872, would prove fatal, establishing a pattern in Indo-Guyanese resistance: five were killed and seven wounded. Workers would complain about inadequate earnings; their grievance deemed spurious by managers; they often sought redress by marching to the office of the Immigration Agent General or one of his district agents; the police would be called in to stop the march; tempers became inflamed, culminating in workers being fatally shot by the police. Men and women resisted. Mangru documents the militancy of the women at Devonshire Castle:

> A fascinating feature of the unrest was the active participation of indentured women who were armed with *hackia* sticks. They, too, complained of long hours and insufficient pay and refused to disperse when ordered to do so. An eye witness claimed that they 'screamed and cursed in a most diabolical manner' and waved their hands frantically in the air. The fact that Indian women were prepared to die with their husbands seemed to indicate gross dissatisfaction with working conditions.[13]

Resistance to perceived injustices, especially after the depression of 1884 through to 1905, was a fact of Indian life on the estates. Between 1886 and 1889 no less than 100 strikes were recorded. In October 1896 five workers were killed and 59 wounded at Non Pareil, East Coast Demerara; in May 1903, at Friends, East Bank Berbice, six were killed and seven wounded; in April 1913, 14 were killed at Rose Hall, East Canje, Berbice. In April 1924, 13 were shot at Ruimveldt, East Bank Demerara. Virtually every year there were strikes on the sugar plantations; this was a culture of resistance. In 1916, for instance, there were 23 strikes; in 1920, 15. There would be more killings at Leonora in 1939 and Enmore in 1948.

Apart from the shootings at Rose Hall in 1913, strikes were comparatively rare in the county of Berbice. Infamous exceptions were Mara and Friends, dying estates in a derelict riverine district: workers on these two estates had no rice lands. Accommodation between workers and management was generally more commonplace in Berbice; possibilities for supplementing wages were greater. But in British Guiana as a whole, it is arguable that by the 1920s-30s a predisposition to radical change was consolidated among Indian plantation workers.

Social, Cultural and Economic Change in the Community over Time: Hinduism has no centre of ecclesiastical authority. And in Guyana, in the latter half of the 19th century, away from the constraints of customs and the tyranny of village ways, Brahmins – no more than 2% of all indentured labourers – could venture on a subversive course. Confronted with rampant proselytizing by Christian missionaries, Brahmin priests began ministering even to those known to be of the lowest castes, in their homes. Moreover, they partook of their cooked food. This was sacrilegious in India. It is true that self-interest precipitated the Brahmins' radical stance, for the plantation regime applied secular criteria in allocating leadership roles; Brahmins were often supervised by lower caste men. Therefore by facilitating the ritual entry of low-caste people into the mainstream of Hinduism in Guyana, Brahmins were creating a vast body of devotees who reciprocated by paying obeisance to them – a massive compensation for their diminishing status on the estates, but equally a source of lucrative livelihood.

In India, Brahmins had a monopoly on the interpretation of the scriptures. Therefore, it is inconceivable how religious functions, life-cycle rites and complex ritual elaboration could have been sustained without these Brahmin *pandits*. Hinduism atrophied in Jamaica and the Windward Islands (Grenada, St Lucia and St Vincent), minor destinations of indentured labourers, because of a paucity of Brahmins. These Indians were less fortified against Christian missionaries. The assimilation process was accelerated; the erosion of cultural moorings also tended to retard, if not thwart, social and economic mobility.

In Guyana and Trinidad, however, the challenge from Christian evangelists elicited resistance and flexibility from their viable Brahmin minorities, a more instrumental approach to Hinduism. This was the context in which they adopted those of the lowest castes – Chamars, Dusadhs, Doms, Bhangis – into the orthodox mainstream, *Sanatan Dharma*. And these low-caste people responded without equivocation, as Chandra Jayawardena observes: 'Since it was a "higher class cult" it was an attraction to the low castes who had traditionally belonged to cults and sects with distinctive gods and rites because they had been excluded...The redefinition of Hinduism as one religion common to all Indians led to the acceptance of *Sanatan Dharma* by the smaller groups.'[14]

Orthodox Hinduism has retained its appeal in spite of the missionary efforts of the reformist Arya Samaj, since the late 1920s, because it was not characterized by austerity, philosophical excesses or exegetical preoccupations. Its preference for the more accessible classic, the *Ramayana*, engendered substantially more popular empathy than the less penetrable *Mahabharata* or the *Vedas*. Besides, the accessibility of the Gods in people's homes, the evocative *murtis*, the so-called idols of Christian infamy; the carnival of rituals; the exposition of the text accompanied by the infectious rhythm of the music (at *kathas*); the bacchanalian spirit of festivals (the spring festival of *holi* and the harvest festival of *diwali* especially), invested so-called orthodox *Sanatan Dharma* with a lightness of touch: a chaotic, consuming spontaneity.

Because of the difficulty of reclaiming land, many more Indians in Guyana – Hindus and Muslims – remained on the plantations than in Trinidad. This has fostered unprecedented solidarity between them. The plantation as 'other' is more enduring. A community spirit has transcended ancient religious incomprehension and inspired a continuity of secular purpose. This was the foundation of the mobility aspirations of many Indo-Guyanese, conducive to the rise of a middle class, based on rice, cattle, commerce and western education.

Wet rice culture was transplanted here and soon became a successful venture. By 1903, 17,500 acres were being cultivated. Most of the rice was grown in villages in the vicinity of plantations. The gradual reform of laws relating to the purchase of Crown Lands, during the 1890s, when the sugar industry faced a prolonged crisis, precipitated a significant rise in land-ownership among Indians. Numerous predominantly Indian villages emerged in all three counties: Essequibo, Demerara and Berbice. However, the acquisition of some land formerly owned by Africans in the villages tended to exacerbate the latter's fear of Indian ascendancy, deepening the resentment spawned by indentureship.

It was during the First World War, with the inaccessibility of rice from India and Burma, that Indians in Guyana stepped in to fill the vacuum. The acreage expanded from 33,888 in 1913 to 58,090 by 1917,[15] while exports increased from 7,709 tons to 14,367 tons respectively. The value of exports rose impressively, from $519,544 in 1913 to $1,422,806 in 1917. The progress of the rice industry was accompanied by the progressive rise of cattle-rearing by Indians. The figures are not reliable, as Indians tended to deliberately underestimate the size of their herds in order to elude taxation, but of the cattle on the coastland in 1917, conservatively estimated at 87,000, a very high percentage was owned by Indians.

By the mid-1930s rice acreage had increased to 85,522. In 1936 *Indian Opinion*, organ of the British Guiana East Indian Association, celebrated the farmers' tenacity:

> '[W]ith the exception of the sugar estates, no scheme has yet been evolved by the powers-that-be whereby rice-growers can make use of the valuable water from...[the] rivers. The [rice] industry, carried on chiefly by East Indians...and to whose indomitable pluck and energy its development is largely due, is dependent entirely on rainfall...the fortunes of the rice farmer are largely at the mercy of the weather, and floods or droughts may cause very serious damage or total ruin. At one time his crops may be burnt out and on another occasion washed out.[16]

The partial drought in the latter part of 1930 and the floods in 1934 wrought havoc on the rice industry. The acreage reaped in 1930 was 64,252, but in 1931, with adequate rainfall, it rose to 78,424; in 1934 it declined to 55,112, yet the following year, with better weather, 85,522

Joseph Barran (1925-2003), my uncle, ploughing our rice fields, mid 1970s.

Harvesting our rice, late 1970s: my brother, Roy (with speckled hat); my grandfather, 'Skipper' is on the extreme right

The 'caste' calling survives: my brother (Sunil) tends our cattle, early 1980s

acres of rice were harvested. In spite of perennial problems of drainage and irrigation, the dream of the landless 'bound coolies' from the United Provinces would have been realised by many Indians (though far from a majority) in Guyana by the 1920s-30s.

The Indian middle class had its origin in the rice and cattle industries, bolstered by the advancement of those who had progressed further, into commerce, in Georgetown, the capital, and New Amsterdam, the main town in Berbice. It is arguable that the absence of an entrepreneurial group among Africans constitutes a major divergence in the mobility trajectories of the two peoples. It is also a key factor in perpetuating African resentment of perceived Indian ascendancy. A major reason for the rise of the entrepreneurial elite among the latter was the consolidation of the joint family as a corporate economic unit by the First World War. The patriarchal family could mobilise the labour of sons and daughters-in-law, occasionally even daughters and sons-in-law, during the embryonic stages of a business, for the crucial task of capital accumulation. Moreover, some wealth was a prerequisite to being a good Hindu or Muslim: both religions, as practised by Indians in Guyana, required considerable expenditure on religious functions, marriages, life-cycle rites as a whole. Communal ritual feastings sponsored by families, also, were an onerous aspect of being a good Hindu or Muslim. Thrift, therefore, was indispensable to obligatory ritual extravagance. Among Hindus, Lakshmi, the Goddess of wealth, was revered. Religious and commercial imperatives intersected.

The Indian middle class was established by the 1920s. They were also pioneers in education, funding the professional pursuits of at least one son, initially, in law and medicine. They were aided immeasurably by the Canadian Presbyterians (the Canadian Mission), who commenced work in Trinidad in 1868, exclusively among Indians, and had initiated a similar mission in British Guiana in 1885. Their skilful manipulation of cardinal Indian cultural symbols conferred on western education unprecedented attraction to Indians in both colonies, their general resistance to Christianity notwithstanding. The Canadian Mission encouraged the wearing of *dhoti* and *sari*, the use of Hindi, the singing of *bhajans* (Christian hymns in Hindi), the holding of cottage meetings in Indian homes, where *Yesu katha* (the story of Jesus) was narrated. Canadian missionaries were expected to speak Hindi; interesting Bible stories were rendered in the language. Indian catechists were trained in the colony, and they were tutored to cite the Hindu classic, the *Bhagavad-Gita*, as 'the authority for the claims for Jesus Christ', thus rendering Him worthy of worship by Indians. *Yisu Masih* (Jesus Christ) was lauded as *Ishwari-ji* (the Lord) and *Shri Bhagwan* (God). The principal architects of mission work in Guyana were Rev J.B. Cropper and Rev J.A. Scrimgeour.[17]

The Canadian Mission, more than any other denomination, facilitated the accelerated education of Indian boys in the colony. Scrimgeour in particular, a gifted teacher, was able to reach the imagination of many. He even resisted the inclination of Cropper to prioritize the saving of souls over the educational component. Scrimgeour had unimpeachable credentials in the education of Indians in Trinidad; and in the 1920s, at the Berbice High School (for boys), opened in 1916, he replicated his achievement by enhancing the perception by Indians of education as another instrument of mobility in Guyana. Just as path-breaking was the Berbice Girls' High School, opened in 1920. This offered education to several gifted Indian girls: Marie Khan, Katie Kowlessar, Helen Khan and the sisters, Irene and Clara Ramdeholl. Clara qualified as a lawyer in London in 1939. While on her way home to Guyana the next year in the *Simon Bolivar*, the ship was torpedoed by the Germans; she did not survive. Credit is due also to the Canadian Mission primary schools, in villages and plantations, which offered some Indian girls a rudimentary education. With the removal, in 1933, of the obscurantist Swettenham Circular (passed in 1902), which had sanctioned the non-attendance of Indian girls – a religious concession ostensibly – the Mission expanded its work significantly. But as the Director of Education observed on that momentous occasion, 'it is an advance desired by the Indians themselves, and an acknowledgement of the position they hold in the community today.'[18]

Demographic Changes and Gender Relations:

Although 238,909 indentured labourers from India went to British Guiana between 1838 and 1917 and only 75,808 (31.7%) were repatriated, the Indian population in the colony did not reach 239,000 until 1956. Guyana was chronically malarial until the late 1940s, and Indians were the most susceptible to that disease. In 1891 there were 105,563 Indians in the colony (38.9% of the total population) and 115,588 Africans (42.7%); the census of 1911 recorded 126,517 Indians (43.8%) and 115,486 Africans (39.9%). The census of 1921, however, revealed that the Indian population had declined to 124,928 (43.3%); Africans numbered 117,169 (40.6%). In the census of 1931 130,540 Indians and 124,203 Africans were returned, or 41.9% and 39.9% respectively. The returns at the next census, in 1946, were as follows: 163,434 Indians (43.5%) and 143,385 Africans (38%). With the eradication of malaria by the late 1940s, the next census, in 1960, revealed a remarkable demographic change among Indians in Guyana: 267,840 (47.7%), an increase of nearly 104,000 since 1946; whereas the African population of 183,980 represented an increase of only 40,000. Africans now constituted only 32.8% of the Guyanese population.

The eradication of malaria, principally the work of the great malariologist, Dr George Giglioli (1897-1972), was the single most significant advance in the social history of Indians in the colony. On the occasion of the country's independence, in May 1966, the *Guyana Graphic* observed: 'The era of Guyana's growing pains is pockmarked with incidents none the least significant of which has been the battle against the scourge of malaria. And in the battle one man's name stands out boldly – Dr George Giglioli, famed malariologist whose dedicated service in the cause of ridding Guyana of this dreaded scourge, is a story of single-minded purpose and unflagging determination'.[19] As Jay R. Mandle observes, whereas the crude birth rates between Indians and Africans were 31.9 and 30.1 respectively between 1911 and 1920, between 1946 and 1950 these had improved to 46.1 and 35.1 respectively; between 1956 and 1960 the birth rates were 49.4 and 38.6 respectively.[20] This continuing disparity fuelled the escalating political rivalry between Indians and Africans, towards the end of empire. The comparatively positive economic and social indices identified earlier, for Indians, were enhanced by these demographic advantages in the 1950s-60s. The emergence of highly talented Indo-Guyanese cricketers (such as Rohan Kanhai, Joe Solomon and Ivan Madray) was both a symptom of social progress and a major contribution to Indo-Guyanese self-confidence. The political pendulum had been swinging increasingly in favour of Indians since the late 1940s; but the 'ethnic balance' was disrupted.

Another important aspect of the Indian population was its distribution: although the proportion resident on sugar plantations remained high, it had declined from 48% in 1911 to 38% in 1946; the urban Indian population had hardly changed: 5.8% in 1911, 5.9% in 1946; but Indians resident in villages had increased from 46.2% in 1911 to 56.1% in 1946. While Indians constituted 85.6% of the estate population in 1911; in 1946 they were nearly 90%.

The 40:100 woman/man ratio of recruitment under indentureship had resulted in a chronic shortage of women. This bred prolonged instability in family structure, especially on the plantations. But the freedom which women had sought by migrating was reflected, in part, in a greater tendency for women in the 19th century to choose their partners, or leave them if they so wished. Because Hindu and Muslim weddings were not deemed legal, some women left their husbands for a variety of reasons: lack of financial stability, alcoholism, violent behaviour, even sexual inadequacy. A minority who were prostitutes in India capitalized on the shortage of women in Guyana to augment their earnings. The virtual elimination of caste taboos meant that women could consciously seek to marry a man of known higher caste, especially if the financial consequences were perceived as advantageous. Moreover, women were workers in their own right; this enhanced their freedom to choose. It was certainly a substantially freer environment for women than in UP and Bihar. However, this freer state was fraught with dangers, especially when wives deserted husbands whose wealth was concentrated in the gold jewellery in their possession. Even amidst the early sexual instability of the plantations, the honour of men was deemed sacrosanct: many wife-murders, especially before the 1920s, were rooted in the shame occasioned by the perceived sexual infidelity of wives.

Sexual freedom was a tenuous and ambiguous one for Indian women on the plantation, for it was subversive of the Brahminic patriarchal ideal, which had reasserted itself in the context of resistance to evangelical Christianity, after the 1870s. The Sita construct of loyalty to mothers-in-law, husbands and sons so permeates the Indian imagination that most women could not elude its web. Meanwhile the virtual equalization of the sex ratio, by the 1920s, conferred on the reasserted patriarchal ideal the means of realisation: the proportion of Indian women to men in the villages was about 84 to 100; on the plantations, 76 to 100, improving to 82 to 100 at the end of the decade. Land-ownership was crucial to livelihood, so families on the sugar plantations were inclined to marry their daughters into families that owned land, in the villages. Women tended to join the patriarchal/patrilocal families of husbands. These marriages were solemnized by Brahmin priests steeped in ancient codes: the indissolubility of marriage vows, marital fidelity and loyalty to the patriarchal family. As in India, divorce was virtually impossible; it brought shame and the idea of a woman returning to her mother's family was no less disgraceful in Guyana.

The tenuous freedom for women on the plantation was now being exchanged for status, however circumscribed, within the Hindu or Muslim joint family. The woman now belonged to the husband's family which functioned as a corporate economic unit. It was the key instrument in exploiting diverse niches in the Guyanese coastal environment. The paterfamilias would seek to mobilise family labour for a range of seasonal economic activities. In the villages especially, family labour, male and female, was deployed into rice, cattle, market-gardening, sometimes rural commerce – a general store and/or a rum shop. In poorer families, work in the village was supplemented with strategic employment on the sugar estates, during the cane harvest. This regime necessarily entailed curbing the fledgling freedom of women, but in the context of Brahminic Hinduism, the status conferred by a stable marriage, a degree of financial security within the joint family, and the prospect of becoming the wife of the paterfamilias, in later years, were infinitely more attractive in an agrarian society than the capricious freedom on the plantation, to choose or leave one's partner.[21]

Naipaul says that the joint family 'protects and imprisons'.[22] Once the Brahminic code was reconstituted in Guyana, the sanction against female rebels was immutable. Often, the few who dared to flee the perceived prison, desperately unhappy arranged marriages, became rudderless: washed up, beyond the pale – whores. But the prostitute, though marginalised and maligned, played an ambiguous role in Indo-Guyanese society. Her sexual services had provided a degree of stability on the plantations, under indentureship. The reconstituted Brahminic code now sanctioned early marriage: often boys, 17 or 18, would marry girls 13 or 14; and female virginity was an imperative in marriage. Bereft of sexual experience – even basic social competence with women beyond the immediate family – the anxieties of these young men, on the verge of marriage, were raw; nerves taut. So although whoring was not condoned, the whorehouse, as an institution, paradoxically, was a ballast of this rigid sexual morality. Patriarchal assumptions would quietly concede a space for it. The whore was the singular refuge for the male novice seeking the rudiments: he could spend a whole night with her, unhurried, blundering towards a modicum of competence. Rooplall Monar's novel, *Janjhat* (1987), gives a truthful portrait of the consequences of sexual ignorance in a new marriage.[23]

However, within the interstices of the family's draconian frame, the options thrown up by Christianity allowed a few women to move beyond the mould, finding a space beyond the domestic sphere: a secondary education, then a job as a schoolteacher in a Canadian Mission school. A few would discover leadership skills within the context of family businesses. But it would take several decades before some entered university. A new persona for women was really taking shape: it accommodated substantially greater exposure to the public sphere than in India, even if it were still heavily circumscribed by patriarchal assumptions. Today there are thousands in Guyana and in the large Guyanese diaspora, in Canada and the United States, who have charted successful careers in diverse fields: law, medicine, business, academia and the international civil service. The mass migration of Indo-Guyanese women since the post-colonial decline, from the late 1960s, has provided increased options for autonomy.

Major Events and/or Episodes in the Life of the Community:
Intellectual resistance was seminal in the making of the community. This was first exemplified by the Anglo-Indian missionary and writer, Rev H.V.P. Bronkhurst (1826-95). In books such as *The Colony of British Guyana and its Labouring Population* [1883], *The Ancestry or Origin of our East Indian Immigrants* [1886] and *Among the Hindus and Creoles of British Guyana* [1888], he documented the great secular achievements of ancient India thus demonstrating that the 'coolie' phase of Indian life, in British Guiana, was 'a microscopic episode' in the longevity and opulence of Indian civilisation: art, language, philosophy, architecture, cave paintings, sculpture, poetry, and other manifestations of refinement. Embedded in Bronkhurst's writings on Guyana is an ambivalence bred by his mixed race identity; but his pride in the diverse treasures of the great Indian civilisation is unambiguous:

> [W]hy should the young man of the colony, in whose veins runs the Indian blood, lag behind, or in any way appear to be inferior to other races in the colony? Let us be worthy descendants of our forefathers, whose aims were far higher and more sublime, and in whose veins ran the milk of humanity, who maintained the freedom of men and women alike. If we are truly proud of being the sons of India, then let us try to be a true pride of India, the home of our ancestors, whence in bygone days enlightenment and civilisation travelled to the other parts of the world.[24]

One person who attributed his provenance to Bronkhurst was Joseph Ruhomon (1873-1942), the first Indian intellectual born in Guyana. His seminal pamphlet, *India: The Progress of Her People at Home and Abroad*....[1894], the first published by an Indian in the Caribbean, was profoundly influenced by the magnanimous strand in Bronkhurst's idea of India: celebrating her magnificent legacy of learning. Bronkhurst and young Joseph Ruhomon were able to provoke a rudimentary Indian consciousness in Guyana, at the end of the 19th century. In this pantheon of Indian pathfinders, Bechu, the 'bound coolie radical', an unremitting critic of the indentureship system, has also earned a place.[25]

Between March 1897 and February or March 1901, when he left British Guiana, Bechu's provocative letters to *The Daily Chronicle* were a medium of embryonic democracy, in a society where the franchise was very limited and the planters' power to shape policy was still considerable. Bechu's letters in defence of Indian rights were a catalyst for debates on the key issues of the day. He was unflappable in the face of threats from the goliaths of privilege and unmindful of his own security. He was uncompromising in his cause: the rights of Indians in the colony. Like all visionaries he was not averse to varnishing the truth in dramatizing his case; to challenge certainties; to disrupt complacency; evoke guilt. Ruhomon recorded his impressions of the man in February 1897. He deemed Bechu 'the redoubtable, invincible… champion of his race', and commended his 'fearless and straightforward' articulation of his people's grievances.[26]

The rehabilitation of India – its ancient heritage, bolstered by Gandhian India seen to be in revolt against imperial rule – brought pride to the Indian middle class after the First World War. They founded three key organisations: the British Guiana East Indian Cricket Club (1915), the British Guiana East Indian Association (1916) and the Wesleyan East Indian Young Men's Society (1919), of which Peter Ruhomon (brother of Joseph) was for nearly two decades the leading light. The latter two organisations did the bulk of their work in the 1920s-30s. They promoted the educational and intellectual elevation of Indians while celebrating India's historical and contemporary achievements. The membership of all three bodies comprised Christians, Hindus and Muslims. They were not apologetic in articulating a categorically Indian perspective. A bifurcated ethnic nationalism was taking shape: one Indian, the other African. These might intersect occasionally but attitudes were hardening.

This was reinforced by the Colonisation Scheme in the 1920s, aggravating African fears that it was a ruse to flood Guyana with Indians. Supported by the plantocracy and sections of the Indian community in the colony, the scheme was an attempt to revive immigration from India after its termination in 1917. The foundation of African apprehension was a meeting between the multiracial British Guiana Colonisation Deputation and officials of the India Office, in London, in 1919. Chaired by the Under-Secretary of State, Lord Sinha, an Indian, J.A. Luckhoo, the first Indian legislator in the colony, advocated the creation of an 'Indian Colony' in British Guiana. In the presence of the African-Guyanese delegates, Luckhoo stated:

> [I]n British Guiana, although we form 40% of the population, we feel and we have always felt that we are scattered sons of India, and that India should stretch her hands across to us and lift us up. The only way of doing this is to increase our numbers in the colony...*We hope that in future British Guiana will become a great Indian Colony.* ...We appeal to the Head of the India Office, and to the leaders of Indian authority and opinion to give us their help. We feel that you have our destiny in your hands, and we ask you to remember [that] those people who emigrate to British Guiana will have the same rights, and that if they will come in sufficient numbers, we shall be able to build up an Indian Colony which will be a credit to India and the Empire [emphasis added].[27]

Luckhoo and Dr William Hewley Wharton, the Indian members of the Deputation, also issued a pamphlet in London, *British Guiana Imperial Colonisation Scheme*, which restated their case for an 'Indian colony'. They met Gandhi in India in 1919-20, but he did not support the scheme. When they tried to resurrect it in 1923-4, the principal African organisation in Guyana, the Negro Progress Convention (NPC), dispatched a memorandum to the Colonial Office (in February 1924) denouncing the scheme as 'a distinct act of discrimination' against Africans, who should have been offered 'first consideration' to recruit African immigrants, as they were the 'pioneer settlers' of British Guiana. The NPC feared for the future of Africans if the Indian population were augmented inordinately by the scheme:

> 'It would tend to rob them [Africans] of their political potentialities as they would be in the minority in any voting contest: the Indian voters would become more than or equal to the votes of any two of the other sections of the community; it would be detrimental to good government and the preservation of the peace of the country...All this makes it necessary that the different sections of the subject races should be as near as possible balanced.[28]

The ominous contours of Guyanese politics were already discernible.

Race would become the dominant force after the Second World War. Indians were in the ascendancy, but the journey to independence would be fraught with many imponderables.

The Nature and Role of Political Participation – Party Politics, Political Leadership and Ideology:

Escapism has always had its use in coping with the harsh Guyanese reality. Indians were doubly fortified. The golden age of the *Ramayana* met the extravagant promise of El Dorado,[29] deepening the mythical proclivity of the Indian mentality: the millennial is irrepressibly seductive. An element of Aryanism had seeped into the seminal thoughts of Joseph Ruhomon in the 1890s. In the 1920s, J.A. Luckhoo's idea of an Indian Colony was permeated by the messianic; it would be followed in the mid-1930s by the fantastic ideals of the first Indian trade unionist in the colony, Ayube Edun. After the Second World War, Indians would put their faith in the greatest dreamer of them all – the implacable Marxist, Cheddi Jagan.

In Guyana the sugar plantation was ever evocative of enduring hurts. In 1939 and 1948, at Leonora and Enmore respectively, Indian workers were again gunned down. The formation of the first trade union by an Indo-Guyanese visionary, Ayube Edun (1893-1957), had politicized many Indian workers by the end of the 1930s. The intransigence of the plantocracy, which sought to strangle embryonic unionism, had stirred these workers' wrath. The shootings in 1939, while the Moyne Commission was sitting in Georgetown investigating abysmal social and economic conditions in the British West Indies, hastened the recognition of Edun's Manpower Citizens' Association (MPCA). Armed with a journal, *The Guiana Review*, Edun unleashed a searing critique of colonial society generally, and the plantation in particular. But permeating Edun's philosophy for change was a utopian strand that would be replicated even more extravagantly in the thoughts of Cheddi Jagan. In his book of 1935, *London's Heart-Probe and Britain's Destiny*, Edun advocated the reforming of the British Empire by the creation of a Rational-Practical-Ideal state, the 'inviolable controller' of production and distribution that would 'mobilise the citizens' in order to cater for 'each citizen's equal needs'. This ideal state would also have sole responsibility for the education of children, taking the place of parents.[30]

The unchanging perception of the plantation fed the messianic vision among Indo-Guyanese, thus laying the foundation for the rise of the Marxist leader, Cheddi Jagan (1918-97). His crusade against the evils of 'bitter sugar' would sustain his mission for over fifty years. Cheddi was an industrious, honest man. He was an indefatigable fighter for the working class against those whom he defined as the 'sugar gods': capitalist 'exploiters' epitomised by Booker, which owned most of the sugar plantations. But

Jagan's long-term political failure stemmed from the intractability of the race issue, between Africans and Indians in Guyana; his political inflexibility, especially after Castro's revolution of 1959; his inability to cultivate strategic allies (such as Jock Campbell, the head of Booker, a reformer; and Iain Macleod, the liberal Tory Colonial Secretary); and his incapacity for clear thinking marked by a tortuously doctrinaire propagation of his beliefs, which alienated many potential allies. Cheddi was an indefatigable campaigner against the 'evils of colonialism and imperialism' – the inveterate gadfly – not a statesman. As a somewhat uncharitable observer noted, he found it infinitely more satisfying to travel than to have arrived.[31]

This flaw would lead to the saddling of Guyana with the dictatorial regime of the African leader, Forbes Burnham (1923-85) and his successor, Desmond Hoyte, between 1964 and 1992. For some of this time as president, Burnham, a Machiavellian, affected a radical posture, in order to consolidate and prolong his dictatorship. By strategically embracing Marxism and Fidel Castro – the core of Jagan's creed – he reduced Jagan to impotence. Moreover, conscious that elections in Guyana are ethnic censuses, Burnham rigged them all: in 1968, 1973, 1980 and 1985 (the latter by Hoyte, his successor). Rigging was deemed imperative to stall the political and economic ascendancy of Indians. The latter evoked in most Africans deep foreboding – a reflex triggered by old fears: loss of land to Indians; the 'Indian Colony' idea; Indian commercial success; their cultural resilience and triumphal identity with 'Mother India'. Substantial educational advances by Indians, after the Second World War, exacerbated that fear as it threatened the last citadel of African supremacy: the professions and the civil service; so did their demographic leap (with the eradication of malaria in the late 1940s) and the granting of universal suffrage in the early 1950s.

Jagan's PPP won the elections in 1953 and 1957. But in March 1960, although the British granted Cheddi internal self-government, with independence in a couple of years virtually assured, he tactlessly repudiated the 'imperialists' for not giving immediate freedom to British Guiana. He knew that independence was there for the taking, and that internal self-government was an established prelude. Yet he denounced the new constitutional proposals in language unbecoming of a statesman: 'They [the British] were prepared to adorn me with the title of Premier and I threw it back in their faces, because I was not asking to become Premier but to have cabinet status as in Trinidad'.[32]

He promptly announced that he was going to Cuba to learn how Fidel was doing things. Buoyed by what he saw there, Jagan alluded sarcastically to Prime Minister's Macmillan's recent 'wind of change speech' (with regard to Africa), in proclaiming his renewed faith in the communist creed: 'The East wind was blowing over the West and because of this the West is forced to liberate colonial peoples. The British are breaking up fast, not because they want to make us free…Two years from now there will be no more colonies'.[32]

Jagan probably infuriated the British by his irresponsible rhetoric after 1960, and was obviously lacking in magnanimity when he repudiated Iain Macleod, the Colonial Secretary, who granted him internal self-government against the reservations of many in the Conservative Party. Yet when Macleod met Kennedy in early 1961 and the President cautioned him not to move too quickly to independence for British Guiana, Macleod responded: 'Do I understand, Mr President, that you want us to decolonise as fast as possible all over the world except on your own doorstep?' President Kennedy laughed and said: 'Well, that's probably just about it.' Macleod replied that while he appreciated the President's concern, the policy of taking British Guiana to independence was irreversible. [33]

In October 1961, Cheddi went to Washington and made a fool of himself, provoking an ideological exchange with President Kennedy that placed him unambiguously in the communist camp: 'This philosophy of the West, I argued, could not help the underdeveloped countries.' Earlier, on American television, with the President watching, Cheddi had sought to vindicate his creed: 'Life in the Soviet Union is growing day by day better and better. The standards of living are improving, and as such, we are concerned. We want to know how this is done'.

After 1962, Kennedy's pressure on the British to get rid of Jagan (before independence was granted) was so relentless that they reluctantly agreed to comply, in the summer of 1963. Kennedy had visited Macmillan in England specifically for that purpose. The CIA had been subsidizing a regime of violence by Burnham's African supporters, including the trade unions, in 1962-3. Jagan was acutely vulnerable to this pressure. This was the context in which he was tricked by Duncan Sandys, the right-wing Colonial Secretary, in the autumn of 1963, into signing a document empowering him to change the electoral system to proportional representation. This brought Burnham's People's National Congress (PNC) to power in December 1964 (in a coalition with the anti-communist party, the United Force), and paved the way for the destruction of the Guyanese economy, its democratic institutions (including the judiciary), as well as its rich educational heritage.[34] Out of office, Jagan felt emboldened, in 1969, to embrace his ideological beacon, the Soviet Union: 'a kind of homecoming', he called it. His tactlessness would guarantee Burnham's survival in spite of his own flirtations with the communist bloc.

It is ironic that it took the collapse of the Soviet system for Jagan to return to office, after 28 years. With the end of the Cold War, the United States no longer saw him as a threat. Through the intervention of Jimmy Carter, the PNC Government was prevailed upon to hold free elections. Jagan's undiminished support from Indians combined, for the first time, with that of the indigenous Amerindians, ensured his victory in October 1992.

The Contemporary Situation: Issues, Challenges and Opportunities in Economics and Politics:

It is arguable that this was a pyrrhic victory for Jagan's People's Progressive Party (PPP), as the best educated and skilled Guyanese had long fled overseas. Another set of mediocrities, including party hacks whose intellectual nullity was compounded by their moribund Marxist creed, had come to power. Free and fair elections had come, but Burnham's dictatorship has left a dark shadow over this land. Its democratic institutions have been gravely undermined: parliament, the judiciary, the police, the army, the public service. It is believed that the official economy, based on sugar, rice, forestry, bauxite and gold, is dwarfed by drug-related activities. Guyana is a key place for the transhipment of drugs, from Brazil and Colombia to North America. A small minority, comprising Africans and Indians, have become unimaginably rich; and their money laundering comprises a major part of the capital invested in the country. Moreover, people at the highest levels are now thought to be compromised. The escalating culture of crime has its roots in the drug trade. In this respect, the society is even more criminalised than during Burnham's regime, as armed criminals terrorise vulnerable people with impunity.

Guyana is a land of fear, but the problem has been compounded by the fact that the racial divide, between Africans and Indians, is worse than it has ever been. Indians have the numbers to win elections; but they harbour unprecedented fear, vastly more than Africans, of being victims of violence. The African People's National Congress (PNC) could not be elected even if they were able to win over the Amerindian minority – a remote probability. Yet Africans dominate the army and the police, while accounting for a sizable section of the public service. But with their party out of office since 1992, they are so alienated that it is not inconceivable they will feel that peaceful options are no longer viable unless there are constitutional guarantees that the winners (Indians for the foreseeable future) do not continue to take all. There was violence in the aftermath of the last two elections, in 1997 and 2001, as African supporters of the PNC burnt several businesses owned by Indians in Georgetown. They alleged, erroneously, that the elections were rigged. Africans know that they can never win in free and fair elections. They are desperate, hence susceptible to those who contend that Indian political domination will only be stopped by a violent challenge to their perceived supremacy. The constitutional option is deemed closed. Moreover, the fact that Indians also dominate the commercial sector is eternally inflammatory to African sensibility: it explains why their businesses are the instinctive target of black rage.

Another grave problem is the massive decline in educational standards since the 1970s. The colonial education system, assiduously developed over more than a century in some of the best elite schools in the Empire, was deemed incompatible with a socialist Guyana. Elsewhere, in the Anglophone Caribbean less prone to fantasy, it has been adapted to meet the needs of modern democratic states. In Guyana, however, illiteracy is rampant as many leave school barely able to read or write; many teachers are only marginally less incapacitated. The University of Guyana, too, which had produced many fine scholars in diverse fields, has contributed prolifically to the Guyanese diaspora in North America. Staff and gifted students were continually lured into flight with tales of the financial success of relatives and friends in New York and Toronto.

These daunting problems are aggravated by the susceptibility of the country to floods and droughts. Economic and political decay, over many decades, bred chronic neglect of the complex hydraulic system. Catastrophic floods, in January 2005, undermined this system further, increasing Guyana's vulnerability to a capricious climate, apparently the result of the relentless destruction of the Amazonian rain forest. Meanwhile there are no signs of a speedy alleviation of Guyana's economic woes. The subsidies from the European Union that ensured its viability as a sugar producer are coming to an end, as those countries disengage from guarantees grounded in residual post-colonial sympathies. Moreover, the corrosion of the society by drugs, money laundering and perceived corruption of key officials render prospects for economic regeneration remote.

As *Stabroek News* observes, the past is a millstone on all Guyanese:

> All the elections in Guyana suffer from the legacy of the shameless rigging [by the PNC] in 1968, 1973, 1980 and 1985. This baggage brings with it on the one side [African] an unexpiated guilt for that systematic plundering of votes and on the other [Indian] a desire for revenge for those long years in the wilderness. It is not a propitious setting. By a peculiar inversion the PNC now sees rigging where often none exists.

Nothing illustrates this futility more than the stark fact that the population of Guyana, estimated at 815,000 in 1974 had declined to 767,000 in 2004.

Major Challenges at the Beginning of the 21st Century:
Indians are vulnerable in spite of their comparative political and economic strength in Guyana. The PPP have failed to attract Indians into the army and security forces: the pay is poor; the job has no prestige; it is seen as black people's work. This, combined with their lack of support among African-Guyanese, is their Achilles heels. Meanwhile the rate of migration of Indians continues to denude the community of its best and brightest. The ambition of most Indians in Guyana is to seek a better life in Canada or the United States, where established family

networks enhance strategies of adaptation. That is not likely to change unless their long-term political and economic security in Guyana is assured.

The biggest challenge for Indians, at the beginning of the 21st century, is to achieve a stable government of national unity; to explore areas of cultural and political co-operation with Africans in order to create a confidence-boosting environment; to become engaged in a long-term programme for protecting a fragile environment; and to promote an anti-drug/anti-corruption culture that facilitates the rule of law and normal economic activities, including the attraction of foreign investors to boost employment. The escalating crime-rate is seen by most Indians as being perpetrated by Africans against them. This problem cannot be resolved independently of a comprehensive programme of national development which engages Africans in the political and economic rehabilitation of Guyana.

The future looks ominous for Indians. Their distrust of Africans is so deep that a few years ago even a little book by an African Guyanese academic, which locates perceived Indian prejudices against Africans in ancient notions of caste,[35] did not provoke a debate on the merits or demerits of her case, but immediately evoked assertions of racism. Indians are a majority in Guyana, but Africans form a substantial minority. The country is ungovernable without a culture of negotiation, give and take, justice seen to be done. Indians are perceived by Africans to be in the political and economic ascendancy. They, therefore, must be seen to be conciliatory. But this is not happening, as is evident from the letters of two correspondents to the *Stabroek News* on 16 February 2005: one a prominent African (Clarence F. Ellis), the other Indian (Mohan Singh). Ellis wrote in support of the book referred to above; and he accused an African on the government-appointed Ethnic Relations Commission of failing to understand Africans' fears and aspirations. He was really challenging not only the government, but all Indians, to a debate on a critical issue:

> It is his refusal to engage Africans in intellectual discussion that is so infuriating and that will lead to an *explosion* [emphasis added]'. He reasoned: 'The…fundamental consideration…is that of the religiously sanctioned hierarchical stratification of caste. While it is true that caste may have weakened or even disappeared in…[Guyanese] society, the inegalitarianism that gave rise to caste is deeply entrenched in Hindu culture…The issue needs to be studied and dysfunctionalities in the philosophy should be expunged. This is happening in some parts of India.

Singh was reacting to the PNC's advocacy of power-sharing : African stake in governance. He saw no merit in it:

> 'I would support the idea…but anyone who is willing to assess the distribution of power can see that it is very well spread between PNC

supporters (predominantly Afro-Guyanese) and PPP supporters (predominantly Indo-Guyanese). If anyone doubts this just walk into any government office and see who is running things. Walk into a police station or any town council meeting. About a year ago President Jagdeo [Indian] announced that seventy-five percent of government payroll goes to Afro-Guyanese... This call for shared governance is only a smokescreen by the PNC to bring the country to a standstill because that would be the result of giving the PNC control of ministerial portfolios. Judging from the PNC's record of wasteful spending, corruption, racial discrimination and the current poor state of affairs in its administration of region four [East Demerara], one can only imagine the huge steps backward this country would take were the PNC in control of any portfolios.'

He had, probably unwittingly, resurrected Indian stereotypes of Africans being incapable of handling money, unfit for rule. Indians must be seen to be supportive of greater African participation at all levels of Guyanese society, notably central government and entrepreneurial activities. Time is not on their side. Guyana is sitting on a volcano. This land of fantasy is in dire need of some quick, hard thinking as well as a sense of history.

It is noteworthy that several generations of African Guyanese schoolteachers contributed immeasurably to the accelerated advancement of Indo-Guyanese in the sphere of education and the professions; and African Guyanese midwives delivered many thousands of Indian babies over many decades. Yet we are still imprisoned by a lack of mutual magnanimity. Guyana will progress only when all its peoples are engaged in the process of building a nation, all its people feel that they belong and are inspired to work towards the shaping of this elusive nation. But this is a process; it will take time, patience and mutual recognition of each other's aspirations, shortcomings and fears. I believe that Indo-Guyanese, as I argue in my book, *Mother India's Shadow over El Dorado* (2011), have benefited enormously from an enduring engagement with their ancestral land, however imagined their conceptualisation of that land and its legacy. African Guyanese, like those in other parts of the region, have sought continually to engage with an imagined Africa in building self-esteem. However, that link has been less vigorous for a number of reasons, but that does not invalidate the endeavour, as I argue in my book of 2007, *Muscular Learning*. That process must be encouraged and accelerated, by the Guyanese state, because Guyana's long-term security and prosperity is predicated on its diverse peoples building self-confidence within their groups, if they are to have the courage and resolve to collaborate in building a nation. There is no quick fix, and indices of reconciliation must be seen to be pursued all the time, with conviction.

In August 1936 the Indo-Guyanese intellectual, J.I. Ramphal (1903-66), commented on the notion of a Guyanese identity. He did not subscribe to 'sectarianism' or 'sectionalism'; he wanted 'Guianese first, Indian after'; but he recognised that it would be idealistic to elude references to 'racial problems… for a while yet' in British Guiana. He was very aware that building a nation was an aspiration; it would be a protracted process with many potential pitfalls. He elaborated:

> We want the Negroes of the country to have a real Negro consciousness until they find their footing. After that they will be qualified for a real Guianese consciousness…[But] we want Negro-controlled organisations to work for the benefit of British Guiana, giving expression to the peculiar contribution which that race is endowed to give to the world. We want Indians and other races to give their peculiar contribution also. *In a mixed community like this…the process of country consciousness is necessarily slow, and in our opinion has to pass through the stage of section-consciousness to country-consciousness*. What we can do is to minimise as much as possible the time at the sectarian stage, and proceed quickly to the greater and better stage. It is only then that British Guiana can come into its own, only then mutual respect and mutual love will follow. Then there will be a Guyanese consciousness. Until then the term Guyanese is only a wish [emphasis added].[36]

Nearly eight decades since J.I. Ramphal penned these profound thoughts, Guyana, unfortunately, has not moved beyond the 'sectarian stage', our Marxist experiments notwithstanding – our endeavour to prioritise class over ethnicity. The term Guyanese remains 'only a wish'. A few years ago Professor Clive Thomas spoke of 'the importance of the promotion of our [African] culture in enhancing self-identity, group cohesiveness and non-conflictual modes of behaviour among African Guyanese and between African Guyanese and other groups'. This remains a valid goal. Therefore, the biggest challenge for Indian Guyanese, as we approach the 50th anniversary of Guyana's independence in 2016, must be to explore and accelerate areas of cultural and political co-operation with Africans to forge mutual ethnic comprehension and security and to reduce fear and mistrust – to begin to shape the rudiments of a nation; to collaborate, in the pressing context of climate change, in a long-term programme for the conservation of a fragile ecosystem and the rehabilitation and expansion of a crucial, but delicate, hydraulic system; and to promote an anti-corruption culture that engenders respect for law and order and legitimate economic activities that open up possibilities for all-round development for all ethnic groups. With respect to the latter, it is important to recall that in October 1992 Cheddi Jagan, a man with impeccable credentials of incorruptibility, told the people of Guyana that 'corruption is a cancer which my Government is determined to eradicate'. All Guyanese could do well to ponder – and act – on these words of that great Guyanese.

It is imperative that Guyana be open to vigorous debate. It is paramount that we seek, actively, to build a nation. We are a sovereign state but are yet to create a Guyanese nation to which all our peoples feel a sense of belonging. When you live in multiracial, multi-religious, multi-tribal societies, it is crucial that you have an on-going dialogue encompassing all groups. The time to talk is when the voice is not silenced by the sound of violence and the futility of despair. It is very important, therefore, that the dominant group is seen to be listening to those groups which see themselves as subordinate or suppressed. If you want people to live and share with you in peace, if you do wish to create a nation, you must engage others in organisations that seek to cross ethnic boundaries; and, sometimes, you do have to face things that are quite painful, even about yourself, about your history.

Notes

1. Michael Swan, *British Guiana: The Land of Six Peoples* (London: HMSO, 1957), p. 29.
2. V.S. Naipaul, 'A Handful of Dust: Return to Guiana', *The New York Review of Books*, 11 April 1991.
3. Cheddi Jagan, Interview with Frank Birbalsingh, 24 October, 1984. See Birbalsingh, *From Pillar to Post* (Toronto: TSAR, 1997), p. 106.
4. Quoted in *Report of a Commission of Inquiry into the Sugar Industry of British Guiana* (J.A. Venn, Chairman), (London: HMSO, 1949), p. 9.
5. *Ibid.*
6. Walter Rodney, *A History of the Guyanese Working People, 1881-1905* (Baltimore, Maryland: The Johns Hopkins University Press, 1981), p. 3.
7. The phrase about maidenheads come from Walter Raleigh's The *discovery of the large, rich, and beautiful Empire of Guiana, with a relation of the great and golden city of Manoa* (which the Spaniards call El Dorado), published in 1595. Two of Guyana's novelists offer powerful visions of the fatal consequences of the Guyanese susceptibility to the myth of El Dorado. In Edgar Mittelholzer's *Shadows Move Among Them* (1951) an utopian commune reveals itself as a quasi-fascist dictatorship eerily foreshadowing Jonestown. Jan Carew's *Black Midas* is the archetypal portrayal of the pork-knocker's rags-to-riches-to-rags pursuit of gold.
8. The phrase comes from Joseph Beaumont, *The New Slavery: An Account of Indian and Chinese Immigrants in British Guiana* (London, 1871)
9. See Brij Lal, *Girmitiyas: The Origins of the Fiji Indians* (Canberra: Journal of Pacific History, 1983). And see Chapter 4 of this collection for a discussion of the similarity of origins of the North Indian indentured labourers to British Guiana and Fiji.
10. V.S. Naipaul, 'Reading and Writing', in *Literary Occasions: Essays* (London: Picador, 2004), pp. 6-8.

11. See 'The Legacy of the *Ramayana*', in my *'Tiger in the Stars': The Anatomy of Indian Achievement in British Guiana, 1919-29* (London: Macmillan, 1997), pp. 44-52.
12. Basdeo Mangru, *A History of East Indian Resistance on the Guyana Sugar Estates, 1869-1948* (Lewiston, NY: The Edwin Mellen Press, 1996), p. 73.
13. *Ibid*., pp. 74-5.
14. Chandra Jayawardena, 'Religious Belief and Social Change: Aspects of the Development of Hinduism in British Guiana', *Comparative Studies in Society and History*, Vol. 8, No. 2 (1966), p. 228.
15. See also Part III of my *'Tiger in the Stars'*: 'Economic Achievement in a Hostile Environment: Indians and the Development of the Rice Industry, 1919-29'.
16. *Indian Opinion*, 1936.
17. See 'Changing Attitudes to Education and the Emergence of Indian Professionals with Special Reference to the Work of the Canadian Mission', in my *'Tiger in the Stars'*, pp. 274-95.
18. *Ibid*.
19. See Denis Williams, *Giglioli in Guyana 1922-1972* (Georgetown: National History and Arts Council, 1973).
20. The statistical data is taken from Jay R. Mandle, *The Plantation Economy: Population and Economic Change in Guyana, 1838-1960* (Philadelphia: Temple University Press, 1973).
21. The best study on the subject is Patricia Mohammed, *Gender Negotiations among Indians in Trinidad, 1917-47* (Basingstoke: Palgrave, 2002). It needs virtually no revision with respect to women in British Guiana.
22. This is captured brilliantly in Naipaul's great novel of 1961, *A House for Mr. Biswas*.
23. See Rooplall Monar's novel *Janjhat* (Leeds: Peepal Tree Press, 1987) for an acute portrayal of the consequences of sexual ignorance in a new marriage.
24. H.V.P. Bronkhurst, *Among the Hindus and Creoles of British Guyana* (London: T. Woolmer, 1888). p. 212.
25. See my introduction to the reprint of Ruhomon's essay (Jamaica: University of the West Indies Press, 2001)
26. *Ibid*., pp. 134-5: Joseph Ruhomon's letter to the *Daily Chronicle*, 9 February 1897. See my *Bechu: 'Bound Coolie' Radical in British Guiana, 1894-1901* (Kingston, Jamaica: University of the West Indies Press, 1999).
27. This is from a Colonial Office file, accessed from the India Office records: CO111/633 [India Office], J&P 6588/1920, 11 October 1920.
28. CO111/652, Thomson to Thomas, confidential, 9 April 1924, encl.: Memorandum of 'Resoned Statement' Submitted by the Negro Progress Convention.
29. See my *Sweetening 'Bitter Sugar': Jock Campbell, the Booker Reformer in British Guiana, 1934-66* (Kingston, Jamaica: Ian Randle Publishers, 2005), Chapter 7: 'Ayube Edun, the *Guiana Review* and the Birth of the MPCA, 1936-9: Sugar Workers Find a Voice'.
30. *London's Heart Probe and Britain's Destiny* (London: A.H. Stockwell, 1938.

For more on Ayube Edun see Clem Seecharan, *Mother India's Shadow over El Dorado* (Jamaica: Ian Randle Publishers, 2011), passim.

31. *Ibid.*, Chapter 31: 'Kennedy's Obsession: Jagan, Castro and the Decolonisation of British Guiana, 1960-63', and see my essays in this collection, 'Whose Freedom at Midnight' and 'The Anatomy of Cheddi Jagan's Marxism'.
32. V.S. Naipaul, 'A Handful of Dust: Return to Guyana', *The New York Review of Books*, 11 April 1991, p. 19.
33. See note 31.
34. See, too, the essay in this collection: 'Whose Freedom at Midnight?'.
35. See Kean Gibson, The Cycle of Racial Oppression in Guyana (Maryland: University Press of America, 2003).
35. J.I. Ramphal, *The Daily Chronicle*, 2 August 1936.

INDIA'S AWAKENING AND THE IMAGINING OF THE 'EAST INDIAN NATION' IN BRITISH GUIANA

Notions of Mother India have been at the core of the shaping of Indo-Guyanese identity. From the 1890s, with the emergence of a small Indian middle class (several of whom were converts to Christianity), they sought to belong to their new homeland although they were not at ease with its creole sensibility. This tended to disparage them as 'coolies' (barbarians) whatever their social status. But an emergent India, retrieved from historical ignominy by European scholarship (Indology) that established her ancient achievements in diverse spheres, was the foundation of the 'idea of India' (Sunil Khilnani) and the dawn of a national awakening. This inspired pride amongst many Indo-Guyanese that a resurgent motherland was capable of self-governance. The construction of an Indo-Guyanese identity, though defined within the creole milieu of the colony, would henceforth be refracted through an imagined India: part fact, part fantasy. It was a potent instrument for challenging the persistent 'coolie' stain.

Because of the astounding diversity of peoples in India – a multitude of races, linguistic groups, religions, castes and sub-castes, tribes – the articulation of nationalism, however nuanced, inexorably excluded many. The fact that this new idea of India was grounded in a pre-Muslim, largely 'Aryan' or Vedic past, Hindu in its essentials, rendered the nationalism of the Indian National Congress (founded in 1885) inherently flawed, however sanctimonious its professions of secularism. In the end, its *raison d'être* was a procrustean Hindu construction of Indianness. Although the modern idea of India would hasten the end of Empire, it also had to confront its potential contraction: the notion of two nations, culminating in 1947 in the creation of Pakistan, the Muslim nation. The unitary idea of India – mapped by Empire – was difficult to sustain without the imperial presence. It was caught between exaggerated assertions of cohesion and its fissiparous reality. The essentially Hindu foundations of Indian nationalism made it ill equipped to bridge the powerful fault-line between Hinduism and Islam.

British rule had invented both the space and the intellectual underpinnings of that idea of India. Sunil Khilnani has explored the thinness of that idea and its imaginary dimensions:

> [B]efore the nineteenth century, no residents of the subcontinent would have identified themselves as Indian. There existed intricate, ramified vocabularies of common understanding, which classified people by communities of lineage, locality and sect; but 'Indian' would not have figured among its terms... What made possible the self-invention of a national community was the fact of alien conquest and colonial subjection. It was the British interest in determining geographical boundaries that by an act of Parliament in 1899 converted 'India' from the name of a cultural region into a precise, pink territory... The arbitrary precisions of colonial administrative techniques thus brought forth an historical novelty, a unified and bounded space named India.[1]

For the Indian in British Guiana, the amorphousness of Indianness was largely unconsidered. But whereas it was the foreigner, the British 'other', against whom the idea of India cohered in the motherland, it was primarily the African 'other' that engendered the comprehensive Indianness of Indo-Guyanese, whether Hindu, Muslim or Christian; north Indian (UP and Bihar) or south Indian (Tamil). Indeed, their conception of self as *not* African – the distinction at the core of their identity as Indians in the Caribbean – gave them a flexibility to adopt diverse constructions of India ('many Indias'), several more or less imagined, a compound of fact and fantasy. Indo-Guyanese could appropriate these Indias tendentiously for the ever-shifting requirements of their identity construction, the quest for self-affirmation in a plantation society. The pejorative 'coolie' 'otherness' was not amenable to easy dissipation; but the idea of India, with its multiple articulations, became a potent instrument of self-assertion, as Indians selectively challenged their exclusion from mobility in Guyana's social structure, whilst asserting their reluctance to assimilate to a Euro-African creole sensibility. In the process, Indians in the Caribbean would grope towards a tenuous belonging, fortified by the example of Mother India. For middle class, Christianised Indians, identity with India was no less imperative than for the 'bound coolie' (indentured labourer) anchored in the India of the *Ramayana* – its anthropomorphic Ram, Sita, Lakshman, Hanuman and Rawan, apprehensible and manipulable to suit every local exigency. For within this seeming paradox, between the Christian Indian lawyer or doctor and the 'bound coolie' engaged in a common project of claiming a redemptive idea of India was a common denominator: the 'coolie' stain, which clung like barnacles to all Indo-Guyanese. Yet the confidence generated by identity with Mother India prolonged the incredulity of other Guyanese with regard to the authenticity of Indo-Guyanese loyalty to British Guiana.

In the early 1880s Rev H.V.P. Bronkhurst,[2] an Anglo-Indian Wesleyan missionary in the colony, bemoaned the tendency among creoles, even educated blacks and coloureds, to see all Indians in the colony as 'savages or semi-civilised barbarians': 'You, sammy; you coolie!' were the common

H.V.P. Bronkhurst's book of 1888: one of the Anglo-Indian missionary's studies of Indians and Africans in British Guiana in the late 19th century

Joseph Ruhomon (1873-1942), the first Indo-Guyanese intellectual; a disciple of Bronkhurst

demeaning epithets thrown at them. Bronkhurst rejected the pervasive crude perceptions of Indians, although he, too, often used the opprobrious term, 'coolie': 'Whatever may be the defects and blemishes seen by the people of the colony in the coolies around them, I have no hesitation in saying that I have found a large number of them to be a very hospitable and courteous people. They surpass every other nation in this respect…'.[3] But the ascription of Indian indentured labourers to low caste status with a proclivity for criminality, mendacity and turpitude was resilient. The following assessment of 'coolies', from the *Berbice Gazette*, in August 1882, was characteristic of attitudes towards all Indians in the colony, although their caste background mirrored the caste diversity of the United Provinces (UP) whence most had come:

> The present labourers from India, with very few exceptions are all pariahs and the low castes. Perhaps it may be suggested that as labourers do not come here for any other but agricultural pursuits it is no matter who comes… but when we review the crimes that are being committed by the coolies, we are led naturally to suggest otherwise, and speak in favour of better labourers to our colony than the present set. We apprehend that most of the labourers embarking from India… are always the lowest castes… chamars, domes [doms or cremators of the dead], mathurs, harries, pariahs and half-caste Mussulmans [Muslims]. We… should try to get coolies from the western provinces of India [Punjab, Rajputana and Bombay].[4]

This erroneous impression emanated from the county of Berbice, where Indians were comparatively better off. Forty-two years later, in 1924, in their report on conditions of Indians in British Guiana, Pillai and Tivary, the delegates sent from India, were appalled by the stubbornness of the 'cooly' stain. They did concede that Indo-Guyanese could 'acquire property or carry on business without let or hindrance'; indeed, that 'no disabilities have so far been imposed upon…[them] on merely racial grounds', yet they deprecated what they deemed 'considerable race-prejudice' towards Indians:

> Every Indian, high or low, rich or poor, is a cooly [sic]. This contempt against East Indians is partly racial and partly economic, and is the direct outcome of the conditions under which East Indians used to be taken from India and made to work… [under] the indentured system… We asked Mr Lukhoo [sic] [J.A. Luckhoo, the first Indo-Guyanese legislator and twice a Colonisation Scheme delegate to India] whether the following statement… in 1917, was true of British Guiana…: 'It is known fact that the general body of Europeans in the colonies consider Asiatics as racially and fundamentally inferior to them… the latter is reduced to that of mere cattle…' Mr Lukhoo stated: 'Of course, "cattle" is a strong word to use but that is exactly what is thought of Indians here'… He added that Indians were considered to be inferior in intelligence to others, including the Negros [sic]. The prevailing idea has been that the East Indian is fit to serve only as labourer and nothing more.[5]

The *Daily Chronicle* of 24 March 1924 concurred: 'Here is an ugly aspect of local conditions; but no one can deny their essential truth'. As Edgar Mittelholzer, who grew up in New Amsterdam, Berbice (after the First World War), next door to the most distinguished Indian family in British Guiana, the Luckhoos, recalls: '..."coolies" we called them, whether they were labourers or eventually became doctors or lawyers or civil servants'.[6] Consequently, educated Indians, particularly Christianised ones like Joseph and Peter Ruhomon (cousins of the Luckhoos), and J.I. Ramphal, a respected educationist and journalist, would seek assiduously – over five decades – to use the tools of western scholarship and the knowledge of India unearthed by it, to establish that Indians had minds, that they were not all 'coolies' or menial jobbers; that their ancestors were makers of great ancient civilisations. The process of intellectual rehabilitation, the necessity to transcend the 'coolie' universe of humiliation, had begun as early as the 1890s, with the formation of the ephemeral British Guiana East Indian Institute, in Georgetown (in 1892), 'the first society of East Indians in the Caribbean', according to its founder, the British Guiana-born Indian, Dr William Hewley Wharton.

The founders of the organisation were largely Christian Indians, the first generation with the learning and confidence to challenge creole rejection of their claims to belonging. But they would assert a wider Indian inheritance, even inchoate claims to Indian nationhood in the colony, in seeking credence for their distinctive place within creole society. This paradox was engendered by the pervasive tendency in British Guiana to deny them the capacity for intellectual discernment, to ridicule any suggestion of a civilised temperament. And because most creoles (whites, coloureds, blacks, Madeiran Portuguese) were bred on the assumption of British cultural superiority, mastery of its principal idioms was indispensable to claims of belonging to the colonial space. The shaping of Indian identity in the colony would be conditioned by a complex, sometimes contradictory, interplay between the pursuit of colonial indices of civility and culture, on one hand, and identity with the high civilisation of Mother India, on the other. That imagined India could not have been constructed without the affirmation of Indology, and only the westernised elite in British Guiana were trained to apprehend and maximise its intellectual legacy. Such were the founders of the British Guiana East Indian Institute: Veerasawmy Mudaliar (a student of H.V.P. Bronkhurst); F.E. Jaundoo, J.R. Wharton (later a lawyer) and his brother, William Hewley Wharton (later a medical doctor). As aspirants, too, to colonial mobility, they were astute enough to identify with Indians who had gained recognition in the West. The caste or religious background of the successful ones overseas was immaterial, and Indo-Guyanese would have appreciated some reciprocal recognition from them, however minimal. Yet it was not an imperative, for their notion of

Indianness, including the appropriation of indices of Indian achievement, was germane solely to the shaping of their identity in British Guiana.

A memorable illustration of this was occasioned by the case of Dadabhai Naoroji (1825-1917), the first Indian elected to the British House of Commons. On 28 July 1892 the *Daily Chronicle* in British Guiana carried the following terse item on the unique achievement:

> An interesting figure in the next Parliament will be the Parsee, Naoroji, whom Lord Salisbury [the Tory Prime Minister] held up to mistaken ridicule as a 'black man'. Naoroji's victory in Central Finsbury, by three votes, was challenged by the Conservatives, but a recount confirmed Naoroji's poll. The National Liberal club men, with whom the genial Indian is popular, greeted his victory with volleys of hurrahs.

On 1 October 1892 the British Guiana East Indian Institute forwarded a congratulatory letter to Naoroji, expressing 'exceeding joy and gratification' at his election, which they viewed as 'an honour... [to] our race in this remote part of Her Majesty's dominions'. Furthermore, they considered his election to the House of Commons an honour to 'the East Indian nation'. The idea of that imagined nation permeates the letter (reproduced in the *Daily Chronicle* of 7 October 1892), thus substantiating my argument that this extraordinary achievement could be appropriated as an antidote to the calumniation of the 'East Indian' in the colony as 'coolie'. There was no equivocation in claiming Naoroji for 'the East Indian' nation. They were unabashedly triumphal:

> We are fully conscious of the multifarious difficulties you must necessarily have had to surmount in order to secure your success in this, to our nation, memorable election, and that fact alone impels us to doubly prize the honour which the East Indian Nation has, through your meritorious instrumentality, attained an event unparalleled in the annals of the History of India. We need hardly say that although we are thousands of miles separated from you, it will be our foremost interest to read of your career, and earnestly trust that success will attend your undertakings... and we further venture to hope that the example which you have so nobly set will be fruitful in actuating others of our ancient race to follow; and thereby rid themselves and countrymen of the political oblivion [into] which they have been presumed hitherto to be sunk. In concluding our humble quota of the many manifestations of pride at your entrance to such a traditionally illustrious house... we fervently hope that Almighty God will direct your every movement in your elevated sphere, and thereby ensure a brilliant and happy career for one in whose veins courses our kindred blood.

Their imagined East Indian nation – a concept that would have had no resonance in any part of India – was designed to satisfy the yearnings of a people who had lost their old moorings, however restrictive and oppressive, and were groping towards a new self-definition. It is noteworthy that although the idea of the East Indian nation was vague in relation to India, it was suggestive of a potential extension of it: a greater India, within the Empire. It was certainly not creole in conception and would not have inspired empathy by Africans or other groups in British Guiana. There is no evidence that Naoroji responded; indeed, that he was even aware of the existence of Indo-Guyanese. Although he would become President of the Indian National Congress thrice, he could not have comprehended what 'the East Indian nation' meant; and, as a Parsi (a Zoroastrian of Persian descent, however remote), it is doubtful whether he considered himself a member of 'our ancient race...in whose veins course our kindred blood'. They, however, had defined him as 'East Indian', a son of Mother India – not a 'black man' as Lord Salisbury had defined him – whose eminence could absolve them of some of the stain of an extant bondage (indentureship), while endeavouring to shape an identity in British Guiana.

Naoroji, whose example exerted a seminal influence on Gandhi when he was studying in London (1888-91), was being constructed as their leader, at the highest level of Empire, who could hasten and inspire a political awakening in Mother India and, therefore, among her scattered children. Ideas of India (many Indias of the imagination) were ever at the heart of Indo-Guyanese self-definition. By humbling themselves before Naoroji, they were embracing the aura generated by his meteoric rise in order to challenge their many local detractors. The problem, of course, was that African, Coloured or Portuguese people would not have been enamoured of 'the East Indian nation' in British Guiana, however abstract. Although it offered Indo-Guyanese a degree of self-belief, it conveyed to others a communal aspiration at variance with creole sensibility.

The unpalatability of the notion of 'the East Indian nation' to African Guyanese would have been exacerbated by the absorption of ideas of Aryanism by some Indo-Guyanese, particularly as articulated in the works of Professor Max Muller and Rev. H.V.P. Bronkhurst, the Anglo-Indian missionary in the colony. As early as 19 November 1885, Bronkhurst had echoed Max Muller's thesis on the remote common ancestry of Europeans and Indians, from an original Aryan stock in central Asia. His paper, entitled 'The Ancestry and Origin of our East Indian Immigrants', was no doubt intended to evoke enormous rehabilitative pride among the despised 'coolies' of British Guiana:

> [Indians] are unmistakably the oldest people now living in the civilised world...The ancient name of [their country] was ARYA-VARTA, literally the abode of the Aryans... Even in British Guyana [sic]... where they are employed as labourers, we find the Indians more prolific than any other race... They are, as a race... a comely and tractable people, possessing intelligence – a large number of them exhibiting cultured minds – and a natural capacity for civilisation... Civilisation then is natural to the Hindu race... The ancient Hindus were an enterprising people, and they were

> always on the move, migrating or voyaging to distant countries... The modern Hindus have traditional accounts of their forefathers crossing the 'Seven Seas' in search of wealth, fame, home, etc., and thus establishing themselves in different parts of the globe...[7]

Bronkhurst underlined the supposed common ancestry of Indians and Caucasians, the thesis of the so-called Aryan race:

> Heathenism and superstition have... blinded the eyes of the modern Hindus as to their origin and relationship to the Europeans, but... they will wake up to the fact that they... are related to each other, by the closest ties. The descendants of the ancient Aryan-Hindus will claim relationship with the Germans or Germanic races in Europe, and the descendants of the Tar-Aryans... [and] the Tamil population of southern India, will claim relationship with the English or the Saxons of Great Britain...[8]

Those Indians in British Guiana who read Bronkhurst's paper were quite possibly buoyed by his celebratory reflection on their antecedence, which must have assuaged some guilt for crossing the *kala pani*, the dark waters of modern Hindu opprobrium. They would also have been flattered by his assertion of a common ancestry between themselves and the ruling imperial race. Lightness of skin is an imperishable Indian preoccupation; it is prized. The illusion of racial affinity with Europeans, however, must have banished the dark African further from the Indian imagination, thus compounding their own deep-seated caste bigotry, permeated by notions of ritual pollution and sexual contamination. Moreover, because many Indo-Guyanese were dark themselves and of low caste origin, their instinct for distancing themselves from blackness would have been magnified.

Like the myth of Rama Raj, the blissful rule of Lord Rama in the *Ramayana*, the Golden Age in the kingdom of Ayodhya, and the myth of El Dorado, so resonant – and necessary in a hard environment – in British Guiana, the myth of Aryanism answered the urgent needs of the 'coolie' angst. It elevated the Indian to kinship with the British ruler, thus short-circuiting in the imagination the pedestrian, measured creole route through education, religion and cricket, to a kind of Englishness. It compensated for gnawing inadequacies and self-doubt on the weary road to creolisation in colonial society. No wonder the first Indian intellectuals in British Guiana, Joseph Ruhomon (1873-1942), and his brother, Peter Ruhomon (born 1880), Dr. William Hewley Wharton (born 1869), founder of the British Guiana East Indian Institute, and several westernised Indians would fall for the allure of Aryanism.

Joseph Ruhomon's discovery of India, through Bronkhurst, was seminal to Indo-Guyanese identity in the 1890s. His pamphlet of December 1894, *India and the Progress of Her People at Home and Abroad and how those in British Guiana may Improve Themselves*, was deeply inspired by his pride in ancient India's diverse intellectual achievement. Ruhomon was pained by the educational backwardness of Indo-Guyanese, and he exhorted them to take pride in the legacy of ancient India and contemporary progress in Mother India.[9] Forty-three years later, in 1937, Joseph Ruhomon recalled the context of his seminal pamphlet. He was 'shocked at the intellectually and socially backward state of my people in comparison with their advanced and still advancing Negro brethren, and I thought I would sound a clarion call for a forward movement'. He elaborated:

> [I]ts great objective was to arouse local Indians from their lethargy or indifference in respect of their intellectual and social interests and to stimulate them to action, after first comparing them with their more progressive brethren in the Motherland and in other parts of the world...I [also] pointed... to the achievements of black and coloured people [mixed race] in the realms of education, of intellectual, cultural and social movements, of professional practice, of politics, and of village administration; and on the other hand, I pointed to the fallow-fields of Indian soil in those same realms awaiting still the ploughshare of intelligent husbandry to make them rich and fertile... I emphasised...the urgency of the matter and demanded... the establishment of some institution that would be both cultural and representative of Indian interests...[10]

To counter the 'coolie' stigma, he extolled the cultivation of the intellect. He was inspired by the reported oratorical and philosophical exposition, as well as the acclamation, of India's Swami Vivekananda at the World's Parliament of Religions in Chicago in 1893, as he was by the election of Dadabhai Naoroji to the House of Commons the previous year. In both cases Indians had earned the recognition of the West through merit. Joseph Ruhomon, too, was claiming Naoroji's achievement as his own, and that of 'the East Indian nation'. As the following excerpt shows, there was also a millennial strand in his imagined nation, redolent of the golden age. Moreover, his 'East Indian nation', more than that adumbrated in the East Indian Institute's congratulatory letter to Naoroji two years earlier, clearly encompassed all Indians, 'at home and abroad' – a greater India:

> We, East Indians, should feel supremely proud of the fact that the members of our own race are practically showing the world today by their example that the great East Indian nation is no mean nation. Our people have been great in the past and they will be greater yet in the future. The signs of the times point to the brilliant future of the East Indian race. Let prejudiced-eaten races say what they will... but we know that there is a golden harvest to be reaped by East Indians... I am not only convinced... of the greatness of India as a country, and the greatness of her sons and daughters as a people, but I am joyfully and confidently anticipating the time when in intelligence, in culture, in morals and intellectual attainments, the great East Indian Race shall be second to none in the world.[11]

Then, having advanced claims for the intellectual sagacity of Indians, he endorsed the then popular notion of Aryanism, as if to validate his postulate of cerebral equivalence to Europeans, through a putative common racial pedigree. The 'coolie' persona was being transcended in Joseph Ruhomon's formulation of Aryanism: 'I may add... that we also in British Guiana with all our ancestors in India are closely allied by blood relationship to the British nation, as the following poem by Ben Elvry entitled "To India"... will show':

> Brave brothers, of the sun-kissed face
> Heirs of the ancient Arya name;
> Like heritage with you we claim,
> Our tongue betrays our kindred race.
> Far sundered had our wanderings been,
> By depths of dusk and ways unknown;
> Glad now we join once more to own
> One Mother Empress – Kaisar – Queen[12]

But Ruhomon would not acquiesce in 'the East Indian nation' being under the indefinite governance of their 'fair-faced brothers'. He acknowledged that the latter were making a salutary contribution to the intellectual awakening of India; and that Indians 'at home' were acquitting themselves magnificently in many spheres of European scholarly and professional endeavour. He considered British rule a period of apprenticeship in mastering the skills for the regeneration of 'the East Indian nation'.

When Joseph Ruhomon's pamphlet was published in Georgetown in December 1894, the conservative *Argosy* of 29 December challenged his contention that Indians had the capacity to govern themselves in the near future. They observed that although 'a Hindoo or a Negro' had the same scope for advancement in the Empire as the British, it was premature to assume that they were ready for self-government. Subject races had to be tutored for responsibility, necessarily an incremental process. Furthermore, they contended that Ruhomon's extolling of India's achievements redounded more to the credit of the British than to any inherent native capacity for self-improvement. In a sarcastic allusion to Ruhomon's affirmation of Aryanism, the kinship of Indians and the British, the *Argosy* cautioned Indians (and Africans) with pretensions to self-governance that their apprenticeship was far from over:

> In an absolutely free country like the British Empire, a Hindoo or a Negro has equal opportunity with the Anglo-Saxon to rise to eminence, granted he has the same capacity for taking pains; but it is in this sternly-necessary qualification that the hundreds of millions of the tropical and sub-tropical races are defective. Here and there in the present day, just as it was in the past centuries, spring up a commanding genius whose exceptional career only throws into deeper shade the utterly blank and purposeless lives of the teeming millions; but it is open to all of us to

> hope and believe, as Mr Ruhomon says he does, that in course of time the genius, intelligence and industry of the East Indians as a people, will gain for their country [India] a foremost place amongst the nations of the world... We notice that the lecturer is constantly measuring the East Indian with the Anglo-Saxon... that the former is at least the equal of the latter... Granted this to be true, it is the fair-faced brother who has most reason to rejoice in it. It was he who liberated, as far as he could, both the Negro and the Hindoo...

Ruhomon recalled later that he was not at all actuated by 'jealousy' or ingratitude towards the British, as 'that fine old Scotsman [Thomson, editor of the *Argosy*]' had asserted. He was simply arguing that Indians had the ability to compete with Anglo-Saxons intellectually: '...the equality of the two races in respect of mental capacity, in order to encourage our own people to try to realise their possibilities in the intellectual world.'[13] This was why the incisive and provocative letters of Bechu (the Bengali 'bound coolie radical in British Guiana'), to the liberal *Daily Chronicle* between 1896 and 1901, made such an impact on all Indo-Guyanese. It was not only the insurgent tenor of his challenge to the sugar planters, but also his mastery of the English idiom – the language and the conventions of debate, his demonstrated nimbleness of intellect – that resonated with them. The fact that Bechu was of humble origins, an iconoclastic indentured labourer, would have added immeasurably to the self-esteem of his compatriots in the colony.[14]

It is comprehensible, therefore, why Indo-Guyanese would envision 'the East Indian nation' essentially in terms of an ever changing and perceptibly resurgent Mother India. They still lacked the confidence to create their own ideas; they were not at ease with a creole sensibility but they could not elude it; they were despised as languishing in a state of barbarism. It was the idea of a renascent motherland, reinventing herself through her ancient greatness, which gave them the strength and an emerging confidence to shape a new identity. This was fraught with danger in creole society, but the power of India to mould attitudes in the new space was immense – and inescapable. And the fact that indentureship was not abolished until 1917 enhanced the motherland's moral authority in the tortuous process of self-definition.

In India, as well as with Indo-Guyanese, European recognition of India's ancient legacy was received with pride. This is evident in the response of William Hewley Wharton (the first Indian born in the Caribbean to study at a British university) to an assertion of their mutual Aryan antecedence by a distinguished Scotsman, in December 1899. Wharton was born in British Guiana on August 20, 1869; his parents were indentured labourers from India. He was the founder of the short-lived British Guiana East Indian Institute, in 1892, the demise of which is probably attributable to his departure for the University of Edinburgh in 1893. Throughout his university years (1893-9), he identified closely with Indian affairs; in 1896 he was elected secretary of the Edinburgh Indian Association. A unique honour was thus conferred on him, an Indian born outside the motherland, when he was elected president in 1898-9. But the cherished commendation would come on the occasion of the annual dinner of the Association, on 7 January 1899, from the guest speaker, Professor Sir Thomas Grainger Stewart, Physician-in-Ordinary to Queen Victoria. More than 40 years later, in his entry for *Who is Who in British Guiana, 1945-8*, Dr. Wharton reproduced the accolade of the eminent professor from that Edinburgh evening in 1899. It must have had a profound impact on his life, erasing the 'coolie' stain:

> Here is a young gentleman who was born in British Guiana, possesses an English name, fills the chair at this banquet with much dignity and grace, and still insists on calling himself Indian. I may as well call myself Indian, as we both belong to the same stock – the Aryan family.

In British Guiana, where thousands of Indians were still under indentureship, Max Muller's writings on Aryanism, however fictive, aided the small Indian middle class to ease their gnawing self-doubt and self-deprecation. Max Muller's influence ran deep in the colony, as it did in Victorian India. Nirad Chaudhuri assesses the eminent Anglo-German's scholar's contribution to India's awakening. He was referring not only to Aryanism, but also his indefatigable labours in translating the ancient Vedic works from Sanskrit. Chaudhuri explains:

> The human urge in all his scholarly work was that, becoming aware of their great past and drawing on their legacy... [Indians] would revitalise their contemporary life, and shed the dead wood which had accumulated through the centuries'. He cites a Bengali writer who, as early as 1874, had dramatised the impact of Sanskritic studies in Europe and comparative philology in reshaping British attitudes to Indians: 'We were niggers at one time. We now become brethren... The advent of the English found us a nation sunk in the mire of superstition, ignorance and political servitude. The advent of scholars like Sir William Jones found us fully established in a rank above that of every nation as that from which modern civilisation could be distinctly traced... We should know that it is to the study of the roots and inflexions of Sanskrit that we owe our national salvation... [15]

The idea of 'the East Indian nation', a construct by the small Indo-Guyanese elite at the end of the 19th century, flowed from similar promptings. The lowly image of Indians in the colony gnawed especially painfully at the dignity of the educated minority – an experience shared by the educated elite in India. The discovery of ancient India with its seminal accomplishments in diverse spheres of high culture – initially, almost wholly the work of scholars such as Jones, Colebrook, Wilkins and others in the Asiatic Society of Bengal – imbued Ram Mohan Roy, Dayananda, Vivekananda,

Tagore, Ruhomon and Wharton with the means to redefine themselves. This gave them the self-belief to challenge imperial definitions; indeed, to begin to reinvent India and challenge imperial supremacy. In this sense, Indo-Guyanese in the short-lived East Indian Institute were right to speak of an East Indian nation, however impractical it would prove to be in the colony later. It reflected their pride in a resurgent Mother India that was beginning to stir at the end of the 19th century.

The stature of Mother India was heightened by the fact that colonial authorities tended to respond to educated, articulate men from India who visited the colony with arrogance and paranoia: they were deemed subversive. For instance, Pandit Parmanand Saraswat, a distinguished Arya Samaj missionary from the Punjab, arrived in British Guiana on 28 December 1910. The government would not permit him to deliver a lecture at the Immigration Department, an institution with ambiguous resonance within the Indian community: indentureship was still in force. The problem originated with the Government of India, which deemed him 'a dangerous man', and sought intelligence on his activities overseas, including British Guiana. Parmanand's offence was an intellectual one: he was celebrating the achievements of ancient Hindu India. This was conducive to a resurgence of Indian self-respect and self-confidence, thus kindling notions of their capacity for self-governance. However, Parmanand was eventually allowed to deliver his lecture, 'Ancient India', at the Town Hall, Georgetown, on the evening of 12 January 1911.

The missionary's stature was enhanced immediately: he was seen by all Indians, whatever their religious persuasion, as an emissary of the new India. This was magnified by the enthusiastic response of a wide cross-section of Guyanese society who attended the lecture. It was chaired by the distinguished English-born historian of the colony, James Rodway, the author of a three-volume history of British Guiana as well as several other works. Among the prominent non-Indians present were: Hon W.C. Crawford, a member of the Executive Council, Dr W.W. Campbell, the 1894 Guyana Scholar, Rev. J. Dingwall of the Moravian Church and Venerable Archdeacon Josa of the Anglican Church. Rodway's erudition was unassailable in British Guiana, so his acclamation of the legacy of ancient India must have been deeply appreciated by Indo-Guyanese. He cited the scholarship of Professor Max Muller in bringing India to the European imagination, adding that 'India had taught Europe a great deal'. He reportedly argued: 'The old Greeks and Romans were very sharp in a great many things, but they knew nothing about Arithmetic, nothing about the cipher or the nought; and on account of not having the nought, they could not carry on commercial business. About the year 1200, the Arabs brought to Europe figures up to 10, from India, and from that time Europe began to become mercantile. The basis of mercantile calculation, the decimal system, came from India'. Rodway concluded thus:

> Another thing India had given, was still giving and would give to the world, and that was the basis of its religion, the basis of humanity – loving kindness. No people in the world were like the Hindoos for their loving kindness...[16]

Parmanand, too, referred to Max Muller, noting that if India's contribution to warfare, imperial conquests or the political history of the world was not impressive, she had more than recompensed by virtue of her pre-eminence 'in the religious history of mankind'. She was, indeed, 'the mother of religious thought'. He then addressed the intellectual universe opened up by European discovery of the language of Aryan India, Sanskrit, which has to its credit seminal achievements in drama, poetry, literature and philosophy. Sanskrit also provided the foundation of comparative philology that led scholars to the supposed commonality of origin between it and Greek, Latin and the Indo-European languages. Parmanand observed that the rich Sanskrit legacy was epitomised by the *Rig Veda*: 'the oldest book of mankind'.

He was arguing that ancient India was the source of civilisation because her literary and philosophical texts reflected originality of thought several thousand years ago. He concluded with a portrayal of the ancient motherland as a veritable utopia; this would have struck a chord with his Indo-Guyanese audience, buoyed by the recent cascade of credits for their antecedents. It was also congruent with their conception of the rule of Lord Rama, the Golden Age, in the *Ramayana*. But Parmanand, while celebrating their ancestral religious legacy, counselled them, like Joseph Ruhomon, to pursue western education:

> India influenced humanity through the Persians, Greeks and Arabians, and when India exerted her influence through Buddhism... seven centuries before Christ, the standard of morality was so high, they did not require locks for their doors, did not lie, and were sober and industrious... [He discussed] the teachings of Buddhism...comparing it with the teachings of Christianity... [arguing] that they should not force the East Indians to accept the latter religion, but should educate them and make them better citizens... [Western] education was the only thing to better their condition... [17]

S. Radhakrishnan, once Professor of Eastern Religions and Ethics at Oxford, has commented on the importance of the influence of the West in equipping Hindu India with the means of self-assessment, the foundation of India's regeneration and nationalist assertion:

> It is the tragedy of India that while its culture produced individuals who had something undeniably attractive and superior, it did not develop a high civic or national sense...As a designer of national life, Hindu civilisation was not a success... [The] disparity between Hindu ideals and practices

> became manifest when India came under the influence of the West after the advent of the British. Her thinking men felt the undemocratic character of many of the institutions associated with Hindu religion, and traced the weakness of India to lack of social sense and imagination. Western influence widened the horizon of the Indian mind, opened up fresh channels, and gave it a more universal direction.[18]

This was true of British Guiana as well. India and Europe were both seminal in the shaping of Indo-Guyanese identity.

Notes

1. Sunil Khilnani, *The Idea of India* (London: Penguin Books, 1998), pp. 154-155.
2. See also pp. 73-74 for a discussion of Bronkhurst's significance.
3. Rev. H.V.P. Bronkhurst, *British Guyana and its Labouring Population*. (London: T. Woolmer, 1883), pp. 268-269.
4. Quoted in the *Colonist*, 16 August 1982.
5. [Pillai and Tivary]. *Reports on the Scheme for Indian Emigration to British Guiana, Part I – Report by Dewan Bahadur P. Kesava Pillai and V.N. Tivary*. (Simla: Government Press, 1924), pp. 55-56.
6. Edgar Mittelholzer, *A Swarthy Boy* (London: Putnam, 1963), p. 155.
7. H.V.P. Bronkhurst, *The Ancestry or Origin of our East Indian Immigrants*. (Georgetown: The Argosy Press, 1886), pp. 3; 5; 15.
8. Ibid., pp. 67-68.
9. Clem Seecharan, *Joseph Ruhomon's India: The Progress of her People at Home and Abroad and how those in British Guiana may Improve Themselves* (Kingston, Jamaica: University of the West Indies Press, 2001), chapters 1-3.
10. Joseph Ruhomon, 'The B.G. East Indian Association, or 1894-1937, and the Years Between', *Indian Opinion* (Christmas Number, 1937) p. 23.
11. Seecharan, *Joseph Ruhomon's India,* pp. 62-63
12. Ibid., p. 63
13. Joseph Ruhomon, 'The B.G. East Indian Association...', p. 24.
14. See Clem Seecharan, *Bechu: 'Bound Coolie' Radical in British Guiana, 1894-1901* (Kingston, Jamaica: University of the West Indies Press, 1999).
15. Nirad C. Chaudhuri, *Scholar Extraordinary: The Life of Professor the Rt. Hon. Friedrich Max Muller* (London: Chatto and Windus, 1974), p. 318.
16. *The Daily Chronicle*, 14 January, 1911.
17. Ibid.
18. Sir S. Radhakrishnan, 'Hinduism and the West', in *Modern India and the West: A Study of the Interaction of their Civilisations*, L.S.S. O'Malley, ed. London: Oxford University Press, 1941.

SUGAR IN MY BLOOD

> Our most personal attitudes are deeply affected by elements in the environment which seem to have no connection with them at all.
> —Walter E. Houghton (1957)

As my introduction records, from around 1990 to 2002, I worked on a study of the activities of Jock Campbell (1912-94), the radical Chairman of Booker Bros, McConnell and Co [Booker] in British Guiana between 1952 and 1967. This essay is drawn from the first chapter of the book published in 2005 as *'Sweetening Bitter Sugar': Jock Campbell, the Booker Reformer in British Guiana 1934-1966*. It was an attempt to reflect on my biographical relationship to my subject, how, like Campbell, I have sugar in my blood, though we got it through different veins. For six generations, as he would often say, his family had grown rich on the labour of African slaves and indentured Indian 'coolies' in British Guiana. I am the great-grandson of indentured coolies brought from the United Provinces of India, between 1875 and 1909, to labour on the sugar plantations, some on Plantation Albion, one of the Campbell estates, on the Corentyne Coast, in the county of Berbice.

Jock spent 18 months at Albion during his first sojourn in the colony, between 1934 and 1937. On his first tour of that plantation, escorted by the manager, James Bee, an autocratic, humourless Scot, he encountered the hovels of the resident Indian workers, the infamous logies or ranges, with roots in African slavery. Neighbouring these was a more pretentious building – clean, painted, obtrusive. Jock enquired who lived in the hovels: 'Our coolies', replied Bee. He then asked of the residents of the smarter building; Bee said: 'Oh! We keep our mules there.' A naïve 22-year-old Jock asked flippantly: 'Why don't you move your coolies to the mules' palace and put the mules in the hovels?' A stunned Bee exclaimed cryptically: 'Mules cost money, sir!"

My father's maternal grandfather, Sewnath (1881-1956), was an indentured child-labourer on this Campbell estate. He was taken from Kharaura village, Ghazipur District, eastern United Provinces [Uttar Pradesh]. He embarked at Calcutta, bound for British Guiana, on October 8, 1892, aged eleven. Nothing is known of his parents other than that they were of Ahir caste, the traditional cattle-rearers of Uttar Pradesh and Bihar, the Hindu

Jock Campbell (1912-1994): the Booker reformer who responded to Cheddi Jagan's crusade for change.

My paternal great-grandfather, Sewnath (1881-1956), a child labourer at Albion (owned by Jock Campbell's family), and my great-grandmother, Etwarie. He was a Hindu, born in India; she in British Guiana of Muslim parentage, and probably changed her name at marriage.

heartland in the Gangetic plain of North India. Sewnath was accompanied by his older sister, Sonbersi, aged 22, and her husband, Raghu, aged 30. They were all indentured to Albion. So one of those ghastly logies – 'pig sties', as Jock saw them – would have been the home of my great-grandfather, this child-labourer.[2]

By the time Campbell got to Albion in 1934-35, Sewnath had long left the plantation: sometime before the First World War. Frugal to the bone, he had saved enough from his puny wages to buy a property at Palmyra Village, seven miles from Albion, on the north-western perimeter of Rose Hall estate, a Booker sugar plantation. He left behind those derelict ranges that, more than two decades later, were to make an enduring impression on young Jock Campbell. As he would relate time and again, and as he did to me four days before he died on December 26, 1994, the guilt festered. It became the principal prompting of his life, a reflex – the notion of debts unpaid, of wealth extracted by sordid means, the taint of slavery and indentureship – and a compunction to compensate, belatedly, for ancient wrongs. Over and over, in numerous speeches and interviews, in casual conversation, he would repeat the following almost verbatim – a mantra of his Guyana awakening:

> The conditions in which past members of my family had... made considerable fortunes came as a great shock to me. Conditions of employment were disgraceful; wages were abysmally low; housing was unspeakable; workers were treated with contempt – as chattels. Animals and machinery were, in fact, cared for better than the workers because they cost money to buy and replace... the sugar industry had been founded on slavery, continued on indentureship and maintained by exploitation.[3]

For me this was no abstraction. It was etched on the weary bodies of my great-grandparents, whose aching bones I was often bribed to massage, a task I played at purely for the reward. Sewnath and his wife, Etwaria, my father's maternal grandmother, had an amazing consistency of purpose – as labourers in the cane-fields as well as in their own rice-field and provision ground, as cattle-rearers, too. My mother's paternal grandfather, Sohan, was indentured to Plantation Rose Hall in 1875, but he, also, had bought a small property and was rearing cattle at Palmyra; this eased his dependence on the sugar estate but it never eliminated it. My mother's maternal grandfather and grandmother were 'bound' to Rose Hall in 1908 and 1909 respectively. Unremitting toil on the estate, coupled with extraordinary thrift bordering on miserliness, enabled them, too, to buy land at Palmyra. Although they continued to live in the logies, the old barracks, at Rose Hall, they had moved their cattle to Palmyra where my maternal grandmother, their only child, married Sohan's youngest son in 1930. She was 14 years old. As I explore in greater depth in the essay, "Girmitiyas...", my people were mainly Ahir, from eastern Uttar Pradesh, whose frugality enabled them to squeeze savings to sustain their ancestral caste-calling – the cow had made the crossing.[4]

So, by the time Jock Campbell was serving his apprenticeship in sugar, at Albion, in the mid-1930s, most of my family were settled away from the plantation, at Palmyra village. As he drove his two-seater Ford V8, fast, to New Amsterdam, the county town, he would have passed them grazing their cattle along the edge of the road or planting or reaping rice and vegetables. They had become masters at exploiting every niche in the village economy, but proximity to the estate and access to the joint family as a unit of production, allowed them to tap into opportunities on the estate also, often surreptitiously, with practised ease. They stole grass, wild vegetables and wood from the cane-fields and canals, or garnered a rich harvest from the flood-fallowed cane-fields teeming with fish; they stole water, too, during the dry season (there was no artesian well in the village until the late 1940s). Jock was familiar with the rhythm of Indian village life, its work-cycles and consuming rituals, festivals and weddings, which shaped a sense of community in the new land.[5]

These were hard times, the 1930s: poor sugar prices ate into the meagre wages of the sugar workers, the first victims of austerity during the Depression. Meanwhile, the absence of a recognised trade union until 1939, impeded their ventilation of grievances as it stifled concession of basic rights by the plantocracy. An impotent rage festered, which juxtaposed vivid, poignant tales of oppression on the estate with the idea of a mythical idyllic India, drawn largely from the stories of the *Ramayana*.[6] The stories of oppression were reinforced daily by the supercilious manner of most white managers and overseers in our midst: remote, incomprehensible Scottish men, invariably in cork hats and short khaki pants, exaggeratedly whiskered and stockinged, on horseback – awe-inspiring colossuses, evocative of older oppressions.

The great divide between coolies and 'backra', the white elite on the estate, had no more enduring symbol than the impressive colonial bungalows of the latter, with their white picket-fences protecting cultured lawns, verdant fruit-trees and gardens ablaze with flowers, separated by a canal from patched-up ranges, 'barracks', reeking in a sea of slush and refuse during the heavy rains – order and power on one hand, decay and subservience on the other. This, too, lodged in Jock Campbell's memory.

I was born in 1950. Jock's family firm, Curtis Campbell and Co, had been acquired by the giant sugar company, Booker Bros, McConnell and Co, in 1939; so had he. His rise in Booker was astounding: in 1943 he became a director; managing director in 1945; in 1947, aged 35, he was made vice-chairman. In 1952, Jock, aged 40, was made Chairman of Booker. My memories of sugar culture in British Guiana and Plantation Rose Hall in particular, one of Booker's best estates in the late 1950s-60s, are still fresh. I grew, up on its periphery, at Palmyra, amidst a large, extended family, many of whom continued to work some of the time on the sugar estate. But my memories of sugar, one generation away from the Great Depression, though mildly tainted by the remorseless tales of suffering and deprivation, are essentially happy ones: not images of the bitterness of 'King Sugar' but of hope, of possibilities as capacious as the Corentyne sky which Jock Campbell adored: 'the great big skies; those marvellous skies, immensely unclaustrophobic', he would recall. My vision, too, was as expansive as the sugar-cane fields of Rose Hall that met those of Albion, touching those skies, in my boyhood imagination.

The smells, the tastes, the spirit of the plantation cling to me; they are inseparable from my conception of self – the construct I am. My oldest recollections are from around 1955, the year I started school. The cane-fields of Rose Hall began across the main road from our house at Palmyra. This road was separated from our yard by a narrow ditch where I learnt to fish with hook and ink earthworm for lure. We *kept* our catch; we ate it, except for yarrow, a pariah snakelike, flat-head, fish, which we relished slaughtering. Behind our house, the rice-fields began a two-mile journey to the foreshore, where the mighty Berbice River, belatedly, only just before it entered the Atlantic, made room for its tributary, the Canje. This little river watered the big Corentyne plantations: Albion, Port Mourant, Skeldon and our own Rose Hall. The latter's cane-fields, to our eternal dismay, were protected from us by a broad, deep canal, which spoke of King Sugar's power to define.

From our veranda I would survey the sea of cane. The smoke belching into the sky from the factories at Rose Hall and Albion spoke of the annual cycle. By the age of five or six, I could read the rhythm of the sugar culture: flood-fallowing; the release of the water after nine months and the fishing carnival in the muddy fields; planting, manuring, weeding; the prolific cane-arrows on the eve of the harvest; the burning of the cane and its evocatively syrupy rich smell; the amazingly quick reaping by raucously loud cutters and loaders who never ceased to enthral us as acres of cane disappeared. I was already conscious of the order, the higher skills of sugar, on one hand, and the chaotic, eclectic character of our rice and vegetable plots on the other. But rice culture, too, had its own rhythm with its peculiar evocation of smells and images, its own rich tapestry of tasks, feverish activity and accompanying Hindu rituals for a good harvest, to placate our gods.

In August, during our school-holidays, the cane-fields in our village were harvested. A consuming expectancy claimed us all. Impatiently, we awaited the burning of the cane to remove the thick undergrowth, the impenetrable thrash which colonised the ground as the cane reached 12 feet or more. The aroma of burnt cane and scalded cane-juice was seductive. It was a signal for *our* harvest to begin. The night before the cane was cut, in darkness or in moonlight, our reaping of choice, juicy stalks, provided sheer bliss through many hours of cane-sucking, heightening the peculiar freedom stolen by boys in the night. The navigation canal between the road and the fields quickly exuded a cocktail of foetid odour of decaying cane-tops, muddy water churned up by the iron cane-punts, and decomposing crocodiles crushed by colliding punts. It was most satisfying to steal cane from the punts as they were tugged to the factory – at one time, lazily, by mules; later, swiftly, by tractors, 'Farmall', a skeletal tractor, almost a toy.[7]

The lush contact of machete on juice-saturated cane began before dawn. Soon cutters, blackened by ash, would be haranguing each other. Invariably this had nothing to do with work; the source of the animation would be more elevated – sex, whorehouses, rum and cricket. Subtlety would have been out-of-place. The raucousness and crudity of the exchange must have helped to lighten the hard tasks, made more burdensome by bodies smeared with the sticky cane juice, ash and sweat in the remorseless heat.[8] It always astounded me how fast the forest of cane would disappear, yielding its daunting secret: a complex hydraulic system of canals, drains, ditches, dams, *kokers* – geometric precision, symmetry, etchings on the heavy clay, as if to ease the monotony of this flat land. Holland in the tropics, I call it elsewhere.[9]

At the time I could not have made the connection between this complexity and the use of the land. I could not have grasped how tenuous was our grip on the Guyana coastland; but something lodged in me in those innocent, spacious days. For, over and over, I would sketch, badly but avidly, scenes from the cane-fields: men cutting; women manuring; boys leading mules tugging punts to the factory belching smoke; men manoeuvring big machines like toys to the edge of the water. But always, the crudity of execution was marred further by the canals and trenches, which I hated to sketch, but somehow could not leave out: it would not have been real.

It was many years later, into my young adulthood, that I learnt to read this landscape, to begin to conjure up the monumental feats of the imagination, skill and brawn-power expended in its original construction.[10] This suggested the scale of discipline and will – consistency of effort – central to the maintenance of the drainage and irrigation system. Even now I can see half-clad men, specks in the huge fields, clearing a drain, adding earth to a weak dam, adroitly locating, under water, a potentially serious leak. These seemingly trivial acts of little men, many of whom I knew, were crucial in the minding of the larger plantation order. I took all this for granted then, so did most Guyanese, in the Campbell years, in the late 1950s and early 1960s.

Soon after the harvest, the trash, the stripped leaves, were burnt; then young men and women would spread manure on the new shoots, the ratoons. Replanting was only done every five or six years. As the canes sprouted, water was pumped into the fields to speed up the process. Quickly, this astounding, man-made landscape was reclaimed by the lushness. Women would then begin weeding the grasses and parasitic plants that retarded sugar-cane growth. Periodically, invisible but vocal men ensconced in the big cane, could be heard as they checked on water-levels in fields and canals, or mended a leaking *koker* or piled dirt on weak sideline embankments. The days when a small plane visited, spraying chemicals on the growing cane, at what seemed like touching distance, were magical. A supposed nod from the pilot made our day.

Flood-fallowing times were especially trying for our parents; numerous domestic routines were evaded or skimped only after a fashion by us children. We were too enthralled by the mechanical wonder in the fields: we, therefore, had to 'supervise' the ploughing and the carving out of the drains and ditches. By the mid-1950s, 'TD18' Caterpillar tractors and draglines gave these tasks a magical dimension, but we still felt an intimacy with this process because many of the operators of these machines were known to us. It was exhilarating to watch men whom we knew as inept cricketers or 'rum-suckers' (boozers), who cursed and stumbled and went to 'hutel' (whore houses) on Saturday nights, manipulate these stupendous machines to the edge of canals, five or six feet deep. We were entranced by these feats of control and timing, although we felt they were exaggerated specially for the young women, drawn to men and machines.

We had sugar in our blood. At play we mimicked all these fascinating facets of the sugar culture. We were also drawn to the roles of power on the plantation – playing at being managers and overseers, affecting what we thought was the white man's accent, as incomprehensible to us as the Scottish brogue was to the workers. We pretended to be stockinged white men, smoking pipes; a thick cake of dried white mud up to our knees, fitted us for the former role.

We had no idea that every square mile of cane on our flat alluvial coast, several feet below sea-level and vulnerable to flooding and periodic drought, required 49 miles of drainage ditches and 16 miles of high-level waterways.[11] Even ,older people appeared to take this for granted. Although the workers seemed to be on strike often in the 1960s, cane-cutting, a job saddled with associations of slavery and indentureship and with failure in school – the end of the road[12] – had acquired a sudden gloss. From the 1950s many young Indian men saw it as a remunerative job, however demanding. One could earn enough to buy a piece of land, build a little wooden house and paint it. Indeed a job on the plantation acquired a new meaning: generally, it no longer spoke of subjugation or failure; it now carried suggestions of mobility, even ambition.

By the late 1950s, we knew people who worked in the estate's office as clerks or typists, or were skilled workers in the factory or 'tractor field', servicing those giant machines which mesmerised us. Some were supervisors in field and factory: one woman from our village, Iris Ramjeet (Auntie Baba), a distant relative, represented women workers as a trade unionist, at home and abroad – she was sent to Brazil, 'on union business', the papers told us. By the early 1960s, many cane-cutters owned brand new 'Triumph' bicycles, shining machines with yellow dusters dangling ostentatiously from the stems of the saddles. Another relative of mine, a cane-cutter at Rose Hall (we called him Bullet), told me in 1960 that Booker made them an irresistible offer, enabling them to become bicycle owners: they could make a deposit of $1 and pay instalments, only during the grinding season, of a $1 per week.[13] He showed up with a 'Triumph' a few days later, yellow duster knotted inside of his shirt collar in the triumphal manner of our great cricketer, Rohan Kanhai, from Plantation Port Mourant. Bullet quickly added a contraption that emitted an annoying melody from a Hindi movie, in order to impress a girl whom he fancied. He inscribed, in red paint, on the fender by the rear light: 'My Desia'. The bike brought the cane-cutter much pride: Jock Campbell was good at seeing 'the importance of small causes'.

I shared in Bullet's romance with his bike. I had the rare privilege, in March 1960, of being towed on his crossbar to the new, impressive cricket ground and community centre, at Rose Hall, to watch our county, Berbice, play England – it was fantastic to read 'Berbice v. England' on the giant, freshly-painted scoreboard. We were proud of the fact that our team had three West Indian Test batsmen – Basil Butcher, Rohan Kanhai and Joe Solomon, all of whom came from Port Mourant, one of Jock Campbell's estates.[14] It seemed as if our whole village was there, including some of the older boys who were studying at the Booker Training School for Apprentices at Port Mourant.

Sugar was in our blood. But growing up in an Indian village at the edge of a thriving sugar estate, when the stature of our charismatic Indian leader, Cheddi Jagan, also from Port Mourant, seemed unassailable, around 1959-60, with three of our cricketers in the West Indies team, and a battery of lawyers and doctors returning from England, it was easy to take sugar for granted, to assume that its profits were limitless. Further, despite rising living standards, it was easy to absorb Jagan's messianic doctrine that the 'sugar gods' were preventing us from reaching the stars.

The perceptible improvements in the sugar worker's condition simply reinforced what Jagan taught us, that the profits accruing to sugar were huge; that we were given the crumbs, to placate us. Only nationalisation of the 'commanding heights of the economy', starting with sugar, could get us to the promised land. Of course, we all knew of Sir Jock Campbell. We heard that he was a better man than anybody hitherto involved with sugar;

that he was more responsive to our people's needs than his predecessors. But immersed in the anti-colonial euphoria, after the freedom of 'Mother India', and dazed by the millennial message of Cheddi Jagan – a simple, credible tale of King Sugar's insatiable greed – we could see nothing redeeming in Campbell's reforms. To have attempted to give any credence to his programme for change was to let the side down, to be seen as a stooge of the 'imperialists', a traitor. Jock understood this perfectly:

> It is easier for a Campbell to pass through the eye of a needle than for Booker to be loved; we wish to be understood and, respected and worthy of respect.[15]

A plantation people, many of us still barely a generation away from the logies – coolies – our world was dramatised and made intelligible for us by Cheddi. His utopian vision told us that Booker kept us back, that our universe was perfectible if only we would expel the 'sugar gods'. His message spoke to us in the way the *Ramayana* did, promising a kind of *Rama Rajya,* the rule of Lord Rama, a golden age. We could muster no patience for reason, for notions of gradualism, incremental change. We were nurtured on El Dorado, visions of illimitable possibilities: we could not be held back by being told about the hazards of the Guyanese environment, about the minutiae of sugar agronomy or the monumental organisational effort required to sustain large-scale production on this harsh land.[16]

In May 1967, one year after the British gave independence to the African Guyanese leader, L.F.S. Burnham, a man for whom Campbell often expressed private contempt, he resigned as the Chairman of Booker. The inflexibility of Jagan's Marxist illumination and racial violence between 1962 and 1964 had taken its toll. By the early 1970s virtually every local politician was supporting nationalisation of Booker, the panacea of all our ills. It was a quick fix. With the support of Jagan, Burnham nationalised the sugar industry in 1976 – hailed by most as the greatest step in the reclamation of the nation's dignity.

In 1982 I returned to Guyana for four months and stayed for four years: I experienced the most repellent phase of Burnham's dictatorial rule. I quickly realised that the nationalisation of sugar was a massive, backward step. This was an empty harvest, engendered by the sterile dogmas and El Doradean dreams about sugar's perennially bounteous returns.[15] Production slumped to less than half its level at nationalisation: from 330,000 tons to 129,000 tons. The delicate, complex hydraulic system had been gravely undermined on most estates. Most of the technical people, trained since Campbell's time at Booker, had fled to America and Canada, while Burnham's incompetent hacks tried to explain away the failure and Jagan's people, asserting a monopoly on communist infallibility, called for authentic 'workers' control' – and more nationalisation – 80% of the fragile economy was already state-controlled.

I despaired. It was then that I started to appreciate the pernicious effect of dogmas and the centrality of good management. Slowly, reluctantly, I recognised some of the merits of the culture of reform of Campbell's Booker in the 1950s-60s – a change of perspective that evoked opprobrium from many of my compatriots. I was beginning to grow wings, to escape the limitations of the Marxist theology that had imprisoned my thoughts for years. My reassessment led me to the work of Jock Campbell in British Guiana, for which many expressed private respect but were afraid to say so in public: it was the time of the zealots.

In June 1985, Ian McDonald, who had worked with Booker and Campbell since 1955, sent me a copy of a book on Guyanese sugar by M. Shahabuddeen, Burnham's attorney-general.[18] I had come to respect this author's intellectual vigour. Now, however, it pained me to discover that he had no backbone: he was unable to transcend his master's frame of reference. He did not have a word to say about Campbell's obvious contribution to the advancement of the sugar industry and his role in postwar change in Guyana. In a footnote at the end of his book of more than 400 pages, Shahabuddeen belatedly assembled a few quotes – prompted and provided by McDonald – reflecting the progressive temper of Campbell, and he concluded, rightly but limply, that a biography of the man 'should form a good part' of any history of British Guiana.[19]

I wrote *Sweetening Bitter Sugar* as an attempt to comprehend the work of a complex, progressive, contradictory, compassionate man, and its effect on British Guiana, in the exciting period between the mid-1930s and the mid-1960s: the time of nationalist stirrings, mobilisation for decolonisation, the fragmenting of the nationalist coalition and the descent into racial hatred and violence. It is about hope, passion and the death of a dream to forge a nation. Jock Campbell's work was essentially an exercise in exorcising the ghosts of what Jagan called 'bitter sugar'. Campbell realised that he could not erase the whole sordid legacy of King Sugar and he felt guilty about this; but he had a passion to ameliorate it, to sweeten it at least, in a radical independent Guyana.

Three days after Campbell died in December 1994, my father wrote to me from Palmyra: 'I am sorry to hear of Sir Jock Campbell's death. He was a giant of a man. He came here to shape the destiny of East Indians.'[18] Whether one agrees or not with this sentiment, the man deserves a place in Guyanese history.

Notes

1. Jock Campbell, interview by the author, Nettlebed, Oxfordshire, May 9, 1990, Tape 1.
2. See my *'Tiger in the Stars': The Anatomy of Indian Achievement in*

British Guiana, 1919-29 (London: Macmillan, 1997), xx-xxii.
3. See, for example, 'Sixth Generation Reformer', *The Times Review of Industry and Technology'* (September 1964): [Appendix 1]; 'Men of Note: Lord Campbell of Eskan', *Jamaican and West Indian Review,* (June 1966): 23; Lord Campbell of Eskan, 'Private Enterprise and Public Morality', *New Statesman,* May 27, 1966; Lord Campbell of Eskan, speech to the Fabian Society, October 22, 1969, (mimeo.), pp. 18-20.
4. See note 1.
5. Interviews with the following relatives, Palmyra, East Canje, Berbice, Guyana: Ramdularie (1916-85), May 1982; Latchman Sohan (1908-89), December 1985; Sarran Jagmohan (1920–2005), April 1986.
6. For an assessment of the *Ramayana* as a text of exile in British Guiana, see my *'Tiger in the Stars',* 44-53.
7. Although my recollections are based on Rose Hall, knowledge of other plantations in Berbice and Demerara acquired in the late 1960s confirmed that these images were representative of all estates.
8. See David Dabydeen, *Slave Song* (1984) for a poetic evocation of the power of this crude estate 'coolie' idiom.
9. See my 'The Shaping of the Indo-Caribbean People: Guyana and Trinidad to the 1940s', *Journal of Caribbean Studies 14, nos.* 1&2 (1999-2000): 61-92.
10. I started to think about this hard land and its impact on the Guyanese psyche after I had read, in 1971, the introductory chapter to Donald Wood's book, *Trinidad in Transition* (London: OUP, 1968).
11. This is a classic quote that the Venn Commission of 1949 had used to dramatise the hazards of the coastal environment; see *Report of a Commission of Inquiry into the Sugar Industry of British Guiana,* Col. No. 249 (London: HMSO, 1949), 9. See also A.C. Barnes, *The Sugar Cane* (Aylesbury, Bucks.: Leonard Hill Books, 1974 [1964]), 119-21, 161-2.
12. See Rooplall Monar's story, "Dhookie" in *Backdam People* (Leeds: Peepal Tree Press, 1985), where the headmaster "shake he head and say, "Dull or brilliant, they all end in the sugar-cane field", and Jan Shinebourne's novel, *The Last English Plantation* (Leeds: Peepal Tree Press, 1988), set around Rosehall estate, where at twelve, June Lehall, just started at school in New Amsterdam on a scholarship, knows her friend from primary school, Ralph Brijlall, has begun full-time work in the canefields.
13. See my essay, 'The Tiger of Port Mourant – R.B. Kanhai: Fact and Fantasy in the Making of an Indo-Guyanese Legend', in *Indo-West Indian Cricket,* Frank Birbalsingh and Clem Seecharan (London: Hansib, 1988), 41-77.
14. We need to remember that in those days the British Guiana dollar exchanged at $4.8 to the pound sterling, not over $320 to the pound as in 2015.
15. Quoted from a mimeographed biographical sketch Campbell drafted some years after he had left Booker. It was among the papers he gave me in 1992.
16. These hazards had been articulated by Jock Campbell in a letter to the *New Statesman and Nation* (October 24, 1953), after the suspension of the constitution.

17. See note 7.
16. M. Shahabuddeen, *From Plantocracy to Nationalisation: A Profile of Sugar in Guyana* (Georgetown: University of Guyana, 1983).
17. Ibid., 410 [footnote 120a].
18. Personal correspondence from Sydney Seecharan, Palmyra, Guyana, December 29, 1994.

GIRMITIYAS AND MY DISCOVERY OF INDIA[1]

About 1880, in the ancient town of Ayodhya in the United Provinces of India, a young girl of the Parray clan gave birth to a son. She must have been deeply disgraced, because she was willing to go alone with her baby to a far-off island to which other people of the region were going. That was how the Parray woman came to Trinidad. She wanted her son to be a pundit...[2]

I know very little about my ancestors in India...All that I shall ever know about my parents before they reached British Guiana [in 1901] is what is stated in the records of the now defunct Immigration Department [Ships' Registers]. They came from Basti in Uttar Pradesh, about sixty miles from Allahabad, Jawaharlal Nehru's birthplace.[3]

I

DARKNESS

I grew up with many Indias, a tapestry of images – part fact, part fantasy – that have helped to shape me. I was born in British Guiana in 1950, on the edge of the plantation where several members of my family were taken, as 'bound coolies', from India, between 1875 and 1909. They were, like most of those who went to Fiji, girmitiyas: indentured labourers. I was given no idea of the India in which my people originated, no clue as to why they left. I imagined India as an undifferentiated place, vastly bigger than British Guiana, but not as big as England. I was claimed by the popular lore that the girmitiyas were tricked by *arkatis* – the evil recruiters in India – into 'a new slavery': they took the place of African slaves in the colony. We learnt nothing of our ancestral background; nothing beyond the embroidered tales of deception and kidnapping that were the unassailable explanation for their presence in British Guiana. We did not reflect on the emotions, the pain, probably still lingering in the rickety frames of the dwindling girmitiyas in our midst, in the late 1950s. We did not explore the terminal break with the 'motherland' – for most, a one-way journey. That recent India was an area of darkness; we did not try to comprehend it. Indeed, the India of the great Hindu classic, the *Ramayana*, the constructed India in Bombay movies, Gandhian India in revolt against British rule, and free Nehruvian India, had greater resonance for us than eastern Uttar Pradesh (the United Provinces) which, I would learn much later, was the home of my ancestors. If I had any notion at all, of the Indian provenance of my ancestors, it was that they were *not* Madrasis (Tamils): darker people whose rituals were alien to ours. We felt superior to them.

In 1966 I learnt from Cheddi Jagan's book, *The West on Trial*, that his people had come from Basti District, in eastern Uttar Pradesh[4]; that had prompted me to ask about the place where our family originated. I learnt nothing; the void remained, and no one seemed perturbed by it. My early years had been spent among several of my great-grandparents, former girmitiyas, yet the carnival of images in the boy's imagination must have considered them strange – companions of the framed Hindu gods and goddesses on our wall who looked over us: pictures that belonged to an India of magic. I must have seen them – these speakers of that funny language of our Hindu rituals – as somewhat mythical, evoking in me something surreal and timeless, as if, long ago, they had wandered too far away from home, got lost in the bush, and found themselves, purely by chance, on a sugar plantation in British Guiana: a long journey over land, among strange peoples. And even when I was told, as late as 1955, that the last batch of former 'bound coolies' were returning to India, by a big boat which was pointed out to me in the newspaper, the boy of five still imagined them retracing those faint steps in the bush, walking for months, possibly years, through places with tigers and elephants and flying chariots.

Such were the labyrinthine fantasies the girmitiyas stirred in me! They persisted into my adolescence. They came not from a precocious imagination but out of 'historical darkness'. We really had no conception of this recent India that was the home of the girmitiyas. Inquiry, such as it was, fell for the tale – perpetuated by the girmitiyas – that they were all duped into going to British Guiana. There curiosity ceased. The *arkati*, the infamous recruiter, still casts a long shadow. V.S. Naipaul (born 1932), whose people went to Trinidad as girmitiyas from eastern Uttar Pradesh, recalls that he, too, was imperturbable about the 'historical darkness':

> I grew up with two ideas of history, almost two ideas of time. There was history with dates. That kind of history affected people and places abroad...But Chaguanas, where I was born, in an Indian-style house my [maternal] grandfather [a Brahmin girmitiya] had built, had no dates. If I had read in a book that Gandhi had made his first call for civil disobedience in 1919, that date seemed recent. But 1919, in Chaguanas, in the life of the Indian community, was almost unimaginable. It was a time beyond recall, mythical. About our family, the migration of our ancestors, I knew only what I knew or what I was told. Beyond (and sometimes even within) people's memories was undated time, historical darkness. Out of that darkness (extending to place as well as to time)

> we had all come. The other where Gandhi and Nehru and the others operated was historical and real. The India from which we had come was impossibly remote, almost as imaginary as the land of the *Ramayana*, our Hindu epic. I lived easily with that darkness, that lack of knowledge. I never thought to inquire further.[5]

The 'India from which we had come', was, in fact, more imaginary and remote than the land of the *Ramayana*. We, too, were comfortable with that darkness. But, as if to atone for this and the timelessness of the narratives we told ourselves, I became obsessed with time and dates – punctiliousness about time in my daily life: punctuality; and a passion for apprehending chronological time: the sequence of events and their contexts, the rudiments of an historical temper. I would lose patience with my own people for not being able to date things, even their own dates of birth or those of their children. I was also frustrated by the absence of a chronological sense. This, I suppose, was what gave me the yearning for a sense of history, and is the genesis of my efforts in recent years to teach and write aspects of Indo-Caribbean history.

It started with the historical darkness in my family: not until the mid-1980s was I able to establish the precise place of origin, in India, of most of my family. And it was not until Brij Lal's *Girmitiyas: The Origins of the Fiji Indians*[6] peeled back the shroud, casting unprecedented luminosity on our historical darkness, that this India which had eluded me whenever I pursued my great-grandparents' antecedents, began to cohere. My discovery of this book in early 1989, in the library of the Royal Commonwealth Society, five years after its publication by the *Journal of Pacific History*, gave me my first conceptions of 19th century eastern Uttar Pradesh. *Girmitiyas* also gave me the context for examining my great-grandparents' attitudes, including their motives for flight. Like an illumination, it unclogged my mind so that I could begin to see the efforts of the 'bound coolies' and their descendants in the Caribbean as an achievement worthy of celebration – though not of triumphalism. *Girmitiyas* is a foundation of my contribution to Indo-Guyanese history. It belongs with Nehru's *Discovery of India* and C.L.R. James's *Beyond a Boundary* – these had cast a spell on me since the mid-1960s. *Girmitiyas* lit up my intellectual path away from the consuming historical darkness that had delayed my creative spirit for a long time. I craved a history of our own – 'a history with dates'.

Professor Brij Lal (born in Fiji): the finest historian of the Indian indentured experience and the Indian diaspora

The second edition of Brij Lal's classic, *Girmitiyas* (republished in Fiji), of which this essay was the foreword.

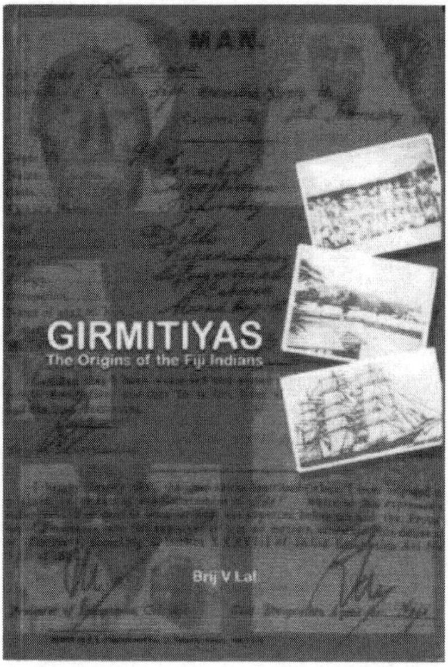

II

SUBMERGED ANCESTRY: KAILA'S WORLD

It was my illiterate maternal great-grandmother, Kaila (1889-1956), who sparked something in me. She kindled my curiosity for the antecedents of the girmitiyas. When she died I was only six years old, but she still occupies a niche in my memory: a mythical persona almost, in my pantheon of Hindu goddesses, however dimmed by time and decades of unfaltering atheism. I think this idealised image of Kaila is a compound of the adulatory recollections of my extended family, and my own faded snapshots and later embellishments of her. But there were grounds for the construction of this somewhat ethereal persona: her abundant sacrifice for the family that betrayed no selfish motive; the absence of petty jealousy – that bedevilling feature of many Hindu joint families; the inexhaustible energy that fed her resolve to make life better for my maternal grandmother, her only child, and her five children. The fact that Kaila never flinched from what she saw as duty to family, until the day she literally dropped collecting firewood in the cemetery, enhanced the persona of unsullied magnanimity. It was a life of total devotion to the building of a new family, in a new place far away from home, for she had journeyed alone to British Guiana as an indentured labourer, in 1909, aged 20. She would never have contact again with anyone in India.

Much of what I remember of Kaila is a blur, but it is a haziness that is of a piece: there is much that is immanent and suggestive in the faded image. It still has the power to evoke in me eclectic visions, to draw me into its shifting meanings and inner complexities – its subtle narratives – while intimating ways of self-reflection that speak to a larger context: the dynamic of our Indian community in colonial Guyana. I vaguely recall her visits to my grandmother, on Saturday afternoons, walking the six or seven miles from Plantation Rose Hall to Palmyra, and repeating the journey on Sunday afternoons. Palmyra, the village of my birth, was also the village of my maternal grandfather's family, the Sohans. Kaila and her husband, Jagarnath (1888-1958), had bought several plots of land there, as well as cattle, for my grandmother, Ramdularie (1916-1985), after she married my maternal grandfather in 1930, aged 14. But they continued to work and live at Plantation Rose Hall, in the rent-free 'logies' or barracks in the 'nigger yard', some of which were built during slavery – and looked so. Abstemious to the bone, every penny earned was guarded. That was why Kaila walked those miles to and from my grandmother's at weekends, whatever the weather. Yet she was unstinting when it came to her daughter, her grandchildren and me, her first great-grandchild, apparently the apple of her eye. She always brought fruits, sweetmeats, clothes, various things she made, for us.

A black, little woman, she was not quite of the Guyanese landscape: after nearly 50 years, she still looked and dressed as if she were from a foreign place. She belonged to that remote, incomprehensible India that possessed my boyhood. In my imagination she fused with those surreal Hindu images that looked out of the walls of our living room – the gods and goddesses that seemed to hover in mid-air. They awed me. As I played at being a boss, a white overseer on the sugar plantation, ordering menial toilers about, my strange boyhood gift for wonder would magically transport Kaila to this India of which I knew nothing – the way Hanuman, the monkey god, fetched the mountain of curative herbs, in his hand, in the framed picture on our wall. But there were ordinary, day-to-day images, too. Kaila was adept at the minutiae of wet-rice culture, as she was adroit in weeding and manuring sugar cane. Even now, nearly 50 years on, I can still place her on the *kharian* or threshing floor, driving our big-horned bullocks in endless cycles, tethered to a pole around which were packed tight bundles of freshly cut rice stalks (*padi*, unhusked rice). I can still see this busy little woman winnowing the *padi*, or helping to fill it into jute bags, for the mill, sweeping up every grain, with practised frugality. Nothing was wasted: the straw was fed to cows, the husk and broken rice to fowls and ducks, the cow cakes were dried for cooking or manuring the vegetable garden. The draconian thrift of village India had not been squandered in the comparative comfort of village Guyana. Fact and fantasy were inextricably interwoven in my apprehension of Kaila. One thing I did know for sure: she retained a deep affection for the girmitiyas, especially the few with whom she had made the crossing.

I remember her being in tears a few times; this stayed with me; and many years after she was gone I asked my grandmother, Ramdularie, the reason for her sadness. She said it had to do with the recurring deaths of several of her friends from India, who were passing away month by month by the mid-1950s. They saw themselves as *jahajins*, ship-sisters, to the end. They were like blood relatives, their children forbidden to intermarry. On several occasions she had to upbraid Kaila for being so deeply pained that she would wail inconsolably at the funeral of one of her *jahajins*, imploring her to 'take' her soon: she could not wait to join them in the next life. Such was the bond of these girmitiyas! It grew stronger as they became fewer, in the late 1950s. Brinsley Samaroo has reflected on the making of this bond:

> On board ship the castes and regions of India were mixed as in the depots, and the common tasks, assigned with little respect to persons, served as a great leveller. The only separation on board was by gender and marital status...[r]eplacing the previous ties of caste and region was a new form of bonding which was started in the depots and strengthened on the ship. This bonding became greater on those ships which underwent difficult passages, for example in the churning, swirling waters of the

> *Pagal Samundar* (Mad Sea) so often encountered off the Cape of Good Hope. This brotherhood/sisterhood of the boat (*jahaji bhai/bahin*) was cemented when the immigrants joined together to resist ill-usage by European seamen. For this reason, the Indians resented being separated into different colony batches when they arrived in the Caribbean.[7]

It is not surprising, therefore, that the enigma of Kaila has accompanied me throughout my life, sustaining curiosity, as if there was something hidden in her life that belongs to me: a kernel of truth that was at the core of my being. I learnt to call this *identity*, an exercise of the imagination that spoke to one's essence, grounded in family as well as a wider context: community, belonging. But that was a mature consideration arrived at after much internal conflict and agony on the meaning of India – many imagined Indias that still find ways of drawing out a strange loyalty. Kaila and my other girmitiya great-grandparents are its source.

But Kaila's India remained elusive to my curiosity. From time to time my grandmother had tried to coax fragments of that past out of her, hoping to draw something from lapses in her taciturnity. She did not get beyond the exhausted tale that she was deceived into going to Demerara (British Guiana) to 'sift sugar'. Kaila was twenty when she went to the colony; she was 'single' and travelled alone. How credible was her fragment of a story? Was she married in India? Did she have any children? What was her mother like? Did she have a happy childhood? What did they do for a living? Did she miss those she would never see again? Did she dream of returning one day? Why did she leave home? Did she tell anybody that she was going away to work, possibly never to return? Why did she travel alone, unaccompanied by any relatives? How did she find the strength to break completely from her past and establish a foundation for people like myself to acquire ambition and self-belief? Some area of darkness! These questions, if asked at all over the years, were never answered. The gnawing secrets are interred with her. But, for me, the questions would not go away. They were sustained by my liberal education and the emerging historical temperament that was tormented by the historical darkness. That darkness that shrouded this woman, whose quiet consistency of purpose must have lodged in my imagination, fed my intellectual curiosity. It would later endow my pursuit of Indo-Caribbean history and historiography with the aura of a mission. This submerged history, which was Kaila's and mine, had to be written. The problem was how.

Joseph Ruhomon[8], Dwarka Nath[9] and Peter Ruhomon[10], local Indian amateur historians, had made a bold start. However, the girmitiyas, as individuals, were silent in these pioneering studies. Even Bechu's fearlessly partisan writings on their behalf, in the late 1890s[11], had not sought to remedy this, although there were many thousands in British Guiana. Agency was denied the 'bound coolies'. Amidst the supremacy of imperial institutions and definitions and the omnipotence of the colonial bureaucracy, individual lives, as well as the universe of the girmitiyas, were rendered voiceless. The intellectual means did not exist for the exploration of Kaila's world, including her inner promptings. After a while, curiosity just dried up. Everything would be subsumed under the resilient *arkati* thesis of deception and kidnapping, which brought closure on the imponderables. But, unlike Naipaul, I could not 'live easily with that darkness'. It grew worse the older I got. My intellectual *raison d'etre* was animated by this gaping void in self-knowledge, a strangled sensibility – a fault-line in my identity.

It would be a circuitous route to comprehension of Kaila's world. A few years ago I reflected on this passion to know: 'My family grew rice but they had been cattle people for nearly a century in British Guiana. I took this for granted. It was many years later, in the 1980s, when I became deeply involved in my father's cattle business that I began to explore this family obsession with cattle. I turned to the National Archives in Georgetown [Guyana], to the Ships' Registers of indentured labourers'.[12] This helped me to detect the vague contours of my girmitiya ancestors. I quickly ascertained that much of their caste instincts had accompanied them to the Caribbean; it was a major force in shaping their new world. The Ship's Registers[13] had lightened the historical darkness; that elusive India was just peeping through its Himalayan clouds.

My first ancestor in the colony was Sohun (Sohan),[14] my mother's paternal grandfather, who went to British Guiana as a 'bound coolie' in the ship, *Rohilla*, which left Calcutta on 11 February 1875. He was 22 years old and came from Doobaree Village, Azamgahr District, in eastern Uttar Pradesh (UP). He was indentured to Plantation Rose Hall, the same sugar estate to which Kaila and Jagarnath were taken later, in 1909 and 1908 respectively. When Sohan left the estate, sometime in the late 1880s, he bought some land at Palmyra Village, the place of my birth, on the edge of that sugar plantation. He started to graze cattle on the common pasturage, which abounded before the meteoric rise of rice cultivation during the First World War. But Sohan continued to work as head cattle minder on neighbouring Plantation Prospect, an estate owned by a Mr Gill, one of the many Scotsmen in the district. I felt as if I had cracked an ancient code when I discovered in the Ship's Register that Sohan was of Ahir caste, the celebrated cattle rearers of Uttar Pradesh and Bihar. I grew up with knowledge of our Ahir caste provenance, but that had engendered incredulity in me, from time to time. I needed official corroboration in order to accept our cattle pedigree as unimpeachable. The need for authentication was aggravated by the absence of any caste rituals that would have anchored the claim.

Many of Sohan's children, grandchildren and great-grandchildren were also cattle rearers. A few became infamous cattle rustlers. My maternal grandfather, Latchman Sohan (1908-89), was not unimpeachable. The last of Sohan's ten children, born when his father was 55, he was a spoilt child, pampered by his creole Indian mother, Surat, Sohan's second wife. He turned to heavy rum-drinking early and retained that passion all his life. He was also prone to violence in the home. Outside of the home, Latchman was a warm, magnanimous man, prodigal with his generosity, if a bit of a rogue, something of a folk hero. He was known as Skipper Ding; most called him Skipper; this was done out of affection. That he was a legendary cattle herder – masterful at the lasso – sustained a heroic image long after he had passed his best. The image in the home was less heroic. In the late 1930s, already a father of five, he would deftly escape pressing domestic chores, especially the demanding seasonal tasks of rice-planting and rice-harvesting. Skipper was not overly concerned with the maintenance of his young family, a task stoically assumed by his wife and her parents, Kaila and Jagarnath, over many years.

A skipper's life was one of perpetual flight. Escape through booze and excess of all sorts; escape to the hinterland of British Guiana, to the inhospitable grasslands of the Rupununi, on the Brazilian border, encountered in Evelyn Waugh's *Ninety-Two Days* of 1934 and *A Handful of Dust*, his novel of the same year. For many years in the late 1930s-early 1940s, Skipper drove cattle on the Rupununi Cattle Trail, the 180 miles from Dadanawa, through Surama and Kurupukari, to Takama, on the Berbice River. Often, after that drive through the rain forest – heat, mosquitoes, sand-flies and a million things that bite, itches and sores, the dog tiredness – he would abandon himself to a week's whoring in the brothels of Takama, until body and money were spent. He would hitch a ride back to Dadanawa for another drive. The cycle could be repeated several times, before he returned home. Something of the Ahir had fused with the spontaneous anarchy of the Brazilian *vaqueiro* and images of the hard-drinking, brothel-hooked cowboy of the American west. To Skipper, money was a handful of dust. Eventually, he would drink his way home until he was broke. He was known to pull out his gun, threatening to shoot his whole family; wife and children would scatter into the darkness and the bush. The bravado spoke of futility: belated assertiveness in a home that had learnt to do without him. He never fired the gun, except once – when he killed a 'tiger' (probably a jaguar) and made it into the newspaper. He had become a legend.

I was groping towards the diverse forces reshaping us, removed from that India we could not apprehend. Yet, somehow, India still mattered. Throughout the 1960s I came under the spell of one of Sohan's other sons, Kaywal [Kilpax (1901-72)], a self-educated man who gave me another kind of India. A reformist Hindu, an Arya Samajist, he devoured several daily newspapers, apart from the writings of Gandhi, Nehru and Swami

Vivekananda. A chain smoker, possessed by the World Service of the BBC and All-India Radio, he was glued to his little light green 'Ferguson' radio, as it crackled into the night. Next day he would seek me out early, to survey world events: Nehru's speech to the Lok Sabha on Pakistan or China; President Johnson and Vietnam; trouble in the Congo; Castro, Sukarno, Nkrumah, Ben Bella, Nasser; and, inevitably, back to Nehru, Gandhi and names that I learnt to associate with India's freedom struggle: Motilal Nehru, Gopal Krishna Gokhale, Madan Mohan Malaviya, Abdul Kalam Azad, Sarojini Naidu and others. Jawaharlal Nehru, of course, was infallible. Kilpax had lots of time. When I thought we had exhausted the political deliberations of the day, he would deftly throw in a name to conjure with, and start firing again: 'Krishna Menon! Weak! Too much talk! And now the Chinese have walked into India! Ladakh stolen!'; or 'Jagjivan Ram, a Chamar, and Defence Minister!' I was drawn into his web. Another India, Nehru's, was taking shape in me. Kilpax was giving me his passion for argument and his enchantment with the spoken word, in English. And throughout my apprenticeship, he treated me like his equal, although I always called him *nana*: maternal grandfather.

Skipper's and Kilpax's father, Sohan, this patriarch who died in the mid-1920s, had left a very rich legacy, indeed. His youngest daughter's grandson, Len Baichan (born 1946), was a Guyana and West Indies cricketer. He toured India and Pakistan in 1974-5 and Australia in 1975-6, and played in three Test matches. In his first, in Lahore, in 1974, he made a century. He did not play a Test in India, but he travelled widely there and brought back lavish tales of the subcontinent, from the Khyber and Kashmir to Karnataka and Kerala, of legendary cricketers and film stars, of great palaces and maharajas, which he shared with me during many spacious hours, over rum, under that big samaan tree in the village. The cascading visions of India battling in me could not dry up. The curiosity, too, would not die. So my journey through the Ships' Registers, in 1985, had become an imperative. It would throw light on some things, feed new questions, but leave many unanswered. But it was a journey that had to be made.

I discovered that my father's maternal grandfather, Sewnath (1881-1956),[12] like Sohan and Jagarnath, was an Ahir. He came from Kharaura Village, Ghazipur District, eastern UP, and embarked at Calcutta on 8 October 1892, aged 11. He went to British Guiana in the *Avon*, accompanied by his sister, Sonbersi, aged 22, and her husband, Raghu, aged 30. Raghu, also, was an Ahir. It is noteworthy that the Register has them as the parents of Sewnath. That was incorrect; nothing is known of his parents, but they did not go to the colony. The assumption of parenthood by his sister and brother-in-law was a ruse to evade scrutiny of his case: he was a minor and would have needed the approval of his parents to board the ship at Calcutta.

The trio were indentured to Plantation Albion, on the lower Corentyne Coast, about 12 miles from Rose Hall. Young Sewnath soon acquired a formidable reputation on the estate as a shovelman. Sometime during the First World War, he had moved from Albion to Plantation Rose Hall where he continued as a shovelman. His earnings were better than most fieldworkers, and his astounding frugality and gift for spotting a bargain or a niche for profitable investment, enabled him to buy several properties at Palmyra and neighbouring Sea Well, at the junction of the East Canje and Corentyne districts. Sewnath, like Sohan and Jagarnath, retained the Ahir's passion for cattle: he bought several heads and soon established a subsidiary source of income.

A self-assured, orderly and meticulous man, Sewnath was scrupulous with his time. He often said things in parables; many centred on a theme: time is money. He had little time to spare, and was impatient with those who wasted his time. He managed that time dextrously, combining estate labour with cattle, sheep and poultry rearing, rice farming, the cultivation of fruits and vegetables, and money-lending. The idea of a holiday or a slack period did not sit easily with Sewnath and his wife, Etwarie. On Sundays, whatever the weather, they would work on their vegetable farm at Blendaal, on the west bank of the Canje River, several miles from Palmyra. Only the rapid descent of the solid darkness would stop them: the weary miles home were made in their donkey cart laden with plantains, eddoes, sweet potatoes, cassava, pumpkins, mangoes, sour-sop, sapodilla, a range of other fruits and vegetables. As their first grandson, Sarran Jagmohan (born 1920), narrated to me this tale of resilience, industry and utter devotion to the welfare of their eight children, he recalled: 'that donkey cart, with a small lamp dangling from the axle, had enough to fill a market. They grew most of what they ate; and they ate well, although they were very careful with money'. He added that they treated boys and girls with impartiality: some of the produce of their farm was always reserved for their married daughters.

Etwarie, my father's maternal grandmother, was a creole Indian, born in British Guiana around 1883. She was a Muslim; but when she married Sewnath in 1898, she took a Hindu name. She was hardworking, energetic and thrifty. I remember her, in her last years in the late 1950s-early 1960s: a wiry old woman, skeletal. I never saw her sitting still. For many years she was a weeder at Rose Hall, but her reputation as a rice planter was legendary, deemed the fastest and neatest in the area. Both Sewnath and Etwarie were impelled by a passion to uplift their children. They gave one of their properties to their eldest child, Sukhia (1899-1969), my paternal grandmother, and her husband, Jagmohan (1891-1938), whom she married in 1913, aged 14. Their second daughter was married to Jagmohan's younger brother, Mangal, who owned the best shop in the village in the 1930s. Etwarie died in August 1961, on polling day, having just voted for

Cheddi Jagan. It was totally in character that she should have done her duty before moving on; her reliability, resilience and consistency of focus were as unfaltering as Kaila's. Unconsciously, I must have absorbed her habit of according girls the same respect she gave to boys. She could hold her own in any argument and never flinched from plain speaking or firm decisions.

The background of her first son-in-law, Jagmohan,[16] is fascinating. It is enshrined in family lore. The tale is told of a man named Harpal (1846-1934), an Ahir girmitiya who had returned to India with his eldest son, Balgobin, in 1888. He had left his wife in British Guiana, having counselled her that if he did not return by a certain *jahaj* (ship), she should feel free to take another man. He did not return by that ship, and his wife, a Brahmin born in the colony, my father's paternal grandmother, soon invited a Brahmin man, another former girmitiya, Ramsarran Maharaj, to live with her. In early 1891, unannounced, Harpal (with his son) returned from India and went straight to his home at Warren (East Coast Berbice), as if nothing had happened. There he met the wife he had left behind pregnant by Ramsarran. Harpal had an amicable discussion with him and implored him to return to his home in a neighbouring village. Ramsarran pointed to the problem thrown up by the pregnancy, but Harpal assured him that he could handle that: he would bring the child up as if it were his own. Ramsarran left. This child, Jagmohan, my paternal grandfather, was born on 15 August 1891. He became a cattle herder, fathered 13 children and died prematurely, of pneumonia, on 17 September 1938, aged 47. He and his eldest son, Harold, who also died of pneumonia, were buried on the same day. Jagmohan grew up at No. 7 Village (East Coast Berbice), and worked for many years on Harpal's cattle farm. In his last years he was a cattle herder on an estate, Goldstone Hall, not far from Plantation Rose Hall. Ramsarran Maharaj returned to India for good, around 1898; there is no evidence that he had anything to do with his son Jagmohan's upbringing. The latter – a full Brahmin by birth – had taken to Harpal's Ahir calling, so that when he married my paternal grandmother, Sukhia, Sewnath's eldest daughter, Harpal probably saw that as keeping within the Ahir fold, his mother's Brahmin stock and the Muslim upbringing of Etwarie notwithstanding.

I had gone to the Ships' Registers looking for my girmitiya ancestors in chronological order, so Jagarnath and Kaila came last on my roster. My mother's maternal grandfather, Jagarnath (1888-1958), went to British Guiana in the ship, *Ganges*, which arrived there from Calcutta in late 1908. He was indentured to Rose Hall. He was twenty years old and, like Sohan, also from Azamgahr District in eastern UP; his village was Azampur. He was Ahir, like Sohan, Harpal and Sewnath, my other great-grandfathers. I was not aware how far the Ahir pedigree permeated the family. From time to time people spoke of our Gwalbans Ahir background, but the Registers had established for me that our obsession with cattle was not fortuitous. It had its roots in ancient caste promptings; and our settling on a section of the British Guiana coast, with ample land for grazing, must have rendered the ancient calling irresistible. We would pursue it assiduously for some 120 years, until one by one our numbers dwindled as we fled hapless Guyana for the greener pastures of the Indo-Guyanese diaspora: New York and Toronto primarily.

Kaila's story, however, broke this Ahir monotony. I had not anticipated this. She went to British Guiana in the *Ganges*, in September 1909. She came from Bhagwanpur Village, Gonda District, eastern UP, next door to Basti, on the border with Nepal. As noted before, she was 20 years old, and travelled alone; no relatives, man or woman, accompanied her. The Register gave her caste as Pasi. I had never heard of this, so it took me some time to discover that it was a low caste of palm tappers and catchers of wild birds and small game. It quickly dawned on me that her very dark complexion was, indeed, a badge of her low caste status. Pasis were an aboriginal caste, black people, so her name, Kaila, was probably a corruption of 'Kala': black. I learnt that the name Pasi comes from a word meaning, noose, used in trapping small game. I reflected on this often, and concluded that by escaping her low caste ascription, this remarkable woman had, indeed, escaped the noose.

My maternal grandmother had just died when I discovered Kaila's caste background; a very dark woman herself, I have no idea what her reaction would have been. My mother was not very pleased with this belated revelation. She did not belabour the point; but said that I should not make this public. Although I was aware of our Ahir roots, my caste instincts had never cohered; yet I recall a tinge of disappointment on learning of Kaila's low caste. This had surprised me. I must have felt vindicated, having discovered the strength of our Ahir antecedents, for I had become a passionate cattle rearer in my last years in Guyana, in the early 1980s. However, I like to think that the belated establishment of the diversity of my roots – Ahir, Brahmin, Muslim, Pasi – however submerged, has made me a broader person, equally proud now to claim a wider legacy. This, I suppose, has made me a better Guyanese and West Indian, more at ease with diversity and hybridity, better able to appreciate the achievements of the people of African descent in the region. It was a journey that had to be made; I had learnt much from it, but it left me with far more questions than when I started.

The curiosity grew thicker with my assembling of the fragments of my great-grandparents' Indian background. But the darkness over the real India which they had left, including their reasons for leaving, was not amenable to speedy dissipation. It was my discovery of Brij Lal's *Girmitiyas* that slowly opened for me sealed doors to the opaque world of the indentured labourers. It provided, at last, windows unto Kaila's world that had eluded me since I was a child. This book would be the foundation of my belief that an Indo-Caribbean historiography was possible; and that it would debunk Naipaul's infamous dictum that the history of the 'West Indian futility' could not be written because history was 'built on achievement and creativity; and nothing was created in the West Indies'.

I was fortified for the journey. This is what I wrote in 1997, reflecting on the place of *Girmitiyas* in the project:

Towards the end of the 1980s I endeavoured to recover the real India of these north Indian 'bound coolies' in British Guiana. A fount of rare illumination presented itself with my encounter of Brij Lal's *Girmitiyas: The Origins of the Fiji Indians*. Here, in a refreshingly lucid and dispassionate way, the unexamined dogma of deception and kidnapping is scrutinised and largely debunked. Lal had unearthed compelling socio-economic reasons for their leaving...[and] their role in shaping the temperament of the indentured labourers and their descendants in the sugar colonies. *Girmitiyas* also had a seminal influence on my way of seeing. The resilience of the Indians in Guyana, their thrift and ambition for their family – their achievements – are rendered more intelligible because we now have an authentic overview of real eastern UP and western Bihar, from the latter half of the nineteenth century.[17]

This is a magnificent legacy. How precisely did *Girmitiyas* help me to comprehend Kaila's world?

III

DISCOVERING *GIRMITIYAS*: OUT OF HISTORICAL DARKNESS

At the beginning of the book Brij Lal makes it clear that he challenges many of the standard assumptions about the girmitiyas and the world whence they came. It is, indeed, a fine scholarly achievement, revolutionary in its execution. He examines all the emigration passes (embarkation slips) of the 45,439 north Indian indentured labourers, who embarked at Calcutta for Fiji, between 1879 and 1916. He gave me hope at the start of *Girmitiyas*: '[O]ur discussion has relevance for many other Indian labour importing colonies, particularly the West Indies, which drew their supplies from the north'. He repeats this at the end:

> [M]uch of what has been said...also applies to those other Indian labour importing islands, in the West Indies especially, which drew their supplies from north India. All the British colonies operated under the same, or very similar, regulations and many of them shared the same facilities

in Calcutta. Sometimes the same emigration agent officiated for several colonies simultaneously, and even the sub-depots and recruiters were shared.[18]

No examination as thorough as this had been undertaken for British Guiana or Trinidad; this is still the case. The story he was telling was also the story of my people; this was the light I had yearned for most of my life. Buoyed by this, I turned to a seminal article by the British social anthropologist, Raymond Smith, done in the late 1950s on the origins of the girmitiyas to British Guiana.[19] Smith's study was based on a sample of 9,393 emigration passes of north Indians, between 1865 and 1917, but the correspondence between his findings and Lal's is so compelling that any doubt that *Girmitiyas* does not constitute an accurate account of the origins of Indo-Caribbean girmitiyas as well, is dispelled.

The only major difference between Fiji and British Guiana is the paucity of Madrasis (Tamils primarily) in the latter. Smith estimates that they comprised 4.4% of the migrants to British Guiana. Lal states that they were 6.3%. He is nearer the mark: Madrasis numbered 15,065 of the 238,909 girmitiyas taken to British Guiana between 1838 and 1917. In Fiji they were 23.8% of all migrants. However, this disparity is not replicated for north Indian migrants. Smith estimates that 85.6% of the indentured labourers to British Guiana originated in Uttar Pradesh (UP) and Bihar: 70.3% in the former, 15.3% in the latter. Lal states that 86% of north Indian migrants to Fiji originated in this area: 75.5% in Uttar Pradesh, 10.5% in Bihar. Both Smith and Lal observe that eastern UP and western Bihar primarily, were the sources of these migrants, especially the former.

Nine districts in eastern UP, and a neighbouring district, Shahabad, in western Bihar, contributed 51% of those migrants to British Guiana who originated in these two states. It is noteworthy that nine of the ten principal districts that supplied labourers to the two colonies are identical. In British Guiana the five principal districts of recruitment were: Basti, Azamgahr, Ghazipur, Gonda and Fyzabad. In Fiji, Basti, Gonda, Fyzabad and Azamgahr were among the five principal districts that contributed north Indian migrants; the other was Gorakhpur, neighbouring Basti, on the border with Nepal. Three of these districts had special resonance for me: Sohan and Jagarnath were from Azamgahr, Sewnath came from Ghazipur and Kaila originated in Gonda. They were becoming less remote, no longer imaginary. I could now locate them on the map – real places. My exploration of the girmitiyas was acquiring intellectual validity.

Brij Lal also establishes that, contrary to popular opinion, an overwhelming majority of the migrants were not from the lowest castes and outcastes. Raymond Smith corroborates this. Lal states that Brahmins and other high castes (Kshattriyas) comprised about 14% in Fiji; middling agricultural and artisan castes were 39%; low castes and outcastes contributed 28%; Muslims were 15%. Smith estimates that Brahmins and other high castes (Kshattriyas) accounted for 13.6% of the migrants to British Guiana; middling agricultural and artisan castes were 38.8%; low castes and outcastes were 31.1%; Muslims 16.3%. Not only was there a remarkably high correspondence in the caste distribution of the two sugar colonies, but, as Lal observes, this also corresponded with the representation of the main castes in Uttar Pradesh. The low caste Chamars, the largest single component among girmitiyas, contributed 12.9%, 13.4% and 12.4% to British Guiana, Fiji and Uttar Pradesh respectively, in 1901. Kshattriya castes constituted 9.2%, 10% and 7%; Ahir 9.7%, 9.2% and 8%; Kurmi 5.6%, 5.1% and 4.1%, Pasi 2.2%, 2.4% and 2.6%, and Muslims 16.3%, 15.1% and 13.5% in British Guiana, Fiji and Uttar Pradesh respectively, in 1901. Brahmins, however, were less inclined to go to the colonies as girmitiyas: they comprised 2.0% and 3.7% of unindentured migrants to British Guiana and Fiji respectively, but they accounted for 8% of the population of UP in 1901. Lal summarises his findings:

> It is obvious that the evidence calls in question assertions about the predominantly low caste origins of the indentured migrants. Low castes, of course, contributed a large percentage of the total numbers migrating, but the proportion of high and middling castes is noteworthy…It is clear that for most castes, with the exception of Brahmins, there is a broad correlation between their strength in the United Provinces and their contribution to the emigrating indentured population… Muslims and Chamars, who constituted the largest component of UP society, also furnished the largest number of migrants. Kshattriyas and Ahirs, too, feature prominently.[20]

Lal also establishes that, contrary to accepted dogmas, by the latter half of the 19th century, the impoverished districts of eastern UP and western Bihar were already immersed in a culture of migration: to Assam tea plantations, jute mills and myriad industrial destinations in Bengal, especially Calcutta, even Bombay textile mills. Many people were already on the move, when they engaged for indentureship in the sugar colonies. The penetration of their agrarian economies by the British rendered many of the traditional caste skills superfluous; there was immense dislocation. Pressure on this old land, in eastern UP, was intense: the density of population in 1891 in Fyzabad, Azamgahr and Jaunpur districts, for instance, had reached 702, 790 and 816 per square mile respectively. The problem was exacerbated, with the demise of many caste occupations, because virtually every non-agricultural caste was forced upon the land. This was a region of chronic land hunger and destitution for many people from the lowest and middling castes, but some high caste people were not immune from this plight.

In 1911, in UP, only 9.2% of Ahirs were returned as earning a living principally from their traditional caste occupation: 'pastorals, cattle owners, breeders, dealers in milk produce'; 73.6% were listed as cultivators. Among Brahmins, only 7.9% gave 'priesthood' as their principal means of livelihood; 73.6% as well were returned as cultivators. Among Kaila's people, Pasis, a mere 0.5% still pursued their caste job; 63.3% were cultivators; 23.4% field labourers. The low caste Chamars had also virtually abandoned their ancient, despised trade, leather-working: 39.1% were returned as cultivators, while 35.9% and 9.6% were field labourers and general labourers respectively. It is significant that Kurmis and Koeris, the premier cultivators of the eastern districts of Uttar Pradesh, indicated little occupational shift: 84.3% and 87.9% respectively were cultivators. But the influx of virtually every caste, seeking subsistence from the land, would have aggravated their land-hunger as well as their vulnerability to the notoriously usurious money-lenders.[21]

By the late 19th century Kurmis, Koeris and Ahirs had earned a formidable reputation as cultivators, but the land was still monopolised by the high castes: Brahmins and Kshattriya (Rajputs and Kayasths). In the late 1880s these upper castes owned 79.8% of the land in Basti, 83.2% in Sultanpur, and 67% in Azamgahr. Yet Brahmins were not enamoured of agriculture and attributed ignobility to working on the land. In 1901, in Basti, the single largest source of migrants to British Guiana and Fiji, Brahmins comprised 12.6% of the Hindu population and owned 19.3% of the cultivated area. They owned more than any caste although considered 'inferior agriculturalists owing to their prejudice against handling a plough'. The incompetence of Brahmins contrasted with the meticulous husbandry of Kurmis, Koeris and Ahirs, who were responsible for 24% of the cultivated land; they were deemed of the 'greatest importance in the economic condition of the district'. Ahirs held 8.2% of the cultivated area, and were considered cultivators 'of a high order'. However, the crown for agricultural excellence was reserved for Kurmis. Dr Voelcker, an authority on agriculture in eastern UP at the end of the 19th century, had praised their 'minute methods'. He was deeply impressed with the husbandry of the agricultural castes as a whole:

> [N]owhere would one find better instances of keeping land scrupulously free of weeds, of ingenuity in device of water-raising appliances, of knowledge of soils and their capabilities, as well as the exact time to sow and to reap, as one would in Indian agriculture, and this not at its best alone, but at its ordinary level. It is wonderful, too, how much is known of rotation, the system of mixed crops, and of fallowing. I...have never seen a more perfect picture of careful cultivation, worked with hard labour, perseverance and fertility of resource...[22]

Yet all these cultivating castes were at the mercy of landlords, hence the necessity for prudence in financial matters, if they were to elude the trapdoor to permanent debt-bondage.

In Ghazipur District, the home of my paternal great-grandfather, Sewnath, his caste of Ahirs formed 'the backbone of the cultivating community', and were deemed 'hard-working and successful farmers'. Yet they experienced acute land-hunger, most being tenants of the Brahmins, Rajputs and Kayasths. In 1906 the upper castes in this district owned 82% of the land; Ahirs owned a mere 2,283 acres although they were responsible for 14.3% of the cultivated area. In the neighbouring district of Azamgahr, the home of my maternal great-grandfathers, Sohan and Jagarnath, Ahirs were also among the best cultivators, but they owned very little land: 7,601 acres or 0.6% in 1879; 10,637 acres or 0.8% in 1906. However, they believed that their ancestors were once the ruling race, holding the same high status as Rajputs and other Kshattriya castes. In view of the contemporary political ascendancy of Ahirs (Yadavs) in Uttar Pradesh, it is not far-fetched to suggest that this belief in past supremacy must have been conducive to self-esteem and the sustaining of effort. The achievements of my girmitiya ancestors in British Guiana would seem to substantiate that. Their thrift and passion to own land certainly have their roots in the frustrated agricultural initiatives, the stifled skills, of Ahirs in eastern UP, as cattle rearers and farmers. I am unable to ascertain whether my Ahir great-grandparents' families, in Azamgahr and Ghazipur, had continued to pursue cattle rearing as their principal occupation despite the demise of their traditional calling, but the passion with which they pursued it in British Guiana suggests continuity, not merely the resuscitation of a folk practice. In any case, they would also have combined it with cultivation, as was the pattern with most Ahirs in UP. But their land hunger must have been acute, their indebtedness probably chronic.

As I read the *District Gazetteers* of eastern Uttar Pradesh and other sources, animated by the emerging universe to which *Girmitiyas* had led me, I began to grasp the context in which my people's attitudes and skills had been shaped. For instance, the following by E.A.H. Blunt, an authority on eastern UP, on their capacity to pursue several activities simultaneously, in order to combat land-hunger and the yawning trap of the moneylender, struck a chord. I readily set Sewnath and his wife, Etwarie, into this milieu. It is true that the latter was born in the colony and was of Muslim stock, but Muslims often manifested, even more than some of the other groups, a passion for thrift, entrepreneurship and ingenuity in performing several subsidiary occupations simultaneously. I could also appreciate the role of the joint-family in the process. I was better able, too, to comprehend why land was at the heart of their endeavour. Blunt had written:

> A subsidiary occupation is a matter of great economic importance for it makes, especially amongst agriculturalists, all the difference between poverty and comparative ease... There are, in fact, many peasants who have other sources of income: dairy work, selling grass or fuel, basket

> weaving, the making of rope, gur (coarse sugar), and tobacco, the ginning, spinning and weaving of cotton, etc...[T]he economic unit amongst the Hindus is not the individual but the joint-family...[O]ne or more of its members are often in separate employment and earning an income of their own, of which they usually remit a part to the common pool of the family.[23]

There must have been a consuming fear among small cultivators of the *mahajan* or moneylender: because of land-hunger and the smallness of their plots, they were perpetually vulnerable to him. As Lal observes, debt-burden in these eastern districts of UP was pervasive and deep-rooted, a perennial nullification of effort and enterprise. I could now better understand the reason for flight from this region to other parts of India and to the sugar colonies. I could see, also, why most of my girmitiya great-grandparents harboured such a passion for thrift, driven by that imperative for landownership:

> Debt was indeed one of the major problems for the small cultivator. The full extent to which the peasantry was indebted was revealed by an enquiry into the subject in 1868-9...[I]n most districts indebtedness was pervasive...in Lucknow, between 66 and 90% of the cultivators were estimated to be in debt; in Unao and Fyzabad 90%; and in Sitapur between 60 and 80%... *over three-quarters of the peasantry were shackled with debt*... Sometimes the debt had descended from father to son, while sometimes it was contracted for a marriage ceremony or to pursue a law suit. In addition...the peasants also had to borrow for agriculture or related purposes... *The cycle never ended; the cultivating tenant, one observer noted, 'is born in debt, increases his debt throughout his life and dies more hopelessly in debt than ever* [emphasis added].[24]

Lal made me reflect further on the despair which must have claimed my people in the late 19th century eastern UP, and the will of a few to escape. I could see that indentureship in British Guiana, though initially darkened by its bonded element, was not a static state: within a decade or so after their arrival, they became landowners and cattle farmers. Released at last, their skills and ambition could grow, even flourish. This was my story, and I could no longer accept double-billing on the historiography of oppression: to see indentureship as 'a new slavery'. It was absurd to equate Indian indentureship with African chattel slavery; to do so was to trivialise the brutality of the latter. Besides, the plantation experience of Indians, however oppressive, was certainly not a journey into despair. This bleak, somewhat political, interpretation – to assuage African fears of perceived Indian economic ascendancy – did not accord with the experience of my family in the colony. Lal had also made me think of my people in the context of the 200 famines in India between 1860 and 1908. I tried to locate Sohan, Harpal, Ramsarran Maharaj, Sewnath, Kaila and Jagarnath in that India where the 'constant and menacing spectre of famine... stalked the land with increasing frequency and stubbornness'.[25] This was a land of real slavery for landless people, whose traditional occupations had disappeared. This was probably the fate of the low-caste Pasis, Kaila's people, landless labourers, many of whom would have been *sewaks* (bonded slaves). In fact, in 1905, as the *Gonda Gazetteer* recorded (Kaila's home district), many Kori agricultural labourers, possibly slightly higher in status to the aboriginal Pasis, were *sewaks*: 'practically the slaves of their employers'. Brij Lal sketches the anatomy of this form of slavery in eastern UP:

> Many landless labourers led the lives of bonded slaves. This status began with the taking out of a loan by low caste men such as Chamars and Dusadhs. They then committed themselves and their descendants in perpetuity to the landlord until the loan was repaid. In return the landlord allowed the *sewaks* (bonded slaves) an agreed share of the produce of the field that they cultivated. In most cases, the share was barely sufficient to feed the *sewak* and his family. The landlord therefore provided further supplies, their value being added to the principal loan. The son of the *sewak*, once old enough, shared, and at his death succeeded to, his father's bond. In the meantime, the principal loan was perpetually being increased by the addition of the value of the food supplied by the landlord, and there was little prospect of the debt being repaid.[26]

The poverty of Kaila's people would have made them especially vulnerable to myriad diseases that were rampant, assuming epidemic proportions, in the latter half of the 19th century. In her home district, Gonda, cholera was endemic after 1875; violent epidemics were common. Between 1872 and 1881 this disease accounted for 11.5% of the total mortality of her district. There were bad outbreaks in 1873, 1876, 1877, 1878, 1881, 1886 and 1888 – 10,000 died in the latter year. In 1893, 16,000 died from cholera. Smallpox visitations were also common in Gonda: there were epidemics 'of great intensity' in 1876 and 1880. Famine struck in 1874, 1877 and 1897.

This was the context, Lal argues, in which some people, men and women, in eastern UP and western Bihar, became enmeshed in a culture of migration. By 1900, for instance, migrants from these areas had monopolised the jobs in the jute mills and factories of Bengal. The five principal districts from which they came were Benares, Azamgahr, Ghazipur, Jaunpur and Allahabad. In 1911 a quarter of the UP migrants in Bengal were women; by 1921, at the end of indentureship, a third in Calcutta were women.[27] Lal explores the phenomenon and concludes that it is incorrect to attribute blame on the *arkatis* for duping vulnerable people into migrating overseas. He contends that although an element of deception was necessarily embedded in the recruitment process, there were potent economic forces that sustained the culture of migration, internally and externally. He confers 'agency' on the girmitiyas, autonomy as actors:

> [T]here was great upheaval in rural Indian society in the 19th and early 20th centuries, and this ultimately had its origins in the character of British

> rule in India. All strata of Indian society, the high castes and the low castes, the landlords and the landless labourers, were exposed to, and affected by, the widespread changes sweeping the Indian countryside. Many adjusted to their declining fortunes and stayed on in the village in the hope that things might improve. Others, from all groups and of differing social gradations, thought differently and left. *The recruiters may have painted rosy pictures of glorious prospects in the colonies, and may, thereby, have attracted many into their net. But there were forces at work in Indian society itself that were cutting the peasants off from the safe moorings of their traditional society. Not only men but women* [as individuals] *and families also migrated* [emphasis added].[28]

Girmitiyas is probably most revolutionary in its treatment of women indentured labourers. This enabled me to reach Kaila's elusive world. Over and over, I could see how these extraordinary women were suffused with the strength of character manifested by Kaila, as well as creole women like Etwarie and Ramdularie. Raymond Smith estimates that 43 women were recruited for every 100 men who went to British Guiana between 1865 and 1917: 82% were between 10 and 30 years old; 52.6% were between 20 and 30. Among men, 85.6% were between 10 and 30. Lal's figures for Fiji corroborate Smith's with regard to the sex ratio as well as the age structure. It is clear that most of these people were very young; their whole lives were ahead of them. What is surprising, however, is the high incidence of women who migrated, as individuals, unaccompanied by any relatives. Lal states that while 86.8% of the adult males who went to Fiji were 'single', 63.9% of the adult women were 'single'. Nearly two-thirds of the women were registered as single. I do not know what proportion of the girmitiya women to British Guiana were single, but in view of the remarkable correspondence of the statistical evidence from the two colonies, it is reasonable to assume that it was as high as Fiji. Kaila was in this 'single' category, although she was twenty years old when she landed in 1909. The incidence of single women is very surprising indeed. In 1891, in UP, 90% of females were married between 10 and 14; between 15 and 19 only one in fifteen was not married.[29] In British Guiana, my creole-born paternal great-grandmother, Etwarie, was married at 14; my paternal and maternal grandmothers, Sukhia and Ramdularie, too, were married at 14. Lal's explanation of the high incidence of single girmitiya women is persuasive.

He rejects the notion that these women were primarily from the lowest castes, that they were mainly whores or women of loose morals. As with men, the women who went to Fiji were drawn from a broad cross section of castes in UP: 4.1% were Brahmins; 9% Kshattriyas; 31.4% from middling agricultural castes; 31.9% from low and outcastes; 16.8% were Muslims. He also observes that a high percentage of women migrants were registered outside of their home districts: 59% from Basti, 66.5% from Gonda and 'the overwhelming majority' from Azamgahr and Sultanpur.[30]

He contends that this was so not because they were tricked by *arkatis*, but because many had already left home or were driven out of their homes after the death of their husbands, during recurring epidemics. Indeed, many women were already on the move, going 'east', to Bengal and Assam, seeking a new life:

> Migration was not a new or unknown phenomenon for Indian women; thousands had left their homes before they met the recruiters and were shipped to Fiji and other colonies; had moved to other parts of India (Calcutta jute mills, Assam tea gardens, Bihar coalmines, Bombay textile mills) in search of employment, either on their own or in company of their male relatives. The journey to Fiji was part of a larger process of migration.[31]

Although Lal acknowledges that an element of deception permeated the indentureship system, he does not see these women as 'helpless victims', merely 'pawns in the hands of unscrupulous recruiters'. He recognises them as 'actors in their own right'. He gives agency to these women. They were still very young, immersed in a hopeless environment, but with a broader vision of new possibilities spawned by the culture of migration of the late 19th century. Exposure to a wider world and anonymity, beyond their villages, expanded their horizons, and endowed the more enterprising with notions of escape from the ancient despair. Lal observes that some young women were in a desperate situation because their husbands had migrated and had obviously decided not to return; others were young widows or young wives marooned in a pitiable existence in the homes of their in-laws. He concludes:

> The fact that women were prepared to part with a life of drudgery and unhappiness for the largely unknown would seem to me to suggest that many of them must have been individuals of remarkable independence, enterprise and self-respect. These were certainly the values they nurtured and lived by in the colonies.[32]

This could easily have been a commentary on Kaila's life in British Guiana, between 1909 and 1956. It led me to William Crooke's contemporary account of the role of women in agriculture in UP at the end of the 19th century. I had no doubts now of the pedigree of Kaila and Etwarie – the source of their meticulous cultivating practices, in rice or cane field, their continuity of focus, their balance and sense of proportion, which helped to guide their menfolk and rescue them from the excesses of plantation life. Crooke observed:

> Among a large section of the cultivating tribe the women freely assist the men in field labour; in fact, the effectiveness of husbandry may be to a large extent measured by the degree to which this is the case. You will constantly see the wife of the Kurmi or Jat sowing the seed grain as her husband ploughs, weeding or assisting in irrigation by distributing the water from one little patch to another, if she does not take a more

> active share in the work by helping to empty the well bucket or raising the water lift…[S]he milks the cow, feeds the calves, picks pottage herbs in the fields, collects firewood or makes the cow-dung into cakes for fuel. She has to grind the wheat or barley, which is the chief food of the household, husk the rice or millet, and do all the cooking, besides taking her share in field work, and scaring the parrots and monkeys from the ripening crops. If she has any leisure she can devote it to ginning cotton or spinning thread… If she misconducts herself she has to endure hard language and sometimes blows.[33]

This is also the source of their resilience and initiative, for although women were expected to endure and stoically perform their 'duty' to mothers-in-law, husbands and sons, they were not all compliant. A minority, pushed by the futility, became unlikely rebels. As noted above, because of the recurring epidemics in the late 19th century, many girls, married at 11 or 12, were widowed at 13 or 14. These girls became drudges, virtual slaves in the households of their late husbands. Remarriage was impossible; it was a disgrace to return to their parents' homes. They were washed up; there could be no worthy life ahead. They carried the stain of widowhood as if they were the authors of the premature demise of their husbands. Others were girls deserted by husbands, who had fled family debts or other communal exactions. Some were accused of sexual infidelity, which meant disgrace and ostracism in village society. The main difference between the latter half of the 19th century and previously was the possibility of escape: internally and overseas.

That explains why nearly two-thirds of the women who went to Guyana and Fiji travelled alone: 'single'. Many of the men, also, reportedly single, probably were in similar circumstances. As I noted in my essay 'Sugar in the Blood', in this collection, men and women had a lot to hide, much of it unimaginably painful. But it was easier for them to learn to forget when they were all in the same boat, to come to believe their constructed narratives that attributed all blame for migration to the *arkatis*, the ignoble recruiters. A collective amnesia was crucial to the building of a new persona and a new life. That was why the India of the girmitiyas was quickly claimed by historical darkness. That real India was too problematical for easy narration; it harboured too many secrets; it was reinvented as mythical; it had gone beyond scrutiny. The mythical India of the great Hindu classic, the *Ramayana*, with several of its named places located in contemporary UP, was constructed as an authentic representation of the motherland. The real eastern UP and western Bihar disappeared from the radar. The India of the *Ramayana* has endured, as I have written elsewhere, because it is a narrative that answered many of the monumental, urgent needs of the girmitiyas:

> The theme of Lord Rama in exile in the Dandak forest is resonant among Indians in the diaspora. His triumphal return to Ayodhya has a freshness; it offers a long reign of enlightened rule, when harvests were bounteous

> and 'mothers wailed not in their anguish for their babes'. It is an evocation of hope and renewal, even of their own triumphal return, however illusory. Essentially, it answered the yearning for a new beginning, reassurance that there was life after despair. It gave more – the Golden Age, a vision of a perfect India that eclipsed the dark, familiar one. That Hanuman, the monkey-faced loyal servant of Lord Rama, could scale and uproot mountains to get curative herbs to save a wounded Lakshman, Rama's devoted brother, made him the great shaper of possibilities; and his role in the rescue of Sita, the wife of Lord Rama, from the evil Rawan, made him the great defender not merely of chastity, but of *dharma* (Hindu duty) itself.[34]

I explain the special resonance of Sita with girmitiya women and their descendants thus:

> Indian women in the Caribbean empathised with a Sita of human proportions: the machinations of her husband's co-wife; exile; privations in the forest; kidnapping and imprisonment in Rawan's Lanka; and as related in the Valmiki version of the *Ramayana*, aspersions cast on her sexual purity, lingering suspicion and further banishment. The pathos is exhausting but the Sita persona spoke to women who were in virtual exile, had severed all links with their families in India, had to endure aspersions cast on their sexual life on the plantations (occasionally ending in murder by jealous partners), while toiling to reshape a life and recreate a family in a distant land. But even beyond the dark shadow of the plantation, this Sita endures among Indo-Caribbean women – a symbol of resilience – *not* merely a tendentious patriarchal construct of compliance.[35]

This Sita could absorb the guilt, the submerged pain of loss, the trauma of 'kidnapping' and 'exile'; the amnesia so essential to the reinvention of self. This Sita could fill the void of the recent past and allay the fears of the present. Sita had transcended the mythical state.

It belongs to our family lore that among the few things Kaila took to British Guiana in 1909 was a copy of the slim *Hanuman Chalisa*, a celebration of the heroism of Hanuman. She could not have read it; she was illiterate. In my youth I recall seeing this tattered, incense-stained, booklet among the family's religious paraphernalia. No one ever read it: that would have profaned it. It was enough that it spoke of the great shaper of possibilities and the defender of Hindu faith. It celebrated something seminal to the world that my girmitiya ancestors had made in British Guiana. And the fact that Kaila supposedly brought the booklet from India also endowed it with sacred properties. Indias of the imagination were at the core of this new world.

I could not have arrived at the self-definition I have grown into, in the last fifteen years, without *Girmitiyas*. It has helped me to find the centre. But this book has also been at the heart of my work in Indo-Caribbean historiography; and I am proud to claim it as a seminal text of this new chapter in Caribbean historiography.

Notes

1. This is an introductory essay to Brij Lal, *Girmitiyas: The Origins of the Fiji Indians* (second edition), (Suva, Fiji: Fiji Institute of Applied Studies, 2004)
2. V.S. Naipaul [on his paternal great-grandmother], *Finding the Centre: Two Narratives* (London: Andre Deutsch, 1984), p. 65
3. Cheddi Jagan, *The West on Trial: My Fight for Guyana's Freedom* (London: Michael Joseph, 1966), p. 13
4. Cheddi Jagan, *The West On Trial: My Fight for Guyana's Freedom* (London: Michael Joseph, 1966), 13-4, 24. Cheddi was born on 22 March 1918 at Plantation Port Mourant, Corentyne, Berbice. His people were Kurmis. His birth certificate gives his name as 'Chedda'; just below that is recorded: 'Illegitimate'. His father was: 'Jagan, Calcutta Immigrant, 88470, *Elbe*, 1901'. His mother was: 'Bachaoni, Calcutta Immigrant, 88316, *Elbe*, 1901'. (I am grateful to Professor David Dabydeen for a photocopy of this document.)
5. V.S. Naipaul, *Finding the Centre: Two Narratives* (London: Andre Deutsch, 1984), pp. 58-9.
6. All quotes cited from *Girmitiyas* are taken from the original, published in 1983.
7. Brinsley Samaroo, 'Chinese and Indian "Coolie" Voyages to the Caribbean', *Journal of Caribbean Studies*, Vol. 14, Nos. 1 & 2 (Fall 1999-Spring 2000), p. 19.
8. See Clem Seecharan [Introduced with notes and appendices], *Joseph Ruhomon's India: The Progress of her People at Home and Abroad and How those in British Guiana may Improve Themselves* (Kingston, Jamaica: University of the West Indies Press, 2001 [1894]).
9. See Dwarka Nath, *History of Indians in Guyana* (London: The Author, 1970 [1950]).
10. See Peter Ruhomon, *Centenary History of the East Indians in British Guiana, 1838-1938* (Georgetown: The East Indians 150th Anniversary Committee, 1988 [1947]).
11. See Clem Seecharan, *Bechu: 'Bound Coolie' Radical in British Guiana, 1894-1901* (Kingston, Jamaica: University of the West Indies Press, 1999).
12. Clem Seecharan, *'Tiger in the Stars': The Anatomy of Indian Achievement in British Guiana, 1919-29* (London: Macmillan, 1997), p. 22.
13. These Registers are in the National Archives, Georgetown, Guyana. There are 188, 917 individual embarkation slips, bound in 358 volumes, with the name of the ship and the year of the voyage embossed on the spine. These slips have the names of the immigrant, their ship's number, any peculiar identification mark, their village of origin, as well as their tahsil (sub-district) or district. They also state their place of registration, and the nearest of kin, if any, accompanying them. The plantation to which they were sent is pencilled in.
14. I have relied heavily on the following two people for information on Sohan, Jagarnath and Kaila: Ramdularie (1916-1985), Palmyra, East Canje,

Berbice, interview, May 1982; and Latchman Sohan (1908-1989), Palmyra, interview, December 1985.

15. I have relied heavily on Sarran Jagmohan (1920-2005) for information on Sewnath, Etwarie, Harpal, Ramsarran Maharaj and Jagmohan: Palmyra, interview, April 1986; personal communication from Toronto, Canada, dated 21 July 1994, 14, 16 March 1995.
16. *Ibid.*
17. See note 12.
18. *Girmitiyas* [1983], p. 131.
19. See Raymond T. Smith, 'Some Social Characteristics of Indian Immigrants to British Guiana', *Population Studies*, Vol. 13, Pt. 1 (1959).
20. *Girmitiyas*, pp. 70-1.
21. *Ibid.*, pp. 72-3.
22. Dr. Voelcker quoted in William Crooke, *The North-Western Provinces of India: Their History, Ethnology, and Administration* (Karachi: OUP, 1972 [1897]), p. 330.
23. E.A.H. Blunt, 'The Environment and the Distribution of the Indian People', in Blunt (ed.), *Social Service in India: An Introduction to some Social and Economic Problems of the Indian People* (London: HMSO, 1938), pp. 30-1.
24. *Girmitiyas*, pp. 83-4.
25. *Ibid.*, p. 88
26. *Ibid.*, pp. 87-8.
27. *Ibid.*, p. 64
28. *Ibid.*, p. 89.
29. *Ibid.*, p. 103.
30. *Ibid.*, p. 108
31. Brij V. Lal, 'Kunti's Cry: Indentured Women on Fiji Plantation', *Indian Economic and Social History Review*, Vol. 22, No. 1, (1985), pp. 57-8..
32. *Ibid.*, p. 114.
33. See note 22.
34. Clem Seecharan, 'The Shaping of the Indo-Caribbean People: Guyana and Trinidad to the 1940s', *Journal of Caribbean Studies*, Vol. 14, Nos. 1&2 (Fall 1999- Spring 2000), pp. 64-5.
35. *Ibid.*, p. 65.

IN SIR VIDIA'S SHADOW, OUT OF HISTORICAL DARKNESS

> I come from a people who were immemorially poor, immemorially without a voice.
>
> — V.S. Naipaul, *The Sunday Times*, 16 September 1990.

> Away from this world of my grandmother's house… there was the great unknown – in this island of only 400,000 people… As a child I knew almost nothing, nothing beyond what I had picked up in my grandmother's house.
>
> — V.S. Naipaul, 'Two Worlds', Nobel Lecture, 7 December 2001.

> To write was to learn.
>
> — V.S. Naipaul, *Finding the Centre* (1984).

In an interview in 2002 Nobel laureate, Sir Vidia Naipaul rejected what he deemed mimicry in contemporary Indian historiography. This, I believe, was aimed at the 'subaltern school'. Naipaul rarely names what he despises; he never acknowledges those for whom he has no respect. He observed:

> There is this great sense in India of needing to catch up with what is being done in the world outside. Now they are trying to write this kind of academic history, to keep up with the jargon. There's no human interest, no interest in the people, only interest in the movement – a most abstract interest.[1]

One ignores the great man at one's peril, even when he is at the peak of his arrogance because, ineluctably, a kernel of truth, an uncomfortably illuminating shaft, permeates his most seemingly trite, provocative assertions. I think what repels Naipaul most is the desiccation of learning by the pressure in academia to conform to the reigning theoretical fad. He is revolted by a sort of tyranny of theory in literary and historical studies and the loss of clarity of exposition.

In Naipaul's later travel writings, on India, the American South and the 'converted' peoples in the Islamic world, the diverse narratives of the people he interviews speak for themselves. The character of the societies and their animating impulses are suggested by the verbatim or reported testimonies of his informants (page after page); but the old certainties of judgement do not obtrude. As he explained in 1990, after the publication

Young V.S. Naipaul: a seminal influence on me, from as early as 1962

Naipaul and his second wife, Nadira, when he received the Nobel Prize in 2001: his writings continue to inspire me.

of *India: A Million Mutinies Now*: '...I thought it was better to let India be defined by the experience of the people, rather than writing one's personal reaction to one's feeling about being an Indian and going back'.[2] The generalising impulse gives way to 'a million mutinies': what is knowable is necessarily limited by the complexity and diversity of the human condition. Naipaul has no time for social scientists, even academic historians: '[Real] scientists matter. Not the arts courses... People should read in their own time. I should like to see all those arts courses closed down... I think universities should be for science and mathematics'.[3]

Naipaul holds these arts courses responsible for the decline of the mind: thought clogged by jargon; language despoiled. The basis of his rejection of contemporary historians in India, therefore, seems to be that while claiming to confer agency in history to marginalized men and women, their obsession with academic credibility in the West has driven them into a theoretical quagmire. The so-called subaltern – mired in jargon – is no less submerged. Jargon 'turns living issues into abstractions... jargon ends by competing with jargon...'[4] He feels that his own attempt at writing history, his book of 1969, *The Loss of El Dorado*, goes beyond the theoretical vapourings of these academic historians. He is not enamoured of their 'overly abstract way of dealing with history'. He explains: '[F]or the two years I lived among the documents, I sought to reconstruct the human story as best I could'. But he does not eschew an 'overarching approach', the possibility of discovering what J.H. Plumb found in *The Loss of El Dorado*, 'truths about society that are... profound and moving'.[5] The problem, though, is how does Naipaul integrate the 'human' approach – the verbatim narratives of his informants – and the 'overarching' approach with the necessity to generalise (even theorise)? How does he prevent his 'million mutinies' (the testimonies that he sedulously presents), from hanging in the air: valid narratives, arrived at through much toil and skilfully arranged which exhaust you with their particularity? How does he find the centre?

It is now ten years since my book, *'A Tiger in the Stars': The Anatomy of Indian Achievement in British Guiana 1919-29* was published. It is not encumbered by theory; it is not driven by 'abstract interest', but it does generalise. It is a book about the achievement of Indians in colonial Guyana, a very difficult environment: for me, a very personal history, very 'human', with elements of the 'overarching' approach. But I am certain Sir Vidia would not waste time on 'this rubbish kind of writing', on a place where 'nothing was created': to speak of achievement there is 'bogus'. Yet I am able to see what drives his writing: revulsion against the certainties of 'believers' and the death of reason: rejection of knowledge earned and fear of letting the side down – a return to 'tribal wallow'. Although we may arrive at different conclusions about the people we seek to comprehend, I think where Naipaul and I do connect is 'racial' and intellectual.

What are the 'racial' commonalities and intellectual promptings that link us? We are both descendants of Indian indentured labourers from eastern Uttar Pradesh, taken to sugar plantations in the Caribbean in the late 19th century. Naipaul's people went to Trinidad in the 1880s, mine to Demerara (British Guiana) from the 1870s. They were Brahmins; mine Ahirs [contemporary Yadavs], the traditional cattle-herders of Uttar Pradesh and Bihar. His people, though poor, would have made the journey certain of their high place in the Hindu social order; mine did so in despair that their agricultural skills counted for nothing because of chronic land-hunger and caste prejudice in eastern Uttar Pradesh. My people were no less ambitious than his, abstemious in their zeal to own land in British Guiana; jealous, too, of other people's achievements. This was a harsh, highly competitive environment; invidious comparisons were rife but a spur to effort. For the first time, they could use their skills, as cultivators and cattle-rearers, in a relatively free, achievement-oriented society. They had escaped to an area of possibilities. They sought wealth no less passionately than they practised Hinduism; the discovery that they could achieve so much made them open up, made them less inward looking, more flexible. They became adept at exploiting every niche conducive to gain.

As I have explored in more detail in the essay above, 'Girmitiyas and the Discovery of India', my illiterate maternal great-grandmother, Kaila (1889-1956), journeyed alone to British Guiana, as an indentured labourer in 1909, aged 20. She was from a low Shudra caste, Pasi (often associated with crime), but she married an Ahir on the plantation, started to buy a few head of cattle and was soon able to acquire land, in a neighbouring village, the place of my birth. Only now am I able to reflect on what this would have meant to a woman who was probably married at ten and widowed soon afterwards (away from her village, Bhagwanpur, in Gonda District) – therefore, a virtual slave henceforth. She could even have been driven into flight by a hopeless child-marriage and oppressive in-laws. Hers, in any case, would have been a life of eternal darkness if she had stayed in India. Her only child, my maternal grandmother (born in British Guiana in June 1916), often said that she tried for years to coax fragments of that past, in India, out of her. She learnt little beyond the tired tale that she was deceived into going to Demerara, to sift sugar. It was her way of dealing with the escape and the severing of all links with relatives in India; her way of assuaging lingering guilt, seeking to forget that past of unimaginable pain. Was she married? Did she have any children? What was her mother like? What did they do for a living? Did she miss those she would never see again? All this remained an area of darkness; the gnawing secrets were interred with her. It was easier to reach Rama's and Sita's India of the great Hindu epic, the *Ramayana*, than to touch Kaila's recent India.

Naipaul's Brahmin grandparents would have been little more forthcoming about their past:

> I grew up with two ideas of history, almost two ideas of time. There was history with dates. That kind of history affected people and places abroad...But Chaguanas [in Trinidad], where I was born, in an Indian-style house my grandfather had built, had no dates. If I read in a book that Gandhi had made his first call for civil disobedience in India in 1919, that date seemed recent. But 1919, in Chaguanas, in the life of the Indian community, was almost unimaginable. It was a time beyond recall, mythical. About our family, the migration of our ancestors from India, I knew only what I knew or what I was told. Beyond (and sometimes even within) people's memories was undated time, historical darkness. Out of that darkness (extending to place as well as to time) we had all come. The India where Gandhi and Nehru and the others operated was historical and real. The India from which we had come was impossibly remote, almost as imaginary as the land of the *Ramayana*, our Hindu epic. I lived easily with that darkness, that lack of knowledge. I never thought to inquire further.[6]

Whether Brahmin or Ahir, Pasi or Chamar, these indentured labourers ('bound coolies') in the Caribbean had a lot to hide. As I was to learn much later, they came from one of the most impoverished parts of India, virtually lawless – feudal in its social organisation and ossified by the immutability of caste prejudice. They were escaping from a chronically moribund and stultifying environment. (The heavy hand of the landlord, as I discovered recently on my visit to eastern UP, is well tutored in its ancient aptitude for instant justice.) Even Brahmins could become impoverished, indebted to landlords and moneylenders; besides there were many personal, domestic reasons why some would have wanted to flee: men and women. As Naipaul discovered later of his paternal great-grandmother, a Brahmin girl:

> About 1880, in the ancient town of Ayodhya in the United Provinces in India, a young girl of the Parray clan gave birth to a son. She must have been deeply disgraced, because she was willing to go alone with her baby to a far-off island to which other people of the region were going. That was how the Parray woman came to Trinidad. She intended her son to be a pundit...[7]

Trinidad and British Guiana, certainly by the 1870s, offered them mobility, reward for merit, the initial travail on the sugar plantations notwithstanding. For the Brahmin, there was scope for acquiring both wealth and enhanced status. As noted in the essay 'Indians in Guyana', lower-caste Hindus and outcaste Chamars, who could not have dreamt of the Brahmin ministering to them, in India, had now acquired that privilege. Part of the reason was the flexibility of the new society and the fear, among Brahmins, that rampant Christian proselytising would steal their flock. To stem this, they became sacrilegious: ministering to even the lowest of the low, performing *puja* (religious ceremonies) in their homes; and partaking of their cooked food.

The Brahmin was answerable to no central authority in the 'motherland'; no body of ecclesiastical dogmas challenged his iconoclastic approach to Hinduism in the Caribbean. The elaborate rituals, the dramatic temper permeating the communal readings from the *Ramayana* and the *Mahabharata*, and the carnivalesque tenor of some of the festivals in orthodox Hinduism, such as Divali or Phagwah, appealed to labourers and farmers, as it did to the children. The ritual elaboration, in celebratory space – music and sumptuous feasting in the 'yard'; outside – minimised the monotony of plantation toil. It also magnified the aura around the Brahmin priest. Indeed, the Brahmin in the Caribbean became even more entrenched in his dominance of Hindu society. Lower caste and outcaste Indians, having achieved a degree of material progress, and hungry for enhanced status within Hinduism, probably felt deeply honoured by their access to the Brahmin – and the privilege of paying obeisance to his status and, therefore, tended to reciprocate generously – emotionally and financially. This was the context of the rise of Naipaul's family in Trinidad at the end of the 19th century: 'My [maternal] grandfather had done well in Trinidad. He had bought much land – I continued to discover 'pieces' he had bought; he had bought properties in Port of Spain; he had established a very large family and in our community he had a name'. [8]

But the rapid ascendancy of the Brahmin came with a price. He had to maintain a certain distance in spite of the egalitarian propensity of Caribbean Hinduism: 'On the island, in our [Indian] group, we were set apart'.[9] The life was still circumscribed by many taboos. In contrast, my own Ahir people could lose control – drink hard, curse and fight publicly, frequent whorehouses, be seen to eat meat, including pork, while selling their cattle to Muslim or African butchers. There were virtually no sanctions against such behaviour.

Vidia Naipaul was born in 1932, the same year as my late mother; the sanctions on him, a Brahmin, the custodian of Hindu tradition, would have been very rigorous, even if he were 'born an unbeliever'. Brahmins were superior but they did not have the freedom, the easy access to excess of the lower castes. This fused them into certain attitudes in the Caribbean. Their superiority complex transmuted the fear of contamination by dark, lower-caste people onto black people, Africans. In the Brahmin's universe, the latter were relegated to beyond the pale, to the subordinate space formerly reserved for Chamars, Doms, Dusads and Bhangis, the outcastes in North Indian villages. Colonial society's own obeisance to light skin reinforced this Indian obsession. Although most Indians in the Caribbean tended to be darker than their Brahmin compatriots, the Indian's partiality for light skin did not diminish. The Brahmin's fear of pollution by the 'Negro' became universal, a reflex among most Indians, including Muslims and converts to Christianity. Even the broader vision engendered by a liberal education could not lessen this corroding impulse. Nothing could shift it, not even Cheddi Jagan's Marxist endeavour of nearly fifty years, his construction of the Guyanese condition, in a countervailing idiom, in terms of class and the class struggle, against local and foreign capital.

I am of the generation after Naipaul. I was not subject to the social constraints required of the Brahmin. I did not grow up in an extended family, a large group of kin occupying a shared space – in Naipaul's evocative assessment, 'an enclosing self-sufficient world absorbed with its quarrels and jealousies, as difficult for the outsider to penetrate as for one of its members to escape. It protected and imprisoned…'[9] But both of us grew up in a void with regard to our Indian antecedents, and a longing to look back, heightened by the presence, everywhere, of former 'bound coolies' from India. My boyhood, in the 1950s, is inextricably interwoven with their final years in colonial Guyana. Even now I recall my imagination being provoked by the last of those enigmas: scaling seas and mountains, like the monkey God, Hanuman, yearning to reach this mythical land of India whence they came. India was not amenable to scrutiny; it was fused into a construct of religious inviolability. Naipaul and I start from this void. That is why his notion of India as 'an area of darkness' is more than a standard Naipaulian disparagement, his instinct for the negative. It is also a comment on our consuming ignorance of a place, so close to our lives yet remote, but never susceptible of being ignored. As Naipaul recalled after his first trip to India in 1962:

> To me as a child the India that had produced so many of the persons and things around me was featureless, and I thought of the time when the transference was made as a period of darkness, darkness which also extended to the land… And even now though time has widened, though space has contracted and I have travelled lucidly over the area which was to me the area of darkness, something of darkness remains, in those attitudes, those ways of thinking and seeing, which are no longer mine.[11]

It is from this area of darkness, too, that I have felt a passion for inquiry. But unlike Naipaul, for whom the journey 'broke my life in two',[12] my regular trips to India, to Kerala, Karnataka and Tamil Nadu in the south, and Himachal Pradesh, Punjab, Rajasthan, Madhya Pradesh and Uttar Pradesh in the north, have dissipated much of this darkness. I have been studying India, on my own, for many years, although I know no Indian languages. My experience of India was totally different. I felt as if I had been there before: in the south as well as in the north, separate worlds. I connected so readily it made me feel that those seminal experiences of my Indian boyhood planted something in me – communion with the spirit of the place. Even the fading mythical images of my youth seemed to belong.

Where Naipaul and I depart is our way of seeing. His was shaped by the narrow Brahmin boyhood. In spite of the precision of the writing, the magnificent gift for detail, the intellectual sagacity that makes him so prescient even when he is cynical – Naipaul lacks empathy. That is why, although he denounces historians in India for aping theoretical fads, for having 'no human interest, no interest in the people', he cannot really reach the cultural and religious promptings at the heart of human endeavour. Naipaul's Brahmin boyhood turned him away from religion, rituals, festivals, the spirit of place, the capacity for trust and friendship. It fused him into a way of seeing that is clinical in its perspicacity, but fundamentally mean in spirit. The revulsion against his own boyhood: the surfeit of Brahminic certainties; the emasculation of his own father, 'imprisoned' in his in-laws's compound (the worst possible fate for the male Hindu); the sheer ubiquity and claustrophobia of the huge joint family, all this bred in him a hardness. The individual had no place in 'Lion House' [Hanuman House of *A House for Mr Biswas*]. To claw back a semblance of self, required cultivation of that hardness, fighting early against the grain; an impulse; an iron will *not* to belong. The young mind became attuned to distancing itself. In his novel of 1979, *A Bend in the River*, set in central Africa, it is poignant that the protagonist, Salim, can reflect thus:

> So from an early age I developed the habit of looking, detaching myself from a familiar scene and trying to consider it as from a distance. It was from this habit of looking that the idea came to me that as a community we had fallen behind. And that was the beginning of my insecurity... I was without the religious sense of my family. The insecurity I felt was due to my lack of true religion...[13]

Naipaul was acquiring the means of self-assessment, astounding powers of observation and attention to detail, but this young mind had had its childhood attenuated. Pessimism came early; laughter did not come easily; when it did it was sardonic. In his novel of 1967, *The Mimic Men*, the protagonist reflects on the void in the childhood:

> For Cecil childhood was the great time; he would never cease to regret its passing away. It was different with me. I could scarcely wait for my childhood to be over and done with. I have no especial hardship or deprivation to record. But childhood was for me a period of incompetence, bewilderment, solitude and shameful fantasies. It was a period of burdensome secrets... And I longed for nothing so much as to walk in the clear air of adulthood and responsibility, where everything was comprehensible and I myself was open as a book. I hated my secrets. A complying memory has obliterated many of them and edited my childhood down to a brief cinematic blur. Even this is quite sufficiently painful.[14]

The man had come too soon to the child. He lacked a sense of the absurd, which comes out of grounding, belonging, security: roots. Even those works of humour and irony of the early years, 'when the jokes came fast', as he recalled with a touch of self-deprecation, are a cover for an essential pessimism: eschewing the pain of happiness; fostering the hardness so essential to the pursuit of his craft. Yet the certainties of the Brahmin boyhood had residual powers, Naipaul's persistent disavowal notwithstanding. They evoked yearning for that old security, however flawed, in Hindu Trinidad, as he meandered tortuously towards a fragile, constructed English persona. Here is Naipaul's 'narrator' of *The Mimic Men* again:

> Coming to London, the great city, seeking order, seeking the flowering, the extension of myself that ought to have come in a city of such miraculous light, I had tried to hasten a process which had seemed elusive. I had tried to give myself a personality. It was something I had tried more than once before, and waited for the response in the eyes of others. But now I no longer knew what I was; ambition became confused, then faded; and I found myself longing for the certainties of my life on the island of Isabella, certainties which I had once dismissed as shipwreck.[15]

I did not have to endure or negotiate those Brahminic certainties. I was not marooned ('shipwrecked') in the Brahmin's universe of rituals and ceremonies; neither did I have to endure people in the mass, day after day, under the same roof. I did not have to take preferential treatment or adulation for granted. I could not become complacent: my people had to earn whatever respect seeped their way, so did I. Therefore, in spite of Naipaul's rejection of his Trinidadian Brahmin roots, it planted in him snobbishness, a lack of manners, a hard certainty, superciliousness with regard to his own intellectual powers and an incapacity for magnanimity or gratitude. Maybe all of this is a mask for an underlying cultural insecurity, but the hardness has kept him going. The hardness has sustained the mission. The hardness has enabled this great mind to work single-mindedly, undeterred by its many detractors, over several decades. It has given the way of seeing its pertinacity.

The following self-assessment by Naipaul is, I feel, permeated by the germ of this unfaltering pursuit of the craft, and the way of seeing – an instinct for difference and a fear of closeness:

> We ate certain food, performed certain ceremonies and had certain taboos; we expected others to have their own. We did not wish to share theirs; we did not expect them to share ours. They were what they were; we were what we were... Everything beyond our family had this quality of difference. This was to be accepted... But the moment any intercourse threatened, we scented violation and withdrew... I came of a family that abounded with pundits. But I had been born an unbeliever. I took no pleasure in religious ceremonies... [T]hough growing up in an orthodox family, I remained almost totally ignorant of Hinduism. What, then, survived of Hinduism in me? Perhaps I had received a certain supporting philosophy... Examining myself, I found only that sense of the difference of people... a vaguer sense of caste, and a horror of the unclean.[16]

It can be argued that such seminal instincts of caste superiority, and the accompanying fear of pollution, bred in the man an incapacity for empathy, not only with outsiders, but Indians, too. This has been exacerbated by the thinness and tenuousness of his 'supporting philosophy'. All peoples have a need for rituals; a yearning for communal authentication and reaffirmation of identity, manifested in life-cycle rites, festivals, communal feastings and the commemoration of designated historical events. Naipaul consciously erased these from his own life; he is repelled by the 'wallow' of the 'tribe'; he hates crowds. Yet he would travel widely, in Africa and Asia, to collect material for his books. He would seek out the unclean: he would visit the slums; he would observe Indians chewing, spitting and shitting; he would see the bush taking over, everywhere in Africa; he would admit that he fucked whores regularly. His art has constructed and thrived on a whole 'turd world', to use his late brother Shiva's disparaging play on that concept. It is as if the thinness of his philosophical and cultural moorings needs frailties, fundamental flaws everywhere, in order to validate the self. The vulnerability breeds the dark vision. The empathy is missing, the later narratives saturated with voices of the 'subaltern' notwithstanding; he really cannot relate any more to Indians than to Africans. In 1981, Shiva Naipaul admitted that he himself was 'a very vulnerable construction':

> If I was like a fish out of water at a Hindu rite, I was no less a fish out of water at a drive-in cinema scented with the vapours of hotdogs and hamburgers. Such definition as I do now possess has its roots in nothing other than personal exigency. As a result, I understand how vulnerable a construction I am.[17]

This needs no revision with regard to Vidia. Out of the private void flows the deficit in generosity and empathy.

I think that the best way for me to explore this vulnerability is to contrast the Naipaulian experience of Hinduism with mine. My largely Ahir family was massive. I knew, personally, at least 2,500 people to whom I was related or who claimed me as a relative. In colonial Guyana, in the late 1950s-60s, we used to gather once or twice a year at the Hindu weddings of our wealthy rice-growing and cattle-rearing relatives on the Corentyne Coast. These weddings went on for a week. I was a gregarious adolescent; I yearned for the big event, dreaming of the pretty girls I would meet, identifying a few special ones for greater attention. I was profoundly shaped by these assemblies of the clan: the food, music, laughter, the pranks, the freedom of boys and girls in the night – discovering the beauty of girls, and adult women, too, men's wives; feeling at ease with the other sex. It was a whole world continually yielding its riches to an impressionable mind: curious, bold and mischievous. It was an education and it continues to inspire and animate my life, as I grope towards a kind of adulthood. In the village, too, this spirit was alive: we talked all the time, loudly, men and boys in clumps, often late into the night, about cricket, politics and sex. The men would boast about sexual conquests and their adventures in whorehouses. We listened, pretending not to understand; but we would invent our own sexual tales, later, among ourselves.

My boyhood, outside of the home, was exhilarating: full of little subversions. But I could return to the solitude of home and books; my nuclear family was small. Naipaul's world, in his formative years, was hemmed in, 'protected and imprisoned' by the fortress-like 'Lion House', the compound of his maternal grandparents:

> The entrance gate was at the side… It was a tall gate of corrugated-iron on a wooden frame. It made for a fierce kind of privacy. So as a child I had this sense of two worlds, the wall outside the corrugated-iron gate, and the world at home – or at any rate, the world of my grandmother's house. It was the remnant of our caste sense, the thing that excluded and shut out… It made for an extraordinary self-centredness. We looked inwards… the world outside existed in a kind of darkness; we inquired about nothing.[18]

As a self-contained life it shut out the riches of the diverse, complex colonial universe; it had no curiosity for what it did not encompass or could not comprehend. It was threatened by it: 'we scented violation and withdrew'. This static, orthodox world of the Brahmin Hindu joint family – Naipaul saw it as a mass of humanity – lacked the sensibilities and civilities that grow out of the necessity to negotiate, to compromise with a wider community – the alien. This was what Naipaul missed, and with it the social graces that can come with such contact.

My Hinduism was eclectic, and though my mother was somewhat devout, she did not try to impose her religiosity on me. I could lapse and catch up if I so desired. Some Sunday mornings I went to the Presbyterian or Canadian Mission church; often, on Sunday evenings, I would go to the much freer, more chaotic, Hindu *mandir* (temple), as I did on the many festival days that fill the Hindu calendar. But I did not go home to a world of rituals, a world of pandits, like Naipaul. I could take what I wanted out of my diverse experience. Around the religious festivals there was always scope for secular fun. We would pull at the girls' *orhni* or headwear in the Hindu temple, tickle their feet or hide their slippers; we would go outside to have a pee or a smoke and rejoin the activities, which would go well into the night oblivious of the impending routine of the next working day. The occasion was enriched by the enchantment of the big tropical moon or the fear inspired by the comprehensive tropical darkness, before electricity arrived. The rituals, the festivals, the feastings, the sense of community gave focus to our individual lives.

I grew up with a capacity for happiness, curiosity and a sense of wonder, humour, talk and a gift for mischief. I suppose I was always an extrovert. I chatted with cane-cutters, fishermen, women rice-planters and weeders in the cane fields, ordinary women. I would fall in love with them. Naipaul has spoken often of his sexual ineptitude and his being ill at ease with women. For me there was no world strictly segregated by gender. I enjoyed the banter and flirting with older women. I talked to some of them about virtually anything. This was evidently outside Naipaul's frame of reference. The colonial world was shut out, even its Hindu variant. He could only see it as limited and limiting. He missed a lot. Even when he returned to Trinidad, briefly, after Oxford and publishing the first few books – those in which the 'jokes came fast' – he could not transcend the strictures of his Brahmin boyhood. For all his delicacy of observation, he could not apprehend the richness and fullness of the life he could have found around him. He doubted whether the history of the West Indian islands could be written: history was based on achievement, he observed, but nothing was created there. These were 'half-baked' societies. They could not be taken seriously:

> [N]othing was created in the British West Indies, no civilisation as in Spanish America, no great revolution as in Haiti or the American colonies. There were only plantations, prosperity, decline, neglect: The size of the islands called for nothing else... How can the history of this West Indian futility be written? What tone shall the historian adopt?... The History of the islands can never be satisfactorily told. Brutality is not the only difficulty. History is built around achievement and creation; and nothing was created in the West Indies.[19]

He reflected again on this, in his book of 1994, *A Way in the World*; he had no reason to change his mind:

> I used to feel – in the way of childhood, not putting words to feelings – that the light and the heat had burnt away the history of the place. I distrusted the ideas of glamour that were given to us by postcards and postage stamps (ideas repeated by local artists)... Many years later I thought that that feeling of the void had to do with my temperament, the temperament of the child of a recent Asian-Indian immigrant community in a mixed population: the child looked back and found no family past, found a blank. But I feel again now that I was responding to something that was missing, something that had been rooted out.[20]

The damage of that Trinidadian Brahmin boyhood, the arrogance and hardness bred into the boy, is encapsulated in the following recollection of an early response. His father had moved to Port-of-Spain, in the mid-1940s, and one day had taken the boy to his tailor, a Muslim Indian, to have his trousers made:

> The tailor's name was Nazaralli Baksh... He was a small slender, Indian man... He had a fined-down face, with dark shining eyes set in darker sockets, and with his thin hair brushed back flat: a severe man, friendly to my father, but more matter of fact with me than I expected adults to

> be. I expected adults who had been properly introduced to me to be a little awed by me, and my "brightness ".[21]

The boy has long been contained in the man: this supercilious Brahmin boy. The subtle physical features of the tailor are deftly drawn, but nothing redeeming about the man: no little act of generosity. Had I been taken to such a tailor, my father would have expected me to show good manners to this man; I would have addressed Mr Baksh as 'uncle' or *chacha*. If he were courteous, that was fine; but I had to show deference to an adult or face the wrath of my father all the way home. That was the normal way, the Indian way that shaped us.

In the early 1990s, a Belgian woman, a journalist, tracked Naipaul down, to his sister's house in Trinidad, and eventually procured an interview. Later, they were returning from a drive into the forest and were approaching a rum shop, that institution at the heart of the West Indian gift for talk and laughter. Naipaul could see nothing redeeming in it. He sneered: 'Look at them sitting there. Sitting and drinking'. The woman enjoined perceptively: 'And talking… I've seen that – the men are always discussing things'. Naipaul put an end to that shaft of illumination: 'Talking! They have nothing on their minds'. He had told her that he hated carnival, the music, the noise: 'I have never danced in my life, not once'. He was out of place; he had little in common with Trinidadians: 'They don't work with the mind'.[22]

I knew many years ago that the great mind was missing a lot; the basis of comprehension was flawed. The empathy, crafted by my childhood, does not belong there. His experience, beyond the 'fortress', was puny. The talent alone could not fill the void; the travels, later, could not escape the original darkness:

> We knew nothing of Muslims. This idea of strangeness, of the thing to be kept outside, extended even to other Hindus… [T]he habits of mind engendered by this shut-in and shutting-out life lingered for quite a while. If it were not for the stories my father [Seepersad Naipaul] wrote I would have known almost nothing about the general life of our Indian community. Those stories gave me more than knowledge. They gave me a kind of solidity. They gave me something to stand on in the world. I cannot imagine what my mental picture would have been without those stories. The world outside existed in a kind of darkness; and we inquired about nothing.[23]

Naipaul has had amazing mileage from this second-hand knowledge; but outside of *A House for Mister Biswas*, the absence of experience, the thinness of the 'solidity', shows.

In the late 1950s-1960s a trickle of historians, black and white, began to write the history of the region, from a Creole, and sometimes an Afrocentric perspective. This was an eloquent challenge to Naipaul's famous dictum about nothing having been created in the West Indies. While at university in Canada in the early 1970s, I started to read their books: Donald Wood's *Trinidad in Transition*, Walter Rodney's *A History of the Upper Guinea Coast*, Philip Curtin's *Two Jamaicas*, Elsa Goveia, *Slave Society in the British Leeward Islands at the End of the Eighteenth Century*, Edward Brathwaite's *The Development of Creole Society in Jamaica*, Orlando Patterson's *The Sociology of Slavery*, Alan Adamson's *Sugar Without Slaves*, Richard Dunn's *Sugar and Slaves* and, later, Bridget Brereton's *Race Relations in Colonial Trinidad*. There were a few books by local amateur historians, Dwarka Nath and Peter Ruhomon, and the work of social anthropologists Morton Klass, Arthur and Juanita Niehoff and Chandra Jayawardena, but no professional historical works specifically on Indians in the region, though Wood's book had given me an idea of how it could be attempted – and how daunting the challenge was. But I discovered that a couple of books had been written on aspects of Indian indentureship, and in the mid-1970's I read one, with immense encouragement: Hugh Tinker's *A New System of Slavery*. This is a comparative study of Indian indentureship, with total empathy for the 'coolie'. It revived in me the idea of writing, writing about Indians in British Guiana. This had come to me many years before, in the early 1960s, after reading Naipaul's *The Middle Passage* (1962) and *A House for Mister Biswas* (1961). Later, Jawaharlal Nehru's *The Discovery of India* (1946) and C.L.R. James's *Beyond a Boundary* (1963) kept this early prompting alive.

'Uncle Joe' Dhanna (1909-96), a self-educated man of words (he always carried a small well-used Collins dictionary in his bag), who read Hindi and English, had lent me a tattered, coverless copy of Jawaharlal Nehru's *The Discovery of India*. The book had obviously done the rounds. I had grown up with images of Nehru, this handsome man whose picture and that of Gandhi looked out from the walls of every Indian home in my village. I felt as if they were there to protect us; that they belonged to the pantheon of Hindu gods and goddesses, who also graced our walls. So that when Uncle Joe lent me this book, in 1965, during India's war with Pakistan, I read passionately, for days. It was a big book. I discovered that those few old 'bound coolies' lingering amongst us belonged to a great tradition; and I recall that, even then, my awakening to India's past of high achievement came with an appreciation for Nehru's elegant writing. I wanted to write like him. And the fact, as Uncle Joe related, that he wrote the book in jail, made it feel almost divine, not just a great book. I had no conception of the research that would have preceded the writing. I was seeing it as a kind of illumination given to Nehru: he sat in jail and over a few weeks he just wrote the whole thing out, page after page, as if he were under a spell. The printed word has long entranced me; I still see magic in the final product. A book.

We came, Uncle Joe notwithstanding, from a bookless world. None of my great-grandparents, 'bound coolies' from India, could read or write,

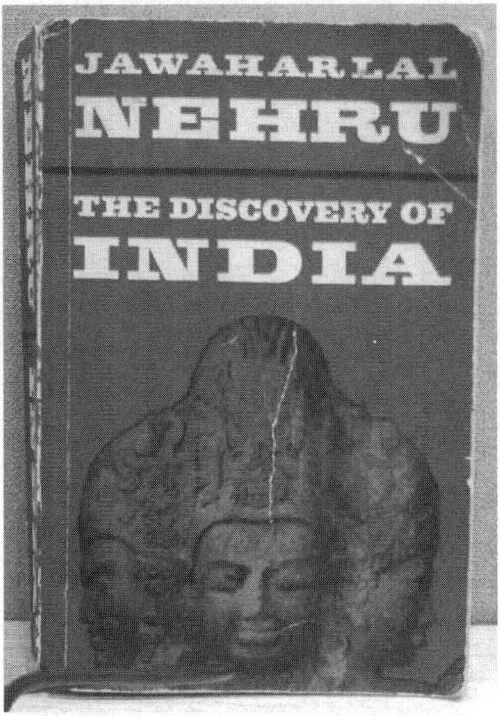

Jawaharlal Nehru's *The Discovery of India* (1946), an inspirational book in my life: I discovered it in 1965.

C.L.R. James's *Beyond a Boundary* (1963): I first read it in 1966 and have done so over twenty times.

Hindi or English. But I recall that the first notion of a book I encountered was a rag of a stained, gnarled booklet in my maternal grandmother, Kaila's house. As I have described in the essay, 'Girmitiyas' this booklet, the *Hanuman Chalisa*, had supposedly been brought from India by her mother, rendering it magical. It resided among the religious paraphernalia, in a corner of my grandmother's house; it exuded incense; no one seemed to read it; I never saw it opened. To do so would no doubt have profaned it.

Visions of Kaila's long journey to British Guiana; my own imaginary India, inspired by the *Ramayana*, Hindi movies and fleeting images dropped by former 'bound coolies', all collided in my young mind making India densely incomprehensible. But I could not ignore this place; failure of comprehension added to its charm. But when, in December 1958, two years after Kaila's death, I learnt that our great cricketer, Rohan Kanhai from Plantation Port Mourant, ten miles from where we lived, had scored a double century in a Test match in India, it was as if all the images of this remote place, irreconcilable in my head, began to fall into place. Kanhai's conquest at Calcutta, the port where most of the 'bound coolies' had embarked, could carry everything for me. I felt as if I, too, had gone 'home' triumphantly: the years had not been squandered. This was a much awareness; but India, cricket, words, books: these were slowly lodging in me.

In 1966, when I was in high school in Georgetown, came my discovery of C.L.R. James's masterpiece of 1963, *Beyond a Boundary*. From the first reading, there was something about the way he spoke of his discovery of books, cricket and cricket writings that impressed me, . I have read the book over a dozen times since and it never fails to trigger something new. After the second reading, following quickly on the heels of the first, I had jotted down several verbatim quotes from the book. Only two really stayed with me because I missed much of what James was saying, but these two excerpts must have spoken to a seminal intellectual yearning:

> Me and my clippings and magazines on W.G. Grace, Victor Trumper and Ranjitsinhji, and my *Vanity Fair* and my puritanical view of the world. I look back at the little eccentric and would like to have listened to him, nod affirmatively and pat him on the shoulder. A British intellectual long before I was ten, already an alien in my own environment among my own people, even my own family. Somehow from around me I had selected and fastened on to the things that made a whole.[24]

The other excerpt I noted was on W.G. Grace. It spoke of reverence at the summit of the game – in England. The idea of cricket in England would have fed my sense of wonder. Besides, I must have liked the sound of the words, the style:

> On his fifty-eight birthday he played for the Gentlemen at the Oval. He made 74 and hit a ball out of the ground. When he hit a stroke for three he could only run one, and the runs were worth a century. Of all

> his innings this is the one I would choose to see. He had enriched the depleted lives of two generations and millions yet to be born. He had extended our conception of human capacity and in doing all this he had done no harm to anyone. He is excluded from the history books of his country. No statue of him exists. Yet he continues warm in the hearts of those who never knew him. There he is safe until the whole crumbling edifice of obeisance before Mammon, contempt for Demos and categorising intellectualism finally falls apart.[25]

My view of the world was definitely not puritanical: the eclectic Hinduism of my boyhood had a facility for not seeing what went against the grain: petty subversions, even graver ones. In my young mind, W.G. and Prince Ranjitsinhji (Ranji) were gods. We had grown up with tales of Ranji, this Indian Prince who had captivated the cricketing world. He was a legend. He had scored a century in his first Test for England, in 1896, and had toured Australia the next year with the English team. I grew up with my father's tale of how the 'racist' Australians responded to him. He would tell the story of how they refused to allow the ship to land with this Indian cricketing Prince on board. Queen Victoria was informed of this and she promptly cabled them that if 'her Prince' could not land, then the whole team must return to England. The Australians relented immediately. I had memorised words from my dad's tale, so I was very upset to learn, years later, that the story was not true. For me, Ranji, like Gandhi and Nehru, belonged to the pantheon of Hindu Gods. I had seen a picture of Ranji in the local paper, and had innocently mounted it, together with a picture of my local hero, Rohan Kanhai, among my mother's framed pictures of Hindu deities. They remained there for some time, until, one day, she was so exasperated with me for having listened to cricket on the radio all day – ball by ball – while our cattle grazed our neighbour's vegetable garden to the ground, that she uprooted them from that sacred space, with exaggerated hauls at the two small pictures, in that moment of uncontrollable anger.

I had started to make clippings from the newspapers since 1960, when I was ten: cricket articles, cricketers' pictures (which I pasted into my scrapbook), and articles from London on new West Indian writers, whom I started to read from around 1961: Edgar Mittelholzer, Sam Selvon, Peter Kempadoo's *Guiana Boy* – not Harris and Lamming: they bored me; the story got lost in the words. But it was V.S. Naipaul, more than anyone, who gave me the idea that books could be written by Indians in the West Indies. We were told he was Indian (from Trinidad); the pictures on the dust jacket of his early books, with the cigarette in his left hand, confirmed this. A note would arrive in the post for me to collect a new book by 'Naipaul, Vidiadhar Surajprasad -1932', reserved some months before. Exhilarated, I would rush to the Public Free Library, in New Amsterdam, anticipating the process that had settled on me. I would play with the book for a while, flicking through the pages, admiring his picture (with the cigarette in his left hand), astounded by the achievement. I thought the cigarette went with the art of composition. I would smell the fresh print, already evocative of another kind of learning, beyond the tattered, mouldy religious books of our India-born Brahmin priest. I would hold the book in what I thought was a scholarly manner, in my right hand with it pressed firmly on my right chest, before the mirror. The reading would come later – slowly, meticulously, interspersed with periodic smelling of the print and reassessments of the author's picture, oblivious of numerous domestic chores. I sat with *Middle Passage*, in a tree, around 1963, reading about Naipaul's visit to my part of British Guiana in 1960-61, recognising the places and some of the people he had sketched with such precision, and the idea came to me that I, too, could one day write books made a fleeting but lasting impression. Coming from a bookless world, this was a kind of fantasy, no different from the visions of India which perennially sprouted in me, changed shape from one day to the next, before merging with or reverting to older ones: a carnival of images of this place which would not leave the boy alone. But it was Naipaul's masterpiece, *A House for Mr Biswas*, which I read around 1964, at the time of our racial troubles, which convinced me that we could write about ourselves. There was a lot of my world on those pages. I must have been moved by my discovery of the 'bound coolies' in Trinidad:

> In the arcade of Hanuman House, grey and substantial in the dark, there was already the evening assembly of old men, squatting on sacks on the ground and on tables now empty of Tulsi Store goods, pulling at clay *cheelums* that glowed red and smelled of ganja and burnt sacking. Though it wasn't cold, many had scarves over their heads and around their necks; this detail made them look foreign and, to Mr Biswas romantic. It was the time of day for which they lived. They could not speak English and were not interested in the land where they lived; it was a place where they had come for a short time and stayed longer than they expected. They continually talked of going back to India, but when the opportunity came, many refused, afraid of the unknown, afraid to leave the familiar temporariness. And every evening they came to the arcade of the solid, friendly house, smoked, told stories, and continued to talk of India.[26]

My first book, *'Tiger in the Stars': the Anatomy of Indian Achievement in British Guiana*, was inspired, paradoxically, by the work of a man who would probably see it as a subject unworthy of serious scrutiny. But he gave me a grand idea, that Indians, people of the cane-fields, latecomers to education in the British West Indies, could write books – and get them published in England: we were no longer a bookless people, 'coolies'.

This discovery of Naipaul, in the early 1960s, precisely the time when the master Indian batsman from my district, Rohan Kanhai, was enchanting Australian and English crowds, made me feel that we now mattered. It was also the time of Cheddi Jagan's ascendancy in British Guiana – on the 'threshold' of Independence we were told – as we triumphantly, and unconscionably, celebrated his victory in August 1961: a victory over Africans. I had already become immersed in a world of words: I would read excerpts, slowly, from *The Guiana Graphic* or *The Sunday Argosy* to my illiterate grandparents and other older people in the village. I would read with confidence, mispronouncing the big words with fluent ease. English words had a special resonance for them – the language of power. They came alive when I read about Nehru or Jagan or Kanhai; and were profusely grateful to me for reading and explaining to them. I saw it as a privilege; I felt like a teacher. I must have taken their achievement for granted: the land they had bought and reclaimed from the swamp; the rice they reaped; the cattle they owned. But my reading to them gave me greater appreciation for words, as well as ambition. I felt I was helping them to make sense of the new world that had crept up on their last years, towards the end of British rule. They had laid the foundation for us to think bigger, to get an education, to go to university. India's freedom was still fresh with us: we celebrated Indian Independence Day, *Swaraj*. Guyana's freedom would soon be our own *Swaraj*, my grandmother had told me. It turned out to be different.

By 1966, our political hero, Cheddi Jagan, had fallen; but his book on 'my fight for Guyana's freedom', *The West on Trial*, appeared in Georgetown, in March or April of that year. I was greatly moved. Strangely, briefly, it seemed to me to compensate for the loss of power. My grandmother gave me $5 to get a copy. I read it over several days, hanging on every word, and was to go back to it many times afterwards. As if by design, Rohan Kanhai's *Blasting for Runs* appeared around the same time. My grandmother gave me $4.60 to buy it. I read it within a day. I then started to read it to the men in my village, as they drank rum under my friend Ole Bai's house. Not only were we achieving, but we were also writing about it – in books. The inspiration of the printed words of Naipaul, Nehru and C.L.R. James was being sustained. I felt vindicated, years later, when I discovered what Naipaul had written in 1963, in a review of James's book: '*Beyond a Boundary* is one of the finest and most finished books to come out of the West Indies, important to England, important to the West Indies. It has a further value: it gives a base and solidity to West Indian literary endeavour'.[27]

I will conclude with an assessment by Andrew Robinson, whose interview of Naipaul I referred to at the start of this piece. It speaks to the power of the man's work whatever one's reservations:

> *Among the Believers*, written in the wake of the Iranian revolution of 1979, was prophetic about the rage of fundamentalist Islam. *A Million Mutinies Now*, published in 1990, was prescient about the sea-change in India of the past decade... In both cases, Naipaul's intuitions and indefatigable on-the-spot research were well ahead of the academic reaction. As for the professional study of literature, there are many who would say that Naipaul's diagnosis is today being proved uncomfortably accurate. Naipaul

> may be savage in his criticisms of academic desiccation, and hardly practical in his solutions to the current malaise in the study of the humanities on both sides of the Atlantic. But no one should make the mistake of imagining that he speaks from mere prejudice. At least this once, the Nobel [P]rize was given to a writer who will always be read – and not just by academics – for his intelligence and insight and for the clarity and elegance of his style.[28]

He has, indeed, been a major influence on me. What would I not do for the clarity and elegance of his style? But I don't envy him the burden of his genius.

Notes

1. *The Times Higher Education*, 9 August 2002.
2. 'Going back for a Turn in the East' [Andrew Robinson interviews V.S. Naipaul], *The Sunday Times*, 16 September 1990.
3. See note 1.
4. V.S. Naipaul, 'Two Worlds', Nobel Lecture, 7 December 2001.
5. See note 1.
6. V.S. Naipaul. *Finding the Centre: Two Narratives* (London: Andre Deutsch,1984), pp. 58-9.
7. *Ibid.*, p. 65.
8. *Ibid.*, p. 60.
9. V.S. Naipaul, *The Mimic Men* (London: Andre Deutsch, 1967), p. 73.
10. V.S. Naipaul, *The Middle Passage* (Harmondsworth: Penguin, 1969 [1962]), p. 88.
11. V.S.Naipaul, *An Area of Darkness* (London: Andre Deutsch, 1964), p. 32.
12. See note 4.
13. V.S. Naipaul, *A Bend in the River* (Harmondsworth: Penguin, 1980 [1979]), pp. 21-2.
14. See note 8, p. 109.
15. *Ibid*, p. 32.
16. See note 10 (pp. 33-5).
17. *The Express* (Trinidad), 20 December 1981.
18. See note 4.
19. See note 9, pp. 27, 29.
20. V.S. Naipaul, *A Way in the World* (London: Minerva, 1995 [1994]), pp. 72-73.
21. *Ibid.*, pp. 12-3.
22. Lieve Joris, 'Home to the Snakes and the Sensitive Plants', *New Statesman*, 17 December 2001.
23. See note 4.
24. C.L.R. James, *Beyond a Boundary* (London: Serpent's Tail, 1994 [1963]), p. 18.

25. *Ibid*., p. 185.
26. V.S. Naipaul, *A House for Mr Biswas* (London: Andre Deutsch, 1961), p. 174.
27. V.S. Naipaul, 'Cricket', *Encounter*, (September 1963), reproduced in his *The Overcrowded Barracoon* (London: Andre Deutsch, 1972), pp. 17-22. The quote is on p. 22.
28. See note 1.

PART III: LOCATING CHEDDI JAGAN

Martin Carter (1927-1997): being sworn in as a minister in the PNC-UF government in 1967 by Governor-General of Guyana, David Rose.

Martin Carter, Guyana's greatest poet, receives the Order of Roraima from President Cheddi Jagan in 1994.

THE SHAPE OF THE PASSION: THE HISTORICAL CONTEXT OF MARTIN CARTER'S POETRY OF PROTEST (1951-1964)

The Colony's best poet is a Marxist leader of the PPP, Martin Carter. His ideology has given his work a passion and intensity.

Michael Swan (1955)

I see no substitute for passion, internally generated, and hard work.

Martin Carter (1960)

I: Radical Promptings of Carter's Imagination, 1939-52

Martin Carter was born on 7 June 1927 in Georgetown, British Guiana to mixed race parents – 'coloured' people as they are still called in Guyana. There was nothing extraordinary about the day of his birth in the colony, but the year is redolent of a measure of infamy. The Colonial Office, in league with the plantocracy and others of the old order, were manoeuvring to deprive the colony of its mildly liberal constitution and replace it with Crown Colony government – more nominated members – presumably more malleable. The pretext was that in the interest of colonial development it was imperative to give the Executive Council, presided over by the Governor and comprising primarily nominated officials and unofficials, greater control of financial matters. The truth is that vested interests in this backward colony had become paranoid at what they saw as an avalanche of potential subversives – popular leaders elected to the Legislature Council in 1926. Most of the representatives of colonial capital had been defeated.

The fear of change was imprinted on the year 1927, but the kindling of protest from diverse sources, also, was an inescapable fact of the Georgetown of 1927. Probably the most articulate protester, a formidable critic of the colonial condition, was Hon. A. R. F. Webber (1880-1932), a coloured publisher and politician seen to be incorruptible. His radical *The New Daily Chronicle*, founded in 1926, was a champion of the underdog; its iconoclasm was shaping a new self-confidence. On 8 June 1927, the day after Martin Carter was born, it carried a leader challenging the official premises for changing the constitution. Webber recommended 'a good, strong, imaginative Executive [Council], inspired by local knowledge and guided by a continuous policy, to take hold of the affairs of the colony…' A few weeks later his paper asserted that 'the quickest way to the realisation of [the political evolution of subject races] is not by suppression but by throwing open avenues of advancement…'[1] The incipient nationalism would not have been lost on Carter's father, a junior civil servant.

Georgetown, in the hard times of the 1930s, was characterised by distinctly ethnic, quasi-political organisations: the British Guiana East Indian Association (founded in New Amsterdam in 1916), and the Negro Progress Convention (founded in Georgetown in 1922). Even the two main trade unions, the British Guiana Labour Union (founded in 1919) and the Man Power Citizens' Association (founded in 1937), tended to bear these features, reflecting the essentially ethnic division of labour which had evolved in the colonial economy since Emancipation. So that even the spate of working class protests from the mid-1930s, Carter's boyhood years, tended to harden racial proclivities.

Indeed, Carter's coloured or mixed race group, because of its comparatively elevated status within the colonial polity, tended to be most punctilious in its defence of their space. This bred a superiority complex, as the Guyanese writer, Edgar Mittelholzer (1909-1965), a coloured man from New Amsterdam, recalls:

> …it was my own class – people of coloured admixture… which looked down upon the East Indian sugar plantation labourers ('coolies' we called them, whether they were labourers or eventually became doctors or barristers or Civil Servants). It was my class which considered the Portuguese social inferiors because of their background of door-to-door peddling, rum-shops, salt-goods shops and pawnshops and their low standards of living. We, too, treated the Chinese sweet-sellers and shopkeepers with condescension because of their poor-immigrant status. We even looked with a certain distinct aloofness upon the young Englishmen who came out to serve as sugar-plantation overseers. We deemed them 'white riff-raff'. And as for the negroes, it goes without saying that they were serving people; that was an accepted tradition dating from slavery days. Only the pure-blooded whites could discriminate adversely against me and my class…[2]

Carter's father, Victor Emmanuel, like many men from coloured families in British Guiana – the van Sertimas, Mittelholzers, McDavids, Westmaases, Sharples, Woolfords – had found a niche in the colonial civil service, below the British who were the heads of departments. Carter's people were also the first people of the book: they celebrated their European side and denigrated – denied, their African side. One could argue, therefore, that European superiority on one hand, and coloured superciliousness in parading their Europeanness on the other, were what nourished the rebel in the young Carter in the 1940s.

Ian McDonald has remarked on the role of learning in the Carter household: 'Carter recalls arguments between his father and his friends about Spinoza and other deeply philosophical subjects. His mother, born Violet Eugene Wylde, also loved books and enjoyed reciting verses'.[3] Carter has also spoken of the bounteous influence of the Bible, its rich allure of language and allusions, its imagery of myth, seeping into his fluid imagination.[4] He had access, in Georgetown, both to the Carnegie Public 'Free' Library and, until its destruction in the fire of 1945, the incomparable riches of the Royal Agricultural and Commercial Society Collection. Besides he would have read, regularly, the two excellent, if conservative, daily newspapers, *The Daily Argosy* and *The Daily Chronicle* – certainly their 'corners' for poets and short story writers. It is not far-fetched to argue that the realms of art, beauty and the personal freedom to think and dream insulated him from the parochialism and what he would later refer to as the 'materialism and philistinism' of British Guiana. His reading also bred a passion for words: their elegance, subtlety, and the seduction of crafting them to give meaning to experience – a process which would have acquired some glamour with the publication of Mittelholzer's *Corentyne Thunder* in 1941, in England.

In the 1940s, British Guiana was a colonial backwater that was stirring. Carter's education had taken him to Queen's College, the prestigious boys' school, in 1938 or 1939; he graduated in 1944. During the 1939-45 war, the preoccupation of the British Government bred a degree of local autonomy. This was stimulated by the liberal Governor from 1941 to 1946, Sir Gordon Lethem (1886-1962), a Scot. Carter's most impressionable years were touched by the large sympathies and imagination of this able man, who believed that good government must transcend the old, insatiable demands of the sugar planters. Lethem was a resolute advocate of drainage and irrigation of the hazardous coastland, where over 90% of the people lived; diversification of agriculture and support for small farmers; interior development. At every stage, however, the plantocracy tried to, and to a great extent were able to, stifle change. Such was Lethem's popularity, that people of all races in the colony petitioned the Colonial Office for him to have a second term. They were rebuffed. Carter's world at Queen's College and his early years in the civil service partook of the exhilaration (and despair) which crowned the Lethem years: the hint of an oasis on the weary road of colonial inertia.

Carter speaks often of the need for passion and hard work. Lethem's endeavours spoke of hope, shoots of possibilities, commitment – daring to change. One commentator's final portrait of the man could explain why he illuminated the lives of so many in British Guiana, possibly even Carter:

> [Lethem] was a lion of a man – great-hearted, formidable when roused, of bounding energy and vitality. Large-minded and generous, he was

> the antithesis of everything petty, mean, meticulous, pedantic. The wide, rough colonial stage of his time was an ideal field for his qualities. His facility with languages and liberal and sympathetic spirit kept him in closest contact with high and low among the diverse peoples with and for whom he worked so devotedly and who in their turn loved and venerated him. His *vividia vis animi*, the faultless verbal memory and power of declamation; his humour and gusto, made him a fascinating leader and friend.[5]

Lethem's perceived purity of motives in British Guiana ought to have enlarged its peoples' sense of the possible, their potential for a fuller life. But this environment – a capricious landscape requiring water now, drainage soon afterwards; then still chronic malaria; the latifundist character of sugar – also bred a hurt and a radical temperament. High hopes and their abrogation during the Lethem years, coupled with the optimism spawned by the Moyne Commission Report and its advocacy of change (1945), expanded the rebellious spirit.

1945 was a pivotal year in Carter's life. He left Queen's College and got a job in the civil service, first at the Post Office, then as secretary to the Superintendent of Prisons, Samuel Baker – a man 'humane to prisoners and scornful of bureaucracy'; a 'great drunkard' and champion wrestler, from Wales.[6] All these features endeared him to Carter; but he was deeply aware that he was hemmed in. Very few colonials, even coloureds in the 1940s, could scale the heights of the civil service; besides, the job stifled initiative and crippled the imagination. But 1945 also brought a new day: A. J. Seymour, another coloured civil servant, founded the first literary journal in the colony, *Kyk-over-Al*. Its aims reflected a deeper ambition: 'an instrument to help forge a Guianese people, make them conscious of their intellectual and spiritual possibilities – build some achievement of common pride in the literary world – make an act of *possession* of our environment... (emphasis added)'[7]

But the 1940s were also marked by an ominous rise in racial consciousness – a situation which was accelerated by the formation of an Indian middle class with a base in rice, cattle and business, and some, by the late 1930s-early 1940s, were challenging the supremacy of Africans and coloureds in law and medicine. This was something of a meteoric rise and it inspired fear among Africans. Even among Indian workers, it was truer to say that their sense of their own possibilities had been buoyed by the relentless march of Indian nationalism in the 'motherland', than by any development in British Guiana. Indeed, in 1944, fear of Indian dominance had led even the veteran African Guyanese trade unionist, Hubert Critchlow (1884-1958), to vote against adult suffrage in the legislature. Carter was aware of these fear, and though he belonged to neither of the two main groups, he was acutely conscious of its destructive properties.

In 1946 Cheddi Jagan (1918-1997), an Indian, his American-born wife,

Janet, H. J. M. Hubbard, a near-white communist trade unionist, and Ashton Chase, a young African trade unionist and assistant to Critchlow, founded the Political Affairs Committee (PAC). One of its aims was to establish 'a strong, disciplined and enlightened Party, equipped with the theory of Scientific Socialism' – a Communist party.[8] Cheddi Jagan was an American-educated dentist, but his roots in the sugar plantations coupled with his experience of American 'Jim Crow' institutions and rampant racism against African Americans, in the late 1930s-early 1940s, enraged him. But, by his own admission, at first he lacked a frame of reference to comprehend the roots of inequality and racism. It was when he met Janet Rosenberg (born 1920), a communist of East European Jewish extraction, from Chicago, that he acquired the rudiments of a Marxist way of seeing. He absorbed it passionately, uncritically, with a convert's zeal.

Cheddi Jagan had found a world-view and he took it and his attractive, politically astute wife to his colonial backwater. He had a young man's enthusiasm and a facility for simplifying the message; oversimplifying it so that it became a millennial vision. His astounding energy, personal charm and evident sincerity made him a hero of the underdog even among many Africans. Hubbard had moved towards Marxism earlier, around 1938-39, as a result of his exposure to the leftist books of two Scottish Presbyterian ministers in Georgetown. Maurice St. Pierre believes that Hubbard's Marxist ideas, ventilated weekly at a study circle in Georgetown, had permeated the Carter household by 1945:

> Reading these books was followed by a number of weekly meetings dealing with the translation of learning into action. Martin Carter, who was subsequently involved with the PAC, grew up in a home (along with his brother Keith who was later involved in the struggle) in which they were enjoined to think and discuss any issue freely. This experience, coupled with the marked propensity of the brothers for reading, soon led to a desire to ask questions and to seek answers about the nature of society, which sought to oppress the majority of the people.[9]

For the young Martin Carter, the analytical perspective and the optimism gained from a non-conventional reading – at variance with his Queen's College orthodoxies – fed the rebellious temperament. Cheddi Jagan and Janet, a first-rate organiser and editor of *PAC Bulletin*, dramatised this new hope; they epitomised the fledgling possibilities. The appeal of the PAC's radical politics was enhanced by Cheddi Jagan's election to the Legislative Council in November 1947, aged 29. For the first time a genuine radical with communist sympathies had won legislative honours and, overnight, he revolutionised people's conception of politics. Jagan recalls:

> Mine was the role of 'politics of protest', with the weapons of exposure and struggle. If the legislature was my forum, the waterfront, the factories, plantations, mines and quarries were my battleground. I brought a new

dimension to the politics of protest. A continuity between the legislature and the street-corner; the legislature was brought to the 'streets' and the 'streets' to the legislature.[10]

Ian McDonald explains how Jagan's vision of freedom reached Carter, in Georgetown, in the late 1940s: 'He had become friendly with many of those, like himself, who had freed their minds and were determined to free their country. He had met the pioneering politician Cheddi Jagan when he heard that Jagan had a marvellous library and went to visit him and stayed to talk and talk'. Indeed, the Jagans frequently invited 'leading intellectuals' to their home to discuss a range of issues. Carter was one of them; he said that the group, deceptively called the Kitty Adult Education Association, was a 'communist front'[11]: it espoused Marxism.

In his first collection of poems, *The Hill of Fire Glows Red* (1951), appropriately, he seems to praise the speaking, guiding hands of Cheddi Jagan, his friend and mentor in those distant, spacious days of unsullied hopes and big vision. Carter recalls: 'Cheddi came back to Guyana in 1943 and began agitating. I used to hear about his agitation and became interested in the movement he had started. He had founded the Political Affairs Committee (PAC), and used to hold political meetings at the Kitty YMCA. I attended those meetings'.[12] This is from 'Looking at your Hands':

No!
I will not still my voice!
I have
too much to claim –
if you see me
looking at books
or coming to your house
or walking in the sun
know that I look for fire![13]

Cheddi Jagan's stature as the prophet of the new day was lifted by the Enmore shootings of 16 June 1948: five young sugar plantation workers were shot by the police – striking men who were among many demanding recognition for the Jagan-backed trade union, the Guiana Industrial Workers' Union. The *PAC Bulletin* covered the tragedy with this caption: 'WE ASKED FOR BREAD! ... THEY GAVE US BULLETS!'[14] Enmore was the catalyst for the rise of the People's Progressive Party (PPP), a Marxist-led but broad-based coalition of diverse races and classes. It was founded in January 1950. It superseded the PAC; and its organ, *Thunder*, replaced the *PAC Bulletin*. Carter became a member of the editorial board of *Thunder*.

Carter's imagery, in his early years in the PPP, fed on Enmore. The 'hill of fire', a transcendent feature of the plantation at harvest time, as the tall sugar-cane is set alight and the avalanche of fire consumes the cane-leaves, undergrowth, insects, snakes, etc., is the infernal motif for the pain, the hurt of slavery and indenture, and fountainhead of colonial being. But it also becomes the symbol of hope: it clears up, cleans, and allows for new shoots of cane, the ratoon, to sprout – the red hill speaks of a new day:

across the dark face of the river
the hill of fire glows red like fresh blood
like the blood of Quamina
flowing through the green forest
the green green forest.[15]

Quamina, the leader of the Demerara Slave Rebellion of 1823, gave his head to free his compatriots; it was displayed on a spike and left to rot. He will be a hero when the new freedom comes to Guiana, the poet is saying.

Carter, however, is declamatory. He mocks the lofty appellation, for British Guiana, 'Magnificent Province', 'Province of mud!/ Province of flood!'[16] The Enmore motif, the bitterness of sugar, is branded on this land. The 'magnificent' is not him, 'with his torn shirt'; it speaks only of those 'in their white mansions' (the great house), 'by the trench of blood'. British Guiana is 'no El Dorado for me'; its catalogue of euphemisms cannot mask its brutal plantation heritage: the 'bruising and battering for self preservation/in the white dust and grey mud' – an allusion to sugar and the harsh coastal landscape of stiff, unyielding clay which imposes eternal toil on slave and freed man. But he will no longer genuflect to poverty: 'now is long past time for worship'. No longer will he be 'kneeling'. He is now armed with 'this hammer of my hand' (the hammer and sickle) and 'this new science of men' (Marxism).[17]

The poet is 'listening to the land'. A voice is being shaped: he hears 'tongueless whispering', 'as if some buried slave wanted to speak again'.[18] He is preparing for the revolution; everyone will become soldiers of freedom – all will be involved:

from the hospitals the lame will come
the mad will be sane again
for the revolution.[19]

But hovering over Carter's euphoria and undammable hope, the enormous gloom, the possibility of despair is there from the beginning. It is as if his personal oscillation – his peaks, his troughs – could not leave the vision well alone. The Lethem promise of pregnant possibilities nestles ineluctably in Carter's poetic landscape with the imagery of drought and oppression, as in the following from *The Hidden Man* (1952):

I stretch my hand to a night of weary branches
feeling for leaves or any twig of blossom:
But the branch is withered with no green leaf for me
and the stalk is brown and has no petal for me
and the root is tap root boring in equator.[20]
. . . .

The potential for the descent of man, the downward spiral, also, is vast.

II: Euphoria and Creeping Self-doubt, 1953-55: Poems of Resistance (1954) and their source

The years after Enmore (1948) and the General Elections of April 1953, the first under adult suffrage, were the fullest time in Carter's life. His dreams were not yet corroded by Guyanese racism and the demonic allure of power. The 'new science of men' fed notions of the weakness of chains, of the inevitability of freedom; most of all it made race an 'epiphenomenon', a temporary evil that true class consciousness would overcome. In this potential cauldron of racism, the 'new science of men', could become a release into fantasy.

In 'All of a Man', in his *The Kind Eagle*, his other 1952 collection, the 'kind eagle' – no American eagle – batters the wall of unfreedom, freeing one suspects even the poet from the dead-end of the colonial civil service:

> O strike kind eagle, strike!
> Grip at this prison and this prison wall!
> scream and accuse the guilty cage of heaven
> hurling me here, hurling me here.

This antithesis of the American eagle, Marxism, has the strength and purity of motives, to enhance freedom for total liberation: 'All of a man can fly like a bird'. Love and hope are the essence of the Carterian new man. The old certainties, the old religion, the whole colonial rationale which shackles – 'the guilty cage of heaven', is being shredded – the declamation of renewal is clean; the kind eagle *will* 'strike': 'The sharp knife dawn glitters in my hand'.[22]

Rupert Roopnaraine has explained the depth of resolution of Carter's work in the early PPP days that fed the intensity of the poetry:

> Between 1950 and 1953 [Carter] and a few others did most of the party educational work in weekend classes. They worked along the coast. An important highlight of this effort was their study of the landlord system in the rice farming village of Golden Fleece, Essequibo. In this study and teaching the young activist was getting down to the anatomy of the estate system on the Essequibo coast. The activists found that there were elements of feudalism alive and well, that often the landlord was the miller and the shopkeeper as well as the moneylender. Carter's righteous anger at these conditions was not ideological in the narrow sense. These were among the discoveries and experiences he accumulated while doing political work off the platform while he was still a public servant. He taught with conviction the part played by labour in production. His scheme was not merely Marxist, but one reinforced with Carterian thought permeated with Guyanese history and experience'.[23]

These years of lofty ideals, in the early 1950s, had seen the trickle of radical sentiments in the PAC of the late 1940s flow with diverse, often discordant streams into the nationalist movement, the People's Progressive Party (PPP), an eclectic multiracial coalition with an anti-colonial mission. It was this coming together of an anti-colonial majority, in conjunction with the suspension of the Constitution by the British, after 133 days, because of the PPP's alleged communist designs, which inspired many of the poems in Carter's finest collection, *Poems of Resistance*, which was published in London in 1954. It is here that Carter's Marxist vision and his optimism that the PPP could shape a free, coherent community from its disparate components, is most discernible. It is here also that one can trace Carter's own quest for an authentic Guyaneseness that is about redefining the past, including slavery. His great poem, 'I Come from the Nigger Yard',[24] is just such an act of redefinition, a reclaiming of the past as an instrument of renewal, a reassertion of humanity as a prelude to the building of the new day. The actual 'nigger yard' might appear to have written the people out of history, but even there the quest for identity, for ancestral moorings to begin to reshape the present, could be seen to have begun:

> It was an aching floor on which I crept
> on my hands and my knees
> searching for dust for the trace of a root
> or the mark of a leaf or the shape of a flower.

Carter's tale documents the pain, but does not despair. He shows us his rage leaping from the material and mental void, with 'coffin space for home' and 'priests and parsons fooling gods with words'. He screams; he is 'stubborn and fierce'; he affirms himself; he becomes. The poem is permeated with hope. He spots 'a tiny star neighbouring a leaf/a little drop of light a piece of glass... like a spark seed in the destiny of gloom'. Like the quivering tension building in a drawn sling approaching release, the language is taut, redolent of aggravated strength; the 'nigger' will write his own history henceforth:

> I turn to the histories of men and the lives of the peoples.
> I examine the shower of sparks the wealth of the dreams.
> . . . .
> From the nigger yard of yesterday I come with my burden.
> To the world of to-morrow I turn with my strength.

Carter is reclaiming his African side; no bouquets here for the European side.

He did not feature directly in the short-lived PPP government of 1953; he did not even win the seat he contested, New Amsterdam. Roopnaraine observes that the seat was unwinnable but Carter 'used the campaign to deepen human relations and to educate people into thinking'. He resigned from the civil service after the 1953 elections, thus freeing himself to work more effectively for the PPP, both as a member of the executive and the editorial board of the party's organ, *Thunder*. Roopnaraine concludes: 'educating people into the habit of thinking may well be his most enduring contribution to our politics'. To Guyana.

Indeed, as the Robertson Constitutional Commission of 1954 reported, Martin Carter was one of at least six of the Party's 'most prominent leaders', who exerted 'a very powerful communist influence'. The report elaborated: this group 'accepted unreservedly the "classical" communist doctrines of Marx and of Lenin: were enthusiastic supporters of the policies and practices of modern communist movements: and were contemptuous of European social democratic parties, including the British Labour Party'.[25]

The suspension of the Constitution and the incarceration of several PPP leaders, including Carter (for three months, towards the end of 1953), and the invasion by British troops, inspired some of the most overtly political poems in *Poems of Resistance*. Earlier, on 29 October 1953, as St. Pierre observes, some of these poems, including 'This is the Dark Time my Love' and 'I Clench my Fist', had been seized by British soldiers from the Magnet Printery in Georgetown. Apparently they had been 'so unnerving to the British' that they were the subject of a despatch from the Governor to the Colonial Office.[26]

Carter's imagery is angry; the hard edge is unforgiving in its denunciation of the British soldiers in the colony: 'All around the land brown beetles crawl about'. Speaking to his young wife, as several of the poems from jail do, they gain in intensity by the interweaving of the harsh political imagery with a pristine love for his wife and their child to whom she has just given birth:

> Who comes walking in the dark night time?
> Whose boot of steel tramps down the slender grass?
> It is the man of death, my love, the strange invader
> watching you sleep and aiming at your dream.[27]

He sees the suppression of the freedom movement in British Guiana as a part of the tapestry of imperialist repression wherever the battle for freedom is waged; but he does not despair. The spirit of his communist brothers and his ancestral brothers, African rebels, descendants of Accabreh, one of the leaders of the Berbice Slave Rebellion of 1763, feeds his zeal:

> O wherever you fall comrade I shall rise.
> In the whirling cosmos of my soul there are galaxies of happiness
> Stalin's people and the brothers of Mao Tse-tung
> And Accabreh's breed...[28]

But Carter, a man of intellect from the coloured middle class, could more readily assess the potential African-Indian confrontation with dispassion. Ominous clouds had settled over the PPP, during crisis week, after the April 1953 election victory, as Cheddi Jagan and L. F. S. Burnham staked their respective claims for supremacy. Carter could see that inherent in this fight were the germs of racial hate – not the nicety of philosophical disputations, however persuasive. This probably accounts for the passion which he brought to his communist vision – an uncompromising path of economic democracy as the foundation for racial equality; no battle against racialism could be won amidst the greed of capitalism and rampant individualism.

Carter had argued in August 1954 against an American officer, Mr. L. E. Norrie, who had written in a local newspaper, *The Daily Argosy* (15 August), that Russia was the 'greatest colonial power on earth' on the grounds that it continued to dominate millions of colonial peoples. For Carter, in 1954, this was poison: the Soviet Union was *the* example – 'the star neighbouring a leaf'; 'the spark seed in the destiny of gloom'. He countered, in *Thunder*:

> ...in 1917 the people led by Lenin overthrew the capitalist state and instituted a system of Soviet Government which guarantees to the people a real chance to live like human beings. Because control of the means of production is in the hands of the people who decide how production should be organised, unlike the USA where the minority class controls everything, the Soviet Government is able to lead the people ever forward to a better life. And because again, the Soviet Union is a socialist country, a country which leads the world in the fight for freedom from imperialism and therefore from colonialism, it follows that Mr. Norrie's statement is viciously false and is cunningly calculated to deceive and mislead...[29]

Earlier, in May 1954, Rory Westmaas, Carter's close friend and junior vice-chairman of the PPP, who, also, had won the badge of communism from the Robertson Commission, had argued that the British suspended the Constitution because the PPP was not a 'reformist' party, like the parties of Manley and Bustamante in Jamaica and Grantley Adams in Barbados. These parties had 'placed themselves completely at the disposal of Imperialism'. Westmaas, like Carter, still believed that the PPP was fulfilling its task as the leader for national liberation: 'Our party in no way resembles these puppet organisations. The PPP, based on the strong working class – peasant farmer alliance with our small businessmen and intelligentsia, truly represents the interests of the entire people. Placing complete trust in it, the people had forged, in a matter of a few years, a sharp weapon for freedom and peace'.[30]

Carter's optimism, also, was not dimmed by the suspension. In a poem published in *Thunder* on 31 July 1954, 'If Today' (apparently never republished), he is still unrelenting in his hate of the soldier/invader, but the struggle sustains the hope:

> If today our city is like a house of stone
> rigid and cold, silent and still
> It is because a soldier walks with a gun
> Not even a friend of the dogs.
>
> And if today the sound of the ocean on our shore
> comes like a rumble of terror
> It is because death rides at anchor in the sea
> Watching until they sleep
> waiting for hope to fade.
> And even if today they try to stamp us down
> flesh into mud, heart into stone
> Are we not still a great generation of struggle
> strong and uncountable
> born to be free?

Carter's certainty of the political vocation in the PPP showed no signs of wear until the 'split' in February 1955, when L. F. S. Burnham, the most gifted African leader in the party, its chairman, and several others who had been designated 'socialists', 'essentially democrats', by the Robertson Commission, left the communist-led (Jagan) PPP. In fact, on the day of the fateful Burnham-inspired meeting in Georgetown, which consummated the split, Carter was still underlining the political vocation – a politics animated by the condition of the working class. The working class child, tomorrow's hope, was in an abysmal condition:

> ...he finds himself locked up in a huge cage of poverty where hardly any opportunity for real individual development exists. Any kind of gift or talent must be immediately sacrificed to the job of putting something in his belly from day to day. And, after a while the grind of life takes over, bright dreams become a bolt in a sugar punt – bent and rusty with the years.[31]

Voiceless people! As Carter would put it in the early 1970s, after he had resigned from Burnham's cabinet, 'the mouth is muzzled by the food it eats'.

By 1955, the rusting of ideals, the corrosion of hope, for Carter (and his friend Rory Westmaas) had begun. Burnham's departure signalled the ominous crystallisation and aggregation of deep-seated racial instincts, sectional prejudices, in this inchoate colonial polity. A united PPP had offered the best hope of stemming a slide into racial obscurantism. The menace of African-Indian incomprehension, fusing around the magnetic personalities of Jagan and Burnham, clouding out meaningful debate, led Carter to argue prophetically in March 1955, less than a month after the split:

> ...[that] it would be better for a person of Indian descent to support Mr. Burnham for ideological reasons than for the same person while agreeing with Mr. Burnham to support Dr. Jagan only because he happens to be an Indian. The same holds good for a person of African descent.

> For this would mean that the action was dictated by reason and not by racialism. In the long run reason would lead to the truth while racialism would lead to disaster.
>
> There is no separate salvation for Indians in Guiana, no separate salvation for Africans. There is only salvation for a united Guianese people fighting as a people against imperialism for National Independence.[32]

The resolve was beginning to crack in the Jagan-led PPP. Even the Marxist assertions were betraying a lack of conviction: catch phrases, dogmas were paraded to paper over the racial divide. Carter observed in September 1955:

> With all this burden in front of us, we tend to become pessimistic and retreat into silence. On the other hand, realising that the only profound solution is the creation of an equitable social order, we tend to repeat worn out clichés, until we ourselves stop believing in their value. Preaching is not going to help us much when all the raw causes remain. Be that as it may, however, one thing we must remember. Without racial co-operation in the face of imperialist menace, we go nowhere.[33]

Two weeks later, impelled probably by what he saw as the growing racism among some in the PPP, he remarked that fear was malleable; it could be embroidered upon, forged as an instrument to fan racial flames. Fear of the other's dominance, his capacity to bend you to his will, has the power of 'corrupting a man's mind, of twisting it into all kinds of shapes'. Fear in the arsenal of the racist in British Guiana, Carter explained, fed a perversion of hope and the liberating principles of Marxism. Inquiry, rationality, the quest for meaning, the shaping of broader loyalties by the reclaiming of history – all were neutralised by the poison of racism. Carter was very worried: 'Instead of going down to the *cause of fear, the racists accept fear and make it a cause* for antagonism… Especially since the split in February [1955], but even before then, these types have been practising their trade. Whether they occur in our Party or in any other Party, they should be dealt summarily, by expulsion on the one hand and exposure on the other'.[34]

By the end of 1955 the racial divide was hardening. A discernible uncertainty, then shoots of despair, crept into his work – the prose and the poetry. To repeat his stark admonition of September 1955: '…one of the strongest emotions that human beings experience is fear. Fear has the terrible power of corrupting a man's mind, of twisting it into all kinds of shape'. This angst spawned three poems which were published in *Kyk-Over-Al* in late 1955: 'Poems of Shape and Motion'.[35] The corrosive power of race, the death of reason and reflection pains him into self-reflection. He is 'wondering' whether he could 'shape this passion' as he pleases, 'in solid fire'; whether he could elude the slide into the racial abyss; whether 'the strength of my heart were enough'. 'Shape and Motion One' speaks of the corruption of ideals. He wonders if 'I could make myself/nothing but fire, pure and incorruptible'.

Carter is 'wondering' whether the primordial loyalties of race, 'the wound of the wind on my face', could be erased by the cause, the broader striving inspired by his politics, 'the work of my life', 'the strife of my days'. He is groping, hoping to find himself in the possibilities; that the 'space in my soul' may 'be filled by the shape I become'. Or is the racial fear too deep-seated, too cancerous ('the roots that spread out in the swamp'), to allow the seemingly untaintable, recent socialist ideals, 'the issuing flower', becoming anything but superficial, ornamental? Is the 'struggle' enough?:

> I was wondering if the agony of years
> could be traced to the seed of an hour.
> If the roots that spread out in the swamp
> ran too deep for the issuing flower.[36]

On 5 November 1955 Carter had reproduced in *Thunder* a poem, 'Shatter this Age-long Shame', by the great Indian poet, the Nobel laureate for 1913, Rabindranath Tagore (1861-1941). He noted that it 'brings home to us the unity of suffering of all people who live under "the indiscriminate feet of dictators". It is a poem that could have been written in Guiana today'. It is tempting to read the poem and Carter's motives at another level, as a declamation against Guyanese obscurantism, the creeping racial scourge:

> Lull me not into languish dreams;
> Shake me out of this cringing in the dust,
> Out of the fetters that shackle our mind,
> make futile our destiny
>
> Out of the unreason that bends our
> dignity down...

By December 1955, when 'Poems of Shape and Motion' appear, Carter disappears from the pages of *Thunder*. He and his friend, Rory Westmaas, are already disillusioned with the PPP, clearly exhausted by what they saw as the atrophy of the higher principles. Dogmas were parading as thought. He had warned, at the time of the split, that 'no one should confuse politics as a social instrument for politics as a social disease'.[37] The latter had already claimed the politics of the land, including that of the Jaganite PPP: their inoculation with Marxist dogmas could not stem the virus of racism.

Writing as a private correspondent to *Thunder* on 28 July 1956, Carter exhorted all Guyanese leaders to treat the issue of race as a matter of urgent importance, central to the survival of the country. It was not enough to be committed to political and economic reform; it was essential to become preoccupied with 'the pure problem of ensuring racial harmony'. Carter advised:

> ...let us have an inward-looking, sincere and determined effort to accomplish racial harmony, and this effort should not be made only to aid political advancement in a general way, as is usually put forward in

> arguments in favour of it, but should be carried out as a task dictated by reason and by the sheer human necessity of creating and wanting a vital community in the deepest and widest sense of the word. For without a community to inherit the triumphs and victories, the most valuable achievements of the present generation will end up like cold night wind blowing through an empty house.

By late 1955, in 'Shape and Motion Three', the despair is growing, but there is still the possibility of redemption: the two are intermingled. The bleak imagery links the poet's identity with 'limping cripples', 'houses tight with sickness', 'dream without the sleep'; he hears himself in 'the loneliness of a child', in a 'woman's grief', 'in coughing dogs' at midnight. A morose imagery permeates the poem. Each stanza, bar one, begins with the line: 'I walk slowly in the wind': this repetition is evocative of one dangling, slowly in the wind. Yet the stanza in which this line does not appear casts the longest shadow of despair:

> Cold huts of iron stand upon this earth
> like rusting prisons.
> Each wall is marked and each wide roof is spread
> like some dark wing
> casting a shadow or a living curse.[38]

A shaft of light – hope not yet extinguished – does, however, penetrate this bleak landscape of the imagination. He can still recognise himself 'in years and days and words that mean so much', in the history of human achievement. He is still able to claim the fruits of universal effort and vision: 'strong hands that shake, long roads that walk'. But the voice is becoming less certain, almost singular as it extends a twig of hope: 'a voice in the soul, a laugh in the funny silence'.

On another level this walk 'slowly in the wind' becomes an older voice, a mature, circumspect one. He concludes: 'I walk because I cannot crawl or fly'. He will not go back to the 'nigger yard' where 'I crept on my hands and my knees'; nor will he return to the illusion of the 'kind eagle', which 'soars and wheels in flight', the messenger of infinite hope: 'All of a man can fly like a bird'. The steps are now tentative, measured, laboured.

But by 1956, politics in British Guiana was becoming 'an empty house' with the loss of Carter – he never joined another political party – and his ideals of bridges across rivers of incomprehension and the perfectibility of humankind. His slide into despair and virtual silence was becoming eloquent. Ian McDonald reflects on the source of the despair: '[he] felt especially deeply, with no self-seeking fervour, the promise of that dramatic time. Thus when the degeneration of ideals and values, and the pettiness and corruption, slowly but surely overwhelmed the promise, Martin Carter's fall into disillusion, and sometimes bitterness, was bound to be deep. His style has carried the mark of this ever since'.[39]

III: The Cauldron of Race and the Crafting of Despair and Bitter Hope, 1956-62

Gordon Rohlehr has observed that life in the West Indies is 'sufficiently chastening to temper most rhetoric into reticence'. In Carter's 'Poems of Shape and Motion', he believes that 'doubt' was 'much more movingly shaped into poetry than his earlier oratorical commitment'. Rohlehr sees an inevitability in this process as 'our lives will from generation to generation be denuded slowly into grief, tiredness and silence'.[40] One is tempted to counter this, in the case of Cheddi Jagan, with the assertion that the rhetoric flowered the more the politics degenerated into aggregations of racial insecurities. Indeed, in September 1955 Carter had already cautioned that dogmas masked reality and crippled thought in the PPP.

While Carter's hopes drained away as racism grew, Cheddi Jagan, in his confidential address to the PPP Congress in New Amsterdam ('behind closed doors'), in February 1956, denounced Martin Carter and his colleagues, Rory Westmaas, Lionel Jeffrey and Keith Carter, Martin's older brother. It was not until 22 December 1956 that Jagan's speech was leaked to *The Daily Chronicle*. (Jagan was confined to Georgetown, so the speech was read to Congress). Significantly, he was silent on Carter's preoccupation with the race issue, while noting that he was one who had sought to change the Party's line on the West Indies Federation; Carter was in favour of joining. The speech was cluttered with extensive quotes from 'Comrades' Lenin, Stalin and Mao Tse-Tung. Ironically, he accused Carter and his friends of suffering from 'left deviationist tendencies', of behaving in 'a mechanistic fashion, copying wholesale revolutionary tactics and slogans of left parties' in the advanced capitalist countries. They had not bothered 'to study carefully our concrete conditions and historical state of development'. Jagan deprecated their 'indiscretions of youthful exuberance', concluding that 'this tendency to left deviationism and adventurism must be combated'.

Jagan quoted from 'Comrade' Mao to underline the damage done to the PPP by 'left dogmatists' such as Martin Carter, before the suspension of the Constitution:

> We allowed our zeal to run away with us; we became swollen-headed, pompous, bombastic... We were attacking everybody at the same time. We tended towards what Mao Tse Tung called 'all struggle and no unity'. This is how Comrade Mao Tse Tung attacks the left dogmatists who during the 10 years (1927-1937) civil war period advocated overthrowing everybody. He said: 'You cannot overthrow those in power, so you want to overthrow those who are not in power. They are already out of power, yet you still want to overthrow those who are not in power...'[41]

Whatever the manifestations of Carter's 'youthful exuberance' in the early 1950s, his 'ultra-leftism' as Jagan labels it in *The West on Trial* (1966), by 1956 he was definitely focused on the 'concrete conditions' – what he saw as the engulfing African/Indian racism, rendering the ideological certainties nugatory. Indeed, it was Jagan whose politics was becoming constipated with a surfeit of indigestible Communist Third International shibboleths – ponderous dogmas to paper over, to wish away the slide into the void of race. His zeal allowed him to virtually pose the question out of existence; the fact that the PPP was permeated by an essential Indianness could be made to seem not to be so. He could tell himself a lie and see it as truth.

But Carter did not fall for the empty words. He shut up. He was a school teacher between 1954 and 1959; he then joined the British firm, Booker, which had deep roots in sugar in British Guiana, as Chief Information Officer. It was he who was free from paralysis of thought encrusted in dogmatic certainties. He was pragmatic enough to move to a successful capitalist enterprise led by a progressive chairman, Jock Campbell (1912-1994), who from around 1950 had inspired Booker to try to sweeten the bitter legacy of sugar.

Between 1956 and 1960 Carter published no poems; no definitive piece of self-assessment or retrospective profundity came from his silent pen. The odd piece of prose, however, was reasoned: the idealism was gone; the voice was older; reflective; circumspect. In January 1958 in an article which epitomised his outlook, 'Sensibility and the Search', he argued that the Guyanese sensibility was rooted in slavery and colonialism. Only the transformation of that sensibility could deliver a new people, and that would come only if the history of slavery, of self-hate, is forged into a source of self-identity: history as midwife; the 'nigger yard' as an instrument of redemption. He elaborates:

> ... this is no easy task. It will call for the emergence of men of genius, men who by a gift of nature are able to assimilate the experience of their heritage and transform it into meaningful symbols and images, so that all of us, on looking at these symbols and images, will be looking into a mirror and seeing ourselves for the first time.[42]

The reasoned, measured tone is evident also in a response on the role of the artist in Guyana. This is from *Kyk-Over-Al*, May 1958: '...the job of the artist and intellectual in the West Indies is no different from the job of the artist and intellectual in every part of the world. We are concerned always with the human condition and the establishment of value. Everything is to be taken in the hand and transformed and given meaning'.[43]

In December 1960, possibly reflecting on his own drought of imagery but relentless in his belief that new poems could not be forced, Carter argued that the notion that young artists should be 'encouraged', was flawed: 'Too often it means that with the best intentions we praise what is third rate and omit to point out that Art requires talent – real talent, and not mere literacy – in any medium. I see no substitute for passion, internally generated, and hard work'.[44]

Carter's drought came to an end in 1961: seven poems, 'Conversation' appeared in *Kyk-Over-Al* in December. By then Guyanese politics was deeply mired in the sterility of racial one-upmanship: Jagan's PPP dominated by Indians; Burnham's PNC by Africans. Presumed ideological differences became a carnival of words, so many masks for the stasis. The elections of August 1957 were won by Jagan; Africans felt excluded from the promise. In March 1960, at the Constitutional Conference in London, the British had granted internal self-government to British Guiana, with the virtual guarantee of independence after elections to be held in August 1961. The posing of the fundamental question of the transfer of power to a Jagan government, kindled old fears of Indian domination, of the death of African political endeavour. Race was the motif of this 'nation' on the threshold of independence, but Jagan's classist rhetoric did not wilt, nor that of the party's organ, *Thunder*.

Indeed, by 1959-60 Jagan and the PPP were animated by a big cause: the Cuban Revolution with its potent symbol of a fresh communist millennium taking on American imperialism – David and Goliath. The hopes were unconquerable. But the PPP's new cause ignited their enemies' flagging hopes. America's fears could now become Burnham's also: anti-communism would be engaged to fetch the real fears of Africans, Portuguese, Coloureds, Chinese (even Amerindians), feeding the will to stall the Indian march to their political Everest. The disastrous American invasion of Cuba to overthrow Fidel Castro, at the Bay of Pigs (April 1961), lent urgency, a discernible panic, to President Kennedy's anti-communist crusade. This reached British Guiana through the American 'Crusade for Freedom', during the elections of August 1961, but the virulent anti-communism could not stem another Jagan victory.

Indian triumphalism, in their country-wide victory parade led by Jagan, deepened the pain and fear of non-Indians. By late 1961, it seemed as if the marginal demographic superiority of Indians had sealed their political control of an independent Guyana.[45] From this sterility, Martin Carter's reluctant voice speaks: 'A poet cannot write for those who ask / hardly himself even, except he lies'.[46] Liars are eloquent. As if responding to the Stalinist rhetoric of the PPP and the undammable invective of race – the death of reason and the futility of words – the poet speaks of trying to speak, of wanting to understand, but failing: 'I barked!':

Speaking with one on a pavement in the city
I watched the greedy mouth, the cunning eye
I reeled and nearly fell in frantic terror
seeing a human turn into a dog.

Recovering, I studied this illusion
and made a stupid effort to be strong:

I nodded and agreed and listened close.
But when I tried to utter words – I barked![47]

All are consumed by the nullity: the Guyanese journey to nowhere. The despair permeates 'Who can share?'[48] also. Politicians, 'loud men who cry freedom and are so full of lies', are lumped with prisoners who rot in jail and drunks who 'dance like shadows'. They are all imprisoned – the politician, poignantly, by deceit, 'so full of lies'. They all crave one thing – freedom, and seem to enjoin the poet in lamentation, 'shouting to God'; but he does not see how God can help them: 'only souls that blaze and burn can win' this freedom. Freedom has eluded all of them; a total rebirth must take place. The authentic voice of freedom is likened to 'true poems': '... we who want true poems/must all be born again, and die to do so'.[49] There could be no hope in the present charade: 'There is no short cut to integrity'.

The times cannot be rescued by words, by rhetorical power, however optimistic, possibly an allusion to his own exhausted words of hope. As Carter frames it: 'Trying with words to purify disgust'. The poet's inviolable craft cannot brighten the vacuous slide, the emptiness of language, the corruption of motives, the death of dreams:

.... it seems I was mistaken
to substitute a temple for a shop.

To see a shop and dream of holy temples
is to expect a toad to sing a song.[50]

Prophetically, at the end of 1961, Carter sees 'a sound of conflict in the sky'. He sees hope only in rebirth: 'I wish this world would sink and drown again / So that we build another Noah's ark'. The big lie is everywhere; fear stalks the land ('The frightened lizard darts behind a stone'); and time is *not* on their side ('...now is the wild assault'). Only the flood, rebirth, renewal, promise freedom: he hopes they can then 'send another little dove to find / what we have lost in floods of misery'. Ironically the poem is called 'So that we Build'[51]: like the poet's words, chiselled and refined over time, the quest for truth, for integrity, is a delicate, difficult process; it is repelled by lies.

Many years later, in 1973, reflecting on the extent to which 'the light of understanding' was put out by lies; how the man who lies to himself cannot discover truth; how lies are the only things he becomes capable of apprehending, Carter wrote:

...what a man believes is contained within the significance of what he consistently does; so that though his declarations of belief may point in one direction, the belief-meaning of his consistent activity may well point in another. While the latter may make clear what he really believes, the former may just be a habit of expression of the codification into acceptable terms of practices that are indefensible.[52]

IV: 'Jail Me Quickly': The Guyanese Futility, 1962-64

By late 1961 President Kennedy was depressed: his obsession with what he saw as the infectiousness of Castroism in Latin America, especially after the Bay of Pigs disaster, rendered Cheddi Jagan's victory in August 1961 portentous. As recently-released U.S. documents show, this obsession fell on British Guiana as well. This colony of lilliputian economic significance to America acquired enormous significance because of Jagan's communist rhetoric – the latter having been confirmed during the Kennedy-Jagan meeting on 25 October 1961, in the White House. So that although the British were prepared to take a risk and grant independence to Jagan, the Americans, after his visit, moved swiftly towards his opponents in British Guiana, L. F. S. Burnham and Peter d'Aguiar, the Portuguese leader – anti-communist alternatives.

In February 1962, Burnham and d'Aguiar launched a campaign against the Jagan Budget, ostensibly because its compulsory savings and capital gains provisions were anti-working class. Most see it now as a strategy of Jagan's enemies to bring his government down. Some see the hands of American trade unionists in the amazing unanimity and involvement of the local trade unions in this violent anti-Jagan campaign. Agitated by Burnham and d'Aguiar, the predominantly African crowds burnt down and looted many of the key businesses in Georgetown on 16 February 1962, 'Black Friday'. Buoyed by American fear of communism, Africans (and Portuguese) were now trying to make the place ungovernable in order to cripple the inclination of the British to give Jagan (Indians) independence. The racial situation had deteriorated to the point where it warrants this crude formulation.

Strangely, in the heat of the moment, Martin Carter sees in 'Black Friday 1962', the first poem in his 1964 collection[53], *Jail me Quickly*, possibilities for renewal:

> ...I was with them all,
> when the sun and streets exploded,
> and a city of clerks
> turned a city of men!
> Was a day that had to come,
> ever since the whole of a morning sky,
> glowed red like glory,
> over the tops of houses.

Carter sees the events of 'Black Friday' as cathartic, as bringing to the open issues which had been submerged by the hopes of 1953, especially race, which had stifled those hopes and fed the split of 1955. Yet, as often in his work, these shoots of optimism are intertwined with the creeping bleak vision:

And I have seen some creatures rise from holes
and claw a triumph like a citizen,
and reign until the tide!

If Carter does not see his optimism as misplaced, he does see it as transitory, 'until the tide' comes up. And in this cauldron of racial suspicion and stammered vision, lies apprehension for the tentative shoots. The clawing of the fleeting triumph quickly descends to the tomb of despair – a prologue to the hate and sterile rage in British Guiana in 1963 and 1964:

Atop the iron rooftops of this city
I see the vultures practising to wait.
And everytime and anytime,
in sleep or sudden wake, nightmare, dream,
always for me the same vision of cemeteries, slow funerals
broken tombs, and death designing all.

In British Guiana, men in despair, even the brightest, would turn to rum; often to the whorehouse, where the drinking was more important. It was not uncommon for fading men of ideas, fuelled by urgent rum, to pontificate incoherently to fellow drinkers and fallen women. Carter draws on this slide for the despair which settled on his sad country, as the potentially cleansing burnings of February 1962 degenerated into an orgy of racial slaughter: blood and mangled bodies, bloated corpses in the river, profound racial hate with its universal signature: rape. The African-Indian incomprehension, in 1963 and 1964, brought Carter to a position of utter futility, to the cemetery of his dreams:

I know this city much as well as you do,
the ways leading to brothels and those dooms
dwelling in them, as in our lives they dwell.
So jail me quickly, clang the illiterate door
if freedom writes no happier alphabet.[54]

He blames no one person, no ideology. Blame is collective: history will not absolve us. He had pointed out at the time of the February 1962 riots that they had 'deeper social and psychological undercurrents'. Like the anti-Portuguese riots of 1856 and 1889, they stemmed from the perceived rise, by Africans, of a new group in the 'direction of the masters'. The riots of 16 February 1962, in which many Indian businesses were burnt to the ground, were rooted in the perceived ascendancy of Indians, late-comers, who, to an even greater extent than the Portuguese, 'developed on the sidelines of the traditional fabric of relationships'. In 1962, virtually at the end of Empire, Africans feared that Indians would inherit the political kingdom. Carter's conclusion then has not lost its relevance to Guyana nor its urgency:

None of the groups in Guianese society is prepared to have any other group ruling it. Not until each group is confident that no other group will rule will there be real peace in this county.[55]

But, as so often in Carter's universe, despair's edge is softened by a trace of hope, a subtle possibility. One week after the riots on 16 February 1962, he could see good coming out of these events when '.... a city of clerks / turned a city of men!' The race question could be faced squarely:

> It is now that, for the first time in the history of the country, we have a chance to initiate things, and to fashion them to our purpose. And without in the least condoning the tragic events of February 16 and their unhappy consequences, it may be, after all is said and done, that what happened on that day is certainly not the worst that could have happened to us in this time and age. For now, at the very least, we know what can happen. And also that the old days are gone forever. The new days are for us to make. Are we good enough?[56]

Carter felt that 'we are witnessing the transformation of a whole society'. As noted above, in the poem 'Black Friday 1962', he is prepared for the despair; he even finds something redeeming in it:

> True, was with them all,
> and told them more than once:
> in despair there is hope, but there is none in death.[57]

Out of the events of 1962 Carter envisaged some compromise – a halt to the slide into the racial morass. This did not happen. By 1963-64, as racial atrocity cascaded upon racial atrocity, his 1962 imagery of 'vultures practising to wait' could well be seen as the central note of his imagination in *Jail me Quickly*: the harvest of the stench. The shoots of hope have wilted in one short year. In 'After One Year' he is resigned to the racial futility of Guyana: 'Men murder men, as men must murder men / to build their shining governments of the damned'.

Carter recalls: 'I had become convinced that this country would not get anywhere because of the racial division'.[58] Imageries of futility permeate the 1964 poems: '... squandered daylight mocks my deep remorse / for seeds that rot, for interrupted love / and hours spent digging hopes out of a grave'. This is a land of 'sharp entanglements' (racism and the ubiquitous barbed wires, in 1964); 'angry streets'; 'frightened stars'; 'bleeding houses'. The whole of the country's being speaks of this futility. The poems ask: 'What can a Man do More?', 'Where are Free Men?'. The poet is asking: 'What is the point of the effort?':

> How utter truth when falsehood is the truth?
> How welcome dreams, how flee the newest lie?[59]

The dream is greater than the effort: 'where are free men?'. In dreams only:

> And what in dreams we do in life we attempt.
> But where are free men, where the endless streets?

> Since we were born our wings have had no rest
> Our prison of air is worse than one of iron![60]

The rage; the declamation; the sometimes arrogant, assertive hope; the circumspect, tentative, even fleeting optimism; the eloquent despair interlaced with shoots of optimism; the cynical, seemingly resigned, but magisterial insights: the 'mouth is always muzzled by the food it eats to live' and 'the shame is greater than the victory'; the futility; the eloquent silences; his repellence by mediocrity and passion for mastery of his craft – they are all of a piece. He could not be diminished by the acquired labels: 'left deviationist', 'ultra-leftist adventurer', 'leftist dogmatist'. Carter's silence spoke more of the diminished quality of the politics and the 'mechanistic fashion' of he who did the labelling. Writing in January 1958, on 'the meaning of writing and reading... to the human condition', the voice from the drought asks his readers to ponder the words of Salzberger:

> Genius, the agent of the dialectical process of history, has to transgress against the laws of moderation which govern the lives of ordinary men, in order to bring to a crisis the conflicts of his age and restore a healthy equilibrium.[61]

The title of Carter's article was 'Sensibility and the Search'. This quote, therefore, may well contain the definitive motive of his art; his politics also: to provoke to reason and reasonableness.

But one tends to forget that sobriety has a place in Carter's passion. As the Chief Information Officer of Jock Campbell's reforming Booker, a redeeming chapter in the dark record of sugar, in some way he helped to make life better for plantation workers. The bitterness of sugar had inspired the art. Campbell was inspired by Carter's poetry of the early 1950s; it must have illuminated his reforming spirit. Now the poet himself was helping to sweeten the bitterness of sugar in the land he has called 'materialistic and philistine'. The pragmatism of his life and the despair of the art, also, are of a piece.

In January 1965 he became editor of *Booker News* and in an editorial soon after, 'On being a Guianese', he commended to his countrymen the response on the subject of one of his compatriots, E. R. Braithwaite, author of *To Sir with Love*. Carter writes:

> ...Mr. Braithwaite reported a conversation he had in Trinidad with a Guianese resident there. After chatting a few minutes he was asked which side he would be on when he returned to B. G. His reply was that he would belong to the side of British Guianese who were concerned first and foremost with the unity of all Guianese. Mr. Braithwaite's reply, in the context of the recent unfortunate years, should be pondered deeply by all who live in Guiana and identify themselves with Guiana.[62]

At the bottom of his art this is what one finds: the dream to make his country a 'nation' – where truth and standards do matter. Instead he has become 'so weary with time' – always trying to 'flee the newest lie'.

The final word on Martin Carter must go to his friend since the early 1960s, David de Caires. Here is his assessment:

> Martin Carter is a large man in every sense of that word. With his strong, brooding presence and his eternal bitter hope he has always represented for many of us a challenge to keep going and to do what we can and a proof of the enormous potential and possibilities in our Caribbean region. His bitterness and despair have been a measure of his hope. In his various undertakings, his trials and tribulations, his long depression he has retained a quality of spiritual integrity without which we would all have been much poorer.[63]

That is why this gifted, paradoxical man's work can transcend the politics, the time, the place, the people: the imagery is not strained; the statements are universal; the craft has been laboured at and refined; the effort springs from integrity.

Notes

1. The *New Daily Chronicle*, 3 July 1927.
2. Edgar Mittelholzer, *A Swarthy Boy* (London: Putnam, 1963), pp. 155-56.
3. Ian McDonald, 'Foreword', *Martin Carter Selected Poems* ([Georgetown]: Red Thread Women's Press, 1997, revised edition), p. 22. Beyond here all references to this book are rendered thus: *Selected Poems*.
4. In 1989 Carter observed: '...when slavery was abolished in 1834 the greatest impact on the population in the sense of language was from the Bible because of the missionaries... So you would find in [the] speech of places like Guyana a tremendous influence of the patterns and vocabulary of the Old and New Testament and I must say of course that one could hardly find a better form to learn from', *Kyk-Over-Al*, No. 44, (May 1993) ['A Martin Carter Prose Sampler', Nigel Westmaas (ed.)], p.144. Throughout this essay I have relied heavily on this excellent collection.
5. *The Times* [London], 20 August 1962. See also the issue of 16 August 1962 (Obituary).
6. See note 3.
7. A. J. Seymour, 'The Biography of a Magazine', *Kyk-Over-Al*, Nos. 46/47, (December 1995), p. 18.
8. *PAC Bulletin*, No. 1, (6 November 1946).
9. Maurice St. Pierre, *Anatomy of Resistance: Anti-Colonialism in Guyana, 1823-1966* (London: Macmillan Caribbean, 1999)
10. Cheddi Jagan, *The West on Trial: My Fight for Guyana's Freedom* (London: Michael Joseph, 1966), p. 95.
11. See note 9.
12. Frank Birbalsingh, 'Interview with Martin Carter', *Kyk-Over-Al*, Nos. 46/47, (December 1995), p. 218.

13. *Selected Poems*, p. 39.
14. *PAC Bulletin*, No. 27, 20 June 1948: 'At 3pm [on 17 June] the procession reached the cemetery. Here the human factor broke loose from its temporary prison and just stared you in the face and tore at your heart. Relatives and widows cried and wailed... on May 7 the Central Demerara representative in the Legislative Council [Cheddi Jagan] tabled a notion asking for the appointment of a Committee to enquire into the dispute, the working and living conditions and into the profits of the Proprietors. Repeated attempts were made to get the Labour Dept. and the Govt. to intervene. The Labour Commission, however, in Olympian aloofness refused to admit that there was a strike...' (Eusi Kwayana [Sydney King] told me that he wrote this article.)
15. *Selected Poems*, p. 36.
16. See 'Not I with this Torn Shirt', *Selected Poems*, p. 33.
17. *Ibid*. See also 'Three Years After This' (Enmore), *Selected Poems*, p. 38.
18. 'Listening to the Land', *Selected Poems*, p. 42.
19. 'A Banner for the Revolution', *Selected Poems*, p. 43.
20. 'I Stretch my Hand', *Selected Poems*, p. 49.
21. *Selected Poems*, p. 64.
22. 'The Kind Eagle, *Selected Poems*, p. 63.
23. Rupert Roopnaraine, 'Martin Carter and Politics', *Sunday Stabroek* [Guyana], 8 June 1997. For a broader reading of Carter's poetry, beyond the politics, as reflected in one poem, 'You are Involved', see Roopnaraine, *Web of October: Rereading Martin Carter* (Leeds: Peepal Tree Press, 1988).
24. *Selected Poems*, pp. 96-98.
25. *Report of the British Guiana Constitutional Commission, 1954* (Sir James Robertson, chairman), Cmd. 9274 (London: HMSO, 1954), p. 36.
26. St. Pierre, *op. cit.*
27. 'This is the Dark Time my Love', *Selected Poems*, p. 94.
28. 'I am no Soldier', *Selected Poems*, p. 80. The other reference to Accabreh is in 'I Clench my Fist' (p. 95):

    British soldier, man in khaki
    careful how you walk.
    My dead ancestor Accabreh
    is groaning in his grave.
    At night he wakes and watches
    with fire in his eyes
    Because you march upon his breast
    and stamp upon his heart.

29. Leader, *Thunder*, 28 August 1954 (*Kyk-Over-Al*, No. 44, p. 46).
30. Rory Westmaas, 'The People against Imperialism', *Thunder*, 8 May 1954.
31. Carter, 'Politics and the Individual', *Thunder*, 12 February 1955 (*Kyk-Over-Al*, No. 44, p. 48).
32. Leader, *Thunder*, 5 March 1955 (*Ibid.*, p. 51).
33. Leader, *Thunder*, 10 September 1955 (*Ibid.*, p. 69).
34. Martin Carter, 'The Racists among Us', *Thunder*, 24 September, 1955.
35. See *Selected Poems*, pp. 103-106.

36. 'Shape and Motion One', *Selected Poems*, p. 103.
37. See note 31. This quote is from p. 49.
38 'Shape and Motion Three', *Selected Poems*, p. 105.
39. See note 3. The quote is from p. 24.
40. F. G. Rohlehr, 'West Indian Poetry: Some Problems of Assessment (Part Two)', *Bim*, No. 55 (July-December 1972), p. 144.
41. Jagan confirmed that the PPP was a communist-led party, as the British and the Robertson Commission had argued:

    Our party is unique in the history of national movements: from its very inception it as under left-wing, Marxist-inspired leadership, uncompromisingly championing the cause of the working class. The right wing, representing the middle and professional class and native capitalists, was in the distinct minority (*The Daily Chronicle*, 22 December 1956).
42. Carter, 'Sensibility and the Search', *The Daily Argosy*, 26 January 1958 (*Kyk-Over-Al*, No. 44), p. 80.
43. *Kyk-Over-Al*, No. 23, (May 1958), p. 20.
44. *Kyk-Over-Al*, No. 27, (December 1960), p. 106.
45. See the following for politics in British Guiana in the late 1950s-early 1960s: Jagan, *op. cit.* [1966]; Peter Simms, *Trouble in Guyana* (London: George Allen and Unwin, 1966); Thomas J. Spinner, *A Political and Social History of Guyana, 1945-83* (Boulder, Colorado: Westview Press, 1984); Maurice St. Pierre, *op. cit.* The latter is the most comprehensive on the role of the Americans.
46. 'They say I am', *Selected Poems*, p. 109.
47. 'Groaning in this Wilderness', *Ibid.*, p. 110.
48. *Ibid.*, p. 111.
49. See note 46.
50. *Selected Poems*, p. 112.
51. *Ibid.*, p. 113.
52. Martin Carter, 'If a Man Lies to Himself, the World will Lie to Him!' (April 1973), *Kyk-Over-Al*, No. 44, p. 84.
53. 'Black Friday 1962', *Selected Poems*, pp. 117-118.
54. 'After One Year', *Ibid.*, p. 119.
55. Martin Carter, 'Recent Events Spring from Social Undercurrents', *The Daily Chronicle*, 23 March 1962 (*Kyk-Over-Al*, No. 44, p. 83).
56. *Ibid.*
57. See note 53. The quote is from p. 118.
58. See note 12. The quote is from p. 223.
59. 'What Can a Man Do More?', *Selected Poems*, p. 120.
60. 'Where are Free Men?', *Ibid.*, p. 121.
61. See note 42.
62. *Booker News*, 5 March 1965.
63. David de Caires, 'A Measure of his Hope', in *All Are Involved: The Art of Martin Carter*, Ed. Stewart Brown (Leeds: Peepal Tree Press, 2000), p. 305.

BALRAM SINGH RAI'S ANTI-COMMUNISM AND CULTURAL IDEALISM

> Jagan survives because he has racial support; he survives on racism, in the same way Burnham survived on racism. Burnham did not survive because of his intelligence... neither does Jagan. They are racist leaders. Jagan owes none of his political longevity to Marxism...
>
> – Dr. Fenton Ramsahoye [interview], London, 25 July 1992.

> In the course of a recent discussion [ca. 1993] between Dr. Jagan and the author [Sallahuddin], the PPP leader, in offering...insights on the factors that sustained the PPP's high political profile during the 1964-92 period, outlined what he described as a process of 'scientific foresight' accompanied by 'appropriate modes of struggle', which the PPP embraced and pursued over the years. In his view 'scientific foresight' involved very thorough and 'concrete analyses' including 'class analysis' of both the domestic and global environment in order to determine 'how the world will develop', then on the basis of the conclusions of such analyses, programmes appropriate to the requirements of the situation 'were formulated and proposed as alternatives to the pro-imperialist policies of the PNC Government'.
>
> – Sallahuddin, *Guyana: The Struggle for Liberation, 1945-1992* (Georgetown: The Author, 1994), pp. 310-11

Dr. Baytoram Ramharack, like the subject of his biography, is a cultural idealist. Over the years, in Guyana and in New York City, he has kept his faith in a reformist Hinduism that is egalitarian and stridently austere in its rituals. It has shaped his resolve for the making of a new political culture in Guyana, which he sees as mired in political and racial obscurantism. Like Balram Singh Rai (born 1921), whom Dr. Ramharack clearly admires, he makes no apology for his commitment to the political cause of the Indo-Guyanese. But it is an endeavour that recognises the multiracial reality of Guyana and the tendency of both African and Indian politicians to pretend that a class-based politics can eradicate deep-seated ethnic insecurity and chronic mutual suspicion, however contrary the evidence. Like Rai, Dr Ramharack starts from the ineluctable fact of Guyana's Indian and African identities, with discrete cultural underpinnings, hardened by generations of scramble for the political spoils and puny economic harvests, in a capricious natural environment.

This depressed land, no El Dorado, cannot afford any more messianic ideological flourishes – grandiose ideas that have led Guyanese on a journey to nowhere. The time demands the shaping of the nuts and bolts of a *modus vivendi*.

A resurgent political culture, therefore, must be animated by a resolve to lessen racial insecurity while establishing a political framework that empowers both major groups. Winner cannot take all in Guyana's electoral exercises, however free and fair and free from fear they may be, for they are essentially racial censuses. A constitution framed consciously to erode the pervasive sentiment of political exclusion harboured by Africans, must be accompanied by the resolute pursuit of an imaginative educational programme that promotes African and Indian cultural security at all levels of society.

In numerous letters to the *Stabroek News*, over the last decade, and in several academic articles, Dr. Ramharack has pursued the elusive goal of shaping a more tolerant political culture in Guyana. In this study of the maverick Indo-Guyanese political leader of the 1950s-60s, Balram Singh Rai, the popular minister expelled from the People's Progressive Party (PPP) by Cheddi Jagan in June 1962, he has explored a life that embodies the hopes and tragedies of the Guyanese political experiment. It is to his credit that he has drawn from this remarkable, if sad, life some crucial lessons for the massive task of building confidence across the racial chasm. If I am correct, he sees Rai's legacy thus: no ideological purity, however zealously pursued, will erase racial insecurity with its potential for violence and instability. Only the cultivation of existing cultural diversity, along with constitutional guarantees of inclusiveness for Africans and Indians, will engender long-term prosperity and a sense of nationhood. As Rai wrote in the foreword to his Justice Party manifesto of October 1964, the recent manifestations of Guyanese racial savagery demanded that the multiracial and multicultural character of the country be recognised as paramount. To deny that diversity – and the absence of a sense of nationhood – would be to bottle up potentially fatal antipathy. He was deeply pained by the escalating racial violence, between 1962 and 1964:

> I have watched with increasing sadness and agony the disastrous events which have befallen our country and our people, more especially the working-class people – of all races. I have witnessed assaults, woundings, death and destruction, helpless to avert such incidents or to stem the swelling tide. I have seen the life's efforts and saving of whole families go up in flames, the hurried dismantling of houses and their attempted re-erection in mud and water; hundreds of people hauled before the Courts, thousands of peaceful, innocent people rendered homeless and made refugees in their own homeland. I have seen people with their few, humble belongings fleeing for their lives and their children's lives and I have attended the cremation and burial of many of our unfortunate

Balram Singh Rai (born 1921): between 1959 and 1962 a minister in Cheddi Jagan's government; founded the Justice Party in 1964.

Rai in Jagan's cabinet, 1961: (left to right): C.V. Nunes, Ranji Chandisingh, Fenton Ramsahoye, Brindley Benn, Cheddi Jagan, Governor Sir Ralph Grey, Ram Karran, Balram Singh Rai, E.M.G. Wilson, C.R. Jacob, H.J.M. Hubbard, George Bowman, Laurence Mann

> ones. On a personal note, I have had to remove my aged father from the home and village [Beterverwagting, East Coast Demerara] in which I was born 43 years ago, and his home is now deserted and abandoned... It is clear that Dr. Jagan and the PPP have made too many costly and major mistakes and have failed in both their domestic and foreign policies.[1]

Rai repudiated Jagan's belief that an ideological struggle guided by a narrowly economist version of Marxism could eradicate 'false consciousness', such as self-definition on the basis of race. He also rejected the kind of Marxism followed by Cheddi Jagan as a supposedly infallible guide to economic development. Although Rai was deeply involved (along with Eusi Kwayana [Sydney King]) in Jagan's first legislative campaign in 1947, he unsuccessfully contested the 1953 elections for the anti-communist National Democratic Party. Indeed, Rai remained opposed to Jagan's communism even when he became a minister in his government, between 1959 and 1962. Dr. Ramharack cites the remarkable case of Jagan's obduracy in the face of a potentially path-breaking deal between Booker and his Government that could have established a benchmark for partnership with foreign capital, while bringing him invaluable political capital at a crucial time. But Rai's moderate counsel could not mollify Jagan's prejudices against private capital:

> Sir Jock Campbell, Chairman of Booker... had met with Jagan, Rai and Benn at a dinner during the 1960 Constitutional Conference... at the Travellers Club in London... While he was opposed to Jagan's extensive nationalisation plan, Campbell made an informal offer to Jagan in which he agreed to make over 49% or 51% of the sugar estates to the government, to be paid out of profits in ensuing years. Rai urged Jagan to consider the plan because he felt it was a good deal rather than pursuing his nationalisation scheme. Jagan, however, refused to consider the plan, and he left at the end of the Conference for Cuba... Jagan's refusal to consider the Campbell offer regarding the sugar industry, despite Rai's urgings, was no doubt clouded by his Marxist ideology... [Yet] Jagan quoted Campbell in a letter he wrote to President Kennedy on 16 April 1963, in an attempt to convince him that there was 'no danger of a Communist dictatorship being established in British Guiana'... [But] Jagan, the Marxist, would not support anything less than total nationalisation, and he saw his plan falling into place when the PNC nationalised the entire sugar industry.

Dr. Fenton Ramsahoye, Jagan's Attorney General between 1961 and 1964, corroborates this, arguing that Cheddi could see nothing redeeming in Campbell's reformist capitalism:

> Cheddi felt that sugar was an exploitative industry in which the planters were making colossal profits. That, in fact, was not the case, and if he had nationalised sugar he would have realised that the profit margins were not that large; that there was a lot of risk involved – that you also needed guaranteed prices which depended upon the goodwill of the politicians in Europe for preferential agreements... Campbell's reforms would not have impressed Cheddi because he felt that they were hiding

> colossal profits, whereas they were not. They were not making such profits but he felt that these reforms were a gift out of excessive profits. But that was never the economic truth... Cheddi had a blind faith in the belief that society is the result of the exploitation of the working class by the capitalist class. It is a very poor analysis. He was a man of faith – Marxism was like a religion.[2]

Dr. Ramsahoye elaborated on why Jagan (Burnham, too) had no patience with private enterprise, why he could not co-operate even with enlightened capitalists:

> He had a misunderstanding of how wealth and employment were created. He felt that the best opportunities for the realisation of these were through a Marxist approach to development. That had been the essence of socialist propaganda from the time of the Bolshevik Revolution. He believed in that propaganda... That was a fundamental flaw in his political thinking... that managerial skills and risk-taking were irrelevant, that state ownership would achieve everything; entrepreneurial skills were not necessary... In other Caribbean countries there was not that extensive hostility to private property, as under Jagan and Burnham... Guyana's two main leaders had a basic antipathy to private enterprise – the private creation of wealth and employment. Those other countries retained their businessmen, bankers, entrepreneurs [after Independence]: people with skills. That set the others apart from Guyana.[3]

As late as the early 1980s, Cheddi Jagan was still railing against the 'tactic of partnership' devised by the 'imperialists'. He argued: 'This policy was also implemented in the Caribbean and Latin America. In pursuit of its objective of maintaining the dependency status of these territories through penetration as distinct from domination, imperialism has resorted to incorporate nationals and even governments as share-holding partners, even to the extent of 51% ownership. This new manoeuvre of joint venture was aimed at creating a wider social base for capitalism-imperialism for the defence of foreign rather than national interest'.[4] The faith was unfaltering and Burnham was exploiting this to the hilt.

But Rai never had any time for Jagan's panacea, his Marxist creed. Indeed, in 1964, in his Justice Party manifesto, his rejection of communism and belief in private enterprise, including joint ventures with foreign and local capital, were clearly enunciated:

> The Justice Party advocates the establishment of a WELFARE STATE – a state in which 'the poor are protected and the strong are just'. It is irrevocably opposed to Communism. It is opposed to State control of all economic activity. It is opposed to the ownership by the State of all means of production, distribution and exchange. It is opposed to the confiscation and expropriation of private property – local or foreign. On the contrary, it will encourage and guarantee the ownership of private property, but it will promote welfare schemes and welfare legislation to promote and safeguard the welfare of workers. The Party is of the view that underdeveloped countries can be most quickly and effectively developed

by private enterprise, both local and foreign, acting under the supervision of and in participation with the Government.

Dr. Ramharack's study illuminates the shaping of Rai's politics, as it does the contrasting forces that made Cheddi Jagan's Marxism. He observes that Rai was a devout Hindu, an Arya Samajist, the reformist Hindu sect based on the teachings of Swami Dayananda (1824-83), the 19th century Gujarati nationalist who sought to cleanse Hinduism of some of its more grotesque excrescences – *sati* or the immolation of widows, caste prejudice, ritual excesses, child marriages, prohibition against widow remarriage (including child widows), sacerdotal monopoly by Brahmins. The bedrock of his reform mission was the reclamation of textual authenticity: a return to the source, the *Vedas.* By rejecting Brahminism, so crucial to Caribbean Hinduism, the Arya Samaj had kindled a subversive spirit among some Indians in the region. It is arguable, therefore, that the germ of Rai's opposition to Jagan's Marxism and his monopoly of Indian leadership stemmed from his immersion in the Arya Samajist creed that was inclined to see Cheddi's politics, though reformist, as Brahminical in its dogmas and inflexibility. It was imprisoned by a received creed. Rai articulated the source of his own politics thus:

> [I]t is my firm conviction that there can be no good government until statesmen and kings are imbued with religion and philosophy... Swami Dayananda's contribution to Indian nationalism, to social regeneration, to religion and to philosophy is immense... Future generations will be grateful to him for the reforms he effected and the attitudes he inculcated. Before his birth in the year 1824... there were many abuses in Hindu society... child marriages, prohibition against remarriage of widows, even child widows, suttee [sati], the inferior position of women in society, image worship, discrimination based on ancestral origin (caste distinctions) and untouchability, spurious scriptures and false interpretations of the scriptures. All this and more the Swami set himself to reform and when his soul departed his body in October 1883... he had boldly tackled these problems and had offered working solutions to them all... He was able to point out that in ancient India women had an honoured position in society equal to that of men, that the *Vedas* did not authorise the practice of idolatry or belief in more than one Deity, that all souls were alike deriving their just position in life not upon any heredity caste system or upon predestination...that child marriages were a social evil having no sanction in the *Vedas*...[5]

So Rai's politics was inspired by this reformist trajectory in his religious provenance, of which he was immensely proud. Therein could be located the fundamental divergence in outlook between Rai and Jagan: the former had a powerful sense of his own internal reverences, the source of his self-belief. Jagan, however, in spite of his orthodox Sanatanist Hindu background, lacked any sense of his Indian antecedence, ritual or secular. He was naked, bereft of similar cultural moorings, thus perilously amenable to external suasion, vulnerable to so-called scientific ideologies. A man without a foundation of cultural autonomy, he became tethered to exogenous sources of comprehension: fatally inflexible, starved of any wellspring of the imagination. Cut off from any substantive Indian sustaining vision and its richly nuanced philosophical tradition, Jagan, paradoxically, was the quintessential true believer: he had no need to revise his thinking; he had arrived at 'total understanding' through Marxism. He would invest its main apostles, Nikita Khrushchev and Fidel Castro, with virtually messianic powers of redemption. Fidel, he said in 1960, was 'not only the liberator of the American continent but also the liberator of this century'. This did not please the Americans who, in the context of the Cold War, kept pace with every word he uttered.[6]

Cheddi could see no merit whatsoever in Africans and Indians yearning for ancestral validity, no merit in their continual pursuit of intimations of ancient ethnic greatness: the quest for imagined homelands that shapes identities. He was in a hurry to erase such supposedly spurious representations of self, evangelical in his impatience with backward manifestations of cultural and ethnic aggregation. The world had been made simpler by his received Marxist creed, answering to the immutable logic of the class struggle that would soon eclipse the false promptings of religion, ethnic foundations of culture and other flawed, eclectic premises of identity formation.

Rai's religious grounding, his cultural security as an Indian and his upbringing in a predominantly African village, made him more amenable to the complexity of ethnic representation as well as its resilience to ideological assaults. He recognised the potential richness of cultural hybridity, if handled sensitively, in shaping the Guyanese imagination. Dr. Ramharack observes:

> The fact that Rai grew up in a 'mixed' village made him aware, from an early age, of the ethnic and cultural boundaries that existed among the various ethnic communities... This early experience led Rai to become acutely conscious of the cultural differences that existed between Indians and Africans, and it was this exposure to the African community that made him more conscious about himself as an Indian. The fact that he was more exposed to other ethnic groups, and grew up with Africans in a mixed village, meant that he was comfortable with his identity as an Indian, and he understood that there were differences between himself and members of other ethnic communities. As such, he did not feel uncomfortable among Africans and had no compulsion 'to prove' his acceptance of other communities. In other words, *Rai was not uneasy about expressing himself as an Indian and felt that Indians had a right to be proud of their heritage, while Africans had a right, too, to be proud of their own history and culture* [emphasis added].

Cheddi Jagan was devoid of such cultural security and lacked Rai's broader grounding that would have helped him to empathise with his

African compatriots. His received Marxist baggage, therefore, was seductive precisely because it filled the void; it enabled him to paper over that deficiency by defining the ethnic problem out of existence as 'epiphenomenal'. Dr. Ramharack adds:

> In contrast, because Jagan grew up in the all-Indian Plantation Port Mourant, the lack of exposure to members of other communities had a different effect on him socially, politically and ideologically. *Jagan was uncomfortable among Africans and his history of political involvement demonstrated that he did not fully understand the African psyche.* This was often painfully obvious during his political career. He was apt to make statements that were sometimes superficial and offensive to Africans, and he found it difficult to assert himself as an Indian [emphasis added].

It can be argued that Jagan's cultural insecurity, the amorphous Indianness, made him exaggerate the class motive in his analysis of Guyanese society; it also fused him into dogmatic, formulaic political attitudes. He lacked empathy, as his former comrade from the early years, Eusi Kwayana, explained for V.S. Naipaul:

> I think he had a cultural problem. If he had been a devout Hindu, even in his youth, he would have had a more workable, a more human, frame of reference. But, having rejected imperialism and all its works along with its culture [the Western intellectual tradition], he got attached to another metropolis which was the Soviet Union. He understood it as it presented itself. So everything he did had to be explained, in his own mind, in the culture of that other metropolis. Once he could do that he felt vindicated.[7]

As I have recounted in more detail in the chapter, 'Anatomy of Cheddi Jagan's Marxism', there is the revealing moment when Cheddi told V.S. Naipaul how the Marxist primers Janet had brought for him from America, nearly 50 years before, had given him instant illumination: 'a total understanding of the world'. There was consequently no need to think things through; no need for the intellectual rigour of revisions, hard assessments, diplomacy: cultural, ethnic and myriad other complexities were temporary aberrations. There was no problem which the inevitable communist society could not resolve – and time was on his side. If internal reverences were lacking, the passion was inexhaustible. Everything worth knowing was now known. He had arrived at scientific truths: the religious and cultural void was filled. The passion could be sustained. Nearly thirty years later, in 1974 – and already 10 years in the political wilderness – he was still enthralled by those truths. In his address to the 18th Congress of the PPP, Cheddi alluded to the superiority of his pure communist faith over Burnham's bogus 'eclectic' brand. In a paradoxically Brahminic way, he was asserting his monopoly on the real stuff:

> The PPP's socialism [is] based on the science of Marxism-Leninism... Practical political work will succeed only when based on *correct theories and ideas* – the ideology of Marxism-Leninism... We must fight for *scientific truths*... Long live the International Communist movement... Marxism-Leninism is a scientific ideology. It will endure. Our party too will endure provided we set our course on this scientific ideology [emphasis added].[9]

Rai, however, was acutely aware of the importance of culture and history in the shaping of people's identities; the eclectic strands and enduring peculiarities could not be wished away by ideological fervour. Moreover, he was appalled by Jagan's hypocrisy of preaching Marxism and the class struggle, while being immersed in a political culture that exploited Indian religious susceptibilities and group insecurities, even violence, in order to sustain his monopoly of Indian votes. It is instructive, therefore, for me to reflect on my boyhood recollection of Rai, how he was perceived in my Indian village, less than 12 miles from Jagan's birthplace in Berbice, Plantation Port Mourant. From 1957 until his expulsion from Jagan's PPP in 1962, he was an icon: young, handsome, fair-skinned (a great asset among Indians of all shades), elegantly dressed, articulate, brilliant, fearless and confident – a 'true Kshatriya', a statesman. The fact that he was not a Marxist like our hero, Cheddi, was immaterial (very few Indians were Marxists anyway). The fact that he was an Arya Samajist, not a Sanatanist like most Hindus in Guyana, was also largely ignored. He was a Hindu and, unlike Jagan, he was devout. This did not go unnoticed in our community; neither was the common view that many Africans respected his integrity. After Jagan, Rai was certainly the most popular Indian leader in the colony. However, we would brook no challenge – from anyone – to Cheddi's leadership, however flawed. Any Indian who dared to do so, in the 1950s-60s and beyond, was a traitor to the Indian cause, instantly excommunicable to the universe of the Chamar, virtually an outcaste – untouchable. As I have suggested in other essays, it can be argued that an unconscious undercurrent of residual caste instincts still lingers among Indo-Guyanese.

So, as soon as Rai impugned Cheddi and Janet Jagan's role in the rigged internal party election, in April 1962, engineered against him ('the foulest ever', in his words), to secure the re-election of Brindley Benn, an African, to the chairmanship on the PPP, he was doomed. Jagan persisted with his anti-Booker, anti-sugar crusade to sustain the 'socialist' image and the fiction of a multiracial PPP. But, surreptitiously, at the 'bottom-house' level, in Indian villages and on the plantations, his party activists heaped opprobrium on any Indian who dared to challenge the infallibility of the leader, represented, ironically, in Hindu imagery as a virtual incarnation of Lord Rama. This was a supposedly Marxist party that garnered every crumb that spilled off the Hindu's table in a cynical exploitation of religion and race. In fact, projections of the PPP's multiracialism, dramatised by the election rigged in favour of Benn against Rai, were bogus. Meanwhile, by

1963, Jagan's pro-Castro sympathies and tactless entry into the Cold War, against the Americans, had driven President Kennedy and the British to conspire to remove him from office, by changing the electoral system to Proportional Representation (PR). Yet the Indians did not turn against him. The fear and paranoia engendered by possible African political ascendancy – privately constructed in terms of the potential savagery of *rakshas* – black violence and sexual assault on Indian women – ensured that Muslim, Christian and Hindu Indians, including Rai's Arya Samajists, would not dare to vote for anyone but Jagan. Indeed, the fact that PR now endowed each vote with unprecedented weight meant that any deviation from loyalty to Jagan, by any Indian, was deemed a betrayal of the race.

I can still recall the ferocity of the demonisation of Balram Singh Rai in 1964 by many of his erstwhile Indian admirers in the East Canje district, where I grew up. We were not allowed to see any merit in his argument. The PPP must win the elections; Rai had no right to challenge the great leader. He had deserted the race; he was on the side of the *rakshas*, the blacks – Rawan's people, the enemy of Lord Rama, the noble ruler, the source of all light. Only in recent years, however, have I started to explore those defamatory images which were daily dumped on Rai – a religious iconography, animated by scorn for the traitor, was skilfully manipulated by the 'Marxist' PPP.[10] His Justice Party was dubbed the 'Jackass Party', and often he would turn up at his scheduled meetings to find several donkeys tethered on the spot. Those who thought about going to his meetings were often warned not to. His candidates and their families were constantly subject to physical and psychological harassment: virtual excommunication from the Hindu fold. They were relegated to the level of the outcaste. Indeed, more venom was reserved for Rai, the Indian 'traitor', than for the powerful enemies of Jagan, who had made the country ungovernable since 1962, Forbes Burnham and Peter d'Aguiar.

An uncle of mine, who had decorated the entrance to his yard, during the 1964 elections, with glowing, triumphal images of Jagan, including a massive red cup, the Party's symbol, inscribed boldly on the public road, in front of his house: 'Death to No. 13', an unmistakable reference to an Indian leader from our village, Partab Singh, who was thirteenth on Rai's party list. Ironically, Jagan's people, having exploited Indian racial idioms to the hilt, now deemed Balram Singh Rai a racist: all his candidates were Indian. When the results were declared Rai's Justice Party polled only 1,334 votes in the whole of Guyana, only marginally better than the Muslim Party's 1,194 votes. Rai failed to win a seat. The PPP polled 109,332. A pattern was already set: for the next 28 years as Jagan and his party became firmly locked into the arid pro-communist sphere of the Soviet Union and its satellites – 'a kind of homecoming', he dubbed his declaration of loyalty – the Burnhamite dictatorship exploited his moribund politics, rigging one election after another and destroying all vestiges of democracy, while America and the democratic Caribbean remained silent. Yet Indians still brooked no challenge to Jagan from any Indian. Whole villages fled into exile, to New York and Toronto, in despair of his sterile leadership, but Cheddi Jagan remained inviolable.

Rai himself went into voluntary exile in 1970, to England, where he has lived ever since, a recluse, damaged by his demonisation by the Indian people of Guyana. Dr. Ramharack, in the course of his research for this book, sought over several years to prise him away from this fatal internalisation of the massive rejection of 1964. No use. Although he was fully aware of the scholar's empathy, he very reluctantly agreed to allow Dr. Ramharack to visit him, briefly, a couple of times in the course of a week in London. But the admirable resolve and humility of the researcher could not persuade Rai to allow him to tape their conversation. He could only take brief notes, but Rai did give him copies of some of his papers. The man was obviously deeply wounded by his encounter with the Indian juggernaut – Jaganism. It can be argued that Rai's political instincts were flawed, and that he also lacked the necessary iron will for the big, long fight. It was suicidal for him to take Jagan on in 1964, for although he sought to gain only a few seats that would have facilitated his bargaining with Burnham and d'Aguiar for a place in an inevitable coalition, he was bound to be seen by Indians as undermining their security. Rai argued that even if all the Indians in Guyana voted for Jagan, he could not get a majority; and he was absolutely certain that Burnham and d'Aguiar did not want Jagan in a coalition government which they intended to form. He, therefore, saw himself as offering a lifeline to Indians to avoid political annihilation. This did not wash.

In 1964, in spite of the electoral hazards inherent in the imposed Proportional Representation system, most Indians still deluded themselves that the PPP would get a majority, however slim, that would enable them to form a government on their own. So Rai's prognosis, though in reality solid, was necessarily interpreted as detrimental to the garnering of every Indian vote Jagan needed for the majority deemed imperative for the security of the race. Many have argued since that had Rai bided his time, and as the PPP slid into virtual obsolescence under an increasingly dictatorial Burnham regime receiving 'critical support' from them, the point might have been reached in the early 1980s when Rai could have mounted a vigorous, popular challenge to Cheddi. It is my own conviction that there was substantial resurgent support for him, or the idea of him, among Indians, during the worse years of Burnhamism, in the early 1980s. By then, however, Rai had long decamped to despair and anonymity in London. Some contend that there must be a serious flaw in Rai's personality, for he was never able to recover from the political debacle of 1964 and the psychological assassination inflicted upon him by Jaganism and some of its ruthless Indian disciples. It is a shortcoming of this admirable work that the flaws in Rai's own political judgement and his personality are not explored adequately. However, it is necessary to record that he was not seduced by the carrots Burnham dangled before him, between 1965 and 1970, when he practised as a lawyer in Guyana. Rai remained incorruptible while many of Jagan's foremost disciples who had calumniated him, including the PPP's brightest Marxist theoretician, Ranji Chandisingh, crawled over to Burnham's carrots.

Ultimately, perhaps Indians in Guyana got the poverty of leadership they deserve. Indeed, that their political immaturity and susceptibility to narrow racial promptings sustained a monumentally inept leader, whose ideological fixation, for over 50 years, was incompatible with their philosophical orientation and detrimental to their welfare. Meanwhile, potentially statesmanlike leadership withered on the vine. But, as Dr. Ramsahoye argues, Forbes Burnham's leadership, too, left African Guyanese nothing to celebrate. This is how he put it to me in July 1992, when the PNC were still in office after nearly 28 years:

> Burnham was a man of ability, but he was totally corrupt. He had neither intellectual nor moral integrity. That was why when he was put in a position of supreme power he made a total mess of it. He has left his supporters an underprivileged, underclass in Guyana, whose fortunes will not improve in the near future unless Guyana gets a multiracial government of really competent people. That is not on the cards at the moment.[11]

Both Jagan and Burnham are dead, but racism is still virulent in Guyanese politics. The volatile situation could be exacerbated soon, as the next election approaches – another ethnic census which Africans will lose again. Unless a constitutional formula is established to secure a government of national unity indefinitely, backed up by a vigorous national programme to promote Indian and African history and culture, to lessen the chronic ethnic insecurity that bedevils Guyanese society, racial division is unavoidable. History and time are not on the side of this sad country! The Marxist ideological experiments of Jagan and Burnham were an unmitigated disaster. A nation is still not in the making: it remains a poor, environmentally hazardous land, mired in racial hatred, with its most educated and skilled in exile. Rai foresaw this, so did a man for whom he had considerable respect, Eusi Kwayana, an incorruptible, principled rival, whom he defeated in the 1957 elections, in the Central Demerara constituency: Rai was a PPP candidate; Kwayana an independent. Neither of these men are racists, as some Guyanese would have us believe; they were realists with a profound sense of the perilous state of race relations. Therefore, in commending Dr. Ramharack's book, I wish to note his assessment of

Kwayana, for his legacy especially with regard to the primacy of the cultural element in shaping African identity and ethnic security (like Rai's cultural/religious focus) has much to offer in the massive task of shaping a nation, still in an embryonic stage nearly 40 years since Independence:

> While King [Kwayana] understood and saw legitimacy in the Marxist analysis as a method of analysing the nature of society and he accepted the programme that flowed from that analysis, he, like Rai, also recognised the ethnic division that existed in colonial Guyana. [But] Jagan could not accept the fact that even the working class could be divided along ethnic lines and would now [after the split in 1955] gravitate towards their own representatives, particularly as the political stakes increased as independence neared. It was partially this primordial sentiment that led King to become the PNC's General Secretary [1958], and to enhance his African culture and mobilise Africans through the formation of the African Society for Cultural Relations with Independent Africa (ASCRIA). To Jagan and the PPP, King's nationalistic sentiments were a reflection of opportunistic and racist tendencies, and were inimical to the party's orientation, much in likeness to the nationalistic Indians who, according to Jagan, were almost '100% opposed to federation' [yet remained in the PPP or were sympathetic to it]... [H]ere was another missed opportunity for the PPP to acknowledge the racial/ethnic division in colonial Guyana, and to accept that this division was much more dominant than the class conflicts that supposedly guided the perspective of its leadership.

In October 1959 Balram Singh Rai, the Minister of Community Development and Education in Jagan's government, exhorted Guyanese to celebrate their diverse heritage and not be distracted by the absence of a sense of nationhood. There could be no short cut to the latter:

> [W]e are not yet a nation and we have no national history in the strict sense of that term... [but] I am more interested in the history of peoples, their social organisation, customs and institutions, their economic and political emancipation, their cultural integration and the spread of their civilisations [African and Indian]. In this way we learn of the aspirations, the struggles and achievements of men and women in society rather than with the wars and conquests and other activities of a personified nation-state...

Like Kwayana, Rai saw richness in Guyanese cultural diversity and was in no hurry to force it through an ideological sieve for the sake of a spurious national identity and short-term political goals. That was why he found communism, indeed, any form of social engineering, so repellent. Nearly 40 years ago, in October 1964, he reflected on where Jagan's lack of imagination had taken Guyana:

> British Guiana is indeed a very sick country at the present time. Her ailments are almost chronic... Today, there is deep racial antagonism between Indians and Africans, virtual economic bankruptcy, mounting

> unemployment, nepotism and corruption in high places, general lawlessness and total insecurity of life and property in the land. All these problems are basically attributable to the wild statements made from time to time by Dr. Jagan and other leading members of the PPP, to the violent behaviour pattern of the PYO, to the external alignments Jagan is forging and to the communist policy he threatens to pursue under the guise of 'socialism'. The false Marxist doctrines of 'class struggles' and 'dictatorship of the proletariat' could never produce harmony in the country or succeed in developing the country's resources and solving or reducing the size of the unemployment problem. Dr. Jagan and the PPP have alienated Western sentiment in favour of the Guyanese people, all of whom, but particularly the Indian section of the community, stand suspect of conspiring with International Communism, thereby posing a security threat to the Western Hemisphere... *The PPP had driven away whatever little African support there was for their party by their open encouragement of the recent bloody and unsuccessful GAWU strike as a result of which Indians killed each other and destroyed each other's property, after which Indians and Africans also maimed and murdered each other and destroyed each other's property...* [emphasis added][12]

Rai then explained the rationale behind his Justice Party contesting the 1964 elections:

> The next Government, we forecast, will be a coalition government of the People's National Congress and the United Force despite mutual criticisms and differences in policy. The PPP can only be in the Opposition... If all persons of Indian descent were to vote for the PPP that Party still cannot win a clear majority of votes, [and] as none of the other parties will work with Jagan in a coalition Government, then he and his Party can find themselves only in the Opposition. In these circumstances, in order to restore racial harmony between the Indian and Negro communities, to banish violence and counter violence and the threat of communism, in order to have a strong and stable Government enjoying both local and international confidence so necessary to the country's development and in order to give some measure of protection and representation to the Indian community, the Justice Party is prepared to work in such a coalition.[13]

As noted above, Rai's 1,334 votes did not entitle him to a single seat: his was a spectacular failure; but so was the PPP's with 109,332 votes and only 24 seats in a legislature of 53. They did not get a majority although the votes Rai received (as well as those polled by the Guyana United Muslim Party) did not cost the PPP any seats. They were excluded from the coalition government of the PNC and the UF, as Rai had predicted. But worse: the Indians were excluded from government for the next 28 years, with devastating consequences for all Guyanese. The body politic was so poisoned by Burnhamism (and Jaganism's impotence in opposition), that little has grown since the PPP was returned to office in 1992, at the end of the Cold War, with the help of America and its Indian majority vote. Neither Africans nor Indians have benefited from the Marxist adventures of Jagan and Burnham. Guyana remains a wasteland, the admirable success of her people overseas notwithstanding. On the 40th anniversary of the racial carnage of 1964 Guyanese could do well to reassess the legacies of Balram Singh Rai and Eusi Kwayana if they are to avert racial warfare.

Notes

1. Balram Singh Rai, Foreword, *Freedom and Justice for All* (Justice Party Manifesto), 7 October 1964.
2. Interview with Dr. Fenton Ramsahoye, 8 August 1997, Georgetown, Guyana.
3. *Ibid.*
4. Cheddi Jagan, *The Caribbean: Whose Backyard?* [privately published, 1985], pp. 117-8.
5. For more on the subject, see J.T.F. Jordens, *Dayananda Sarasvati: Essays on His Life and Ideas* (New Delhi: Manohar, 1998).
6. I explore American fear of Cheddi Jagan's Marxism in the early 1960s and the consequences for Guyanese in *Sweetening Bitter Sugar: Jock Campbell, The Booker Reformer in British Guiana, 1934-66* (Kingston, Jamaica: Ian Randle, 2005).
7. V.S. Naipaul, 'A Handful of Dust: Return to Guyana, *The New York Review of Books*, 11 April, 1991.
8. *Ibid.*
9. Cheddi Jagan, 'Address to the 18th PPP Congress', *Thunder*, (October-December 1974), pp. 21, 26.
10. I am currently researching a book on the role of the United Force and the Catholic Church in the anti-communist demonisation of Cheddi Jagan, between 1960 and 1964.
11. Interview with Dr. Fenton Ramsahoye, 25 July 1992, London, England.
12. See note 1.
13. *Ibid.*

WHOSE FREEDOM AT MIDNIGHT? MACHINATIONS TOWARDS GUYANA'S INDEPENDENCE, MAY 1966

Guyana became independent at midnight on 26 May 1966. But whose freedom was it? For nearly 20 years the Marxist leader of the People's Progressive Party (PPP), Cheddi Jagan (1918-97), of Indian extraction, buoyed by the independence of India and obsessed with the dominance of the British company, Booker, in the colony's plantation economy, had championed Guyana's 'struggle' for independence. Yet, on the big night it was the African leader of the People's National Congress (PNC), L.F.S. Burnham (1923-85), who was the recipient of the prize. His politics, though left-wing, was characterised by a cultivated pragmatism, strategic ambiguity and the facility to 'tack and turn as advantage seems to dictate... his whole political approach is opportunistic', as a British politician had assessed him in 1954.[1] With the aid of the Portuguese and Coloured (mixed race) political party, the United Force (UF), led by a Portuguese businessman, Peter D'Aguiar, a rabid anti-communist, in conjunction with the decisive intervention of President Kennedy himself and the CIA, in 1962-3, the PNC resorted to violence to make British Guiana ungovernable. The latter proved effective: it delayed independence, while Anglo-American collusion brought a Burnham-D'Aguiar coalition to power in December 1964 and independence in May 1966. Cheddi Jagan was a virtual spectator to the celebrations of the country's 'freedom'.

Speaking in the National Assembly on Independence Day, Jagan made it clear that this was not his freedom day. That had to be struggled for: foreign control of the economy had to be eliminated; only his party, the PPP, could achieve real liberation for the country. He meant disengagement from 'imperialism' and the capitalist system and the building of a communist utopia, following the path of the glorious Soviet Union. It was not an auspicious beginning for this troubled land:

> [P]olitical independence has been attained under the continuation and consolidation of foreign economic control and the maintenance of the colonial type economy, based on primary production and extraction. This has already detracted from the living standards of the working people...

> The PPP, the vanguard of Guyana's struggle for national liberation, is convinced that liberty is achieved only when it has been struggled for and won. It cannot be a gift of charity. For the people of Guyana, real freedom is still a prize to be won, and win it we will – as a reunited free people.[2]

Jagan and Burnham, founder-members of the PPP in 1950, had won the first general elections under universal adult suffrage in April 1953. But after 133 days the British suspended the constitution and evicted the People's Progressive Party (PPP) government from office, convinced that Jagan was a pro-Moscow communist bent on subverting liberal democracy.[3] His politics was anathema both to the British Colonial Office and the US State Department, the former of which, at least, could live with the Fabian socialism that was espoused, in name at least, elsewhere in the British West Indies. The tenuous coalition, suggestive of African-Indian unity in the PPP, did not survive the report of the Robertson Commission sent by the Colonial Office to British Guiana in early 1954, following the suspension of the constitution. It sought to make a distinction between the 'communism' of Cheddi Jagan and the moderate 'socialism' of Forbes Burnham. But this was not merely a 'divide and rule' tactic; it was an astute exploitation of the seeds of ethnic division, immanent in the society, and marked by a tendency towards Indian triumphalism and African apprehension, since the freedom of 'Mother India' in 1947. The Robertson Commission argued (mistakenly with respect to Burnham's political cunning):

> Mr Burnham (chairman of the Party) was generally recognised as the leader of the socialists in the PPP and as such to be in rivalry with Dr Jagan for the moral leadership of the Party as a whole... [T]here were many who thought that as the recognised leader of the socialists... Mr Burnham ought to have taken a much stronger line than he did in opposition to the more blatantly communist activities of the Jagans and their supporters. We came to the conclusion that... the ambiguous Mr Burnham... and a number of its less prominent leaders were socialists... We doubt, however, if they had the wit to see the essential difference between themselves and their communist colleagues or the ability to avoid being outmanoeuvred by them.[4]

As early as the elections of April 1953, 30-year old Burnham, a brilliant lawyer with considerable oratorical gifts and already identified as the premier African leader in the colony, had endeavoured to wrest the leadership of the PPP from the Indian leader, Cheddi Jagan. The mutual African-Indian suspicion permeating the colony was reproduced in the Party, Jagan's Marxist dogmas on the primacy of the class struggle notwithstanding. It was so bedevilling a feature of the PPP, in its so-called golden phase of racial unity, that Eusi Kwayana (formerly Sydney King), another founder-member of the Party, an African school teacher from the historic village of Buxton, fearing the escalation of racial rivalry if the assumption

Cheddi Jagan (1918-1997) in the early 1950s: passionate and photogenic

Fraught alliance: Jagan and Burnham with Nehru, New Delhi, 1954

of power were to be confronted precipitately, had counselled that they should not contest more than eight seats. The Party should focus on forging a degree of genuine ethnic unity. He had advised Jagan and Burnham that they should seek *not* to win in 1953:

> Some people like to ignore reality. I had moved in the PPP Executive that *we should not win a majority*, and my reason was that the country was not sufficiently united. I think only Martin Carter [the poet] and I supported the motion that we should *not* go for a majority. I knew we would win a majority, but I didn't think the Party was prepared for it because although the racial unity was there – it was a kind of coalition – it was not well-grounded; it was tenuous. I told Jagan and Burnham we would win the elections. They didn't believe it; they thought we would win about eight seats [out of 24]. I moved a motion that we fight about eight seats and try to do, in a multiple of eight, what Jagan alone had done [since 1947], and really try to unite the country [emphasis added].[5]

Kwayana was correct. African and Indians are separated by a cultural chasm that breeds mutual incomprehension. Indians were not a clear majority, but they constituted the largest group. Africans were afraid that with growing economic and cultural self-assurance, coupled with their demographic superiority, Indians under Cheddi Jagan's leadership would soon lead British Guiana to 'freedom' from British rule. They were therefore apprehensive that independence would herald their permanent subjugation by a wily people. Indian rule was infinitely less tolerable than British colonialism. Indeed African Guyanese would have opted for remaining colonials indefinitely rather than support independence under a party led by an Indian. The instinct to categorise and calibrate everything on the basis of ethnicity is chronic in this polyglot, incoherent place.

Kwayana is a rare example of an individual at the heart of these seminal events in Guyana's meandering path to independence, to speak frankly on racism in the colony. He contends that Jagan failed to address the fundamental fact of African insecurity in the early 1950s. Jagan thought that his Marxist truth, 'scientific socialism', the source of 'total understanding', would dissolve the question of race: a false problem in any case. He failed to comprehend, in Kwayana's evocative phrase, 'the hinterland of suspicion' in the African community. Kwayana explains why the PPP split into two factions in 1955, one Indian (led by Jagan); the other African (led by Burnham):

> The two major groups have stereotypes of each other. Africans tended to see Indians as clannish, as having more money, having an interest in land and a lot of them were selling out their lands to Indians when they went broke. Although they were doing it voluntarily, it also alarmed them. Then there was this rumour that someone from India had come and said who owned the land owned the country… A lot of Africans were unable to go beyond that. They would look at the behaviour of Indians near to them in judging the PPP (the PPP does not understand this until now).

He elaborates:

> If there is an aggressive [racist] member of the PPP in their district, this is how Africans see the PPP. Jagan never… [dealt] with these things at the subjective level, although he ha[d] a lot of rage against Imperialism. That problem was never dealt with; that's one of the reasons why I left the PPP [in 1956, the year after Burnham]. The psychology of the leader is crucial. We had to fight to get Africans to accept an Indian leader [Jagan]. He didn't have that problem. He never had to accept a leader of another race so he didn't know what it is. He talks about revolution, but the personal revolution – nothing. He had a cultural problem. Having rejected colonialism and its intellectual and cultural baggage he had to take something from somewhere else [Russian communism]; he didn't rely on his own personality. If he had Hinduism, it would have made him a different person.[6]

There were no intellectual or cultural foundations to Cheddi Jagan's ideology. He had rejected his Indian cultural antecedents, so he absorbed the received Marxist dogmas uncritically. They took the place of the eclectic Hinduism of his boyhood. Yet, imprisoned by the intractability of racial identities in Guyana, Jagan was discernibly adept at garnering Indian loyalty – and keeping it, manipulating crucial Indo-Guyanese idioms with dexterity. That was why he was able to survive the split in the PPP in 1955, with the departure of Forbes Burnham, as well as that of Eusi Kwayana and Martin Carter in 1956, and proceed, on the basis of Indo-Guyanese invincibility under the first-past-the-post electoral system, to gain re-election in August 1957. Burnham's faction of the PPP was vanquished so he decided to form a party with a less ambiguous identity, the predominantly African, People's National Congress (PNC), in late 1957. Africans were demoralised. This was exacerbated by the fact that in 1960 the Conservative government of Harold Macmillan granted Jagan self-government with virtual assurance of independence, in a couple of years, after fresh general elections. Burnham was rudderless and his African supporters fearful. For Cheddi Jagan, independence was there for the taking. He just had to know how to wait. He did not.

As I have also discussed in the essay on 'Balram Singh Rai's Anti-Communism', Fidel Castro's revolution of 1959 dazzled Cheddi. The circumspection and moderation he strained to project in 1957-9, since his re-election, did not sit easily with him. His Marxist dogmas, the source of 'total knowledge', were battling within him for release. He got the chance to break out of his brief, but stressful, play at moderation, in early 1960, when it became clear that Fidel Castro was a communist, and that the new Cuba would be guided by Marxism-Leninism. Cheddi was over the moon. He would not play ball with the 'imperialists' any longer. Even Iain Macleod, the liberal Secretary of State for the Colonies, who had defied several right-wingers in the Tory Party and committed himself to granting

Fatal attraction: Cheddi and his young hero, Fidel, Havana, 1960

Fatal meeting: Jagan and President Kennedy, the White House, 25 October 1961

America's man: Burnham with President Johnson, the White House, 21 July 1966

Jagan independence by 1962, would be construed as just another imperialist by Cheddi. After the constitutional conference in London, where it had become transparent that no 'struggle' was really necessary for independence, Jagan proceeded to Cuba, his new Mecca, twice in 1960. He was certain that Marxism-Leninism, the purest form of governance devised by humankind, was inevitable. Fidel had vindicated this. The days of capitalism were numbered – the communist utopia was around the next bend. He pontificated:

> I completely support the Revolutionary Government of Cuba... [It] has the support of most of the Cuban people. I have no doubt the revolution will achieve all its objectives. Any revolutionary movement such as this which is tending towards social and economic emancipation will obviously have enemies both inside and outside the country, but if we take into account the times in which we are living, the speed with which the progressive forces of the world are advancing [the communist bloc], and the great support of the majority of the Cuban people, I have no doubts about the Cuban Revolution.[8]

Cheddi boasted in September 1960 that 'the only Government in Latin America which was openly supporting the Cuban Revolution was ours'. He was confident that time was on their side, guided by the Soviet Union and the so-called people's democracies of Eastern Europe. Marxism-Leninism was bound to win; Suez (1956) was a 'turning point in the history of imperialism which is now on the defensive and is losing more and more positions every day. The process will grow not in arithmetic, but in geometric progression'. He predicted that the communist utopia was unstoppable: it would 'emerge triumphant', as capitalism was 'becoming a moribund system'. Communism represented the logic of history; the Cuban Revolution was the watershed in the Western Hemisphere. He could not contain himself: 'Fidel Castro is not only the liberator of the American continent but also the liberator of the century'.[9]

It can be argued that without Castro's Revolution, Cheddi Jagan might have kept his head, to his circumspection of 1957-9; he would not have stirred the Cold War venom of the United States. He would also have deprived his local enemies – Burnham's PNC and the rabidly anti-communist United Force (UF) and their allies, the Catholic Church – of the ammunition that would resurrect their seemingly moribund fortunes. In spite of Jagan's folly, in early 1961 Iain Macleod sought to persuade President Kennedy that Jagan was not a communist; he was more of a Laskiite radical (Kennedy was taught by Harold Laski at LSE): there was no need to be afraid of his political outlook. Meanwhile, the Fabian socialist oriented head of Booker in Guyana, Jock Campbell (a friend of Macleod), had also endeavoured to downplay the signs of Jagan's fatal attraction to communism. This, however, was not easy for Kennedy to take. After the failure to overthrow Castro, the Bay of Pigs debacle of April 1961, it seems that Kennedy feared that he would be seen as being too soft on communism, and still harboured apprehensions that an independent Guyana under Jagan would become a Soviet beachhead for spreading the virus into the continent.

But Jagan was re-elected in August 1961, and it seemed as if the Kennedy administration could be persuaded to follow the British and put up with him, hoping that power would breed responsibility and moderation. However, Jagan organised a tawdry triumphalist parade to celebrate his victory. His jubilant Indian supporters behaved in a manner that was humiliating to African bystanders: they dragged the symbol of the PNC, the broom, behind their vehicles; some displayed small coffins marked 'PNC'. Africans were demoralised by another electoral defeat and deeply apprehensive that Indians were about to collect the big prize. Jagan's pretext for the parade was that it would dispel any doubts the imperialists had of the strength of his support. This was unnecessary: independence was there for the taking – whoever won the elections had earned the right to collect the prize. The shameful display of Indian triumphalism magnified the fears of Africans that dark times were ahead when Jagan got independence. Africans viewed independence with foreboding: freedom for the 'coolies'; slavery for them.

In August 1961 Jagan had all the trumps; few envisaged that he would pull defeat from the jaws of victory. Ever a fantasist, he believed passionately that Marxism-Leninism was superior in comprehending the laws of development – it constituted a science of society – and that the mighty United States was in line for a fall. So his meeting with President Kennedy in the Oval Office, in October 1961, to procure aid for development, was potentially fatal. The British Embassy in Washington had sought to counsel Jagan to moderate his stance when he met the President, eschewing words or expressions that Americans would to construe as synonymous with communism. This proved futile. A little before he met Kennedy, Jagan explained his political philosophy to the Washington Press Club: 'I believe… that the economic theories of scientific socialism [Marxism] hold out the promise of a dynamic social discipline which can transform an underdeveloped country into a developed one in a far shorter time than any other system. We may [therefore] differ from you in the way we [choose to] organise our economic life'.[10] He seemed not to comprehend that it was not simply a matter of differential approaches to economic development, but a deeply provocative statement in the context of the Cold War. He was taking his little country into that global struggle, on the side the Americans deemed abominable a peril to 'freedom' in the Hemisphere.

Jagan did not excel either, in his appearance on 'Meet the Press' on 15 October 1961. The President was watching the programme, and the moderator had asked Jagan whether there was freedom in the Soviet Union and China. Jagan waffled:

> All I can say – I haven't been to China, I haven't been to Russia, but the experts who have been there have said – for instance, you have this chap who is a writer on the question, an expert apparently, who writes for the London *Observer*, I can't recall his name right now. But he has said in his latest book that life in the Soviet Union is growing day by day better and better. The standards of living are improving, and as such, we are concerned. We want to know how this is done.[11]

When he met President Kennedy on 25 October 1961, he virtually committed suicide by leaving the President with no doubt that he was a communist. No aid would be forthcoming, and Kennedy's fear that he was being perceived as soft on hemispheric subversion led to an obsession with the future of little British Guiana. The British must not give independence to Jagan; a second Cuba must not emerge. By early 1962, therefore, Jagan's enemies in the colony were aware that the American President was on their side. The PNC and UF therefore used the budget of February 1962 as a pretext for fomenting trouble: they mobilised African, Coloured and Portuguese resistance to Jagan's government. In Georgetown, a vast section of the commercial district was burnt down. It is noteworthy that Burnham was in favour of independence before the elections of August 1961; by early 1962, with the Americans on his side, he had changed his mind. He was prepared to use violence to make the place ungovernable. His aim was to delay a date for independence, which many had anticipated as forthcoming in May 1962. In fact, Jagan's Government had printed a stamp for official documents that read: 'Freedom Year, 1962'.

Up to this point, Burnham's socialist pretensions, and his craving of Third World credibility, had inhibited his capacity to initiate the subversion of Jagan's Government. In late 1961 he was floundering. He was saved by the United Force and the Catholic Church, which had been propagating a rabidly anti-communist crusade. Although their support-base was small, they had a consistency of focus engendered by a hatred of Castro and 'godless communism', the 'red peril'. In May 1961, for instance, the *Catholic Standard* observed that Jagan's government had never 'uttered one breath of criticism of any of Castro's doings – to them, he is apparently perfect. It means that… they support all of Castro's methods (as well as aims) in Cuba. Among these are: the denial of freedom; the destruction of free trade unions; suppression of the free press; mass arrests.'[12] They also deemed Jagan an enemy of freedom of worship, as the paper cited, week after week, incidents of persecution of the Catholic Church in Cuba. The organ of the United Force, the *Sun*, and a daily newspaper largely owned by Peter D'Aguiar, leader of the Party, the *Daily Chronicle*, sustained this crusade. They were probably also energised by the presence in the White House of the first Catholic President. This was the context, in early 1962, in which Burnham was resurrected. His socialist rhetoric notwithstanding, he dexterously exploited the virulent anti-communism of the Portuguese and Coloured minority in order to make

British Guiana ungovernable. In the process, the Kennedy administration settled on him as their man, and Kennedy put relentless pressure on Harold Macmillan to ensure that independence was not granted to Cheddi Jagan.

As Kennedy's chief political assistant, Professor Arthur Schlesinger, documented:

> [I]n May 1962 Burnham came to Washington. He appeared an intelligent, self-possessed, reasonable man, insisting quite firmly on his 'socialism' and 'neutralism' but stoutly anti-communist... In the meantime, events had convinced us that Jagan though perhaps not a disciplined communist had that kind of deep pro-communist emotion... [that] the United States could not afford... when it involved a quasi-communist regime on the mainland of Latin America. Burnham's visit left the feeling, as I reported to the President [on 21 June 1962], that 'an independent British Guiana under Burnham... would cause us many fewer problems than an independent British Guiana under Jagan'. And a way was open to bring it about because Jagan's parliamentary strength was larger than his popular strength... An obvious solution would be to establish a system of proportional representation [PR]. This, after prolonged discussion, the British Government finally did in October 1963; and elections held... at the end of 1964 produced a coalition government under Burnham. With much unhappiness and turbulence, British Guiana seemed to have passed safely out of the communist orbit'.[13]

But Schlesinger had not told the whole tale: the machinations of the President and the CIA to ensure that their man, Forbes Burnham, would take Guyana to independence. By 1963 the CIA had got into the act, providing funds through diverse front organisations, to fight the Jagan Government's Labour Relations Bill. It was a measure to empower the Minister of Labour to recommend the holding of polls to resolve jurisdictional disputes between contending trade unions. The main reason for the bill was that although the overwhelming majority of the workers in the sugar industry were Indians and Jagan's supporters, they were still represented by a union, the Manpower Citizens' Association (MPCA), which the PPP deemed a company union that was collaborating with Burnham in subverting their Government. The PPP had founded their own union, the Guyana Agricultural Workers' Union (GAWU), and were seeking to get it recognised by a poll as the representative of sugar workers, though even if the Bill was passed, GAWU would require two-thirds of the workers' votes to unseat the MPCA. The PNC and UF took up opposition to this bill as a means of galvanising more resistance to Jagan and delay independence. They claimed that the Labour Relations Bill was framed as a pernicious measure to eliminate unions deemed enemies of the PPP, and a threat to free trade unions. The first half of 1963 was marked by an 80-day general strike ostensibly against the Bill; it was sustained primarily with money from the CIA.[14]

The constitutional conference held in October 1962 had collapsed because the PNC and UF had stalled on all the contentious issues, knowing that the US was on their side. As in 1962, the aim was to delay independence further. The general strike of 1963 degenerated into racial violence throughout the colony. Apart from bringing economic disaster, the strike provoked Africans and Indians into acts of racial hatred and violence, even 'ethnic cleansing' in some districts. This, in conjunction with the destruction of most of the commercial section of Georgetown the previous year, provided President Kennedy with the ammunition he needed to pressure the British to delay independence and to change the electoral system to proportional representation, which, as Schlesinger had argued, was bound to secure the defeat of Jagan.

Kennedy met Macmillan in England on 30 June 1963: the destruction of Cheddi Jagan was the principal item on the agenda. The President made his case forthrightly:

> It was obvious if the UK were to get rid of British Guiana now it would become a communist state. He thought the thing to do was to look for ways to drag the thing out [no immediate independence]... He [argued] that Latin America was the most dangerous area in the world. The effect of having a communist state in British Guiana in addition to Cuba in 1964 [the Presidential elections], would be to create irresistible pressures on the Unites States to strike militarily at Cuba.[15]

Coming after the Cuban missiles crisis of October 1962 and the consuming fear that the world was on the brink of nuclear war, Kennedy's pressure to get rid of Jagan, which the British had hitherto sought to deflect, now carried the force of the imperatives of power.

In delaying independence, Kennedy counselled that they should rationalise it as a necessity to prevent the 'unleashing of racial war', not because of the 'danger of British Guiana becoming communist'. The President was adamant that Cuba would be the major issue in the US elections of 1964; and that 'adding British Guiana to Cuba could well tip the scales, and someone would be elected who would take military action against Cuba'.[16] He was alluding to Barry Goldwater, known for his ultra right-wing views on communism. The British acquiesced; they would delay independence and impose a solution changing the electoral system to proportional representation. But, having suspended the constitution in 1953, they were wary about repeating the exercise ten years later. They therefore decided to hatch a plot, knowing that Jagan's enemies would again stall on all the outstanding issues. In fact, Sandys was anxious for Burnham to spurn Jagan's initiative to get him to enter a coalition, prior to the conference. Burnham was an astute politician; Sandys need not have worried.

Prior to the convening of the constitutional conference in October 1963, Burnham left no stone unturned. He sought to allay whatever lingering doubts the Catholic Church and the UF still harboured about his socialist rhetoric. In August 1963, the *Catholic Standard* felt reassured that there was blue water between Burnham's PNC and Jagan's PPP: 'The statement by the PNC that the Party's brand of socialism is very different from the communism of the PPP is welcome indeed. There has, to our mind, been a distressing ambiguity in the past about the PNC's policy, and we are very glad they have come out with a forthright statement'.[17]

At the second constitutional conference, in October 1963, after the predicted deadlock had occurred, Duncan Sandys, Secretary of State for the Colonies, tricked Jagan into signing a document empowering Sandys to adjudicate on all the outstanding issues. Sandys persuaded Jagan to attend the conference alone on the fatal day when the trick would be perpetrated. Jagan complied and although he encountered Burnham and D'Aguiar at the conference venue – with their teams of advisers intact – an undiscerning Jagan thought nothing untoward. He was the first to sign the deceptive document, lured by the illusion that even if he did not win on the electoral system (staving off proportional representation [PR]) and the voting age (he wanted it reduced to 18), a date for independence would surely be fixed as a quid pro quo.

The illusion of a commitment to early independence was not detected by Jagan because of the skilful construction of the sentence in the second paragraph of the document below, dated 25 October 1963. (I cite it with emphasis.) Read quickly, and bereft of legal scrutiny, it lends itself to the interpretation that an imposition by Sandys would *not* delay independence. It can be argued, too, that the fact that Jagan certainly had no part in its composition (and it therefore warranted his circumspection) was diluted by the phrase: 'we are agreed' – *not* 'we have agreed'. Jagan was ignorant of Kennedy's machinations and the fact that the British were now unreservedly committed to his removal before independence:

TO THE SECRETARY OF STATE FOR THE COLONIES

> At your request we have made further efforts to resolve the differences between us on the constitutional issues which require to be settled before British Guiana secures independence, in particular the electoral system, the voting age and the question of whether fresh elections should be held before independence.
>
> We regret to have to report to you that we have not succeeded in reaching agreement; and we have reluctantly come to the conclusion that there is no prospect of an agreed solution. *Another adjournment of the Conference for further discussions between ourselves would therefore serve no useful purpose and would result in further delaying British Guiana's independence and in continued uncertainty in the country.*
>
> In these circumstances *we are agreed* to ask the British Government to settle on their authority all outstanding constitutional issues, and we undertake to accept these decisions [emphasis added].[18]

Jagan was the first to sign because, as he explained before Sandys announced his decision, he was 'assuming that independence was obviously forthcoming'. He had found the PNC and UF 'very unreasonable', and faced with the futility of the situation broken by the unrelenting chaos of 1962-3, he had opted for an imposition. Even among his supporters, it was rumoured that the alleged infidelity of his wife, Janet, had undermined his capacity for rational judgement. (She had said: 'I am surprised they agreed to sign'.)[19] Yet he trusted the evil imperialists:

> 'I have put my confidence in the hands of the British Government and I hope decisions will be taken on the basis of constitutional principles, on British and Commonwealth precedents and conventions... Independence is absolutely necessary... for the country cannot get anywhere without it'. He noted, without grasping the subtlety of the Machiavellian mind, that Burnham had initially refused to sign but fell in after D'Aguiar had done so.[20]

Jagan would soon be bitterly disappointed. Adhering to Kennedy's request, Duncan Sandys changed the electoral system to proportional representation, just under a month before the President was assassinated. He kept the voting age at 21, and stated that a date for independence *would not* be fixed until new elections were held under PR.

Burnham was the victor. Violence had paid off. Jagan's end was assured. There was no way he could secure a majority under PR. He called for 'a hurricane of protests' to get the British to revoke their iniquitous decision. He argued that he was not bound to abide by Sandys's ruling 'because independence was a condition of his imposing a solution'. It was a 'betrayal of trust'. Belatedly he recognised the foundation of the trick for which he had fallen: 'It is clear that the decision is in keeping with the wishes of the American Government and is subservient to it... The machinations of the Imperialists cannot destroy the PPP. I call upon the people of Guyana to stand firm in this hour of betrayal'.[21] He realised that his enemies were rewarded for their violence; he would now seek to retaliate, to stall new elections scheduled for late 1964 from being held. It was a step inspired by despair. He knew that freedom would soon be the gift of his enemies.

Burnham, ever the slick manipulator, pretended that he was offended by their having asked their colonial masters to adjudicate on the unresolved issues. He claimed that this was an abrogation of the spirit of independence. Having drawn victory out of the jaws of defeat, he was basking in his good luck with feigned regret, while dancing on Jagan's humiliation:

> 'I am pleased about nothing. A nationalist can never be pleased over the indignity of an imposition. We find no reason for jubilation because British Guiana is without a firm date for independence...Perhaps... [Jagan]... should rethink his naïve statement in which he expressed great confidence in the British sense of fair-play and justice... I agree with Dr Jagan that the people of British Guiana should stand firm in this hour of betrayal – of them by him'.[22]

Then, typically, gloating from his self-assured intellectual and political stature over Jagan, he mocked him, noting that Jagan had told the BBC he reposed 'great faith in the sense of justice and fair-play of the British'. He rubbed it in, assuming his legal persona:

> If the Premier is the expert on the wicked machinations of the Imperialists, why did he concede this *volte-face*?... Let me concede, as a lawyer would, that the proposition is correct and that the US Government was particularly interested in the outcome of the conference and preferred a particular outcome so far as the electoral system is concerned. Is it not naïve of the same Dr Jagan who says that the US Government would be interested in a particular outcome, to entrust the political future and the destiny of this country to the greatest friend of the US Government?[23]

I have written elsewhere of Burnham's mockery of Jagan's ignominy – of the Indians' impending fall:

> More of this studied ridicule was to emanate from the sagacious brain of this master manipulator. In February 1964 he told a mammoth crowd in Georgetown of his efforts (spurious... [indeed]) to reach an agreement with Jagan, 'before the fateful document was signed'. He jeered: '[S]ome people have learnt to write... they had a pen and there was ink!' This was especially galling – provocatively evocative of the barely lettered Indian, the *arriviste* 'coolie' pitted against the African scribe.[24]

Jagan launched a well-publicised march by his Indian supporters throughout the coastland of Guyana, to protest the British trickery. He than called a strike for recognition of his union, the GAWU, as the sole bargaining agent for sugar workers. It soon degenerated into virtual civil war, between Africans and Indians. Nothing could change the fact that Burnham was on the way to gaining the prize that Jagan thought was rightly his. D'Aguiar tagged along with Burnham, reluctantly: he was the lesser of two evils. Both he and Jagan were on a journey to nowhere: the exodus of the Portuguese and Coloureds had begun; so too the Indians.

Jagan, in despair, bemoaned in a radio broadcast on 30 May 1964 that the Opposition had been 'recompensed' by the British. He who had toiled for freedom had it stolen from him. Their 'illegal and unconstitutional activities yielded them rich rewards'; all he had fought for 'now hangs in the balance':

> Factional strife strides the land and our movement lies divided and weak. For many years, while others spent their time and leisure in the pursuit of wealth or pleasure and frivolity, I tread every nook and cranny of our wide country preaching the gospel of nationalism and freedom and seeking to infuse in our diverse groups a Guyanese consciousness which would transcend the bonds of race and creed... Today... my hopes of national unity have been cast in the dust... I wish to appeal for the end of racial strife. Racial antagonism is not deeply rooted in this country. But it can easily become so if it is not promptly removed.[25]

He did not know his country's history; very little had been written at the time. Racial insecurity was endemic, and with the ascendancy of Indians after the Second World War, of which his own rise was symptomatic, African suspicion of the motives of Indians was chronic. It was the major factor inhibiting the pursuit of a national identity. Jagan's Marxism was deeply rooted in his aversion to Booker's dominance of the colony's plantation economy. Jagan was an Indian from the plantation. His whole anti-colonial stance had blossomed in this soil of hatred for the 'sugar gods'. But this struggle had little resonance with the African people in British Guiana. Africans, now mostly urban, with few now involved with the plantations, were suspicious of Jagan's anti-colonialism because they thought the end of colonialism would open the floodgates to Indian domination.

Eusi Kwayana elaborates on the pitfalls of a national consciousness in this polyglot colony:

> I lived among very poor [African] people all my life. They were very political. I knew they had a lot of ethnic suspicion although nobody wanted any racial confrontation; that was not there then, not mature enough. *But I knew [also] that they hadn't strong feelings against colonialism – no strong feelings against colonialism – or against Booker because of their monopoly or their treatment of people... The whole idea of rejecting Britain was not very firm.* Indians had it a lot firmer because of the Indian nationalist movement. They had a kind of ideological and cultural resentment against colonialism... [They were exposed to] people coming from India to lecture. Africans did not have this. The link was broken [emphasis added].[26]

Jagan lost the elections under PR on 7 December 1964. Burnham and D'Aguiar formed a coalition government, as expected. The communist Jagan, as the Americans had planned it, was now ousted. He was impotent; he had squandered what he thought were his anticolonial trumps – scientific socialism and the example of the Cuban revolution – having been lavish with them up to the end of 1961. Relieved of responsibility he embarked on a Niagara of nihilistic tactics, characterised by the boycotting of crucial events. He refused to enter the House of Assembly because several of his Party's members were still in detention, Burnham's pretext being that this was in the interest of national security. He boycotted the International Commission of Jurists in 1965, on the grounds that their terms of reference were too broad. He had asked for the redressing of racial imbalance in the security forces; the government decided that the question of racial imbalance be explored in all its dimensions. He boycotted the crucial constitutional conference in November 1965 when the British Government duly granted independence to the Burnham-D'Aguiar coalition. Jagan explained his absence as a protest against the violence and deceit fomented, to ensure that the prize was seen as being awarded to the lackeys of imperialism. He told the BBC: 'I do not wish to lend support to the formal promulgation of decisions already taken [independence] which are gravely inimical to the interests of the Guianese people'.[27] The date for independence was fixed for 26 May 1966. Jagan also boycotted the visit of the Queen to Guyana in February 1966. The reason: '...solidarity with the 4,000,000 Africans in Rhodesia... now suffering from white minority rule' under Ian Smith. The PPP accused Her Majesty's Government of 'lacking in its duty to Africans to crush the rebellion... [Smith's unilateral declaration of independence].'[28]

Percy Armstrong, a veteran anti-PPP columnist, reflected on the implications of such boycotts. His views were congruent with those of Burnham:

> All this means that the forthcoming celebrations, like those of the Queen's visit, will be largely a celebration of Africans, while people of the Indian community will perhaps huddle themselves in their homes, peeping through creases and cracks and giving furtive glances over their shoulders to see whether terrorists from amongst them... are lurking in the rear... The main aim behind all these boycotts is to convert the Indian community into a dissident group which will become an irritant in the body politic of the newly independent state of Guyana, to be used like putty by the Communist international organisations.[29]

Jagan's reaction to Burnham's winning the prize of freedom was to veer outrageously to the left, claiming the ideological high-ground – authentic Marxism, which in the long-run was bound to supersede the moribund pro-imperialist and capitalist stance of the PNC-UF coalition. Jagan was setting himself up for terminal marginalisation, long-term irrelevance and exclusion from power. He had boycotted the Independence Conference in London, but attended the Tri-continental Conference in Havana, from 3-15 January 1966, where long-term revolutionary tactics against American imperialism were debated. In March 1966, the organ of the PPP, *Thunder*, made it clear that they were combatants in the Cold War and that America was not only Cuba's enemy, it was theirs also. Kennedy and Sandys could have declared themselves vindicated:

> The delegates had, above all, a clear-cut objective – how in the face of a ruthless and immoral enemy to unite all the progressive forces for simultaneous confrontation... The establishment of a tri-continental organisation with provisional headquarters in Havana, Cuba, and a continental (Latin American) organisation was a stunning blow to US imperialism. Cuba represents to the national liberation movements two symbols. Firstly, the symbol of a small country successfully confronting the giant colossus of the north and exploding the myth of US omnipotence and invincibility. Secondly, a symbol of ideological unity. The Cuban Revolution encompasses in a brief period revolutionary nationalism, socialism and communism.[30]

Jagan had played into Burnham's hands. He kept 17 PPP activists in detention, arguing, falsely, that they were agents of communist subversion trained in Cuba. Thereafter, the Burnham Government continually renewed the state of emergency on grounds that it was an imperative necessitated by the subversive programme of Jagan's PPP. Guyana became independent in May 1966 with the state of emergency still in place. In January of that year, Dr P.A. Reid, the Deputy-Prime Minister, speaking in the House of Assembly on the rationale for extending the emergency, observed: 'We want to make it known that this Government has no one detained for political reasons. They are not political detainees. If we lift the emergency, we have no control over the movement of explosives which is the basis of the trouble'. He was astutely defining them as terrorists precisely at the time Jagan was attending the Tri-continental Conference.[31]

In April 1966 Prime Minister Forbes Burnham sought to reinforce the Government's projection of the PPP as an organisation committed to subversion: 'When lawlessness prevails Government must exercise control of the source from which senseless and irresponsible acts are inspired... PPP member Dr Ramsahoye... described the extension of the emergency as a disgrace for a country going into independence... It is not for those who participated in Tri-continental conferences to criticise actions by the state, permitted by the constitution and aimed at protecting the community at large'.[32]

Shortly afterwards Jagan announced that the slogan of the PPP, for the Independence celebrations, was: 'Independence Yes! Celebrations No!' He explained the rationale:

> The PPP opposed the fraudulent constitutional arrangements which resulted in its removal from the government in 1964. It did not take part in the rigged constitutional talks in London in November 1965. And it was not consulted on the date for independence. The party's attitude to the independence celebrations is therefore coupled with mixed feelings. On the one hand it is happy that on May 26 our Guyana flag will replace the Union Jack, that we will have our own national anthem and coat-of-arms. But independence has meaning for us not only in symbolic terms. Above all we want also the substance of independence. The substance has been denied the Guyanese people. For the following reasons, we cannot celebrate independence. Firstly, full powers have been transferred to the puppets of the imperialists [the PNC and the UF] by a rigged constitutional arrangement. Secondly, the imperialists who have a stranglehold on our economy are being further strengthened. Thirdly, independence is being ushered in under a state of emergency. The main purpose is to silence the political opposition and to intimidate the working class. Fourthly, on independence day comrades who have fought vigorously for independence during the course of several years will be in detention. [33]

Jagan and his son did attend the flag-raising ceremony at midnight on 26 May 1966. That was the totality of their participation. But they certainly were not planning to subvert the Government. The truth is they were clueless. They would now seek the moral high ground, claiming that they were the true practitioners of a pure Marxism: the source of genuine liberation and independence. But it was indicative of their impotence rather than their commitment to revolution. Even the anti-communist *Weekend Post and Sunday Argosy* observed that the tendency to project on to the PPP subversive motives after Independence was an exaggeration; it was beyond their capacity even when they were in power.[34] But Burnham would return continually to the question of violence and the PPP, using the 'Tri-continental stick' to give credence to his assertions, in the absence of concrete evidence that they were fomenting revolution. Jagan's revolutionary rhetoric notwithstanding, the accusation against the PPP had a ring of fantasy and massive hypocrisy given Burnham's role in the 1961-63 subversion. In June 1966 Burnham addressed Jagan:

> If ... [he] genuinely wishes to unify our peoples and insure their future happiness and well-being, he can readily do this by openly renouncing, once and for all, his penchant for looking outside our borders for solutions to the nation's problems: by renouncing violence, subversion and armed conflict which he affirmed in his recent utterances at the Tri-continental Conference in Havana; by henceforth ceasing to send his supporters and representatives abroad for 'ideological orientation' and financial assistance; by halting the training of his followers in guerrilla warfare, the manufacture of bombs and by openly giving up his ambitions as an international communist leader.[35]

Jagan had been in office for seven years, from 1957 to 1964. If Jagan had not been imprisoned by his communist dogmas, Burnham could never have got anywhere near the big prize. Jagan was an honest man, but a poor politician. He published his autobiography on the eve of Guyana's independence in May 1966. It was grandiloquently titled: *The West on Trial: My Fight for Guyana's Freedom*. Richard Gott, reviewing it for the *Guardian*, wrote: 'Unfortunately for him, his arrogance, intolerance and political misjudgement made him an easy target for criticism... [even] from those who were not predisposed to believe that he was a communist'. David Holden, reviewing it in the *Sunday Times*, was less charitable: '[I]ts author is an inept politician, with an inflated sense of his own importance, a garrulous pen (and tongue) and a thoroughly woolly mind'.[36]

Jagan would remain in opposition for 28 years as Burnham, having gotten rid of the United Force, proceeded to rig all the elections between 1968 and 1985, with the connivance of the United States. Meanwhile he had stolen all of Jagan's clothes: he adopted the bulk of what Jagan considered his Marxist programme, including nationalisation of 80% of the economy, an anti-American posture and 'fraternal relations' with Cuba and the USSR. Yet Jagan remained loyal to his comrades in the Kremlin. Confronted with a choice between Jagan and Burnham, the United States still opted for the latter, even if their aid dried up. Yet Jagan could not see the folly of his actions. On the 25th anniversary of the PPP, in 1975, he revisited his years in government, between 1957 and 1964. What he had to say was, in my view, pure fantasy:

> [O]nly fools who do nothing make no mistakes. The main burden of their attack is that we should not have openly espoused Marxism and given support to the Cuban Revolution. What they fail to note is that had we not taken a firm patriotic position, a world-view [Marxism-Leninism]...we would not have been able to win over the masses [presumably including Africans – a fantasy!] from the traitors and collaborators [Burnham's PNC] ...The mistake we made was not the espousal of Marxism; it was that we did not fully implement it in practice. The PPP was a party geared to winning elections... It was not until 1961 that we established an ideological school, and only in 1969 that we took a decision to transform our loose mass party into a disciplined Marxist-Leninist party. One of the difficulties encountered was that... there was not enough personnel to man both the government and party administration at the same time. The result was that party work suffered while we were marking time in government without power and being sabotaged at the same time. The mistake we made was to have given priority to government rather than the party, staying in the government too long without independence, assuming responsibility without real power, and thereby undermining our influence, cutting the ground from under our feet...[37]

Burnham ensured that he had 28 years, from 1964 to 1992, for nothing but 'party work'!

Forty-two years after Guyana was granted independence, it remains a poor, backward, racially-polarised, country, its African and Indian peoples still defining themselves primarily by their ethnic identity. Guyana is still not a nation, and with more than half its population having migrated to the United States, Canada, the UK, the islands of the Caribbean – anywhere that would have them – the country lost almost all the Portuguese and the original Chinese communities, many of the best educated and skilled Indians and Africans. The population has, in fact, declined from the early 1970s, when it was estimated at about 815,000; today it is under 800,000. In my village in the East Canje district of Berbice, over 80% of the original inhabitants have gone. Of 60 or 70 of us who completed secondary school, at Queen's College in 1968, I am not aware of a single one who still resides there. The British had created a number of first-rate secondary schools, so it was common for people of a certain age in the former British West Indies, those born during the Second Word War or in the decade or so after it, to speak of their contemporaries from Guyana with open admiration. In this drive to education, the quality of schooling was a prime factor, but so too was the impossibility of the place – its daunting hydrological problems. Together they bred a partiality for education, but also an instinct to escape that was geographical and psychological. This has been exacerbated by

Guyana's racial and political futility. The fatal fantasies of Jagan and Burnham are of a piece. As V.S. Naipaul pointed out in 1991: 'Guyana has always been a land of fantasy. It was the land of El Dorado'.

As early as midnight 26 May 1966, with most Indo-Guyanese, at the behest of Cheddi Jagan, boycotting the Independence celebrations, it was clear that while Guyana was terminating its colonial links with Britain, a nation was still to be born. A Guyanese nation remains elusive.

Notes

1. This quote is from the Labour Party's Patrick Gordon Walker, cited in Cheddi Jagan, *The West on Trial: My Fight for Guyana's Freedom* (London: Michael Joseph, 1966), p. 202.
2. See http//jagan.org/articles.
3. See Cary Fraser, *Ambivalent Anti-Colonialism: The United States and the Genesis of West Indian Independence, 1940-64* (Westport, CT: Greenwood Press, 1994); Cheddi Jagan, *op. cit.* [1966]; my *Sweetening 'Bitter Sugar': Jock Campbell, the Booker Reformer in British Guiana, 1934-66* (Kingston, Jamaica: Ian Randle Publishers, 2005); Thomas J. Spinner, *A Political and Social History of Guyana, 1945-83* (Boulder, Colorado: Westview Press, 1983); and Maurice St. Pierre, *Anatomy of Resistance: Anti-Colonialism in Guyana, 1823-1966* (London; Macmillan, 1999).
4. *Report of the British Guiana Constitutional Commission, 1954* (Sir James Robertson, chairman), Cmd. 9274 (London: Her Majesty's Stationery Office, 1954), p. 37.
5. Interview with Eusi Kwayana, Georgetown, Guyana, 22 September 1992.
6. *Ibid.*
7. V.S. Naipaul, 'A Handful of Dust: Return to Guiana', the *New York Review of Books*, 11 April 1991, p. 18.
8. CO1031/3907 [National Archives], Copy of a translation of the interview of Dr Cheddi Jagan with the newspaper, *Revolucion* [Havana], September 1960.
9. *Ibid.*
10. Cheddi Jagan, 'Towards Understanding…', The Text of an Address to the National Press Club, Washington, D.C., USA, 14 October 1961.
11. CO1031/4177 [National Archives], Cheddi Jagan on 'Meet the Press' [transcript of the interview], 15 October 1961.
12. Leader, the *Catholic Standard*, 5 May 1961.
13. Arthur M. Schlesinger, *A Thousand Days: John F. Kennedy in the White House* (London: Andre Deutsch, 1965), pp. 668-9.
14. For the role of the CIA in British Guiana, see 'Foreign Relations, 1964-8, Vol. XXXII, Dominican Republic; Cuba; Haiti; Guyana'. It may be accessed from: http://www.guyana.org/govt/US-declassified-documents-1964-1968.html.

15. US Government, Meeting of Kennedy and Macmillan, Birch Grove, England, 30 June 1963.
16. *Ibid.*
17. Leader, the *Catholic Standard*, 23 August 1963.
18. *British Guiana Constitutional Conference, 1963,* Cmd. 2203, November 1963.
19. The *Daily Chronicle*, 26 October 1963.
20. *Ibid.*
21. The *Daily Chronicle*, 1 November 1963
22. *Ibid.*
23. *Guiana Graphic*, 20 February 1964.
24. See my *Sweetening 'Bitter Sugar'*, *op. cit.* [2005]), p. 571. The quote from Burnham is taken from the *Guiana Graphic*, 9 February 1964.
25. *Mirror*, 31 May 1964.
26. Interview with Eusi Kwayana, Georgetown, Guyana, 22 September 1992. The quote is reproduced from my 'The Anatomy of Cheddi Jagan's Marxism', in John La Guerre and Ann Marie Bissessar (eds.), *Calcutta to Caroni and the Indian Diaspora* (St. Augustine, Trinidad: The University of the West Indies, School of Continuing Studies, 2005 [3rd edition]), p. 452.
27. *Mirror*, 5 November 1965.
28. *Mirror*, 26 January 1966.
29. *Weekend Post and Sunday Argosy*, 8 May 1966.
30. See 'The Havana Conference: New Stage in the Struggle against Colonialism, Neo-Colonialism and Imperialism', *Thunder*, March 1966.
31. *New Nation*, 16 January 1966.
32. *New Nation*, 3 April 1966.
33. See 'Message from Party Leader: Independence Yes! Celebrations No!', *Thunder*, April 1966.
34. *Weekend Post and Sunday Argosy*, 3 April 1966.
35. The *Sunday Chronicle*, 5 June 1966.
36. The *Sunday Chronicle*, 3 July 1966.
37. See 'Address Delivered to the 25th Anniversary Conference on behalf of the Central Committee of the People's Progressive Party, by the General Secretary, Dr Cheddi Jagan, 3 August 1975'.

THE ANATOMY OF CHEDDI JAGAN'S MARXISM

> Our most personal attitudes are deeply affected by elements in the environment which seem to have no connection with them at all.
>
> – Walter E. Houghton (1957)

> Guyana has always been a land of fantasy. It was the land of El Dorado…
>
> – V.S. Naipaul (1991)

> Imperialism was powerless to arrest the unfolding of the laws of social development discovered by Marx and Engels.
>
> – Editorial, *Thunder*, January-March 1975

> Marxism-Leninism is a science, not a dogma.
>
> – Cheddi Jagan (1990)

Cheddi Jagan was born on 22 March 1918 at Plantation Port Mourant, Berbice, British Guiana (Guyana). His parents were taken to the colony as babies in 1901, by their mothers, indentured labourers from India. Their fathers did not accompany them. The eldest of 11 children, Cheddi trained as a dentist in the United States, between 1936 and 1943. He became involved politically shortly after his return to the colony: first, as founder of a Marxist study group, the Political Affairs Committee (PAC), in late 1946; as legislator from late 1947; then founder, in January 1950, of the first mass-based political party in the colony, the People's Progressive Party (PPP). He was the leader of the short-lived multiracial Government of 1953 (that included Forbes Burnham, the African leader who challenged early for leadership of the Party), which was suspended by the British, after 133 days, alleging that it was communist. He was re-elected in 1957 and 1961 because of the overwhelming support of the larger Indian electorate, comprising Hindus, Muslims and Christians. As documented in more detail in the essay, 'Whose Freedom at Midnight', his defeat, in 1964, was achieved through President Kennedy's machinations and his pressure on the Macmillan Government to change the electoral system to Proportional Representation.[1]

From 1964-1992, the years of rigged elections, executive presidency and party paramountcy, Jagan's Indian supporters were effectively disenfranchised, as he became mired in a sterile, unreconstructed, pro-Moscow communism. When Burnham himself embraced 'Marxism', in 1975, it further compounded Jagan's rudderless-ness. Yet through these dark years, Indian support for Cheddi remained undiminished even as virtually whole villages fled to Canada, the United States, England, Suriname, Trinidad – anywhere that would take them. At the end of the Cold War, and primarily as a result of the intervention of Jimmy Carter, free elections were held in October 1992. Thirty-nine years after the PPP was first elected, Jagan became President of Guyana, a post he held until his death on 6 March 1997. For 50 years he had monopolised Indo-Guyanese votes, despite the fact that few Indo-Guyanese voters shared his political philosophy. He has no parallel in the political history of the Indian diaspora; his longevity apart, most would agree that he was incorruptible: he did not steal; he did not abandon his Marxist creed although the price of his resolve was political suicide. Even the ignominious fall of his glorious ideological beacon, the Soviet Union, did not deprive him of his conviction that communism still offered the best hope for human advancement.

What manner of man was this? What was the source of his uncompromising Marxist creed? To comprehend his passion and inflexibility, on the one hand, and the unfaltering loyalty of the Indo-Guyanese, on the other, requires an exploration of the nature of the Guyanese landscape, its peculiar sugar plantation culture, Cheddi's own experience of plantation life, colonial society generally, as well as the question of ethnic security. To assess his failure one has to explore his Marxist approach to the race question: his inability to reach Africans, to allay their fears.

The late Jamaican novelist, John Hearne, saw a link between landscape and the shaping of a people's temperament: '[W]e must never underestimate the significance of landscape on our lives and perceptions. Like the first stories of childhood, it fashions us in a thousand secret ways'.[2] As I have explored in more detail in the essay, 'Indians in Guyana', the reclamation of the Guyanese coastland for sugar cultivation was achieved only after superhuman effort, and the maintenance of this complex hydraulic system demanded eternal vigilance and great cost. No El Dorado, this strip of land on the north-eastern shoulder of South America!

This hazardous coastland of British Guiana gave slavery its peculiar brutality, culminating in the Berbice Slave Rebellion of 1763 and the Demerara Rebellion of 1823, which hastened the end of the abominable system. The unforgiving land had bred pessimism among early African farmers after the euphoria of the 1840s-50s, when they spent over $1,000,000 acquiring land. Despair, fed by alternating floods and droughts and the lack of a comprehensive drainage and irrigation system, perpetuated the dark memories of slavery and aggravated bitterness towards the plantocracy, who bent the colony to their procrustean mould. Only the large plantations had the resources to remake the land and maintain it, in order to grow sugar-cane.

Their 'empoldered' or reclaimed land stood in stark contrast to the vulnerable African and Indian villages on its periphery. By contrast in Trinidad, where the land demanded no costly hydraulic works, African and Indian small farmers became cane-growers – partners in sugar production. By the 1920s, 44% of the cane was produced by them. In British Guiana 95% of the cane was grown on large plantations. By the late 1930s, one British company, Booker, owned most of these. The plantation retained its malevolent 'otherness', the focus of a general Guyanese antipathy.[3] But agreement on the evil of the plantation did not eradicate mutual racial insecurities among the subordinate groups: first, African resentment of Portuguese commercialism, then the bedevilling African-Indian incomprehension. Indeed, it was part of the contempt of some African Creoles for the Indians that they were 'coolies' trapped in helotry on the estates. Further, the deeper economic vagaries in Guyana tended to exacerbate the fear, harden the stereotypes, towards the end of Empire.

Only the Dutch, with their peerless mastery of land reclamation, could have crafted this bewildering tapestry of drainage canals and fields of clean rectangles, veined with ordered drains, ditches, sea-walls and dams. This geometrical magic spoke of Holland in the Tropics. The feat is truly stupendous, for the Atlantic sits above the land and water from the rain forest 'aback' is a perennial threat. Paradoxically, it was this constructed wonder, with vast bodies of fresh water, which made the colony a haven for the malarial mosquitoes. Guyana needed the dream of El Dorado. It lessened despair and fed dreams of conquest of the unimaginably remote rain forests, watered by mighty rivers that led to mountains of gold. The discovery of pockets of gold and diamond – always tasters – kept the fantasy alive. The millennium is ever round the next bend. The inaccessibility of the interior, the paucity of roads or tracks, the hazards of navigating the big Amazonian rivers, blocked by waterfalls, heightened the fantasies and made the interior almost imaginary. Very few ever got there. The pork-knocker, the intrepid prospector and dreamer who animated the African Guyanese universe, gave it special resonance, a motif of deliverance that fed the notion of this almost mythical space as an area of freedom – away from the coastland: its plantations and resilient images of enslavement; villages of despair, the cemetery of many dreams. It is a dream, as I have noted earlier, dramatised in Jan Carew's classic novel, *Black Midas* (1958).

The Indian, a latecomer to the colony, was not claimed by the pork-knocker's imagination. He rarely got to the interior; but he, too, could not transcend the uses of fantasy in sustaining effort on this capricious land. Fantasy – grandeur masking the commonplace, the ordinary, the lack of wealth – is a vital constituent of the temperament of all Guyanese. In Trinidad, despite the Black Power rebellion of 1970, and the attempted Muslimeen coup of 1990, generally the resources on the ground are real;

the tone of politics mostly less grandiloquent, even self-mocking; ideas more run-of-the mill, though 'bobol' can rise to spectacular heights.[6]

In October 1953, at the time of the suspension of the constitution, Jock Campbell (1912-94), Chairman of the Booker Company, cautioned Guyanese against their millennial reflex, susceptibility to the grandiose politics of Cheddi Jagan. He observed that it was a miracle life was at all possible on the inhospitable coastland. And whilst he alluded to the context of Booker's dominance, he counselled Guyanese not to alienate foreign investment:

> British Guiana is a most imperfect place. But its imperfections are of nature – not Britain or Bauxite or Booker, who are doing their best in formidably difficult physical and economic conditions. The wonder is not that life in British Guiana is not Utopian, but that life and production can exist there at all. Its coastal belt lying below sea-level, a man-made environment reclaimed from the sea by great technical skills and at huge capital expense, fighting a perpetual battle against water, and for years against starvation prices for colonial produce – it is remarkable that inhabited British Guiana can support its ever-growing population at even the present standard of living, low as it is compared with more fortunate countries... Owing to its physical uniqueness there can be no alternative in British Guiana to large-scale planned agriculture. Destroy confidence, drive out capital and skills, and you leave nothing but swamps and starvation.[4]

Jagan rejected Campbell's claim that foreign capital was essential for development. As he wrote in early 1953, on the eve of the first elections under universal adult suffrage, British Guiana did not need Booker; foreign capital was dispensable; it was a yoke. Nationalisation was the way to freedom, he argued in his evocatively titled pamphlet, *Bitter Sugar*:

> Booker is the symbol of British imperialism in B.G... It is represented in all phases of the economic life, so much so that B.G. is sometimes colloquially referred to as Booker's Guiana. It controls a greater part of the sugar estates, and has a dominant position in commerce... The workers are sweated and millions of dollars produced by them find their way into the pockets of sugar 'gods' in England... As a socialist party [Jagan's PPP], nationalisation of the sugar industry, and indeed all major industries, is our objective. In the interim while we are still tied to British imperialism with limited constitutional powers certain reforms have to be undertaken to break the back of imperialism... Join the fight against sugar imperialism.[5]

'Bitter Sugar' would become the motif animating Jagan's crusade in politics. As Campbell explained to me many years later, in 1990, the appeal of Cheddi's Marxist utopianism was rooted in Guyanese antipathy to Booker's 'latifundism':

> Anywhere else [in the West Indies] the sugar industry and business had nothing like the perceived power of Booker because the sugar industry had a lot of [small] cane farmers; they had a lot of people who diversified

> and fragmented it. [In British Guiana] Booker practically owned the colony; it was a state within the state. Barbadians ran the estates in Barbados [whereas] they were all absentee proprietors in Guyana, apart from the Brassingtons and Vieiras. Booker actually commanded a state within a state.[6]

The Marxist message simplified Guyana's problems; it fed into the millennial El Dorado complex, and it allowed Jagan to theorise the grave race question out of existence, to ignore issues of cultural autonomy and the resilience of perceived cultural differences. It accommodated his notion of the inevitable supremacy of class-consciousness over racial, religious or cultural articulation – 'epiphenomena' that are necessarily transcended in the class struggle. 'Bitter Sugar' could be saddled with all the blame for the colony's historical pain, as Michael Swan, who met Cheddi in Georgetown in 1955, observed:

> [Jagan] denies that the Colony's difficulties arise from the problems of its geography. This is an excuse invented by the imperialists to explain why they have not made greater success of the Colony. The difficulties are 'man-made and made by alien control'...Dr. Jagan's answer is ruthlessly to destroy the power of 'King Sugar'. He was himself born and brought up on a sugar plantation [Port Mourant]...and his political principles are guided by a violent hatred of the sugar interests...Generally a courteous and pleasant man in conversation, he will become excited, indignant and lose all powers of proper reasoning when the subject of sugar is discussed.[7]

Unfortunately, Jagan's obsessive anti-Booker crusade unwittingly endowed his Marxist mission with ethnic associations, a fundamental flaw in this multiracial colony. In 1911, 48% of Indians lived on sugar plantations; by 1931 46.8% still resided there. In 1946, the year Jagan founded the Political Affairs Committee, 38% were still estate residents; indeed, Indians comprised 90% of the population on plantations.[11] 'Bitter Sugar' epitomised a peculiarly Indian political agenda, although Booker's 'latifundism' had implications for all Guyanese. Africans, however, did not see this as their main problem, if a problem at all. Their fear of Indian ascendancy was a greater preoccupation.

Jagan's boyhood was shaped on the sugar plantation. His paternal and maternal grandmothers were taken to British Guiana in 1901 as indentured labourers when his father was two and his mother eighteen months. His grandmothers were allegedly separated from their grandfathers by the *arkatis*, the infamous recruiters in India. An 'uncle' apparently accompanied his paternal grandmother to British Guiana. His parents became child-labourers: his father at Albion, one of Jock Campbell's family's estates; his mother at Port Mourant, where Cheddi was born in 1918 and grew up, the eldest of 11 children. His people originated in Basti, in eastern Uttar Pradesh, and were of Kurmi caste. He has remarked that there was no rebel like him in his family tree.[8] What made this rebel in British Guiana? What were the flaws of his rebellion?

Jagan saw nothing noteworthy in his caste provenance, neither did he explore anything beyond the bare facts he retrieved from the ships' registers about his antecedence. As I have recorded at greater length in the essay, 'Girmitiyas and my Discovery of India', nineteenth century colonial officials in the United Provinces [Uttar Pradesh] were effusive in praising the agricultural skills of Kurmis, although most were landless. They were impressed with their thrift, refined husbandry (especially women's meticulous farming methods), consistency of effort and their ingenuity in exploiting diverse economic niches simultaneously. A more recent source noted the practicality of Kurmi's attitude to money and the land, in Basti, the home district of Cheddi's grandmothers:

> Most moneylenders amongst the tenantry are Kurmis. It is reported from one registration office in the Basti district, where the Kurmis are particularly strong in number, that of the total sum which passes from lender to borrower in a certain tahsil (sub-district), the Kurmi contributes a full half. Generally, his own indebtedness is small, and he has money to put by at the end of the year… The Kurmi is always planting whether his crop lives or dies.[9]

Those were the qualities Cheddi's grandmothers and his parents cultivated in the new land. He recalled for me, in 1992, the formative influence of his mother, Bachaoni: 'She taught me the rudiments of finance, of thrift, of how to get along and make do, to survive'. And like the imaginatively gifted Kurmis of Uttar Pradesh, his father's earnings as a 'driver', a field foreman at Port Mourant, were supplemented with rice cultivation, a few heads of cattle and the produce of a kitchen garden. It was from his father that he acquired his leadership qualities. Old Jagan (1899-1960) rose from the ranks of a menial cane-cutter at the age of 14 to 'driver', on merit. Cheddi said he was a good cane-cutter, a strong man, and an even-handed 'driver'; but he had reached the ceiling of his rise on the plantation. The next step up, an overseer, was reserved for white or very light men. He did not want his son's ambition to be similarly thwarted. Cheddi explained: 'He sacrificed everything to give me an education; he realised the value of education. If you want to get out of the estates you had to be educated, so he sacrificed everything to give me a high school education, to go to Queen's College [in Georgetown], and then later on, to give me enough money to go abroad [to America] – a small amount but to him it was a lot of money'.[10]

There is much here to suggest the handing on of what were seen as Kurmi values in Cheddi's own capacity for hard work, a sincerity of purpose that was repelled by graft or financial self-aggrandisement, and a unique thrift including when it involved the expenditure of state funds.

The abstemious boyhood built in him revulsion to extravagance, the frills of high life, which most people in power take for granted. He never drank or smoked or dressed extravagantly, neither did he entertain; he never flew executive class and would take circuitous routes to save on airfare, even when President. But the spartan boyhood also gave Cheddi a conception of learning that was inflexibly utilitarian: a propensity for formulaic underpinnings that shut out the imagination. Once the mould was in place, he felt safe. He was not encumbered by the burden of the perils of original thought and the necessity to compromise, to continually rethink. So, paradoxically, I think, the later Marxist illumination came out of essentially conservative promptings.

The constraints of race and class on Cheddi's father's ambition would soon touch Cheddi's own life. He attended the elite Queen's College, in Georgetown, from 1932 to 1935, but he had to return to Port Mourant for a year, 1935-6, having failed to procure a job in the colonial service, in the capital, because of 'a paucity of godfathers'. Such jobs often went to light-skinned, coloured people, with the right family connections.[11] The 'coolie' from the plantation was not in the frame for prestigious urban employment; for the rural Indian the barricade of prejudice, on racial and class lines, was virtually impenetrable.[12] There was a lesson in race and class on the plantation, too, his own Port Mourant, where the Manager, J.C. Gibson, an Englishman, 'czar, king, prosecutor and judge', an awesome figure. On the plantation, the paths to the planter's mansion and the worker's ranges (logies) did not intersect. This bred in Cheddi a consuming curiosity, later a compulsion, to penetrate and dismantle the world of the 'other'. He often told a powerful tale from his boyhood, six or seven years after the termination of Indian indentureship, as if it were the signature of his humiliation:

> I recall vividly my curiosity about the manager's mansion. I wanted to know what it felt like to be inside the gate. I wanted to know what was going on inside. I must have been about eight or nine years old [1926-7]. I joined the creole [child-labour] gang and went to share in the largesse of the manager. The manger's wife, Mrs. Gibson, stood at the window of the top floor of this imposing mansion. She threw coins down to us and enjoyed seeing the wild scramble for the pennies. This is the way our manager's wife offered gifts to worker's children at Christmas time on a sugar plantation.[13]

This was a seminal moment in the making of Cheddi's passionate hatred for 'King Sugar'. The image of Mrs. Gibson tossing pennies to child-labourers in a frenzied scramble, must have lodged in his imagination, the motif of his crusade against the 'sugar gods'. This, in conjunction with the racial barrier that killed his able father's ambition on the plantation, nurtured the rebel in Cheddi, to fight for the underdog. Although his father was a field foreman, he retained links with the workers as well as the overseers. He said that he 'never completely identified' with the authorities; he always sided with the workers 'in his own quiet way, without jeopardising his position'. Cheddi told me that he acquired boldness, a moral frame of reference, of right and wrong, and a capacity for hard work and sacrifice, from his indomitable father. But he totally rejected his father's habit of hard drinking. He remembers: 'At weekends he just drank; this was the only past-time he had'.[14] Cheddi, as noted earlier, never drank. He did not entertain; he was scrupulous with money. In this land of big drinkers, asceticism is not an asset. He never really acquired personal friends; he was not one for intimacy, although he was always polite, humble and charming. He tended to assess people in terms of his perception of their class background and where they had reached politically – an ideological estimate that did not make for small talk or a lighter judgement; no give-and-take. It was categorical in its political assumptions and exclusions. It did not make for alliances or statesmanship.

His father's position on the estate did not affect Cheddi's relationship with less privileged boys at Port Mourant. He continued to play cricket with them, the ultimate bond among boys his age; but his father's status, in the lower middle stratum on the estate, gave him ambition, the way his principled stance on workers' rights offered him a moral compass. He was the first from his family to go to high school, at Port Mourant, then Queen's College; he was the first from his area to attend the latter. The pressure to succeed must have been immense. The financial burden on his family, the massive expectation on the plantation – the fear of failure – filled him with an intensity of purpose. There would be no deviations or distractions, no broader interests. He did not wander beyond the academically stilted colonial curriculum, so oblivious of the Guyanese environment. His education at Queen's College was about preparing for and passing examinations set in England – to get a good job, preferably a profession, in order to escape the plantation and help his many siblings to do the same. It could not stimulate the intellect; it did not offer the means of self-assessment. It could not have lifted the insecurities of a 'coolie' boy from the backwoods, bereft of a literary tradition.

In Georgetown, as a Kurmi (middling agricultural caste) lodging in the home of a high caste Kshatriya, he was quickly made to know his place: he slept on the floor although there was a spare room with a bed. At the home of another Hindu, his many chores before and after school included 'cutting grass for goats'. He hated that. This was the first time he had encountered the pernicious effect of the caste system. He 'deeply resented' such arrogance, and he 'rebelled against it in many ways'.[15] Cheddi's mother was a Hindu but she was not a fastidious devotee. Rituals were performed, festivals celebrated communally, but there was no intensity: the children could lapse and catch up when necessary. But those Georgetown humiliations, by high caste

Hindus, probably turned Cheddi away from religion, for good. It alienated him from his Indian frame of reference, and rendered him impoverished in terms of cultural grounding. A massive void had claimed an unassailable space in the young man: he would never attain religious or cultural mooring. His Hinduism, if not rooted out, was irreparably vitiated; it would become purely instrumental, exploitable in a political context.

Cheddi left Queen's College with an Oxford and Cambridge School Certificate. He claimed he was 'relatively unscathed'. In fact, he had retreated into his schoolwork, virtually unaware of the potentially enriching cultural and educational strands that were being threaded through the Indian community by a small, but vibrant, middle-class elite in Georgetown. Reflecting on my own immersion in diverse extracurricular activities, in the city, while I was at Queen's College in the late 1960s, I pointed out to Cheddi that during his sojourn in the city, 1932-5, there were already several active Indian organisations. I noted that the [Wesleyan] East Indian Young Men's Society, led by an Indian intellectual, Peter Ruhomon, was opened to all Indians, whatever their religion. They debated cultural and political issues; were drawn to a resurgent India through books on its ancient achievements, as well as the contemporary Gandhian revolt against foreign rule, covered copiously by all local newspapers (at least four in the early 1930s). I noted also the British Guiana East Indian Association, which had been active since 1919, and had ongoing links with nationalists in India. Cheddi replied casually that he was ignorant of any such activities, read no newspapers, and had no interest, then, in the Indian nationalist struggle. But one could question, too, whether there would have been any easy welcome for an estate boy – still a coolie, however bright – amongst that distinctly Anglicised, Indo-Saxon, middle-class urban elite. Whatever, Cheddi read no Indian history, had no intellectual curiosity in the land of his ancestors. He read his prescribed school texts – nothing more. Anything beyond this did not reach him:

> There was no bridge at all, no association – [I was] just going to Queen's College to pass exams; there was no way to mobilise young people like me into that kind of stream. Things were happening but at that stage my consciousness and awareness weren't developed.[16]

Martin Carter (1927-97), the poet, Jagan's young Marxist protégé in the late 1940s-early 1950s, tried to grasp what the Georgetown experience of the early 1930s would have meant to Cheddi. He offered this to V.S. Naipaul, in 1991:

> The sheer area of experience was too much for a young man from a plantation background to deal with. We were even more remote than we are today from so-called metropolitan centres. You could imagine – [Martin Carter looks for a word] the lostness of a young man in those days coming out of a background without a literary culture.[17]

This Georgetown 'lostness' not only left him with a narrow educational compass, it blocked off any wellspring of intellectual or cultural growth. It closed the mind to things lacking perceived utility; it also closed the imagination, so that what was available as potential Indian cultural and religious enrichment was not taken in. It would also shut him out from empathy with African culture and history, the basis of their aspirations, their fears and anxieties. This was exacerbated by the fact that Cheddi grew up on a plantation that was almost exclusively Indian. When he brought his Marxist passion to the political arena later, he could not really appreciate why Africans were afraid of Indian domination, which he himself had come to embody by 1955, when the principal African leader, Forbes Burnham, left the PPP. The 'lostness' stayed. He never did acquire the rudiments of a literary culture, to moderate received certainties. Naipaul assesses this literary void among Hindus in the Caribbean and his transcendence of it:

> We were people of ritual and sacred texts. We also had our epics... we heard them constantly sung or chanted. But it couldn't be said we were a literary people. Our literature, our texts didn't commit us to an exploration of our world; rather, they were cultural markers, giving us a sense of the wholeness of our world, and the alienness of what lay outside... I had a better idea of Indian history and Indian art than my grandparents had. They had possessed rituals, epics, myth; their identity lay within that light; beyond that light there was darkness, which they won't have been able to penetrate. I didn't possess the rituals and the myths; I saw them at a distance. But I had in exchange been granted the ideas of inquiry and the tools of scholarship... I could carry four or five or six different cultural ideas in my head. I knew about my ancestry and my ancestral culture...[18]

Cheddi had none of this 'self-knowledge' that could have led him to Naipaul's critical instinct. He would probably have acquired the means of inquiry if, like him, he had started from some knowledge of Hindu and Indian culture, or some access to Western literary culture. Colonial prejudice and injustice would leave a deep scar in Cheddi. However, the society was stirring: a rebellious spirit was taking shape. A union representing sugar workers, headed by an Indian, Ayube Edun, would emerge by 1937. Labour troubles had engulfed the plantations of British Guiana in 1935, the year before Cheddi left to study dentistry in America. The avalanche of protest, fanned by abysmal sugar prices during the depression, hit Port Mourant as well. J.C. Gibson was still the manager; he had held the post since 1906. Jock Campbell knew him well. As a young man learning the ropes, on their neighbouring family plantation, Albion, Jock visited him often. He concurs with Cheddi that Gibson had an authoritarian temperament, and adds that Mrs. Gibson was 'a terrifying woman'. But he reveals another dimension of the man: though paternalistic, he was a most able administrator. He was 'a tough manager'; but he was 'a just man'. Unlike the Scottish managers who were predominant in British Guiana, rough Highlanders, Gibson was an Englishman of some sophistication. He was 'feared', but the workers at Port Mourant respected him. Campbell respected him, too; he was 'a class ahead of the others'.[19] During his 33 years as Manager, Gibson had helped to shape an independent persona among his workers. It is arguable that this was an element in shaping Cheddi's own courage and resolve.

Ivy Jailall was born at Port Mourant in 1924 and grew up there in the 1930s. She knew Cheddi's father well and remembers him as a compassionate man, who horsed around with the kids. She also recalls J.C. Gibson. She states that he always allowed workers to fish, collect firewood, gather wild vegetables, gave them water for irrigating rice, and myriad other things on the estate. But he was very cross if they abandoned unwanted small fish on the dam, instead of returning them to the canals. She, too, thought he was a 'just man', who helped his workers.[20]

More crucially, Gibson had made land available for workers on the estate to grow rice and rear cattle; housing was generally better, many having built their own cottages with earnings from supplementary farming. He had also constructed a narrow-gauge railway to transport workers to the cane-fields several miles 'aback'. He was a keen cricketer and promoted the game vigorously on the plantation. Even in the 1920s, Port Mourant had a flourishing cricket club. The people played the game with passion; many were accomplished cricketers. Although still under the scrutiny of Gibson, workers had some autonomy in running the club.[21] It is not fortuitous that this plantation would produce a number of West Indies Test cricketers from the late 1940s: John Trim (1915-60), Rohan Kanhai, Basil Butcher, Joe Solomon, Ivan Madray, Alvin Kallicharran and Mahendra Nagamootoo. The annual horseracing meeting at Port Mourant, on 1 August, had become a national event; the Governor would travel from Georgetown to open it. By the early 1930s, this healthier plantation, in an infamously malarial colony, had shaped a discernibly independent, bolder Indian worker. J.C. Gibson's role was paramount. Jock Campbell elaborated for me:

> Port Mourant was a very, very well-run estate. [The people] were big and they were healthy in that area because of the salt air. There was no doubt about it, they were particularly healthy and the malaria was less serious. I think I told you that when we started [peasant] cane farming in my day [late 1950s], the Port Mourant cane farmers were way ahead of any other workers in the industry – they were marvellous people…The labour force was confident.[22]

This spirit of independence, and the unrequited hurt, must have quickened whatever rebellious instincts had taken shape in Cheddi Jagan. His father's 'boldness' and 'humanity', he told me, stayed with him; but his father's life spoke also of hope and its abrogation, as eloquently as the plantation evoked social and racial distances. As noted earlier, he had gone from menial cane-cutter to 'driver', but could go no further because of his race. This lodged in Cheddi's colonial mind, as did the fact that he could not get a job in the colonial civil service after he left Queen's College in 1935, for the same reason. At that point, he had no means of assessing his colonial environment from an intellectual perspective; the raw emotions, however submerged, remained part of his response. Out of sheer frustration he left for Washington in 1936, aged 18, to do dentistry. Naipaul, paraphrasing Martin Carter, reflects: 'Cheddi had no literary culture, nothing that would have helped him to see and understand, and put things in their place. He had simply taken things as they had come'.[23]

But he had the passion fed by the hurt and the injustice of colonial society – an intensity that made for single-mindedness. He did not succumb to despair. The comparatively progressive character of Port Mourant also gave him a sense of possibilities: ambition. The millennial El Dorado – reflex of Guyanese – bred an instinct for escape, flights of the imagination. It gave rise to the hyperbolic, a bravura persona – masks for fear and self-doubts rooted in the hazards of the land, and the incomprehension among its diverse peoples. The literary void, the underdeveloped intellectual gifts for self-assessment and critical evaluation, left Cheddi with little facility for reasoning, analysing, judging on merits – for filtering things beyond the framework he had seized for himself. The imagination and flexibility were not there, but the passion did not wane.

The intensity never ceased. Indeed, the struggle to survive while he trained in dentistry in America, between 1936 and 1943, hardened it; the narrow utilitarian thrust of his education was reinforced. He admired Gandhi and Nehru who sparked some pride in his Indian background, but he was devoid of Indian culture. He had no Hinduism, no conception of, or feeling for, the secular gifts of that ancient tradition: its poetry, art, architecture, music, philosophy. He was just as bereft of Guyanese history: very little had been written as late as the 1930s-40s. In any case, he did not read beyond the strictly utilitarian, what was not schoolwork. He had, at that point, no frame of reference to make sense of the world.

He became very ill in 1943 and was sent to a sanatorium to recuperate. The enforced rest made him reflect on the limitations of his education. He decided to go part-time to the YMCA College in Chicago. There, under Professor Sinha, an Indian, he became interested in political science. He read on the American War of Independence. *The Robber Barons: The Great American Capitalists* (by Matthew Josephson, 1934) made him understand how American capitalism worked. He read Nehru's biography; that inspired him. As he told Naipaul: 'Whatever I do, I do very intensely'. The social science course did not lessen the intensity. He was going beyond the mould of a dentist; he wanted to know how 'capitalism worked'; but there was no room for eclecticism, for works of the imagination, for exploration of human motives or individual motivation.

That is why literature – the probing of deeper personal recesses, inquiry into complex human responses, frailties, a sense of the absurd – meant little to him. The world of the imagination, the intellectual probing into political nuances, the exploration of culture, religious complexities, did little for him. Cheddi was only comfortable with total knowledge; he had a passion for certainties, manuals: *How to Win Races; How to Play Bridge*. The urgencies, the procrustean demands of a hard boyhood, the massive expectations and the fear of failure as a student, in Georgetown, Washington and Chicago – he was the first child; so much was invested in him – bred in him a narrow, rigid, utilitarian mental frame. It also gave him the drive, the sense of mission, the sincerity and consistency of motives – the inflexibility, too. His Marxist creed would be his undoing, having staked everything on it by entering the Cold War on the side of the Soviet Union (and Cuba). He embraced it uncritically, with religious zeal, precisely because he saw it as a science, the key to human transformation: the map to the perfectibility of human kind.

In 1943 he met and married Janet Rosenberg (1920-2009) in Chicago. She was a young Jewish American of East European stock. Like many young people during the depression of the 1930s, she was disillusioned with American capitalism. She became a communist, a member of the Young Communist League. She had read some of the Marxist classics. Her beauty ('love at first sight', Cheddi recalls) and her initiation into 'scientific socialism' struck a chord instantly. His sojourn at YMCA College had given him a 'peep into socialism'. He would soon to be given a frame of reference to comprehend the world, having married this 'exceedingly beautiful woman'. Both the creed and Janet would endow him with the strength to take on the 'sugar gods' and their allies in British Guiana. He recalled that on the plantations 'intermarriage was strictly forbidden'.[24] He had violated their code: his mission against 'King Sugar' was about to be joined. He spoke to me, in 1992, of the ideological awakening – and Janet – in equipping him for war against the plantocracy: 'Marxist literature gave me a total understanding to fit everything together... Janet's influence was on the moral side: she was fed up with middle-class emptiness... middle-class American values, the consumerism, the whole emptiness of it'. One gets the impression that in spite of his passion, without his discovery of Janet and through her, Marxism – the acquisition of total knowledge – he would have become just another middle class professional. Janet's own political instinct, support and capacity for organisation translated Cheddi's passion into a political mission. He told me that she was a major force behind the fact that 'I did not betray my class; money was not my motivation or hers in politics'.[25]

Cheddi and Janet, 1956: comrades in the Marxist crusade

'A kind of homecoming': Jagan and Mikhail Suslov (chief ideologue of the CPSU) and Nikolai Podgorny (President of the USSR), Moscow, June 1969

Cheddi returned to British Guiana in 1943. Janet joined him later that year, in December. She brought him some Marxist primers, which gave him 'total understanding of the world'. In 1991 he recalled for V.S. Naipaul, in a clean, rehearsed narrative, that illumination of nearly 50 years before:

> It was Janet who, when she came here in 1943, brought me Little Lenin Library books – little tracts, pamphlets. It was the first time I had read Marxist literature. And then – as with the bridge books – I began reading Marxist books like mad. I read *Das Kapital* after the Little Lenin series. And that helped me to have *a total understanding* of the development of society. Until then, all the various struggles – Indians, blacks, the American people – had been disjointed experiences. To put it in a way that was *totally* related to a socio-economic system came from reading Marxist literature. For instance, the woman question was dealt with in Engels's book, *The Origins of the Family*. The Marxist theory of surplus value brought a *totally* new understanding of the struggle of the working class – not only that they were exploited. It was exciting to me, an intellectual excitement, because a whole new world opened to me, *a total understanding of the world...* [emphasis added][26]

Cheddi told Naipaul: 'There has always been a division between Janet and me. At the end of the day she can drop everything and read a novel. I take my work home'. He could never see the lighter side: 'Whatever I do, I do very intensely'.[27] An anti-colonial reflex laid dormant for years; it ignited towards the end of the 1940s. Deeply rooted in 'bitter sugar', it was marked by inflexibility, an incapacity for compromise, a fixity of thought that rejected virtually everything from the colonial encounter, the tainted world of the imperialists. Marxism gave him the illusion of 'total' knowledge; its formulaic construction would be accepted unreservedly as the science of human development – the road to perfectibility. What he had seized on was a determinist, Stalinist vulgarisation of Marx, the dogma of Marxist-Leninism made gospel by the Communist Third International. There is little evidence that Cheddi Jagan ever encountered Marx as the radical, Hegelian philosopher of the *Economic and Philosophic Manuscripts of 1844*, or Marx the cultivated literary man for whom Balzac was a crucial witness in *Das Kapital*. For Cheddi, what could be known was now known. He did not have to be lumbered with the perils or uncertainties of new thought. He could bypass the vagaries of intellectual inquiry. Janet, on the other hand, because of her firmer grounding, her home-grown radicalism, an authentic aspect of the American youth culture of the late 1930s, and her exposure to a more rounded, eclectic intellectual milieu, did not have to wear her Marxism on her sleeves. It was there and would become a pillar of their anti-colonial crusade, but it was invariably muted, less dogmatic: subtle but effective. She could read novels and enjoy sensations beyond the austere Marxist-Leninist mould, with its claim to 'scientific' thought.

Impelled by his 'total understanding', Cheddi calculated the 'degree of exploitation' or 'the rate of surplus value' of sugar workers at 142%. He argued that in a 10-hour day the worker's remuneration (wage) was, in fact, covered by 4 hours of work, the sale of his labour power; the other six hours constituted 'surplus value', profit extracted by the sugar capitalist: exploitation.[27] As early as 1946 he asserted that the capitalist was superfluous to production; only the dismantling of capitalism would bring freedom to the working class: 'All these parasitic exploiters are sharing among themselves... the surplus labour value created in production by the wage-earning working class. Only with the complete elimination of the capitalist mode of production and distribution, and its consequent surplus value and the substitution of socialistic means of production and distribution will this exploitation cease'.[28] All this sounds like quotation from one of the Little Lenin booklets.

In 1948 Cheddi identified the new 'People's Government' in Czechoslovakia, headed by the Communist Party, as a model eminently worthy of emulation for eradicating 'bitter sugar' from Guyana. He deemed it a 'new and genuine democracy', and was repelled by allegations of its totalitarianism. Apparently, they were redistributing land to the peasantry; no one could own more than 125 acres. He imagined the demise of the 'sugar gods' in a similar kind of state:

> Transposing this situation to British Guiana would mean that the present slave plantation system of the sugar estates would be completely smashed. The estate land would be divided up and the sugar workers instead of merely working for miserable wages would be the producers of their own sugar cane on their own land. The sugar factories would be owned and operated by the Government.[29]

Just like that 'bitter sugar' would be extirpated.

He did not explore the potential hazards for small farmers, of growing cane in a historically daunting hydrological environment. As noted in the essay, 'Balram Singh Rai's Anticommunism', in 1958 and 1960 Jock Campbell, the Chairman of Booker, did try to meet Cheddi halfway. He offered him the possibility of the state, trade unions and local interests owning 51% of Booker. Cheddi never responded. That went against the grain of Marxist economics. His true position on the matter of joint ownership emerged later, in 1972, as Leader of the Opposition. He was pressuring the Burnham regime to nationalise 'the commanding heights of the economy... foreign-owned and controlled mines, plantations, factories, banks, insurance and foreign trade'. Cheddi argued: '[T]he erosion of imperialist strength and power universally had forced them to design a new economic strategy, an aspect of their neo-colonialism – joint ownership'. He had no time for this ruse, the 'involvement of nationals and even governments as partners in imperialist companies as with Booker Stores, Demerara Company, etc... Local people are involved as shareholders, managers and directors, who ultimately defend foreign rather than national interests and reinforce foreign domination. In Guyana, while the imperialists control the commanding heights of the economy...the government indulges in tokenism and state capitalism...'[30]

By 1975 Burnham had completed the nationalisation of the bauxite industry, given diplomatic recognition to Cuba and had even claimed to have adopted Marxism. The PPP were in a quandary; they were now forced into 'critical support' of the regime. But Cheddi was unrelenting in his determination to get Burnham to nationalise the sugar industry and other sectors of the economy. He saw that as a vindication of his creed. The big prize was 'evil' Booker:

> It must be noted that while the PNC has been forced to take some steps against imperialism, it does not have a consistent, firm anti-imperialist position. Witness that the Booker monopoly remains intact, and the PNC has declared its intention of working in partnership with it. The foreign banks and insurance companies still have a great influence in the field of finance and credit... Today many evils like the Booker monopoly... still persist... [W]e do not see the attainment of socialism without first completing the anti-imperialist process by nationalisation of the Booker monopoly, the banks and the insurance companies.[31]

Burnham nationalised Booker the following year; soon 80% of the economy was under state control and already on the road to ruin. Yet the more Burnham was perceived to be moving to the left, to be embracing 'socialism', the more Cheddi felt that he had to demonstrate the purity of his Marxism. That was aggravated by Castro's conferring Cuba's highest national award on Burnham. As if to preserve his reputation among 'fraternal' communists, Cheddi would continually assert his Party's claim as the true bearer of the mantle of the Soviet Union and Cuba – the inheritors of an unsullied Marxism, the only genuine communists in Guyana. He would become imprisoned by the rhetoric, marooned in a quagmire of received jargon, as he sought at the same time to justify 'critical support' for Burnham's cynical appropriation of the rhetoric of socialism and a command economy that could be plundered by the PNC party elite:

> As Marxists-Leninists we must be scientific and dialectical. This means taking an objective view, seeing things not on the basis of how we feel but how they really are. This means not being dogmatic, rigid or inflexible. If the situation demands it, then we must be fearless in changing our political line... Critical support does not mean unconditional support. It means just what it says – giving support for any progressive measure, opposing any reactionary moves, and criticising all shortcomings... We are glad the PNC has been forced to swallow its anti-communist anti-Cuba sentiments and to advocate Marxism-Leninism.[32]

Ten years later, in August 1985, a couple of days before the death of Forbes Burnham, the PPP passed a resolution proclaiming their arrival in

Forbes Burnham (1923-1985): bright, handsome, charismatic – Machiavellian

Comrades! Burnham visits his new-found hero, Fidel, Havana, 1975

the promise land. They were now recognised as a communist party by the 'fraternal' parties of the Soviet Union and its satellites. They traced their ascent to the pinnacle:

> [T]he Party decided in 1969 to commence a process of transformation from a loose, mass party into a disciplined Marxist-Leninist organisation, capable not only of widely disseminating Marxist-Leninist ideology but also of more effectively organising and uniting all working people in the struggle for a socialist Guyana... Since 1969 a series of steps have been taken to reorganise the Party's structure, promulgate a Programme, develop a disciplined core of cadres and membership imbued with the ideology of Marxism-Leninism, undeviatingly apply the principles of Marxism-Leninism to everyday problems, apply the principles of democratic centralism and criticism and self-criticism and such other principles as were necessary to achieve our objective. In this regard since our decision to transform the Party, our work on the ideological front of the class struggle has been strengthened in the fight against right and left deviationism... Our international work is based on proletarian internationalism... We are generally recognised as and accorded the status of a communist part by all other fraternal parties...The prestige of our Party both locally and internationally, had never been higher. We can say with confidence at this 22nd Congress that our Party has been transformed into a Communist Party.[37]

This arrival did not lessen the obfuscation, the cascade of dogmas and it hardly needs pointing out that at the time when this was written, the Soviet Union was in deep economic and political crisis – the period of Glasnost and perestroika, when Gorbachev had begun, belatedly, to give licence to an internal critique of the dogmatism of Stalinist Marxist-Leninism and corruption within the party. It also speaks of the illusion of a 'disciplined core of cadres' – who, after Cheddi's death in 1997, morphed into the most corrupt, self-serving government that Guyana has ever seen. Perhaps at the time of the 1985 declaration, it gave the leadership of the Party – a sect of tightly-knit 'comrades' several decades younger than Cheddi and Janet – the satisfaction of feeling that they now possessed the truth that went to the heart of the creed, a moral superiority. No belated, bogus Burnhamite affectation! For many of these young Indian 'comrades', the density of the dogmas compensated for intellectual limitations. It impressed them as high learning. The sound of the idioms of the creed had taken the place of Hindu mantras. This was augmented by rituals associated with Congresses; hosting delegates from 'fraternal' parties; paid guided-tours to the USSR, GDR, Bulgaria, Cuba or Mongolia (even the Gobi Desert), to see socialism in action. They belonged to the chosen – a family of true believers. There was a kind of religiosity about it, discernible in Cheddi's repudiation of the 'eclectic', 'opportunist' Marxism of the Working People's Alliance (WPA), the Party of the late Dr. Walter Rodney (1942-80) and Eusi Kwayana. The aim was to demonstrate the ideological un-impeachability of the PPP over the intellectual eclecticism of the WPA. It was nonsense; but the doctrinal tone – the vocabulary of the creed – would have impressed Cheddi's disciples:

> Marxist-Leninist science teaches that 'class dictatorship' exists in a bourgeois (capitalist), a transitional (petty bourgeois, bureaucratic and military strata), and a proletarian (working class) state. 'Dictatorship of the proletariat' is a specific form of state rule at a particular period in the revolutionary process, the transition period from capitalism to socialism. In essence, it is a higher type of democracy than bourgeois democracy (dictatorship of the minority capitalist class) since it has replaced the rule of the minority capitalist class by the majority working class and its allies, the peasantry (farmers) and other non-proletarian strata of working people. *This revolutionary process evolved, as in the Soviet Union, into a socialist democracy, a state of the whole people* [emphasis added].[34]

Not a word about the debilitating race question in Guyana! Not a word about the crisis of the state and the economy in the USSR! The majority of Indians, primarily for reasons of racial security, continued to support Jagan. He never had to worry about that. He could wallow in the ideological morass. But by the 1980s there were very few Africans, indeed, in his communist party. This was the most catastrophic aspect of Cheddi's Marxist mission: one by one, virtually every African of note had quit the PPP, frustrated by what they saw as its pro-Indian bias, even racism, which alienated them from a movement that had ostensibly repudiated racial proclivities. Eusi Kwayana (formerly Sydney King), an African Marxist, had been instrumental in garnering African support for Cheddi in the 1947 elections. He explored for me, in 1992, this debilitating flaw in Cheddi's mission. An austere man, Kwayana epitomises African alienation from the PPP:

> There are these racial insecurities. The two major groups have certain conceptions of each other. Africans tended to see Indians not only as clannish but as having more money, and having an interest in land. A lot of them were selling out their land [to Indians] when they went broke, and although they were doing it voluntarily, it also alarmed them. Then there was this rumour that someone from India had come and said that those who owned the land owned the country. You hear this up to now among older people...A lot of Africans were unable to go beyond that. And they would look at the behaviour of Indians near to them in judging the PPP. The PPP does not understand this until now. So if there is an aggressive Indian member of the PPP in their district, Africans tended to see the PPP through him. Jagan never deals with these things – he never does. Essentially he has a lot of courage against imperialism, but at the subjective level the problem of African insecurity was never dealt with. That was one of the reasons why I left the PPP [in 1956]...*The psychology of the leader is crucial. We had to fight to get Africans to accept an Indian leader. He didn't have that problem. He never had to accept a leader of another race. So he doesn't know what it is. He speaks about the problem of revolution, but there was no personal revolution – within himself –*

> *therefore, he could not deal with the problem of ethnicity. The theory was enough* [emphasis added].[35]

It can be argued that the tendency to millennialism in the Guyanese mind encouraged Cheddi's uncritical absorption of the Soviet creed. For him, the theory was infallible: the race question would evaporate when the society embraced Marxism-Leninism. As early as 1947 he had expressed his simplistic formula thus:

> Labour [he meant socialists]... will have to solve the question of race. *This it can do by replacing the question of race by the one of class.* The rich and the poor of one particular race do not have the same interests. It is the poor and exploited of all races who have a common interest – that of improving working and living conditions [emphasis added].[36]

In fact, in early 1953, as I documented in the essay 'Whose Freedom at Midnight', amidst the euphoria of the tenuous multiracial alliance that was the PPP, Eusi Kwayana, the assistant general secretary, had cautioned that they should not contest more than eight seats in the General Elections. He feared that if they won the elections in a still racially unconsolidated country, the question of racial insecurity among Africans and Indians would have negative reverberations within the Party itself. As I noted in the same essay, Kwayana was equally revealing on why Africans did not necessarily share Jagan's or the PPP's anti-colonial, anti-estate commitments, and were less imbued with the nationalist spirit that Indo-Guyanese had drawn from Indian independence in 1947. Kwayana felt that Jagan's intellectual limitations, fortified by Indian euphoria and loyalty, prevented him from seeing the broader picture. Kwayana observes that the PPP failed to grasp that the racial question was fundamental. Indeed, to raise the issue in the Party was 'to be divisive... to deviate from accepted policy'.[37] Yet, as early as 1951, this matter was 'not absent from the life of the party'. On grounds of race and ideology, 'sections of the party had considered a change in leadership important'. Kwayana explains further the basis of African fears of Jagan's leadership, and the context in which Burnham joined the PPP in 1951:

> The basic misgiving in the minds of the Afro-Guyanese working people was not the policy of Jagan as such, but their uncertainty of the linkages between him and the defensive Indo-Guyanese politicians and public figures of the day. He had been active in the B.G. East Indian Association. Secondly, many did not feel 'equally yoked' without a prominent Afro-Guyanese of equivalent social standing or status. Forbes Burnham, Guyana Scholar, returning from law studies in England, fitted the bill... [He] had been head of the West Indian Students' Union in England at a time when it fought many liberation struggles, and came home with a reputation. His often empty oratory held masses of people spellbound... Burnham's entry into the all but established PPP as its first Chairman [Jagan was Leader] sent waves of relief among Afro-Guyanese... [He] played a leading

role in persuading the sections still omitted from the mass movement that a common agenda had arrived. A certain impatience with depth marked the campaignings of both leaders to whom an anti-colonial victory was more immediate than a consolidating of a deep non-racial understanding… The main area of education [by the PPP] should have been the racial question and arrangements should have been made inside the party for power sharing.[38]

The PPP won the elections with 18 of the 24 seats, and Kwayana's apprehensions were realised. The multiracial coalition of 1953 collapsed; it was on the ropes even before the suspension of the constitution, as Burnham challenged Jagan's claim to lead the newly elected Government. Burnham quit the PPP in 1955. The two race-based parties, the PPP and Burnham's People's National Congress (PNC), thereafter became entrenched. Politics degenerated into the racial carnage of the early 1960s, as Africans and Portuguese, aided and abetted by President Kennedy, resorted to violence in 1962-3, to make the colony ungovernable under Jagan, in order to delay Independence. Indians retaliated in 1964. African-Indian incomprehension became chronic. Yet Cheddi never tackled the race issue frontally; he continued to hide behind Marxist dogmas. In 1974, for instance, he wrote an article captioned 'Race, Class and Ideology'. He was still 'replacing' race with class. The problem could be theorised away:

What is the reality? Those who see only race in politics see only a part of the reality. The 'two monolithic racial blocs' idea, like the 'two superpowers' idea, interprets reality quantitatively, and not qualitatively. *Side by side with race, and more fundamental is class.* What is often forgotten is that the Indian and African racial groups in Guyana are not homogeneous, are not uni-class. At the bottom of each group, consisting the bulk are workers and farmers; at the top, a small percentage of middle-class professionals and capitalists – mainly commercial and industrial capitalists (tied up in some cases with landlordism) in the case of Indians, and mainly bureaucratic-capitalists in the case of Africans… From a mass vanguard party… [the PPP] is being transformed into a Marxist-Leninist party. As a mass vanguard party of the working class, it recognises that apart from the working class, there are other classes and strata – the farmers, intellectuals, students and petty bourgeoisie – which can take an anti-imperialist position… [I]t will work assiduously for action against racism and state-monopoly capitalism [emphasis added].[39]

In February 1974 Cheddi's most loyal Marxist disciple, Ram Karran (1919-90), explained to students at the University of Guyana how the race question would be resolved by the PPP's 'scientific ideology'. This was his master's voice:

Though at a certain stage… [race] might be the dominant force in politics, this can only be a temporary phase. Eventually the economic base and the scientific laws of political economy will assert themselves, and the political situation will be transformed. For this transformation to take

> place and for it to be accelerated, there is the need for a vanguard party such as the PPP. At the ideological level it must put a scientific (Marxist-Leninist) ideology in place of an emotional and/or unscientific and utopian (cooperative socialist) ideology. It must pose an anti-imperialist, pro-socialist programme in place of the PNC's racist, anti-working class and pro-imperialist programme... Only by the attainment of working class power and the complete transformation of the economic structure will racism and the influence of race in politics be finally brought to an end. This has happened in the Soviet Union and in Cuba. It will also happen in Guyana under the leadership of the PPP.[40]

Ten years later, in October 1984, in an interview with Frank Birbalsingh, in Toronto, Cheddi was firm as ever that his Marxism-Leninism 'in relation to the Soviet Union and other Communist countries' was winning. His resolve in not capitulating to imperialism was being vindicated. There was no reason 'for changing course':

> [Birbalsingh]: What... would you regard as your greatest regret over...your long political career of almost forty years? What did not work as you had planned, or as you had hoped?
>
> [Jagan]: I have not many regrets, to tell you the truth. I am a revolutionary and I have confidence, revolutionary confidence in the future, because what I stand for [the Soviet system] is winning. It took a long time in Guyana, but it is winning in the world as a whole.
>
> [Birbalsingh]: You have been in [O]pposition for a long time [since 1964, twenty years].
>
> [Jagan]: That does not matter, because *I am not only fighting for the people of Guyana. I am fighting for the people of the world.* I am contributing to that struggle. That struggle is winning. That is why the United States is so hysterical at the moment, because of that very fact, that what I stand for is winning [emphasis added].[41]

'Guyana has always been a land of fantasy. It was the land of El Dorado', says V.S. Naipaul. It is also a land where Indians have no knowledge of their real Indian antecedence – the reasons for leaving; the places whence their ancestors came; the myth behind the *arkatis*, the infamous recruiters, who allegedly tricked or kidnapped all the indentured labourers; the high incidence of women who went alone to Guyana, about two-thirds. It was a past of darkness in India, and forgetfulness – collective amnesia – helped to alleviate the pain and the need to revisit that past and its secrets. Ignorance persists; but the mythical India of the Hindu classic, the *Ramayana*, depicting a golden age in the just kingdom of Lord Rama – when there was no poverty, no disease – has filled that void in the Indo-Guyanese imagination. There is no memory of Uttar Pradesh and Bihar, their original homes in India. Fantasy, as I have argued, is at the heart of the Guyanese sensibility; and among Indo-Guyanese the El Dorado reflex is augmented by the escapism offered by the *Ramayana*.[42] A millennial strand has coiled itself inextricably in their imagination. Cheddi's own lack of religious empathy and his Marxist utopianism, therefore, may not have been as incompatible with their 'instinctive, ritualised' lives as they appear. His fantasies belonged. They would be inexhaustible to the end. In 1990, with the collapse of the Soviet empire, the *Stabroek News* asked Cheddi whether communism was dying. He replied:

> In Eastern Europe it was not communism (from each according to his ability, to each according to his need) but its first phase, socialism (from each according to his ability to each according to his labour), which ran into trouble. Communism, as a system, has not been tried in any country as yet and remains a highly moralistic and humanistic ideal and destination. Even for the most advanced socialist society it will remain an ideal or goal of the 21st century as admitted distortions and deviations have forced the USSR to literally start all over again along the path of socialism...The goals of socialism and the virtues of Marxist doctrine must not be confused with the failures of those who tried to implement socialism.[43]

One notes that contrary to anything Marx may have intended (he would probably have been horrified) the idea of Marxism as a 'doctrine' remains unshakeable.

Indians in Guyana today continue to vote for the PPP, while Africans still vote for the PNC, at periodic elections – ethnic censuses. Parties that try to transcend the racial mould soon disappear. It is nearly 60 years since Cheddi Jagan founded the Political Affairs Committee, on 6 November 1946, with the aim of 'establishing a disciplined and enlightened Party, equipped with the theory of scientific socialism'. Yet hapless Guyana remains a land marked by racial bigotry, many of its people impoverished, lacking education – washed up – many of the best educated and skilled having fled into exile. His model of perfectibility, which he pursued with religious zeal for nearly half a century, is now a handful of dust.

In the last years, there were perhaps gleams of the kind of pragmatism displayed by the 1957-1962 Jagan governments, but long unvisited. By 1990, Cheddi was arguing that 'foreign capital and certain methods of liberal capitalism...[did not] undermine...the social gains of socialism.' Moreover, he was advocating a 'new partnership with foreign private capital, as the PPP has always advocated for Guyana [sic]'.[44] In 1991, the year before the PPP was returned to government after nearly 28 years, Cheddi told businessmen in Georgetown that his Party rejected 'winner-takes-all politics... and intends to form a plural democratic government to tackle the tasks of reconstruction'.[45]

An honest, passionately dogmatic man, Cheddi Jagan died on the 6th March 1997, aged 78. There was genuinely national mourning and the recognition that whatever his failings, he had made an important contribution in moving Guyana on from its colonial past and creating the possibility, at least, of a nation.

However, at the time of his death, his government had made little progress towards forming a plural, inclusive government that seriously addressed African feelings of exclusion. Since his death, that necessity has retreated ever further, though the two-party blockage in Guyanese politics has to some extent been opened up by the emergence of the Alliance for Change. But it remains a challenge that if Guyanese are to begin to eradicate their racism and build a nation, they must use their imagination to create wealth and devise a wider conception of governance.

Notes

1. For an autobiographical sketch and his version of these events, see Cheddi Jagan, *The West on Trial: My Fight for Guyana's Freedom* (London: Michael Joseph, 1966).
2. See John Hearne, 'What the Barbadian Means to Me', *New World Quarterly*, Vol. 3, Nos. 1-2 (1966-7).
3 This theme is developed in my article, 'The Shaping of the Indo-Caribbean People: Guyana and Trinidad to the 1940s', *Journal of Caribbean Studies*, Vol. 14, Nos. 1-2 (Fall 1999/Spring 2000).
4. Jock Campbell to the Editor, *The New Statesman and Nation*, 24 October 1953.
5. Cheddi Jagan, *Bitter Sugar* (Georgetown: The Author, n.d., [1953]).
6. Interview with Jock Campbell, Nettlebed, Oxfordshire, 9 May 1990.
7. Michael Swan, *British Guiana: The Land of Six Peoples* (London: HMSO, 1957).
8. See note 3 [p. 69].
9. See note 1 [pp. 13-5].
10. E.A.H. Blunt, *The Caste System of Northern India with Special Reference to the United Provinces of Agra and Oudh* (London: OUP, 1931), p. 266.
11. Interview with Cheddi Jagan, Warwick University, Coventry, England, 10 May 1992.
12. Although set in Trinidad, the Guyanese novelist Edgar Mittelholzer's portrayal of the character of Jagabir, and the contempt with which he is regarded by his Creole fellow workers, in *A Morning at the Office* (1950) is acute on the sense of exposure and attendant humiliations awaiting the rural Indian in the urban Creole world.
13. See note 1 [pp. 18-9].
14. See note 11.
15. See note 1 [pp. 23-4].
16. See note 15. See too episodes in Peter Kempadoo's (Lauchmonen) *Guiana Boy* (1960, reprinted as *Guyana Boy* (Leeds: Peepal Tree Press, 2002) and Rooplall Monar's story 'Cent and Jill' in *Backdam People* (Leeds: Peepal Tree Press, 1986) for portrayals of such scenes of intended humiliation.

17. V.S. Naipaul, 'A Handful of Dust: Return to Guyana', *The New York Review of Books*, 11 April 1991, p. 18.
18. V.S. Naipaul, 'Our Universal Civilization', *The New York Review of Books*, 31 January 1991, pp. 22, 24.
19. Interview with Jock Campbell, Nettlebed, Oxfordshire, 23 July 1992.
20. Interview with Ivy Jailall, Sea Well, Berbice, Guyana, 10 February 2003.
21. See note 19.
22. *Ibid*.
23. See note 17.
24. See note 1 [pp. 62-3, 19].
25. See note 13.
26. See note 17 [p. 19].
27. *Ibid*.
28. C.O. 946/1 [Colonial Office], Evidence of Cheddi Jagan to the Venn Commission, 14 January 1949.
29. *PAC Bulletin*, No. 2, 20 November 1946.
30. Cheddi Jagan, *A West Indian State: Pro-Imperialist or Anti-Colonialist* ([Georgetown]: The Author, 1972), pp. 59, 53-4.
31. Cheddi Jagan, 'Address Delivered to 25th Anniversary Conference on Behalf of the Central Committee of the People's Progressive Party, 3 August 1975', *Thunder*, (September-December, 1975), pp. 14-5, 25, 30.
32. *Ibid*., pp. 25, 27-8.
33. 'PPP is Marxist-Leninist', *Thunder*, (Third Quarter, 1985), p. 6.
34. Cheddi Jagan, 'No Future for Pragmatism and Rightist Opportunism', in *Yes to Marxism – No to Rightist Opportunism* (pamphlet issued by the PPP [1985]).
35. Interview with Eusi Kwayana, Georgetown, 22 September 1992.
36. *PAC Bulletin*, No. 20, 17 December 1947.
37. Interview with Eusi Kwayana, 1992
38. Eusi Kwayana, 'More than Survival: Afro-Guyanese and the Nation', (mimeo.), July-August, 1988, pp. 57-8; Kwayana, 'More than Survival: A View of the Indo-Guyanese Contribution to Social Change', (mimeo.), May 1988, pp. 38-9.
39. Cheddi Jagan, 'Race, Class and Ideology', in Cheddi Jagan and Ram Karran, *Race and Politics in Guyana*, (Georgetown: The Authors, 1974), pp. 4, 8.
40. Ram Karran, 'Race and Politics', *Ibid*, p 16.
41. The interview is in Frank Birbalsingh, *From Pillar to Post: The Indo-Caribbean Diaspora* (Toronto: TSAR, 1997), pp. 97-107. The quote is on pp. 106-7.
42. See my introductory essay, '*Girmitiyas* and My Discovery of India', in Brij Lal, *Girmitiyas: The Origins of the Fiji Indians* (2nd edition), (Suva, Fiji: Fiji Institute of Applied Studies, 2004).
43. Cheddi Jagan, *Tracing our Path in a Changing World!* (PPP pamphlet), August 1990, pp. 14, 23.
44. *Ibid*., p. 14.
45. Cheddi Jagan, 'Our Footsteps and our Vision for a Free Guyana', Georgetown, (mimeo.), 8 June 1991, p. 11.

IV: MISCELLANEOUS PIECES

Brian Moore's book of 1995: a major study of 19th century Guyana

CULTURE AND ETHNICITY IN POST-EMANCIPATION GUYANA

Brian L. Moore, *Cultural Power, Resistance and Pluralism: Colonial Guyana, 1838-1900* (Kingston, Jamaica: The Press, University of the West Indies, 1995) xiii, 376pp. £12.50. ISBN 976-640-006-7

Brian Moore's two books on British Guiana (Guyana) between 1838 and the 1890s[1] are marked by a sustained effort to adapt a theoretical framework to his historiography in order to comprehend the colony's racial complexity. The results are abundantly suggestive and provocative. Moore was born in British Guiana in 1948 and was educated at Queen's College in Georgetown between 1959 and 1966. It is arguable that his books have been profoundly shaped by the turbulent racial politics of Guyana in the early 1960s and the continuing resilience of the race factor, as well as by his response to the Marxist frame of reference of several Guyanese politicians and intellectuals, particularly Walter Rodney (1942-80).[2] Indeed, Moore's approach to Guyanese history is an impressive scholarly challenge to the Marxist underpinnings of Rodney's acclaimed *A History of the Guyanese Working People, 1881-1905* (1981).

Between 1966 and 1973 Brian Moore studied history at the University of the West Indies in Jamaica. There his intellectual vision was enriched by the capacious, eclectic and distinctly non-Marxist historiography of his mentors: the late Guyanese historian, Elsa Goveia (1925-80)[3] and the Barbadian poet/historian, Edward Kamau Brathwaite (born 1930), who were the supervisors of his doctoral thesis. Brathwaite's *The Development of Creole Society in Jamaica, 1770-1820* (1971), based on his 1968 doctoral thesis at Sussex, was a major influence. Brathwaite argued that creole Jamaican culture had been shaped by its European as well as its African peoples in the context of slavery. But while this process created 'friction', embedded in brutality, it was 'creative'. Then, alluding to what Moore now calls 'cultural power', Brathwaite suggested that creole whites could have carved a niche for themselves in an evolving Jamaica had they embraced a 'more unrestricted', creative creolization. Instead of relying on a dependent 'bastard metropolitanism', they could have secured their economic and political moorings by empathizing with the rich Afro-creole culture and the liberation of their slaves. On the other hand, the African slaves might have won their liberation earlier had not the elite slaves (i.e. house slaves in positions of trust, skilled workers and supervisors), also, derided this creole culture, particularly its African elements. Brathwaite elaborates:

> Blinded by the wretchedness of their situation many of Jamaica's slaves, especially the black elite [...] failed, or refused, to make conscious use of their own rich folk culture [...] and so failed to command the chance of becoming self-conscious and cohesive as a group and consequently, perhaps, winning their independence from bondage, as their cousins in Haiti had done [...] Whenever the opportunity made it possible, they and their descendants rejected or disowned their own culture, becoming, like their masters, 'mimic men'. (pp. 307-8)

In 1974, in a monograph, *Contradictory Omens: Cultural Diversity and Integration in the Caribbean,* Brathwaite advanced his argument on the power of culture in his assessment of newer 'segments', such as Indians in the Caribbean. He observed that there was a tendency to decry their 'proven cultural resources' as a 'defiance... of our false, inherited order'. He deprecated this, countering that the region had infinitely more to gain by nurturing its historically depreciated diversity. Brathwaite asserts: 'To hold... that a realisation of sectional authenticity as a necessary step towards real integration can lead only to conflict, when in fact the bases of conflict lie within the very folds of non-revelation, is a dangerous falsification...' This would have come as a beacon to Moore, as he grappled with the Guyanese complexity.

In his first book, *Race, Power and Social Segmentation in Colonial Society: Guyana after Slavery, 1838-1891* (1987), based on his Ph.D. thesis of 1973, Moore was at variance with Rodney for 'downplaying race as a key factor in explaining socio-political developments in 19th century Guyana'. He argues that although the settlement of Indians on the land after the 1870s was indicative of their desire to be incorporated into colonial society, 'they remained as sharply differentiated racially and culturally from the other ethnic groups' at the end of the century as when they first arrived. He adds that this condition was perpetuated by their isolation on the sugar estates and their settling primarily in 'racially exclusive villages'. Moore concedes that there was some 'interculturation' between Africans and Indians in 'peripheral aspects of cultural life', but that this 'did *not* extend to the core culture of each ethnic section... religious beliefs, marriage and family, ideas and values'. He concludes, 'despite significant changes which occurred within the social system after emancipation, Guyanese society towards the end of the 19th century has to be classified as being closer to the plural model' (pp. 217-18, 222).

In his second book, *Cultural Power, Resistance and Pluralism,* Moore's central argument is rooted in the assumption that it is not good historiography to seek to explain the social structure of late nineteenth-century Guyana, and by implication beyond, primarily by reference to the economic forces and presumed aggregation of class interests in this plantation polity. For him the universe of culture(s), however complex, transitional, and non-discrete, has substantially more explanatory power. He therefore refines Brian Stoddart's notion of *cultural power*[4] so as to trace the impact of the ruling British elite's projection of its cultural supremacy onto subordinate racial groups in Guyana, as they tried to build identification with the imperial ethos among the disparate peoples – Africans, Coloured, Portuguese, Indians and Chinese. Moore argues that, 'cultural power encompasses the use of legislative and executive instruments, the forces of legitimate violence, propaganda, elite public opinion, religious proselytisation, the cultural content of colonial education, the invention of imperial traditions and symbols, the control of the leisure time of the colonial population, as well as the transmission of sports ethics' (p. 3).

However, Moore contends that the projectors of this *cultural power* did not envisage a demolition of race and class boundaries – absorption or assimilation. Indeed, he suggests that the retention of these boundaries was also central to the sustaining of the imperial ethos: notions of hierarchy and ethnic compartmentalisation were actually fostered. But the subordinate groups were not spineless objects. They contributed to the colonial complexity, even as they were enmeshed in the process of creolization. This was marked by two features: (i) the cultural resistance of each subordinate racial group to the impositions of the dominant British cultural elite; (ii) the resistance of subordinate groups, such as Indians, to perceived cultural 'pollution' by Africans as manifested, for instance, in the demise of the *tadja* festival (p. 224).[5]

Moore observes that the dominant British elite culture was refracted through a range of subordinate groups' cultures – African, Indian, Portuguese and Chinese – however attenuated. This complexity was deepened by the diverse contexts in which these peoples were introduced into the colonial polity. In assessing the 'material and temporal' culture of each group (accommodation, language, dress, food, sex, morality, and domestic life, rites of passage, leisure, and so on), as well as their peculiar 'spiritual' culture (religion, festivals, magic, witchcraft, and so forth), he documents this complexity with unparalleled meticulousness. He also demonstrates how each group was able to employ its own culture as a weapon of resistance in an environment where the Victorian values of the British elite threatened their autonomy.

Change, though endemic, was not uniform. Among African Guyanese, because of their prolonged oppression under slavery, the diversity of their heritage and the end of migration from the motherland, the process of creolization – a syncretism of aspects of African and European cultures – was most advanced. But even here, creolization was on a continuum, with a pronounced Eurocentricity among middle-class Africans and coloureds, and a greater degree of Afrocentricity among poor, rural and urban Africans. Moore concludes that African Guyanese were better integrated into the colonial polity:

> Although there were several cultural institutions, belief systems, behaviour patterns, customs and values that were distinctly Afro-Creole, and which became *foci* of cultural resistance to the dominance of the Anglo-Creole cultural model, the fact remains that the Creoles did share the same *basic* institutions, sociocultural ideas and values as the elites. In this context, Afro-Creole folk culture formed a subculture of the dominant Victorian culture system. (p. 154)

He also identifies this integrationist tendency among some of the successors to the Africans on the plantations – the Portuguese and the Chinese. Among the former, Moore illuminates their resistance to the dominant Victorian culture, especially their sustained resistance to the British Catholic practice of seeking to obliterate the peculiar Madeiran flavour of Portuguese Catholicism in Guyana. Here, also, he interprets rituals and festivals, rooted in the world of the Madeiran folk, as instruments of resistance, 'potent elements of Portuguese ethnicity' (p. 264). However, he remarks that by the 1890s they also shared many of the *basic* institutions with the ruling British elite.

Among the Chinese, who never exceeded 7,000 in the colony – in fact, by 1891, they numbered 4,000 – the shortage of women, the termination of migration from China, the absence of a centralized religion, and rampant Christian proselytizing, led to a less robust resistance to British elite culture. They were, already by the 1890s, on the road to creolization. But, as with the Africans and the Portuguese, the adoption of aspects of Victorian culture did not lead to the eclipse of all aspects of their Chinese heritage. Moore's argument is that although Africans, Portuguese, and Chinese shared the *basic* institutions of the British, this did not result in a diminution of racial consciousness: their respective 'temporal and material' and 'spiritual' cultures were resilient. Indeed, as he demonstrates, the anti-Portuguese riots of 1848, 1856 and 1889, by Africans, underlined that while the elite's exertion of *cultural power* was shaping a generalized, increasingly accessible creole culture, there was sufficient racial compartmentalization of identity to preclude the emergence of a comprehensive Guyanese identity. This, however, did not vitiate loyalty to the Sovereign, the Queen – a manifestation of the 'invention of tradition' and its appropriation by the subordinate races, as exemplified in the celebration of Queen Victoria's jubilees in British Guiana, in 1887 and 1897 (p. 27).

Moore sees Indian culture in nineteenth-century British Guiana as a manifestation of cultural pluralism. He argues that the reshaped Indian culture in the colony, the *Bhojpuri* culture, with its roots essentially in eastern Uttar Pradesh and western Bihar:

> performed a very important role of heightening their sense of ethnic consciousness and solidarity within the predetermined ethnic boundaries that separated them from the other groups... But for a very tiny minority, they shared no cultural institutions or values in common with the rest of society, and one can only conclude that their cultural integration was minimal by the end of the nineteenth century' (p. 240).

Moore shows how the *Bhojpuri* tradition feeds on the Hindu and Muslim (minority) centralized religious traditions of the Indians who retained links with the culture(s) of the motherland because of continual replenishment to the end of indentureship in 1917. The Indian Guyanese, therefore, tried to 'recreate a traditional way of life at a personal, familial, and community level'. This was not a simple transplanting. In fact, it entailed 'a redefinition and reorganisation of their traditional institutions and customs to produce a homogenised *Bhojpuri*-based culture...' Moore contends that this process was 'to some extent accelerated with the establishment of free village settlements in the late 19th century' (p. 205).

He concludes that although there was a 'high degree of cultural integration' among the creole white/coloured/black sector 'around a core of ideas and values which stressed the superiority of Victorian culture', it would be erroneous to support the 'integrationist' position (p. 305). Instead, Guyana by the end of the nineteenth century conformed more to 'the overall picture of cultural pluralism'. Moore asserts:

> Even though the physical and social environment brought some change to the immigrant cultures, for the most part this led to consolidation *within* existing ethnic boundaries rather than cultural integration *across* those boundaries. The amalgam made for a rich diversity of culture, but there was no rapid momentum towards the evolution of a truly *national* Guyanese culture or value system integrating *all* ethnic groups. (p. 306)

This is an outstanding work of scholarship. One feels overwhelmed by its portrayal of the wealth of cultural diversity in a plantation environment still in its ascendancy. Whether he is speaking of the intellectual and artistic effort of the British elite, or African names, dress or food, whether he is grappling with the complexities of Indian castes or Hindu and Muslim festivals, rites, and rituals, or Portuguese (Madeiran) rituals and festivals, or Chinese dress, he is authoritative.

Nonetheless, there are some problematic areas. In his assessment of the shaping of Indian *Bhojpuri* culture in the colony, following Steven Vertovec, a social anthropologist who worked in Trinidad, Moore speaks of 'the wide catchment area' from which the indentureds originated. He adds: 'This wide diversity of spoken tongues meant that communication was at first very difficult among the Indians themselves. But as with other aspects of Indian immigrant culture, a process of homogenization gradually took place leading to the emergence of a... levelled form of *Bhojpuri,* the Hindi dialect of eastern Bihar, as the lingua franca of the Indian immigrants' (p. 162). I am less inclined to stress the diversity because, as Moore remarks, 85% of the Indians in Guyana originated in eastern Uttar Pradesh and western Bihar – basically the same culture area.

Raymond Smith estimates that 70% of the Guyanese immigrants originated in eastern Uttar Pradesh, while 15% came from western Bihar.[6] The *Awadhi* and *Bhojpuri* dialects of Hindi are the principal languages of this area. So that although there was a small minority of immigrants from various parts of India, the overwhelming majority came from essentially the same culture area. This explains why a generalized Indian culture could take root and adapt to the Guyanese plantation environment relatively quickly. There was a core culture, sufficiently homogeneous, from which to adapt. This is corroborated by the Indo-Fijian historian, Brij Lal, whose *Girmitiyas* is the authoritative work on the origins of Fiji's north Indian immigrants; its findings are applicable to British Guiana, Mauritius and Trinidad as well.[7]

Moore mentions the impact of the *Ramayana* on Hindus in Guyana, but does not elaborate. In fact, the *Bhojpuri* tradition is firmly rooted in the universe of this classic: it was set in eastern Uttar Pradesh/western Bihar; many of the places named in this work were known to the indentureds; its evocation of a Golden Age was infinitely more alluring than their real, recent, bleak history of poverty and disease; its theme of exile and triumphal return was especially resonant.[8] The Muslim indentureds would also have shared many of the 'material and temporal' aspects of the *Bhojpuri* tradition. This would have lessened the potential for conflict based on fundamental differences in their 'spiritual' culture – the source of so much ancient hatred in India. The acquired comprehension, between Hindus of all castes and Muslims, helps to explain why an Indian culture cohered in Guyana, as does a caste-like perception of Africans (the *new* outcasts), conducive to the plural framework; the African, the 'other', is crucial to this new Indian identity.

On a more substantive point, Moore's exclusion of spheres of economic enterprise, such as the rice and cattle culture (Indians) and huckstering and shopkeeping (Madeirans and Chinese), already evident by the 1890s, from his notion of 'material' culture is regrettable. He has addressed this elsewhere, in *Race, Power and Social Segmentation in Colonial Society,* and probably felt that it was a beaten path. This, however, could have illuminated further how subordinate groups shaped their own identities in the plantation environment, exploiting peculiar economic niches, adapting their transplanted cultures to enhance economic status to shape their autonomy. After the 1870s, for instance, a mercantile culture brought economic security to some of the Portuguese; this was the basis of the rise of a more authentic Madeiran Catholicism which supplemented the dominant British variety. One could argue also that the upsurge in the construction of temples and mosques among Indians and the elaboration of their 'spiritual' culture in the last quarter of the nineteenth century is rooted in the flowering of the rice and cattle culture and the generation of an economic surplus. This sustained their more or less discrete villages, animated by their peculiar rhythm of work, prayer, and play – a potent weapon of resistance to the assumptions of the British elite culture.

It would have been useful also to allocate space to the evolving culture of the African and coloured middle class; a greater place, too, for the small Indian middle class, people like Joseph Ruhomon, Dr William Hewley Wharton, and others. This might have revealed the extent to which their respective identities were clawing back intimations of ancestral greatness to bolster uncertain, tentative creole personas. Indeed one could argue that constructing an Africa and an India of the imagination – part fact, part fiction – was central to a redefinition, a reclamation of a positive self-image from the shame of slavery and indentureship. As Joseph Ruhomon's 1894 pamphlet, *India; the Progress of her People at Home and Abroad,* and the reported deliberations of myriad African Guyanese associations underlined, creolization was not simply imitative of the cultural elite; the development of the intellect bred a passion for older, ancestral moorings.[9]

Moore's treatment of cricket – the quintessential imperial game adopted by all subordinate groups – suggests how this positive self-image was also fed by imperial streams. The fact that by the 1890s Indians were playing organized cricket with Africans, Portuguese and Chinese could be interpreted as a quest by the incipient middle-class and local-born Indians to establish their 'creole' credentials, to be *of* colonial society. This, significantly, coincided with the garnering of the early fruits of the rice and cattle culture – a measure of economic autonomy, as a settled people.

Moore observes that by the mid-1870s, Brahmanism dominated Guyanese Hinduism. This also was an aspect of Indian resistance, in this case to rampant Christian proselytising. By ministering in the homes of the lowest castes, partaking of their cooked food, the Brahmans had abrogated ancient notions of purity – unthinkable in Uttar Pradesh and Bihar. In creolizing Hinduism, they had brought into its fold many who might have been potential converts to Christianity. But they were less tolerant of Africans, as, too, were Muslim Indians, as Moore argues in explaining the demise of the *tadja* festival from the 1880s:

> The increasing level of Creole [African] participation in what had come to be regarded as the greatest Indian religio-ethnic festivity was evidently perceived as a cultural threat by both Muslims and Hindus. And indeed their initial reaction was to attack the Creole *tadjas* physically. In one such clash at Plantation Leonora in 1873, the Indians broke up the *tadja* and chased away the Creole revellers. When such hostility failed to dampen

> Creole enthusiasm for the revelry, the Indians decided to retreat. This attitude to cultural integration is very interesting. It is very understandable for the Indians to have sought to resist absorbing significant elements or aspects of the host culture, in particular Christianity, which could lead to cultural emasculation; it is quite another matter for them to have resisted Creole assimilation of Indian culture. But it is quite probable that they were sticking out against what they may have interpreted as a desecration of their religions by the Creoles. (p. 224)

The racial boundaries were, indeed, being strengthened – a manifestation both of Indian material progress and the necessity to reinterpret certain basic cultural rules to cope with the new environment – as home, a place of permanence. One could discern a scramble for patriarchal assertion; the clipping of emboldened female wings; the reconstitution of the joint family.10 These, paradoxically, were taking shape precisely when the process of creolization was gaining ground as Indians settled in villages away from the sugar plantations.

Indeed, the problem was not the 'rich diversity of culture', it was the rise of racism. The tightening of the racial boundary by Indians as they became permanent settlers, provided room not only for lower-caste Indians but Muslims as well, within the evolving social space. Whereas in the earlier years of indentureship, Hindu-Muslim rivalry found expression, as Moore argues, in violent clashes during the *tadja* processions, the dwindling of Indian participation by 1880, Hindu and Muslim, coincided with increased African participation (pp. 223-5).

Is this the context of the rise of perceptibly better relations between Hindus and Muslims, so evident in a range of Indian voluntary organisations after the end of indentureship: The East Indian Cricket Club, The [Wesleyan] East Indian Young Men's Society, and The British Guiana East Indian Association? Was the old antagonism between Hindus and Muslims displaced onto the new 'untouchables', the Africans? Given the passion for hierarchical ordering in Indian society, an instinct to exclude, did the construction of an Indian identity in British Guiana relegate Africans to pariah status? To what extent are contemporary African-Indian relations in Guyana rooted in this view? These are some of the intriguing, if uncomfortable, questions suggested by *Cultural Power.*

Did the admission of Indian pariahs (Chamars, Dusadhs, Doms, etc,) into Brahmanic Hinduism in Guyana and the entry of Muslims into the reshaped Indian identity, however incongruously, require the African for its coherence? In his recent study of Hindu-Muslim riots in Hyderabad, India, *The Colors of Violence* (1996), the eminent psychoanalyst, Sudhir Kakar, observes that one of the Hindu groups, the Pardis, formerly a nomadic, hunting people of low ritual status, seemed to need Muslims as the 'other' before they could arrive at 'self-identification' as Hindus. He adds: 'It seems a Hindu is born only when the Muslim enters. Hindus cannot think of themselves as such without a simultaneous awareness of the Muslim's presence.' Kakar then identifies a range of stereotypes of Muslims fostered by Hindus to bolster their tenuous religious identity and dampen the power and claims of their constituent caste identities:

> The image of Muslim animality is composed of the perceived ferocity, rampant sexuality, and demand for instant gratification of the male, and a dirtiness which is less than a matter of bodily cleanliness and more of an inner pollution as a consequence of the consumption of forbidden, tabooed foods.[11]

We have only just begun to fathom the depths of African-Indian incomprehension in Guyana; Brian Moore's work underlines the urgency of this task.

Shortly after the death of Walter Rodney in 1980, Moore made an appraisal of his contribution to Guyanese historiography. There he reminded us of the limitations of a Marxist perspective where the vision of class unity often imposes itself on the historical record. He tempered his admiration for Rodney's 'brilliant and incisive analysis and thorough research' as reflected in his 1981 book thus:

> Throughout his work, Rodney highlighted similarities in the behaviour of the two ethnic groups both on and off the estates and created the impression that the struggle by labour against capital was a common one which transcended racial boundaries. However, [...] the conditions in which the groups coexisted in 19th century Guiana militated against social interaction. Interethnic relations were from the outset affected by the system of state-aided immigration and indenture itself for which the Creoles [Africans] were taxed to finance the introduction of alien workers which lowered wages and reduced employment possibilities. Although Rodney argued that Creole opposition to this system, arising out of self-interest, did not extend to anti-Indian racism, the weight of the documentary evidence appears to suggest that while the Creole leadership may have made such fine distinctions, that was certainly not the case with the vast majority of Creole working people [...] contrary to Rodney's perception, the 'working class' in 19th century plantation Guiana was in fact profoundly divided along racial lines. One might even be persuaded to speak in terms of two working classes reacting, as Rodney observed, in similar ways to the exploitation of the dominant planter class, but separately and independently.[12]

But Moore does not speak of despair. He seems to be warning us against a quick fix, the wishing away of diversity – the perceived cradle of racial conflict. *Cultural Power* is a celebration of cultural diversity at the end of the nineteenth century. Enough of it still remains at the end of the twentieth century and it is to be hoped that Guyana's political culture can avoid the futility of racial conflict by accommodating and celebrating its people's plurality, indeed that it *must* be shaped by the latter.

Notes

1. See *Race, Power and Social Segmentation in Colonial Society: Guyana after Slavery, 1838-1891* (New York: Gordon and Breach Science Publishers, 1987).
2. The best study on this subject is Thomas J. Spinner, Jr., *A Political and Social History of Guyana, 1945-1983* (Boulder, Colorado: Westview Press, 1983). See also Chaitram Singh, *Guyana: Politics in a Plantation Society* (New York: Praeger, 1988).
3. Moore acknowledges: 'I cannot fully express the tremendous sense of gratitude that I feel in respect of the late Professor Elsa Goveia who was the principal supervisor of my thesis, and who thereafter encouraged me to do further research with a view to publishing this work (op. cit., [1987], p.xiii). Elsa Goveia's principal works are: A *Study on the Historiography of the British West Indies to the End of the Nineteenth Century* (Washington: Howard University Press, 1980 [1956]) and *Slave Society in the British Leeward Islands at the End of the Eighteenth Century* (New Haven: Yale University Press, 1965).
4. See Brian Stoddart, 'Sport, Cultural Imperialism, and Colonial Response in the British Empire', *Comparative Studies in Society and History,* 30 (1988).
5. For the adaptation and demise of *tadja in* British Guiana, see Basdeo Mangru, 'Tadjah' *[sic]* in British Guiana: Manipulation or Protest?' in his *Indenture and Abolition: Sacrifice and Survival on the Guyanese Sugar Plantations* (Toronto: Tsar, 1993), pp. 43-58.
6. Raymond T. Smith, 'Some Social Characteristics of Indian Immigrants to British Guiana', *Population Studies,* 13, Pt. 1 (1959).
7. Brij V. Lal, *Girmitiyas: The Origins of the Fiji Indians* (Canberra: The Journal of Pacific History, 1983), p. 131.
8. Vijay Mishra argues: 'the structure of the Tulsidasa *Ramayana* tends to enforce a particular design, a way of looking at the realities of indentured life in Fiji. It also, of course, tended to help the process of 'mystification' which went along with the Fiji Indians' concept of India...

   Both Trinidad and Fiji (one could add to them Mauritius, Guyana, and so on) easily became the forest of Dandak in the *Ramayana*, a temporary state from which Rama and Sita would some day return'. V. Mishra (ed.), *Rama's Banishment: A Centenary Tribute to the Fiji Indians, 1879-1979* (Auckland: Heinemann, 1979), p. 140.
9. See the following by Clem Seecharan: *India and the Shaping of the Indo-Guyanese Imagination, 1890s-1920s* (Leeds: Peepal Tree Press, 1993); and *Joseph Ruhomon's India; The Progress of her People at Home and Abroad... The Centenary Edition, 1894-1994* (UWI Press, 2001).
10. Rhoda Reddock, 'Indian Women and Indentureship in Trinidad and Tobago, 1845-1917', *Caribbean Quarterly,* 32, 3-4 (1986), pp. 27-49.
11. Sudhir Kakar, *The Colors of Violence: Cultural Identities, Religion, and Conflict* (Chicago: University of Chicago Press, 1996), p. 107.
12. Brian Moore, 'Walter Rodney: His Contribution to Guyanese Historiography', *Bulletin of Eastern Caribbean Affairs,* 8, Pt. 2 (1982), pp. 28-9.

'HELPING LIONS LEARN TO PAINT': WALTER RODNEY (1942-80) AND THE POWER TO DEFINE

In June 1988 Eusi Kwayana's booklet, *Walter Rodney,* was issued by the Working People's Alliance (WPA). It comprises two pieces published by him in 1981 and 1985 respectively, focusing primarily on Rodney's last years in Guyana, when he epitomised the resistance to the regime of Forbes Burnham. So they were obviously inspired by inviolable memories of the political attributes of this outstanding young scholar and revolutionary, assassinated on 13 June 1980, allegedly by agents of the said regime. Rodney had returned to his homeland in 1974 to take up a post at the University of Guyana, after nearly five years as a lecturer in African History in Tanzania. However, he was not allowed to teach there because the Government rescinded his appointment. They saw his radical scholarship allied to a discernible political acumen as inherently subversive. The African-backed People's National Congress (PNC) could accommodate the moribund leadership of Jagan's pro-Moscow People's Progressive Party (PPP), the Indian-backed opposition. Both of these established political forces were comfortably lodged within their ethnic cocoons. But they feared the sagacious brain of Walter Rodney, apprehensive that it could challenge young Guyanese to go beyond their racial frame of reference.

Kwayana (born 1924), an incorruptible man of learning, was a close friend of Rodney and shared a passion, in the late 1970s, to unite Africans and Indians in Guyana in order to rid it of the dictatorship of Burnham. They yearned to create a democratic, socialist society. On the occasion of the republication of this booklet, my task is to offer some thoughts on Rodney's conception of self-definition in the process of liberation.

Many of his Guyanese compatriots had read his groundbreaking book of 1972, *How Europe Underdeveloped Africa*, and were exhilarated by his impressive, but accessible, scholarship in locating Africa at the heart of human endeavour and achievement, before European penetration of the continent. Rodney had written from a Marxist perspective, but his analysis was free of jargon; and he provided Africans, at home and in the diaspora, with the reassurance that their ancestral land had not been out of step with the universal accomplishment of humankind, in what the Grenadian T.A.

Marryshow called 'Cycles of Civilisation'. Africa had a great deal to be proud of before the rise of the European slave trade. Rodney argued:

> The first prerequisite for mastery of the environment is knowledge of that environment. By the 15th century Africans everywhere had arrived at a considerable understanding of the total ecology – of the soils, climate, animals, plants and their multiple interrelationships. The practical application of this lay in the need to trap animals, to build houses, to make utensils, to find medicines, and above all to devise systems of agriculture. In the centuries before the contact the overwhelmingly dominant activity in Africa was agriculture. In all the settled agricultural communities, people observed the peculiarities of their own environment and tried to find techniques for dealing with it in a rational manner. Advanced methods were used in some areas, such as terracing, crop rotation, green manuring, mixed farming and regulated swamp farming.

He adds:

> The single most important technological change underlying African agricultural development was the introduction of iron tools, notably the axe and the hoe, replacing wooden and stone tools... The coming of iron, the rise of cereal-growing and the making of pottery were all closely related phenomena... The rate of change over a few centuries was quite impressive. Millet and rice had been domesticated from wild grasses just as yams were made to evolve from selected wild roots. Most African societies raised the cultivation of their own particular staple to a fine art.[1]

Earlier, in his doctoral dissertation of 1966, on the history of the Upper Guinea Coast, written when he was only 24 and published by Clarendon Press at Oxford in 1970, Rodney had remarked on the agricultural sophistication acquired by the people of the Gambian littoral. He observed that they wrested the land from the forests while battling 'intractable swamps'. Moreover, heavy rains that constantly inundated the land precluded many crops from being cultivated there. Yet the irrepressibly ingenious farmers achieved 'agricultural mastery' of this swampy region by striving for excellence in diverse strands of wet-rice culture. This encompassed expertise in drainage, desalination and the protection of reclaimed land from the perennial threat from the sea and tides.[2]

In his didactic manner, Rodney also sought to enhance his people's self-perception by imploring them to learn about Africa's ancient civilisations:

> 'Apart from the states of Egypt, Meroe [Sudan], Axum, Ghana, Mali, Songhai and Kanem...there were many others in different parts of Africa which achieved greatness before the arrival of the white man and before we were snatched away as slaves. On the West African coast the states of Benin and Oyo were famous, in Central Africa we can take as examples Kongo and Monomotapa (Zimbabwe), and in East Africa two of the oldest kingdoms were those of Bunyoro and Buganda. All of these are strange names because we have never been taught anything about them. If we

Walter Rodney (1942-1980): eminent Marxist historian and politician

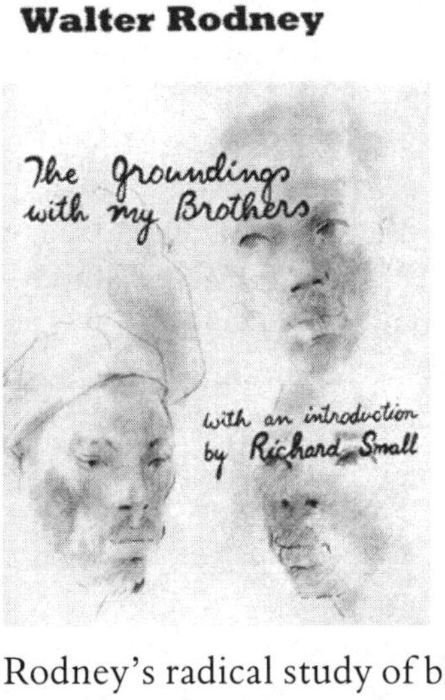

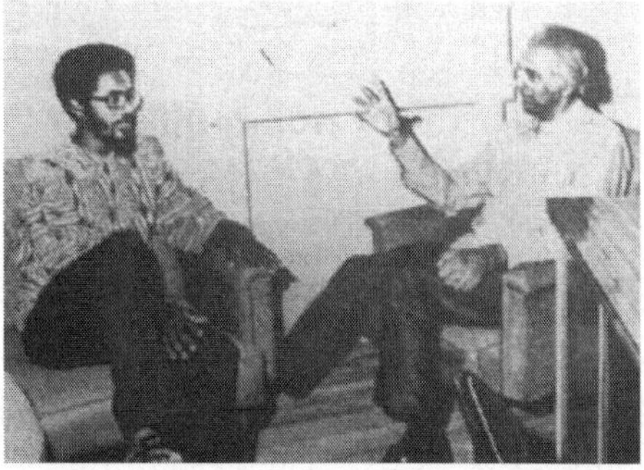

Marxists of different stripes: Rodney and Cheddi Jagan, mid 1970s

Rodney's radical study of black power (1969): the text of lectures that contributed to his expulsion from Jamaica in October 1968, but earned him an international reputation

> want to call ourselves conscious Africans, then we must know the map of Africa, we must remember the names of these great African states, and we must find out as much as possible about them.[3]

But he would often argue, too, in the manner of his African-Caribbean intellectual precursors of the late 19th century, Edward Blyden and Dr T.E.S. Scholes, that while there are numerous examples of high civilisation and grandeur in the history of the African homeland, it was essential to celebrate the achievements of smaller societies, also, and to recognise their adaptation to, and respect for, their specific habitat, manifest in their culture and enshrined in their universe of rituals. Indeed, as he taught his students at the University of the West Indies (UWI), as well as his Rastafari brethren, in Jamaica – 'the groundings with my brothers' in the *dungle* of West Kingston in 1968 – African history must be at the core of their self-discovery; it was a necessary instrument of self-emancipation. I have used the notion of 'muscular learning' elsewhere for knowledge that empowers; it is congruent with Rodney's notion of history/learning as 'a weapon of liberation'.[4]

This was why, after Rodney earned a first class honours in history in 1963 at UWI, he proceeded to the School of Oriental and African Studies (SOAS), University of London, to do a doctorate in African history. Moreover, he thought it imperative for every African in the diaspora to be disabused of the notion of Africa as a 'savage' place – to become familiar with its rich legacy of achievement: the foundation for the making of a new persona. Therefore, unlike many of his colleagues at the University of the West Indies, he discerned in Garveyism and Rastafari philosophy the germ of an ethos of liberation. Rodney identified with their notion of the African homeland as a source of redemption. In Guyana, where ethnic conflict had erupted in a virulent manner towards the end of Empire, in the early 1960s, he conceived of cultural regeneration, rooted in their respective African and Indian homelands, as a fount for enrichment, not as fodder for further ethnic incomprehension. Like his mentor, Eusi Kwayana, he would argue that the latter thrived in the soil of insecurity, particularly cultural impoverishment. Therefore, even before he returned to Guyana in 1974, he had empathised with the aims of Kwayana's African Society for Cultural Relations with Independent Africa (ASCRIA), as he did with similar Indian organisations: both sought to construct and disseminate rehabilitative narratives drawn from Africa and India respectively.

It is apt to recall how Rodney framed the place of African history in the retrieving of her people's self-esteem, in the diaspora. This would have been 1968, in Jamaica, in the context of his 'grounding' with the Rastafari brethren and the magnetism of the black power movement in the United States, in conjunction with the legacy of W.E.B. Du Bois and Malcolm X:

> Every human society has a history and a form of culture, and this includes Africa. Africans in the West have been *deliberately* kept ignorant of African achievements by the white man for centuries. The purpose of their policy was to build up a picture of barbarous Africa, so that we Africans who have been removed from our homes and made into slaves would be afraid to admit even to ourselves that we were Africans... In the West Indies... our knowledge of Africa is got from reading Tarzan comic books. We are the only group in the world who deny ourselves, preferring to be known as 'Negroes' rather than Africans. In order to know about ourselves we must learn about African history and culture... What we need is confidence in ourselves, so that as blacks and Africans we can be conscious, united, independent and creative. A knowledge of African achievements in art, education, religion, politics, agriculture and the mining of metals can help us gain the necessary confidence which has been removed by slavery and colonialism.[5]

Even as a doctoral student at SOAS he went against the grain, challenging the way African history was written and taught by white historians. He felt that the story had to be told from an authentically African perspective; and as he observed in 1975, his writing of *How Europe Underdeveloped Africa* was informed by a conscious endeavour to transcend the academic orthodoxy that he thought perpetuated African inferiority. He was resolved to write a history for African peoples, aimed at retrieving and enhancing their self-respect:

> ...[the book] was designed to operate from outside, in the sense that it would not be sponsored by the people who considered themselves, and whom many others considered, to be the ones at that time who had the last word to say on African history and African Studies. The aim of this publication was to reach our own people without having it mediated by the bourgeois institutions of learning.[6]

It was published simultaneously by Bogle-L'Ouverture (founded in London by his Guyanese friends, Eric and Jessica Huntley) and Tanzania Publishing House, thus accomplishing the task of involving black people at all levels of the creation of this formidable body of knowledge about themselves.

This was what he meant by 'helping lions learn to paint'. Eusi Kwayana recalls, in this booklet, an anecdote passed on by Rodney, around 1975, shortly after his return to Guyana. He was underlining the necessity for working people and minority groups as a whole to pursue education for self-emancipation. Rodney told a tale, hitherto unknown in Guyana, of 'lions who went to view an art exhibition and were amazed at the claims on canvas made by hunters and their glorifiers. A lion shook his head with resignation and was heard muttering: "If only lions could paint!"'[7] Kwayana states that this tale speaks of Rodney's conviction that the power to define is indispensable to freedom. I may add, too, that this is the aim of 'muscular learning': empowering people through education to challenge orthodoxies, shaping their resolve to subvert the received wisdom of their oppressors, thus preparing the foundation for self-realisation.

But Rodney was no narrow defender of Africans; he believed that living in a polyglot society like Guyana, where self-definition was still largely along ethnic lines, it was paramount to be sensitive to the cultural promptings, fears and aspirations of Africans *and* Indians. Positing an inexorable evolution towards a common creole identity is not compatible with the making of a national identity in Guyana. It is crucial to engage with the peculiar sensibilities of each group, while striving for greater national coherence. This is necessarily protracted.

He had addressed this delicate matter in *The Groundings with my Brothers*, at the end of the 1960s:

> There seems to have been some doubts… and some fears that Black Power is aimed against the Indian. This would be a flagrant denial of both the historical experience of the West Indies and the reality of the contemporary scene. When the Indian was brought to the West Indies, he met the same racial contempt which whites applied to Africans. The Indian, too, was reduced to a single racial stereotype – the coolie or labourer. He, too, was a hewer of wood and bringer of water. I spoke earlier of the revolt of the blacks in the West Indies in 1938. That revolt involved Africans in Jamaica, Africans and Indians in Trinidad and Guyana. The uprisings in Guyana were actually led by Indian sugar workers. Today, some Indians (like some Africans) have joined the white power structure in terms of economic activity and culture; but the underlying reality is that poverty resides among Africans and Indians in the West Indies and that power is denied them. Black Power in the West Indies, therefore, refers primarily to people who are recognisably African or Indian.[8]

But, as Eusi Kwayana observes, by the mid-1970s, when Rodney returned to Guyana, with what seemed like a resolve to fight the Burnham dictatorship, 'he had made the natural, or necessary, leap through black power to the science of the revolutionary working class, Marxism. This at first disappointed many who thought he would stop at lending dignity to the Afro-Guyanese presence'.[9] In fact, Rodney's change of stance is hardly surprising, for a Marxist nostrum has enthralled many politicians of note in Guyana since the late 1940s, including Cheddi Jagan (1918-1997) and Forbes Burnham (1923-1985). It seems that the intractable issue of racial insecurity, between Africans and Indians, so well documented in Rodney's Marxist-oriented history of Guyana, *A History of the Guyanese Working People, 1881-1905* (1981), has tended to draw Guyanese towards a millennial reflex. The ethnic suspicion and insecurity were endemic even in late 19th century Guyana. This was aggravated by the massive hydrological problems also documented superbly by Rodney. The natural difficulties of this backward colony, coupled with limited resources, have long sustained the myth of El Dorado: the harsh reality is softened by the illusion of massive wealth around the next bend. It feeds hope, the will to go on; but it also breeds envy and an implacable fear of domination by the other, who could inherit the rich kingdom in perpetuity.

Consequently mutually negative stereotypes of each other cohered around several contentious issues, such as the taxation of Africans to import Indian indentured labourers for the sugar plantations in order to undercut their bargaining position, after slavery; and the acquisition of African land by Indians, consequent upon the stagnation of their villages occasioned by the vagaries of floods and droughts. Later, beyond the period studied by Rodney, the emergence of a confident, often assertive, Indian middle class, rooted in commerce, rice, cattle and the professions and buoyed by Mother India's stature between the Wars, would exacerbate African fears of total domination by the latecomers. Talk of the creation of an 'Indian Colony' in Guyana spawned fervent African apprehension in the 1920s. This would be aggravated by greater Indian demographic growth, with the eradication of malaria by the end of the 1940s, precisely when radical constitutional change towards universal adult suffrage was being debated.

Eusi Kwayana, a long-time Marxist, is a rare example of a Guyanese politician and thinker who has, from time to time (at great cost), advocated a political solution that recognises the necessity for the attainment of economic, judicial and cultural security for all ethnic groups in Guyana. But, often, the mirage of the 'science of the revolutionary working class' – Marxism – would becloud even the clarity of thought and sincerity of motives of this indefatigable man. This certainly appeared to have been the case, also, with Walter Rodney, during his last years (documented in this publication), when he called for the overthrow of the Burnham dictatorship by the end of 1979, his sensitivity to cultural nuances notwithstanding. He, and others before him, had underestimated the resilience of ethnic loyalties and the power of culture to shape attitudes and inform responses: ethnic insecurity and ethnic intransigence. So when Rodney was assassinated in June 1980, the party that he, Eusi Kwayana, Rupert Roopnaraine and others had founded, the Working People's Alliance, was unable to establish itself as a credible force. The PNC and the PPP were able to capitalise on the death of a formidable challenger, thus sustaining their hold on their respective ethnic constituency.

The Indian-backed PPP has been in power since 1992, and the African-backed PNC limps along as a most ineffective opposition. But the bedevilling racial divide remains a chasm. The country is sitting on a volcano. A political initiative that seeks to foster peace and avert racial warfare must focus on refashioning the country's institutions to alleviate the fears and apprehensions of its diverse peoples. There is no quick fix. As the Guyanese historian, Brian Moore, argues, even in the late 19th century, the African-

Indian incomprehension was a powerful force that Rodney seemed to have underestimated in his history of Guyana.[10]

The idea of a Guyanese national identity remains elusive today, nearly five decades since independence in 1966. A solution, certainly, must be predicated on its cultural and ethnic diversity, while recognising the admirable hybridity that has taken shape (creolisation). The legacies of both Rodney and Kwayana speak of a potential for cohesion in the long run based on a creole sensibility that accommodates the cultural variants of Guyana's peoples: the apprehensions, hopes and aspirations fostered by them. At the core of Rodney's politics and scholarship is the vision that the political culture of Guyana would avoid the futility of racial conflict by accommodating and celebrating its people's cultural diversity; indeed, that it must be shaped by the latter in a manner that minimises their ethnic insecurities.

Notes

1. Walter Rodney, *How Europe Underdeveloped Africa* (London: Bogle-L'Ouverture Press, 1972), pp. 47-48.
2. Walter Rodney, *A History of the Upper Guinea Coast, 1545-1800* (Oxford: Clarendon Press, 1970), p. 20.
3. Walter Rodney, *The Groundings with my Brothers* (London: Bogle-L'Ouverture, 1969), p. 36.
4. See Clem Seecharan, *Muscular Learning: Cricket and Education in the Making of the British West Indies at the end of the Nineteenth Century* (Jamaica: Ian Randle Publishers, 2006).
5. *The Groundings*, p. 35, 37
6. *Walter Rodney Speaks: The Making of an African Intellectual* (Trenton, N.J.: Africa World Press, 1990), p. 26.
7. Eusi Kwayana, *Walter Rodney* (Georgetown: WPA, 1988), p. 8
8. *The Groundings*, p. 28.
9. Kwayana, *Walter Rodney*, p. 7
10. Brian Moore, 'Walter Rodney: His Contribution to Guyanese Historiography' *Bulletin of Eastern Caribbean Affairs*, 8, Pt. 2 (1982), pp. 28-29.

EMPIRE AND FAMILY IN THE SHAPING OF A WEST INDIAN INTELLECTUAL: THE YOUNG C.L.R. JAMES, A PRELIMINARY ASSESSMENT

> *Beyond a Boundary* is the product of a true renaissance man. A man steeped in the literature of the ages but also experiencing the realities of life and combining them together with life. Sport, art, literature, politics, economics and life itself cannot be divorced from each other. It is in his denial of categorisation and specialisation and his emphasis upon the interrelationships between all aspects of life that C.L.R. James makes his most important contributions.
>
> – Alan Metcalfe (1987)[1]

1: The British Empire and the Shaping of C.L.R. James

Cyril Lionel Robert James [CLR] (1901-89), the author of *Beyond a Boundary* (1963), is arguably the most acclaimed intellectual in the history of the British West Indies. Born in Trinidad on 4 January 1901 of African ancestry, he was profoundly shaped by the British colonial ethos. His is one of the most fascinating minds made by the British intellectual tradition, in the elite schools of their non-white colonies. Though aimed primarily at producing teachers at the primary and secondary levels and junior functionaries in the colonial civil service, these schools, paradoxically, were the nursery of many radicals, the pioneers of anti-colonialism.

The curriculum in the elite schools of the British West Indies (such as James's Queen's Royal College [QRC] founded in 1859), encompassed the classics (Greek and Latin), English literature and English history. It also included cricket, with its public school ethos intact: respect for its complex rules and the authority of the umpire along with magnanimity towards one's opponents. This was the table at which white creoles and a sprinkling of light coloureds, people of mixed ancestry, had supped as early as the late 18th century. However, white creoles were a small minority in the British West Indies. Even in Barbados, with its unbroken English governance since the 1620s, they constituted no more than 5 or 6 %. Therefore, the coloureds (some could pass for white), in a graduated continuum from the pinnacle of white superiority towards darker shades of fairness, were next in line for the measured rise. But even the educated coloureds, required to fill posts in civil society, were limited in numbers. The dawn of the day for the black middle class had, consequently, become a worthy and attainable aspiration in post-emancipation society. Education, preferably at one of the elite schools of the British West Indies, was the instrument of mobility.[2] Although it would be long in coming and circumscribed by the stubborn primacy of colour (lightness was prized by all, consciously or unconsciously), it bred a penchant for moderation, incremental change: gradualism. It also fostered ambition among the black lower middle class. The revolutionary temperament, so ingrained in Latin America and the Hispanic Caribbean, was alien to the British West Indies.

James's paternal and maternal grandfathers were immigrants from Barbados, who had settled in Trinidad around the 1860s because it was a latecomer to the plantation culture and slavery. Trinidad was Spanish until 1797, but it was virtually neglected by them; their passion was for the Spanish Main: Central and South America. Little Trinidad, off the north-eastern shoulder of the continent neighbouring Venezuela, was a backwater, although it was potentially receptive to the sugar/slave/plantation complex. This was not the sort of thing the Spanish did in the West Indies. But fearing English intrusion towards the end of the 18th century, they offered incentives to fellow Catholics to settle in Trinidad: the French from Martinique and Guadeloupe, and then French planters, white and coloured, fleeing revolutionary Haiti. The French would quickly overwhelm the rudimentary Spanish presence, but the English took the island in 1797. They would terminate the slave trade in 1807. When they abolished slavery in the 1830s, there were only 20,000 slaves in Trinidad. This island did not have to bear the indelible scars of Haiti and Jamaica, infamous for the scale, longevity and brutality of slavery. Black Trinidadians acquired a reputation for ease and self-assurance, an instinctual swagger, seen as arrogance by other West Indians.

After emancipation Trinidad, sparsely populated, needed people – from anywhere – to become a viable colony. It had a lot of land to spare; it became a beacon for land-hungry freed Africans from Barbados and the Windward Islands, desperate to own a piece of land; for indentured labourers from India, too, for the same reason. Barbados had always been English and Protestant with a creole white population of planters and commercial people, who saw themselves as belonging to the island; they harboured a degree of paternalism towards 'their negroes'. This meant that by the late 19th century many black Barbadians were educated at least to the primary level, some to the secondary level; many were trained as artisans, people with pride in their tutored skills. They were more Euro-creolised than in any other island in the British West Indies. They manifested self-respect fostered by competence in, if not mastery of, idioms of the British colonial mission: education and cricket. James's people, Protestant migrants originating in this stratum of skilled artisans, were very proud of what they had become.

James would celebrate this legacy in his magisterial *Beyond a Boundary*, a classic that must rank among the greatest works in English in the 20th century. He has written of his own prodigious intellectual gifts when only ten. He has also portrayed his own family, people of the black lower middle class, as proud of their inheritance. They were cultivated in the spirit of English Protestantism/Puritanism; excellently educated, in a European cultural sense: the Bible, classical music, literature. This made them sensitive to their elevation beyond the plebeian black masses. They were punctilious in maintaining that distance, bearing their acquired culture somewhat ostentatiously. They were driven by the idea (a virtual mission) that they must not be contaminated by the morass of low attitudes they believed endemic to black people in the mass. Theirs was a steep, winding road to a degree of respectability and they were not complacent about it. They could not afford to slide. They would not have celebrated their African antecedence. As James recalls of his paternal grandfather, a Barbadian migrant to Trinidad:

> My grandfather went to church every Sunday morning at eleven o'clock wearing in the broiling sun a frock-coat, striped trousers and top-hat, with his walking-stick in hand, surrounded by his family, the underwear of the women crackling with starch. He fell grievously ill, the family fortunes declined and the children grew up in unending struggle not to sink below the level of the Sunday-morning top-hat and frock-coat.[3]

This grandfather had become a pan-boiler on a sugar estate in Trinidad. It was a technical job that would have been the preserve of white or very light men for a long time. It demanded complex technical knowledge, precision and discipline in the delicate process of extracting, boiling and clarifying the cane-juice from liquid into sugar. James puts this seminal achievement by a black man in the West Indies in perspective: 'This meant that my grandfather had raised himself above the mass of poverty, dirt, ignorance and vice which in those far-off days surrounded the islands of black lower middle-class respectability like a sea ever threatening to engulf them'.[4]

James's maternal grandfather, Josh Rudder, was equally remarkable. He was a Protestant migrant from Barbados who went to Trinidad around 1868 when he was 16. He was the first black man to become an engine-driver on the Trinidad Government Railway. This, too, had been the preserve of white or light men. He had worked his way up from apprentice mechanic to fireman, then through several measured stages to the top. He was obviously a very able man, conscious of his standing; he expected his family to behave in a manner befitting his acquired station. James states that towards the end of the 1890s the sugar factory in Josh's hometown, Princes Town, stopped belching smoke suddenly, a sure sign that something had gone awry. The manager and his engineers laboured frantically to resolve the problem, to no avail. Meanwhile, the sugar-cane, already harvested and stacked high, was deteriorating rapidly. In utter desperation the manager belatedly retrieved from the popular imagination Josh Rudder's astounding affinity with engines; he dispatched his carriage to collect him. Josh answered the call but he asked firmly that he should go alone into the factory. He soon emerged and responded to the manager tentatively: 'I can't guarantee anything, sir, but try and see if she will go now'. The big wheels were soon revolving to their monotonous rhythm. But Josh would not divulge the source of the miracle. Several decades later, on the eve of James's departure for England, in early 1932, he beseeched Josh to tell the tale entrenched in local lore. He did not relent. But this old black man who had reached the summit of his profession – through merit – still nurtured a pride that was inviolable: 'They were white men with all their M.I.C.E. and R.I.C.E. and all their big degrees, and it was their business to fix it. I had to fix it for them. Why should I tell them?'[5]

It was the pursuit of excellence, and the knowledge that their fledgling achievement against the grain spoke for all black people, that was the foundation of West Indian self-respect and an embryonic nationalism. As black pioneers performing mentally challenging jobs, long reserved for white or light men (coloureds) on account of their supposed natural aptitude, they were almost puritanical towards values deemed sacrosanct by their colonial masters. It made for inflexibility, the fear that they could easily lose it all. They dreaded returning to the sugar-cane field, the persistent symbol of slavery in these islands. It bred astringency in James's people which fed the rebel in the young man.

James's paternal grandfather would ensure that James's dad, Robert, benefited from his education; he became a school teacher and a good cricketer. Josh Rudder's first wife, James's maternal grandmother, died young, so Josh sent his daughters, including James's mother, Bessie, to a Wesleyan convent. There she immersed herself in literature so that she became a great reader, 'one of the most tireless I have known'. Her taste was 'indiscriminate'. James provided a sample of the inexhaustible list: Scott, Thackeray, Dickens, Hall Caine, Stevenson, Mrs. Henry Wood, Charlotte Bronte, Charlotte Braeme, Shakespeare… Balzac, Nathaniel Hawthorne, a woman called Mrs. E.D.E.N. Southworth, Fenimore Cooper, Nat Gould, Charles Garvice. He adds: 'anything and everything, and as she put them down I picked them up'.[6]

This was the context in which James's extraordinary life of the mind was shaped: a severe nonconformist Protestantism, with deep roots in Barbados, and a rebellious spirit fostered by the cosmopolitanism of young Trinidad. Cricket would play a crucial role, and many of the colonial verities James absorbed at Queen's Royal College (QRC) between 1911 and 1918, from English Oxbridge masters (themselves votaries of the public school code), would plant in him reverence for many imperial values. Yet the rebel seed was sprouting simultaneously. The unquenchable passion for reading that he absorbed from his mother nurtured a predilection for learning beyond boundaries. His was an eclectic response to the prescribed curriculum at QRC. James pursued cricket, literature, Greek and Latin with rare devotion, but largely through his uncharted adventures in reading, in the public library. This invariably led him away from the measured, tested boundaries of the curriculum. The idiosyncratic learning was magnified by his 'pursuit' of cricket, as he described it, enthralled by the marvellous literature the game had already spawned. He studied its great players, the evolution of styles in bowling and batting and the place of sports in society. He located his peculiar pursuit within the traditions of ancient Greece, and he never tired of asserting its western antecedents. This intellectual curiosity had inspired a fine essay that was published in his school magazine, possibly the first time James appeared in print: 'The Novel as an Instrument of Reform'.[7] The learning was already framed by a libertarian spirit, beyond boundaries. It would make this black man from an obscure West Indian island a world intellectual of the 20th century.

He became a Trotskyist in England in the 1930s, a Marxist theoretician wedded to the notion of world revolution and other absurdities about the revolutionary potential of the workers. It is my view that this would soon distract the great mind from its true intellectual possibilities. But C.L.R. James was never taciturn about the unique depth and breadth of his learning, nor would he deprecate its provenance. In an article written in 1969, 37 years after he first arrived in England, he was still proudly proclaiming:

> I want to make it clear that the origins of my work and my thoughts are to be found in Western European literature, Western European history and Western European thought... I think the people of the underdeveloped countries accept me and feel that I have had a lot to say that is valid about the underdeveloped countries... But what I want to make clear is that I learnt this quality in the literature, history and philosophy of Western Europe... It is in the history and philosophy and literature of Western Europe that I have gained my understanding not only of Western Europe's civilisation, but of the importance of the underdeveloped countries... I didn't learn literature from the mango-tree, or bathing on the shore and getting the sun of the colonial countries; I set out to master the literature, philosophy and ideas of Western civilisation. That is where I come from, and I would not pretend to be anything else.[8]

II: The James Family and the Making of the Eternal Rebel

James got into continual trouble with his teachers and his family while at QRC because, as a scholarship winner funded by the state, he was expected to excel in the conventional sense. He had to play by the rules. He refused to. He was precocious and his approach to learning subverted the established boundaries. One deduces that he was a nightmare to his lower middle class family yearning for a son who would enter the colonial civil service and, in due course, secure a nominated position in the colonial legislature. This was the pattern set by the coloured middle class including James's family. His family was devoted to cricket but they could not accommodate C.L.R.'s unique pursuit of the game, or his view of education. He challenged the colonial and black lower middle-class conception of education as a vocation, a means to a respectable livelihood and acquired status. It is essential, therefore, to quote James at length in order to grasp the peculiar mental universe this young man already inhabited in his late teens. The mould was cast – a life of the mind would possess him for the rest of his life, however flawed his Marxist declamations on the revolutionary potential of the working class:

> When I left school [QRC in 1918] I was an educated person, but I had educated myself into a member of the British middle class with literary gifts and I had done it in defiance of all authority... [A]fter a fearful row with my father, during which I left home and swore I would never go back, he decided to accept me as I was and I became a respectable and self-respecting member of society and have remained so to his day... I have read the classics of educational theory and taken an interest in systems of education. Each suited its time, but I have a permanent affinity with only one, the ancient Greek. When I read that the Greeks educated their young people on poetry, gymnastics and music I feel I know what that means... I did not merely play cricket. I studied it. I analysed strokes, I studied types, I read its history, its beginnings, how and when it changed from period to period, I read about it in Australia and South Africa. I made clippings; I talked to cricketers who had gone abroad. I compared what they told me with what I read in *Wisden*. I looked up the play of men who had done well or badly against West Indies. I read and appreciated the phraseology of laws. It was in that way, I am confident, that the Greeks educated themselves on games with their records and traditions orally transmitted from generation to generation.[9]

But, even as a little boy, James had apprehended the fleeting grandeur in a lower class 'negro' cricketer, Matthew Bondman, whom his family despised. Bondman's family rented from the Jameses. They reeked of the déclassé. His family feared that their respectability, assiduously nurtured, could be dissipated by proximity to the lower orders. James recalls:

> [Bondman] was generally dirty. He would not work. His eyes were fierce, his language was violent and his voice was loud. His lips curled back naturally and he intensified it by an almost perpetual snarl. My grandmother and aunts detested him. He would often without shame walk up the main street barefooted, 'with his planks on the ground', as my grandmother would report.[10]

But Bondman could bat. James reserved a niche for him in his pantheon of seminal cricketing heroes. This crude, otherwise maladroit, character metamorphosed into grace and sublimity as soon as he held bat in hand. James, this little boy watching from his window, discerned Bondman, the batsman, as imbued with majesty. This vulgar young man, down on one knee, could sweep magnificently to leg or slash powerfully, with precision, through the covers: 'my little soul thrilled with recognition and delight'.[11] Young C.L.R. was already going against the grain, seeing things as he wished to, unmindful of being an iconoclast.

The rebel was manifested in other ways that defied family definitions: unflagging respect for the underdog of merit and the artistic genius of the masses as articulated in the calypso. Robert and Bessie James, like many black lower middle-class parents in Trinidad in the early 20th century, were appalled by the ribaldry of the calypso; they deprecated that ascendant medium of popular expression as 'the road to hell'.[12] In spite of its satirical power that animated the common folk by its ridicule of colonial pretensions, James's family saw the calypso as too redolent of the lower class epitomised by the Bondmans. They could not give it any artistic merit. It was to counter this that James, towards the end of the 1920s (before his departure for England in 1932), would exhibit a studied partiality for the underdog. It would draw him towards literary empathy for people in the barrack-yard (slums), marginal folks like those in his short-story, 'Triumph' of 1929, antithetical to James's universe of middle-class aspirations and respectability. The latter was underpinned by a moral imperative of continual demonstration of proximity to, and ease with, idioms of British respectability.

This inflexible framework bred in James ambivalence towards the British. On one hand, he was a great admirer of the colonial education that was at the core of his intellectual firmament; on the other, he became the inveterate rebel against imperialism: a professional revolutionary, often without a secure income. But James's colonial education, as he saw it later, had acquired inviolable cerebral attributes because he pursued it on his own terms. Therefore, while it fed an unquenchable curiosity for learning, it was at variance with the prescribed rules and incrementally measured stages enshrined in the curriculum taught by his Oxbridge masters at QRC and absorbed uncritically by his family. James said that he was 'lectured, punished and flogged'[13] by his father because he played cricket late after school and on weekends. His work in class slipped; he was reported to the

Board of Education. The scholarship boy was letting the whole family down; and in a society where such boys could not elude the island's microscope, it brought shame to the James clan. He would concoct stories in order to play cricket, borrow money and bicycles to get to cricket matches, make up chores supposedly assigned by his masters – all in an endeavour to escape the father's floggings. James has sketched these seminal events that shaped his life:

> I invented beforehand excuses which would allow me to stay and play and take the late train. When I got into the [cricket] eleven, there were matches on Saturday. I devised duties which the masters had asked me to perform. I forged letters, I borrowed flannels, I borrowed money to pay my fare, I borrowed bicycles to ride to the matches and borrowed money to repair them when I smashed them. I was finally entangled in such a web of lies, forged letters, borrowed clothes and borrowed money that it was no wonder that the family looked on me as a sort of trial from heaven sent to test them as Job was tested. There were periods when my father relented and I lived normally. But then bad reports would come, the prohibitions would be re-imposed and I would plan to evade them... When all my tricks and plans and evasions failed I just went and played and said to hell with the consequences.[14]

There is no suggestion here that he ever repaid his debts or agonised over them. James's rebellious spirit against the mould of the family would never leave him. He did not go to university. He never trained for a profession or regular work. He would go to England, write books and become the irrepressible Marxist revolutionary, ever the leader of a small sect of disciples (rarely more than 12), including several beautiful white women. Louise Cripps, one of his white political devotees and lovers from the late 1930s in London, has written about his compelling charm, his learning, his gift for conversation (beautiful words enchantingly modulated), all enhanced by his skilful and sensitive lovemaking. She asserts that he was always deeply aware of his mastery of words and sex, and that he exploited it to the hilt, in his small Marxist groups (in which he was always the peerless talker and sole leader). His earnings, even when he was a cricket correspondent in England for the *Manchester Guardian* between 1933 and 1937, were always small. He depended on his disciples to support him.[15] It was as if he had not left those years as an adolescent rebel; as if he were still outwitting his disciplinarian father, Robert James, and his puritanical mother, Bessie, by pursuing only what he deemed worthwhile. Louise Cripps remembers the scars on his back, a permanent reminder of his father's partiality for the rod. For James, in the 1930s-40s in England and America, dispensing wisdom on the impending socialist revolution on behalf of the working class – the cause – would elicit the same devotion as his obsession with cricket and the classics at QRC, between 1911 and 1918. The boy had not left the man. He would take money from anyone who offered it; he would become the permanent revolutionary (with brief intervals of conventional work), with no remorse, because it was defensible by virtue of the purity of motives and inviolability of the 'cause'. Louise Cripps observes: 'James was handsome and proud… But he was vain… His followers turned him into a prodigy… He was a great lover…[He] was supported for most of his adult life by other people'.[16] But at the peak of his powers, he was peerless at what he did. Both mind and body conspired to make him irresistible to those in his orbit.

Constance Webb (1918-2005), James's second wife, a beautiful white American actress, first met James when he gave a lecture in Los Angeles in the spring of 1939. She has sculpted an enviable portrait of that first encounter with this handsome, irrepressible Marxist rebel:

> He was over six feet two inches; slim but not thin, with long legs. He walked easily with his shoulders level. His head appeared to be on a stalk, held high with the chin tilted forward and up, which made it seem that his body was led by a long neck – curved forward like that of a racehorse on the slip. Shoulders, chest and legs were powerful and he moved decisively. But, as with highly trained athletes, the tension was concentrated and tuned, so that he gave the impression of enormous ease. He was without self-consciousness, simply himself, which showed in the way he moved, and one recognised a special quality.[17]

C.L.R. James (1901-1989) and his second wife, Constance Webb, USA, mid-1940s

And he could talk! About anything! Even V.S. Naipaul (fellow graduate of QRC) came under the spell of C.L.R., in his early days in London in the mid-1950s. In his book of 1994, *A Way in the World*, James's (Lebrun's) enchanting gift for talk is distilled as something of depth and beauty, utterly mesmeric:

> He was born to talk. It was as though everything he saw and thought and read was automatically processed into talk material. And it was all immensely intelligent and gripping. He talked about music and the influence on composers of the instruments of their time. He talked about military matters. I had met no one like that from our region, no one who had given so much time to reading and thought, no one who had organised so much information in this appetising way. *I thought his political reputation simplified the man.* And his language was extraordinary... his spoken sentences, however involved, were complete: they could have been taken down and sent to the printers. I thought his spoken language was like Ruskin's on the printed page, in its fluency and elaborateness, the words wonderfully chosen, often unexpected, bubbling up from some ever-running spring of sensibility... I thought him a prodigy [emphasis added].[18]

James's Marxist obsession (sustained by its niche of devotees) did, in my view, divert and detract from, an exquisite mind with a special gift for apprehending ideas, peoples and places while transcending rigid academic boundaries. At his best, his spoken thoughts went beyond all boundaries. But apart from his great work, *Beyond a Boundary* (and, possibly, *Black Jacobins* [1938]), my view is that what James considered his major publications tend to be bereft of his mental sagacity. Something conspired to render most of his political books irrelevant (at best of transitory value), mired in his pursuit of the mantra of revolution, however unmarred by the dogmas of the Communist creed. I recognise that this is a view not shared by all, on the evidence of the fairly continuous reprinting of many of his books and the spate of academic monographs and critical collections celebrating James as a dialectical thinker. I remain convinced that there was a subterranean fount, rooted in the family's insecurity over money and status and their relentless penchant for discipline and conformity, which made the rebel in James a major flaw. It became a millstone. He had to win the argument. Maybe if he had gone to university, he might have been more secure and reconciled to the fact that one did not always have to win. In his small Marxist groups, his disciples rarely challenged him. He was beyond criticism. He was the creed. Louise Cripps recalls the time in the late 1930s when he was already having doubts about the infallibility of Trotskyism:

> I remained a faithful supporter, but James was already moving away from Trotsky's philosophies... We did not actually quarrel, but it was the first time we were not in complete harmony with each other... He felt that because we could not get married [she claimed to have aborted twice for him, with her own money], I was taking these attitudes that did not

> fit into his own growing anti-Trotskyism. I knew it was not so and that it was just his masculine vanity asserting itself. He was a very proud and, in some ways, a very arrogant man. You had to agree with him on what he thought. We had previously always agreed.[19]

James and Grace Lee Boggs, who were prominent among a handful of James's disciples in the so-called Johnson-Forest Tendency, in America in the 1940s, observe that 'his only roots were in Trinidad', but that 'it was too limited an arena for his fantastic talents'.[20] (Johnson was James; Forest was Raya Dunayevskaya.) Grace Lee Boggs also reflected upon James's fifteen years in America (1938-53) when he published primarily on Marxism (nothing on the West Indies), and was sustained by the adulation and funds of his coterie of devotees:

> Most of his friends and admirers today find it difficult to understand how CLR, who had already made a name for himself as the author of *Black Jacobins* and as a cricket correspondent when he came to the United States in 1938, was content to spend the next fifteen years living and working in obscurity in the small Trotskyite parties, writing and speaking under pseudonyms like J.R. Johnson and AAB. My own view is that they were the happiest and most productive years of his long and extraordinarily productive life.[21]

The reservation that Grace Lee Boggs argues against will not go away for those who cannot share James's political views, who feel the abundant promise of the 1930s was squandered. Robert Hill considers his writing and political engagement in England between 1932 and 1938, before his fifteen years in America, 'a monumental achievement which staggers the mind'. He lists it thus:[22]

(1) *The Life of Captain Cipriani*, 1932.
(2) *The Case for West Indian Self-Government*, 1933 (an abridged version of the above).
(3) Learie Constantine's *Cricket and I*, 1933, which James was largely responsible for writing.
(4) *Minty Alley*, 1936, a novel.
(5) International African Friends of Ethiopia [IAFE], 1935-7.
(6) *Toussaint L'Ouverture* [a play], in which Paul Robeson played the leading role in its London production, 1936.
(7) International African Service Bureau, official organ, formed out of IAFE in 1937 by George Padmore. Editor of *International African Opinion*, 1938.
(8) The first historical account of the Third International, *World Revolution, 1917-1936: The Rise and Fall of the Communist International*, 1936.
(9) English translation of Boris Souvarine's biography, *Stalin*, 1938.
(10) *The Black Jacobins: Toussaint L'Ouverture and the San Domingo Revolution*,
(11) *A History of Negro Revolt*, 1939

If James had not written *Beyond a Boundary* he would not have acquired an international reputation, and without that book the criticism of underachievement and dissipated power could not be advanced. We might wonder, too, whether if James had returned to the West Indies after his productive years in the 1930s in England, he might have arrived at a measure of practicality: learning to give and take. Like effective politicians, such as Norman Manley, Grantley Adams and Eric Williams (his former student at QRC and friend in England), all Oxford-educated, he might have recognised that Marxism is an alien plant in the British West Indian environment; that these small, religiously oriented societies where black people have been in the majority, where social amelioration has been achieved through small incremental changes, have been palpably averse to utopian visions. Radicalism would rarely go beyond the Fabian socialism received from the right wing of the old British Labour Party. But James, his substantial learning notwithstanding, was never comfortable with the so-called 'inevitability of gradualism', espoused by Fabian socialists. Rebelling against the family's definitions was his inheritance for life. Is it possible, therefore, that without a university degree, no profession, James could not face his family in Trinidad? He stayed away for twenty-six years.

In a letter to his second wife, Constance Webb, in July 1944, when he was courting her in America, he hinted at the scars left by his family's inflexible frame of reference:

> I didn't love my parents. I loved nobody. I didn't hate them. I had no grievances [he claimed]. I just didn't feel for them as I was supposed to. Once when my mother was near death I cried because everyone was crying and I thought I ought to cry. But I knew I was faking.[23]

He feared intimacy. Anna Grimshaw (a young English anthropologist) was his personal assistant; she nursed him during his last years in London in the late 1980s. She has written with empathy on the place of the 200 or so letters James wrote to Constance Webb in the 1940s:

> [I]n his correspondence James opened up a free and private space, one in which he could dream, fantasise, admit to needs and desires, explore new dimensions of human experience, discover intimacy, unburden himself, indulge his wit and playfulness in short do all the things he repressed in his public persona. For James, the revolutionary leader, was never anything but reserved and self-controlled, always a master of himself, the situation and the party line.[24]

This great mind lost its creative impulse: 'fiction drained out of me'. It was rarely seen at its best again, apart from in *Beyond a Boundary*; and, privately, in his beguiling conversations which some like V.S. Naipaul had the privilege to savour. Yet there is enough in his great book of 1963, written largely in England and completed in Trinidad (the two countries that possessed his soul), to ensure that C.L.R. James remains one of the great thinkers of the 20th century.

Notes

1. Alan Metcalfe, 'C.L.R. James's Contribution to the History of Sport', *Canadian Journal of the History of Sport*, 2 (1987), p. 57.
2. See my *Muscular Learning: Cricket and Education in the Making of the British West Indies at the End of the 19th Century* (Kingston, Jamaica: Ian Randle Publishers, 2006), Chapter Two, 'The Elite Schools and British Imperialism: Cricket, Christianity and the Classics, the 1860s-90s, with Special Reference to Barbados'. See also Ivar Oxaal, *Black Intellectuals Come to Power: The Rise of Creole Nationalism in Trinidad and Tobago* (Cambridge, Mass.: Schenkman Publishing Co., 1968), Chapter 4.
3. C.L.R. James, *Beyond a Boundary* (London: Serpent's Tail, 1994 [1963]), pp. 7-8. (Hereafter cited as *BB*.)
4. *BB*, p. 8.
5. *Ibid.*, pp. 12-5.
6. *Ibid.*, p. 16.
7. *Ibid*, p. 19
8. C.L.R. James, 'Discovering Literature in Trinidad: the 1930s', in his *Spheres of Existence: Selected Writings* (London: Allison and Busby, 1980), pp. 237-8.
9. *BB*, p. 32-3.
10. *Ibid.*, pp. 3-4.
11. *Ibid.*, p. 4.
12. *Ibid.*, p. 16.
13. *Ibid.*, p. 27.
14. *Ibid.*, pp. 27-8.
15. Louise Cripps's account of her life with James, within the 'Marxist Group' in London in the late 1930s, is permeated by politics and sex. See *C.L.R. James: Memories and Commentaries* (New York: Cornwall Books, 1997).
16. *Ibid.*, pp. 149, 152.
17. Constance Webb, 'C.L.R. James, the Speaker and his Charisma', *C.L.R. James: His Life and Work*, ed., Paul Buhle (London: Allison and Busby, 1986), p. 169. (Hereafter cited as *James*.)
18. V.S. Naipaul, *A Way in the World: A Sequence* (London: Minerva, 1995 [1994]), 112-3.
19. See note 15, p. 80.
20. James and Grace Lee Boggs, 'A Critical Reminiscence', *James*, ed., Paul Buhle, p. 179.
21. Grace Lee Boggs, 'C.L.R. James: Organising in the United States, 1939-53', *C.L.R. James: His Intellectual Legacies*, eds., Selwyn Cudjoe and William Cain (Amherst: University of Massachusetts Press), p. 165.
22. Robert A. Hill, 'In England, 1932-1938', *James*, ed., Paul Buhle, p. 62.
23. 'C.L.R. James on the Caribbean: Three Letters', *C.L.R. James's Caribbean*, eds., Paget Henry and Paul Buhle (London: Macmillan, 1992), p. 21.
24. Anna Grimshaw, 'Special Delivery: The Letters of C.L.R. James to Constance Webb, 1939-1948', http://www.clrjamesinstitute.org/specdel1.html [1996]

INTERVIEW WITH IVAN MADRAY, THE FORGOTTEN CRICKETER

'DA COOLIE GA MEK ABI HUNT LEDDA'[1]

> 'I remember the deep love of the people of Port Mourant who put their pennies to make Rohan and Basil and I what we became... Without them we might all have remained as labourers on the plantation.'

Ivan Samuel Madray, the Indo-Guyanese leg-spinner, was born at Plantation Port Mourant, on the Corentyne Coast in Berbice, Guyana on 2 July 1934. Among his boyhood playmates on the plantation were Rohan Kanhai, Basil Butcher, and Joe Solomon. They all first represented Port Mourant, Berbice, British Guiana, and the West Indies in the 1950s. Kanhai, Butcher, and Solomon had long international careers, playing in 79, 44 and 27 Test matches respectively. Madray played in two Tests, the second and the fourth Tests against Pakistan, during their tour of the West Indies in 1958. He was a competent leg-break bowler who made a fine impression in the Quadrangular Tournament in 1956, which was won by British Guiana, hitherto the Cinderella of West Indian cricket. In the first innings of their match against Jamaica, Madray bowled a record 84 overs, 18 of which were maidens, taking 4 for 168. Against Barbados, in the final, he took 4 for 61 as he and Lance Gibbs, the off-spinner, demolished the great side. It is noteworthy that one of his victims was the legendary Everton Weekes whose batting against the spin of Gibbs and Madray was reduced to a pitiable mediocrity.

Madray's performance was remarkable especially as the West Indies is known for its paucity of top-class leg-spinners. The great Barbados and West Indies batsman Clyde Walcott (1926-2006), who became a coach on the sugar plantations in Guyana in 1954, captained British Guiana during the Tournament. In 1958, he wrote in his book, *Island Cricketers:* 'For this [victory in the Quadrangular Tournament] we had largely to thank our spinners, Lance Gibbs and Ivan Madray, two young players with an undoubted future, who could well assume the mantle of Ramadhin and Valentine in the West Indies one day.' And Walcott, as C.L.R. James wrote, 'is always circumspect in his speech.' Gibbs did, indeed, become the best off-spinner in the world in the 1960s, taking 309 Test wickets in 79 Tests.

My friend, Ivan Madray (1934-2009), during the fourth Test match, West Indies v. Pakistan, Georgetown, March 1958

Madray and his team-mates during the B.G. v Barbados match at Bourda, October 1956: Left to right: Madray, Basil Butcher, Clyde Walcott, Sonny Baijnauth, Rohan Kanhai, Joe Solomon

Three from Port Mourant in the W.I. team, 1st Test, Manchester, 1963: (back row, l to r) Joe Solomon (PM), Lance Gibbs, Joey Carew, Charlie Griffith, Deryck Murray, Basil Butcher (PM); (front row, l to r): Rohan Kanhai (PM), Conrad Hunte, Frank Worrell, Garry Sobers, Wes Hall

But Madray played in only two Tests in which he got no wickets. He left British Guiana in 1958 to play for Penzance in Cornwall. In 1960 he moved to the Lancashire League where he had a successful career until his retirement in 1967. He then attended Leicester College for two years, studying Youth and Community Work. For several years Ivan was a social worker in London, becoming a senior youth counsellor with the Inner London Education Authority (I.L.E.A.). He then established two nursing homes, running them with a measure of success for many years.

In the following conversation with Ivan Madray, at his home in south-east London, the colourful life of the man, his wit and his memorable recollections of his wicked boyhood, his tempestuous cricketing life at Port Mourant, his pleasant experiences as a Berbice and British Guiana bowler, and his aborted career as a West Indian cricketer enlivened and enriched my own life for two days. His great admiration and respect for Clyde Walcott, and his irrepressible adulation of Rohan Kanhai, 'my living god' he called him, flowed like the repetition of a Hindu mantra. Pregnant pauses punctuated the tape as he groped in a frenzy for the elusive imagery to convey his reverence for these two men. There was also a residual, but mellowed bitterness when he recalled his experiences in 1958 with Gerry Alexander, the captain of the West Indies. He believed that if Clyde Walcott or Frank Worrell had been the captain, his brief career in West Indies cricket would not have come to an abortive, unsung end. In his two Tests his figures were 35 overs, 6 maidens, 108 runs, 0 wicket; but he explained that in his debut Test at Port of Spain, three palpable chances were squandered, two by Alexander, the wicketkeeper. He added, '*Wisden* won't tell you so.' He believed that Alexander and the West Indian selectors were determined that he should not succeed, Walcott's high assessment of him notwithstanding. They preferred Rodriguez, a less experienced local white or near-white man. And his non-selection on the tour to India and Pakistan in 1958-59 underlined the futility of his position.

It was a rich, animated conversation with Ivan Madray, much of it delivered in the beautiful, musical vernacular of Port Mourant, spiced with the raw wit, the theatrical inflexions, and the suggestive allusions of these robust Indians of the sugar-cane fields. It is impossible to reproduce this in print; the transcript diminishes it: 'Da coolie ga mek abi hunt ledda' or 'Nuh hurry! Me ga mek fu abi two.'

I last saw Ivan in the summer of 2008, when I interviewed him for my book of 2009: *From Ranji to Rohan: Cricket and Indian Identity in Colonial Guyana, 1890s-1960s*. As usual, we had a few glasses of wine and a superb Indo-Guyanese meal (dal and rice and roti, with prawn curry, salt-fish with tomato, karaila and okra), prepared by his devoted partner of many years, Rohinee Heerah (Ro). He was in good form, but I was also aware that his health was deteriorating. So when he told me in early 2009 that he was contemplating making his last trip to Guyana, I implored him not to undertake the journey. But he was determined to make that last visit of his beloved Port Mourant. Ro told me that a few days before they were to leave Guyana, however, she observed a strange, inexplicable change in Ivan's behaviour, suggesting that he did not wish to catch the plane for London. It seemed as if some alien force had taken hold of him suddenly.

Sadly, on their way to the airport, Ivan had a heart attack and died at the Georgetown Hospital on 23 April 2009. Did he have intimations that this would, indeed, be his last journey? He was buried at his beloved Port Mourant. He always told me that Port Mourant was in his soul: after fifty years in England, he still sounded as if he had just got off the boat, and memories of his rich boyhood experiences, peopled with a cast of colourful characters and eternally fresh, alluring imagery, would flow copiously at the slightest prompting. The humour was consuming and could go on for hours.

Shortly after Ivan's death, I felt a need to catch a glimpse of what Ivan did when he arrived in Penzance, Cornwall, to play his first cricket match in May 1958. There would have been no West Indian or hardly any non-white person in this strange place, a long way from the familiarity of London and its multitude of dark faces, by the late 1950s. *The Cornishman* of 22 May 1958 carried an article captioned:

IVAN MADRAY MAKES IMPRESSIVE DEBUT
WEST INDIES PLAYER WILL DRAW CROWD

> The large crowd that went to the Hayle cricket ground on Saturday to see Ivan Madray, Penzance's 24-year old West Indies Test match professional, were not disappointed. Madray, on a day which certainly could not have suited him, for it was cold and blustery, created a very good impression in all departments of the game.
>
> His bowling figures of 14 overs, 3 maidens, 37 runs, 3 wickets did not represent his skill. Two easy catches were dropped off his bowling, and time and again the ball shaved the stumps with the batsmen completely at a loss.
>
> His batting was share joy to watch. He showed a wide range of strokes all round the wicket, and was not afraid to hit the ball hard from the first delivery he received. He was eventually stumped for a quick 40 when he lost the ball in the sun. His running between the wickets was extremely well judged.
>
> But perhaps it was his fielding which most impressed. Picking up the ball at full speed, he time and again returned it with one movement just over the stumps in a perfect position for a run out. Altogether, there is no doubt he will prove a great attraction and he should make many runs on the Penzance wicket.

> Ivan likes Penzance; he likes the cricket ground; and he likes the people he has met. But he does not like our cold weather!
>
> Of medium height – he is 5 feet 7 inches – Ivan is solidly built and looks as if he is capable of hitting the ball hard.
>
> 'But when it's so cold, I almost feel like running back home', he said with a smile.

It was nearly 51 years before he made his final journey home, and there he will stay, not far away from the cricket ground which possessed his early years and several others of his fellow Berbice, Guyana and West Indies cricketers.

In a piece in 1983 Ian McDonald, the Guyanese writer and poet, sought an explanation of why Plantation Port Mourant had produced six West Indies Test cricketers between the late 1940s and the early 1970s: John Trim, Rohan Kanhai, Basil Butcher, Joe Solomon, Ivan Madray and Alvin Kallicharran. He pondered: 'There must be something in the Berbice air, some special mixture in the soil of Port Mourant, to have grown such a crop of cricketing genius'. It is interesting to recall that in the great Frank Worrell team that toured England in 1963, winning 3-1, the numbers 3, 4 and 6 batsmen were all from Plantation Port Mourant.

I hope that my interview with Ivan Madray, in November 1987, helps in some way to answer Ian's question about this unique sugar plantation that was so extraordinarily endowed with cricketing gifts.

C S: Ivan, what are some of your earliest memories of cricket as a boy at Plantation Port Mourant in the 1940s?

I M: I remember the first time I ever thought about cricket was one day when I went to the Port Mourant Cricket Ground, peeping through a hole in the zinc fence, watching the big men in white play. There was something about their clean, white clothes that made the whole thing look like magic. And as I peeped, with no shirt on and my black ass exposed to the public – my pants tried to hide my willy but it would pop out[2] – I felt like I wanted to be like those men. Yes, it was magic to me. I must have been four or five. I don't remember how I became a cricketer, but at Port Mourant Catholic School I used to practise with the bigger boys. I think I was in the third standard, and I really loved to play with these big boys. In those days only boys from the fifth and sixth standards played for the school. I think I was about ten, and I was so anxious to play, I did everything possible to get into the school team. I remember one day, the pupils played the teachers, and I was asked to play for the pupils; and there was a big hullabaloo about me, this lil [little] boy from third standard, and that I shouldn't play. The teacher, who I remember liked me very much, Sonny Yangasammy, begged for me to play. I did play against the teachers, and I think I made 26 runs. I was a batsman in the eyes of Sonny Yangasammy, and I used to copy his style, bowling off-breaks. I used to admire him. So I began my cricket career playing for Roman School.

C S: As a batsman/off-break bowler?

I M: As a batsman/off-break bowler.

C S: Not as a leg-spinner?

I M: No, as a batsman/off-break bowler. And our first Shield match was Roman school v. Scots school.

C S: Was Rohan Kanhai in the Roman school side?

I M: Rohan wasn't in our side yet. (As a matter of fact, I am about a year or so older than Rohan.) And I played against Scots school and I made 68 runs. I can't remember how many wickets I got, but I remember we won. And some of my best friends, black boys, hailed me, you know, as if I were great, and I was feeling like I was in heaven, and they were lifting me onto their shoulders. Great stuff! I think it was the first time Roman school ever beat Scots school in the...

C S: Gibson Shield?

I M: I think it was the Gibson Shield. I can't remember the name of the shield; but there was a shield. And it went on from there. We won the championship, and our captain, a tremendous chap, a massive fella from Port Mourant – his name was Harry Gokul – ...He was so encouraging; he encouraged me so much, I became close to him – one of his best friends to the day he died, a few years ago. I never looked back. I think the following year Rohan Kanhai came on the scene. And Rohan, as I recall, was a wicketkeeper, and he kept wicket for Roman school[3] that year, and went in to open the batting with me; I used to open the batting. I was the more aggressive player. Rohan was the one that killed everything, the real stonewall. And that suited us because Ro would stay there actually till the end. He would make 15, 20, 30 runs, but you couldn't move him. We never looked back. I remember one time when Rohan and I got stuck together, was Roman school v. ...

C S: The Anglican school?

I M: That's right, the Anglican school. That was the school which Basil Butcher was attending. So you can imagine the battle that was going to take place. Because it wasn't only a battle between the two sides; it was also a battle between the two teachers. In those days, teachers from the respective schools did the umpiring. I remember our teacher – we used to call him Sticky, Mr Francis from Roman school, and from the Anglican school, Makhanlall. English school[4] went in to bat and made 100 runs. I'm positive, dead 100. And we had, I think, about an hour and some minutes to get these runs. We heart been in we mout', and so was everybody at the ground. That same day I became captain of Roman school. And Rohan and I put on a cut-ass pan English school; we slaughtered the bowling all over the place. Then, suddenly, we were told that the match was drawn. The clock showed 6 o'clock; match finish. Look, till I die I won't forget that afternoon. What you think happen? Somebody from the Anglican school moved forward the hand of the clock so that it was showing 6 o'clock when in fact it wasn't. A real war broke out between Roman school pupils and those from Anglican school. Anyway, the crookishness of our enemies was unmasked, and Rohan and I beat the clock this time: we got the runs before it *was* really 6 o'clock. Rohan made 40 something; I got about 60.

C S: So that afternoon Rohan changed from stonewall to stone-crusher[5].

I M: Right. Right. Because I told him, I said, 'Now Ro, is you and me. Yu gat fu knack dis ball rass haad tiday. Yu hear. Nuh worry. We have all the odder boys to come.' And we got the runs. Thank gawd; that day this great genius set out to conquer the world.

I want to come back to that first cricket match I saw through the hole in the fence at Port Mourant Cricket Ground, that day with me bare backside in the air as I peeped through the hole. It wasn't until many years later that I discovered what that big match was all about. It was a final, Flood Cup final.[6] On that day there was a chap playing there who, as if by magic, left a picture of himself in my memory. I was to idolize him in later years. His name was Onkar Naraine, a beautiful batsman and a master fieldsman. A tremendous player, a graceful player; he made everything look so pretty, so complete. And, Clem, it looked so easy. Onkar was from Essequibo.

Another classical batsman who impressed me was a man named Patterson. He was a headmaster, and he played for Berbice. A real treat to watch this man drive and cut and hook! The range of shots! Yes, Patterson was also one of my idols. And, of course, several chaps from Port Mourant. Johnny Teekasingh[7] (I used to call him Johnny Uncle). He was the greatest; he was my God in those early days and even afterwards. There was also Uncle Lutch (Jaggernauth), Uncle Black Etwaroo, and Tam Dadda, my cousin. Always 'Uncle'; you mad call dem by dem name, rass, dem cut yu ass. They were my heroes. I remember coming from primary school in the afternoon – I used to have to cross the ball field to get to my house. And I would put my slate down, anywhere, I couldn't care where, and the big men would send me to keep byes.

C S: Behind the wicket, back-stop.

I M: Back-stop, that's right. So I was getting to know and to adore these men, always Uncle this or Uncle that, and I was starting to see these men as different from other men at Port Mourant. They were bigger than men, and I wanted to be like them. In my dreams I saw them hitting the ball all over the place, and sometimes I saw myself as one of them. The whole thing would come alive in me at nights, before I slept and when I was sleeping. Anyway, one afternoon when the time came for me to bat, Uncle Fielda (Kempadoo) sey, 'Go home. Go home.' Many times this man would repeat this thing, 'Go home, bai. Go a house.' Many people used to be around there. I used to be very angry; and I used to resent this man. Then one afternoon after school, I stopped, as usual, at the ground: Uncle Lutch, Uncle Black Etwaroo and Tam Dadda were there. They always went to the ground early. They would cook 'all-in-one'[8] and would stay on to practise. After they had batted, the three of them, I said I wanted to bat. They didn't allow me to bat. What they did? In those days there were ants' nests all around the ball field. They dug up an ants' nest, took my trousers off, and put my backside on it. This is God heavenly true. And I started to yell, and I was cussing them, 'Yu mudda this, yu mudda that.' And I was crying, screaming in agony.

When I went home, my mother asked me. 'Wa happen, wa happen wid yu, betta [son]?' Me sey, 'Tam Dadda and Lutch Uncle and Black Uncle… When me fe bat, dem na wan' gimme battin'. Den dem dig dis ants' nes'; dem put me batty [backside] pan am.' Me say, 'Me ga wait till pai [father] come; pai ga kill dem.' But the first ting my father said was, 'Yu mus' e a cuss dem bai [boy].' Jus' like da. 'Yu mus' e a cuss dem bai, das why dem bai do da to yu.' And I will never forget it. But I idolized those chaps, and as I grew older I used to be the wata bai,[9] just to be 'round them: they played cricket well, and anyone who played cricket well had to be near to Gawd. And, of course, always 'Uncle'. I always called them 'Uncle'.

C S: You continued to play cricket after you left Roman school?

I M: I wouldn't have known how to stop. I went to Corentyne High School, but I really wanted to play cricket for Port Mourant Cricket Club with Johnny Teekasingh and the others. But I still couldn't make the grade. So I started to play for City Star, a little village club at Miss Sibi (Miss Phoebe). I was about 16.

C S: Miss Sibi, a section of Port Mourant, a smaller club.

I M: Yes. I played for City Star: a good batsman and a good off-spinner. But I wasn't so effective as the competition got hotter and hotter. And something strange happened one day as we were playing underarm for money.

C S: Sponge ball?[10]

I M: Yes. Rubber ball. This was good cricket, good competition, good money. And you bet all your pocket money there.

C S: All the boys were there? Rohan and Basil Butcher?

I M: Everybody. Rohan, Basil Butcher, Joe Solomon. Everybody. We a pick sides. You know, you a play Ankerville, you a play Miss Sibi, Ankerville would play Port Mourant, Port Mourant would play Bung Yaad,[11] and so on. This was underarm; this was fu money: the real, real thing. The other cricket, overarm, hard-ball was the gentleman's stuff; you play there if you fit in there. And I remember Miss Sibi was practising in front of the well; there was a little grassland there. We were practising.

C S: At Port Mourant?

I M: In Port Mourant itself, practising, practising. And I was bowling, going like that, bowling like that, bowling my off-break, as usual, and bowling it fast. And the chap, our batsman, was hitting me nice. Then, suddenly, I decided to do one like that...

C S: On the leg?

I M: On the leg. I decided to do that.

C S: With the wrist?

I M: With the wrist. Just like that. And then I bowled a ball, and it spun so big. I didn't bother then; and I remember the chap went to play like that, expecting my off-break; he didn't read me. I remember his name was Paalo. And he walked down the batting strip and said, 'Yu know wa yu bowl dey jis' now?' Me sey, 'Nuh.' Big chap, Paalo. 'Yu bowl leg-break.' Me sey, 'Wa da?' He sey, 'Bowl am again.' I obliged. That's how I started to bowl leg-break. And I bowled, and I practised, and I practised.'

C S: Under-arm?

I M: Underarm. Then we went to play agains' Bung Yaad; Joe Solomon was playing for Bung Yaad. Butcher was playing for us. I can't remember who Rohan played for. But the whole of Miss Sibi put their money on our side against Bung Yaad: hundreds and hundreds of dollars. Under-arm, the faster you bowl, the better you are. And I remember I came on to bowl, and they were expecting me to bowl my off-breaks. They weren't expecting my leg-breaks. And, Clem, unto this day I can't believe my eyes: I reeled the side out, including Joe Solomon, and that's how it happened that Ivan Madray became a leg-spinner.

I became anxious to put this leg-spin bowling in the proper side. And I remember City Star v. Ankerville, playing for all the gears. The side that won got all the gears; you lost the game, you lost all your gears and you were finished. We went on to play against Ankerville

Cricket Club. Our captain was Isaac Gopie, a player in the Lutch, Black Etwaroo, Johnny Teekasingh era. I made about 5 runs; I was dejected. And as I was walking back, a fella said to me – a big chap, working cut-and- load... (Most of the people playing for City Star were backdam people, cut-and-load people).

C S: Cane-cutters?

I M: Cane-cutters. I was one of the ordinary chaps. I couldn't afford it; so I played for City Star, and thank God I did. Anyway as I was walking back to the pavilion, this chap, Rupchand, I can recall him walking, sleeve rolled up, short chap with a bat in his hand, no gloves. This is one of the hard nuts I am talking about, no batting gloves. And as we were crossing, he said, 'Nuh hurry'? (I don't know if you know the word 'Nuh hurry'? He meant, 'Nuh worry'.) He sey, 'Nuh hurry. Me ga mek fu abi two [for both of us].' I was so sad because that was the first time I ever put a pair of flannels on, long pants, playing for City Star. All the time I used to wear short pants, so I was well-geared for the occasion, nicely dressed, wanting to do well. And I failed as a batsman. But this thing that has stuck with me until today – we remained friends – were the words he used, 'Nuh hurry. Me ga mek fu abi two'. Very touching! He meant he would make enough runs for the two of us.

C S: Where was Rupchand from?

I M: Miss Sibi. Rupchand finished with 145 not out in a total of a little over 200 made by City Star. We went on to bowl Ankerville out for a meagre score. I did well. My skipper called on me to bowl early. He said, 'I want you to bowl leg-break.' I got scared. When I started to bowl my leg-breaks, he put me at the bottom end. Me sey, 'Skipper, nuh. Me want to bowl from tap end.' He say, 'Nuh, de breeze a blow' – these chaps were tacticians, but I was thinking that I wanted my leg-breaks to go down wind, quick like that. He said, 'Nuh. You bowl from de battam end. Me want yu to tass it up.' He wanted me to get the ball to drift against the wind.' And, Clem, that was the beginning; I had graduated from rubber ball to big cricket with my leg-breaks.

C S: Had you ever seen a leg-break bowler before?

I M: Never, never. Yes, yes, yes. That is a lie. Of course, I admired Johnny Teekasingh, Johnny Uncle I called him. He was a superb leg-break bowler. And people at these big games used to shout, 'Johnny, Johnny, Johnny. Fielda put on Johnny.' And whenever he came to bowl, it was like a miracle. And this old man, to me, was one of the greatest bowlers in my time, even when I played Test cricket.

Port Mourant Cricket Club heard of my bowling in our match

against Ankerville. Johnny Uncle came to our house and asked my father for me to join Port Mourant. He said, 'Dis bai a bowl good. If he can bowl like me, dis bai ga play cricket, big cricket.' My father said, 'A'right. Le' dem diduck de money from me pay.' We couldn't afford to pay the membership dues; they had to take it out of my father's meagre wage.

C S: Where was your father working?

I M: My father was working as a field mechanic at Port Mourant Estate, maintaining eight children, sending me to High School. I saw the hardship. So I started to play for Port Mourant, where Uncle Johnny had taken over the captaincy from Fielda Kempadoo. I was very happy about that. You see, Uncle Johnny was the first person responsible for me building the confidence which led me to first-class cricket. In fact, he was a vital force in shaping my life as it developed over the years. And I remember in my first match for Port Mourant as a youth, he brought me on to bowl; and I was very frightened; I didn't want to let him down. He said, 'I want you to bowl just like me.' Me sey, 'Nuh Uncle, me ga bowl off-break.' He say, 'Yu a bowl leg-break.' He sey, 'Yu see dis belt, ya.' That was the word: 'Yu see dis belt. If yu na bowl leg-break, me ga tek dis belt and beat yu.' And right away I remembered when I was younger what Lutch did, what Black Etwaroo did, what Tam did – put me bare batty pan the ants' nes.' And it was the same ball-field. I can't remember who we played against, it could have been Plantation Albion or Plantation Skeldon, but I went on to bowl leg-breaks; and I soon established myself as a top player alongside Uncle Johnny and others…

C S: I recall that Kanhai said that you and he joined Port Mourant around the same time and that Basil Butcher joined shortly afterwards, but that Joe Solomon had already been playing.[12]

I M: Joe was an established player. Looking back, I think Joe should have played first-class cricket before myself, Rohan and Basil. Sonny Moonsammy also should have played before us. But there were also other players at Port Mourant before us who should have played first-class cricket. But can I come back to my relationship with Port Mourant Cricket Club? Some time afterwards, I turned up one Sunday to play – it was an important match – and I was told that I wasn't selected. I enquired why that was so. I was then told that my father had not paid my weekly dues. I didn't know until later that my father had been suspended by the Estate, and therefore no deduction could have been made. I didn't play, but I cried. I cried. I cried. And I remember Lutch, Black Etwaroo, and my cousin, Tam, came and consoled me. Rohan played; Basil played… but I wasn't picked. And I cried; I cried because I wanted to play. I wanted to play because my friends, Butch and Ro and I were so close. We were doing things together all the time: we were practising together with the older ones because the three of us didn't get jobs when we left primary school. I went later to work at the train line, then I went on to Corentyne High School.

C S: Where was Kanhai working?

I M: On the buses, as a conductor.[13]

C S: And Joe Solomon?

I M: Joe was well away on the plantation, working as a distiller.

C S: Bit of a big-shot?

I M: Well, yes. Joe's family was highly respectable. His father had a good job with the Administrative Manager of the Estate. They lived well. Good people, nice people.

C S: And Basil Butcher?

I M: Butch helped his mother, baking cassava pone and so on. And caan pone. And until today if you call Butch, Caan Pone, he will turn round, look hard at yu and sey, 'Whe' yu come from, bai?' Butch false name is Caan Hux; it comes from his making caan pone, cassava pone, coconut pudding and so on. My false name was, my gawd, I remember what the neighbours used to call me, I used to be a very wicked chap then; they used to call me Mudera.

C S: Murderer?

I M: Yes. I put it down, you know, that I was fighting like hell for survival. And Rohan, I remember, they used to call him Kish.

C S: Kish?

I M: Kish.

C S: Why Kish?

I M: I don't know why they called him Kish. One day when we went to play trials in Georgetown, his elder brother, Richard, came to welcome us. (We were staying at a guest house near to the Woodbine Hotel.) He greeted Rohan, 'Hai, Kish!' To me, Kish, I am assuming, is a pet name. Probably when Rohan was a little boy he used to say, 'Gimme kish'. They call him Kish in his family. And Butch, Caan Hux; and me, Mudera.

C S: And Joe?

I M: Joe. I don't know.

C S: Too respectable?

I M: I don't think Joe had a false name. Well, Joe wasn't exposed enough then.

C S: Wasn't one of the rough boys of the village.

I M: I came from rough Miss Sibi, fighting for survival. I used to do a lot of thiefing. I did a lot of thiefing. I thief mainly food.

C S: Not fowl?

I M: Fowl? Oh gawd, yes! Yes. That's regular. Talking about fowl, I remember City Star played a club from Adelphi in Canje, West Canje…

C S: East Canje.

I M: East Canje? And I recall Adelphi had a really good team. People don't remember such good players. There was a beautiful batsman, in the class of Joe Solomon and Sonny Moonsammy. I think his name was Joe Balgobin. They also had a fast bowler, they called him Amazan. He bowled fast, very fast. Anyway we went to Adelphi. We had a lovely time; we stayed overnight. The boys cooked fowl-curry and rice and roti and so on; we had a great time. Shortly afterwards we decided that we would repay the Adelphi boys. So we invited them to Miss Sibi. But City Star had no money, not a blind cent in the till. But we had to put on a show. Each one of us, I remember, went and stole our own fowls. I stole one from our place, and my cousin, Esau, stole one from his mother. And Alvin's grandfather…

C S: Alvin Kallicharran?

I M: Alvin Kallicharran's grandfather, a very strict chap, had a beautiful garden, fruits, plenty fowls and ducks, you name it. We went – we never knew anything of Alvin then – Alvin's father used to be a good cricketer…

C S: Isaac?

I M: Isaac. We went to Alvin's grandfather's place and we stole about five fowls. That is not all. So the boys sey dey ga want aringe [orange] in de morning. Well I sey I know someone – I used to be friendly with this little girl – I know someone who stingy, very mean. They have a aringe tree. Dey sey, 'You mean (a callin' name) Jagat Narine.' (I'm saying this because they are beautiful things now, looking back.) Dey say, 'Yu cyan go dey.' Me sey, 'You watch me.' So, same Paalo, who me fus bowl leg-break to, sey. 'Me ga go een wid yu. Come. Abi ga [we both will] pick.' Me sey, 'Abi ga pick.' He sey, 'Abi naa [won't] pick.' Me sey, 'Abi ga pick.' He sey, 'Abi naa pick. Abi a hall [pull] de tree rass out ah de grung.' An' we tie a rope – this a night time, if you climb up you cyan see fu pick, e daak, no light; an' pimpla [thorns] dey pan de tree – and we pull the tree out, because the place sandy. We pull the tree out, took the tree, lift it up, carry it a water-side, back of all the houses at Miss Sibi. All the fowls that night, Friday night; skin the fowls. Lunch time, chicken curry; Sunday morning, aringe juice.

Pandemonium took place. Me mudda start to cuss me cousin mudda. 'Me fowl go over dey. Me fowl always a go over dey.' Kallicharran, ole maan Kallicharran wife sey, 'Me know who thief me fowl. A Sonny Madray famaly.' Me sey, 'Sonny Madray famaly?' Me say, 'Antie, a wah yu a taak like da fa: Abi [we] na thief nutting from ahyu [all you]. Look ya, somebady thief abi fowl.' And this is how the thing was going. Me sey, 'Look; mus e a Esau dem.' 'Oh Gawd!' Esau sey, 'Me ga tek a cutlish an' chap all ayu fowl rass now.' (Jus, so e ah goh. Esau was a lil madman [a bit crazy].) 'Me ga chap all ahyu fowl rass. Look; people come an' thief abi fowl ya. Oh me mama!' And that is how the thing went. But the beautiful thing was that we didn't steal the fowls just to be wicked; it was too shameful not to reciprocate the way Adelphi had done.

C S: All of this because of cricket.

I M: Beautiful! It was that: (a) the pride, (b) well, the will to get there, to play the game. We are going to let you have a nice time, but we are not going to allow you to beat us. We are going to play fair cricket, even if we are thieves. We all became great friends.

C S: It was a rich village life.

I M: It was rich in a sense...

C S: In terms of experiences?

I M: Not in an economic, material way. But the kind of love that was generated in those days! Tears come to my eyes when I think of it.

I went home to Port Mourant[14] for a brief visit in 1970, at the end of my career as a professional cricketer in England, and after I had completed two years of study in youth and community work. I went home to show my parents me, not Ivan Madray, your son the cricketer; but Ivan Madray, your son, someone you made sacrifices to send to high school and who never made good there, but your son who has now made good in education. I made good in cricket; I earned a living from it for ten years; that was established. But my parents were not there to see me, to listen to me: I made the remarks by their graveside. They had died while I was in England. It hurt. That made me stronger to do something for me, and to their memory. Deep down, I did it for the people to Port Mourant, Miss Sibi in particular.

I had to go back with something, something to say, 'Fu Gawd sake, don't say to me. "Look Ivan, it was a'right fu you. Look how nice yu look; yu haan saaf [your hands soft]; you never work before. And how thing baad in dis place, sey how people a starve." I said, 'I know. Forget about that. In my days there was little food. Yu a taak 'bout wuking in de rice field... I eat me rice sitting down in de wata, an' drink dat wata. Don't worry about who cause this and who cause that. Send your children to school regardless of what. Try and teach your children; educate them, because one day they will do something. Yes, my hand is soft; my hand is nice. But there were plenty, plenty splinters there… and then I had to go and play cricket.'

I didn't do this out of arrogance. I said those things because I love the people of Port Mourant. Because those people, many of them cane-cutters and shovelmen on the plantation, used to collect money on pay-day to buy clothes and boots for us, all of us, Rohan and Basil and I.

C S: Does the poverty of your boyhood still hurt?

I M: When I look back, I don't see poverty. That's not what I remember. I recall that as I got older I became hateful after I was dropped from the Port Mourant team because, as I said, my father could not pay my dues because of his problem at the estate. I felt very resentful, and having seen the man who displaced me, I became enraged. It was a white man, a young overseer. But that was wrong. It was only years afterwards that I realised that I hated the wrong person. And a deep bitterness shifted to the men who made the decision that I must not play, the men on the committee, local men, rising big-shots on the estate. Not my old hero, Uncle Johnny. He was an ordinary man, an instrument for the bigger chaps.

I believe that this incident was related to my father's role in the union on the estate, and the authorities were penalizing me for my father's politics. He was a friend of Cheddi's father. He was very close to old man Jagan.[15] But Clem, no; I don't remember poverty. I remember the deep love of the people of Port Mourant who put their pennies to make Rohan and Basil and I what we became. Joe was better off. Without them we might all have remained as labourers on the plantation. That is what remains strongest within me.

C S: After your problem with Port Mourant Cricket Club, did you continue to play cricket?

I M: Yes. I rejoined my old club, City Star, and I also played cricket for my school, Corentyne High School. But a strange thing happened in the early part of 1954. A letter, addressed to what looked like I. Madray, was delivered to the principal of Corentyne High School, J.C. Chandisingh. It was an invitation for me to represent British Guiana Indians in the Kawall Cup Triangular Tournament between British Guiana Indians, Trinidad Indians, and Surinam Indians, in Trinidad.[16] I was so delighted, I went home and told my mother, my family, and my neighbours. It was a very crucial time. I was preparing to write Senior Cambridge; it was sometime around April. The headmaster protested that I shouldn't go to Trinidad. I was going for four weeks, and that would have meant a big gap, at that particular time, in my education. And so he told my father that I shouldn't go. I made a decision and I went to Trinidad.

C S: Were there other players from Port Mourant who played in the Kawall Cup in Trinidad in 1954?

I M: No. But something dreadful happened when I arrived at the East Indian Cricket Club Pavilion in Georgetown.[17] There was a deafening silence as I entered. But I could not make sense of this. Not until after the tour did I learn that the invitation was sent to the wrong Madray. Apparently the invitation was meant for L. Madray, a good cricketer, an older chap who played for Plantation Albion.[18] So L. Madray, Labrick Madray, found out and was, understandably, deeply hurt. But he did not bear any hatred for me. Afterwards I looked at the invitation again and saw that it was indeed meant for 'L' not 'I' Madray.

Anyway Ganesh Persaud, the captain, apparently insisted before we left, that it was 'I' he wanted. So Ganesh's heart was in his mouth throughout the tour of Trinidad. And in the first match against Trinidad Indians, I got three wickets. I bowled very well; Ganesh was pleased. When we returned to British Guiana, Ganesh told the people at E.I.C.C. (East Indian Cricket Club), 'I told you it was him. I told you how good he is.' I was glad that I didn't let him down, and my performance pleased L. Madray, Labrick, as well. I didn't go back to Corentyne High School, and, of course, it caused a lot of problems with me and my father. Eventually my father stopped supporting me and I had to fend for myself.

C S: I think 1954 was the first year that the Jones Cup Competition among the three counties of British Guiana was started.

I M: That's right.

C S: Did you play for Berbice in the Jones Cup?

I M: We were called to trials. Myself, Rohan, Basil, Joe, Sonny Moonsammy, Saranga Baichu. We were all called to trials. There was also Bickram from Canje. We played trials at the Mental Hospital Ground, and we did very well. I can't remember; I think Berbice won the championship. I bowled very well. Rohan kept wicket; he batted very well; Joe batted very well.

C S: But, by then, Kanhai's reputation as an attacking, attractive player, was it already established?

I M: Oh yes. Rohan was already a polished, flamboyant batsman.

C S: What were your impressions of him then?

I M: Oh gosh! Having grown up with Rohan and played school cricket with him, we learnt to respect each other. We were like two brothers. I would bowl all day to him; he did all the batting. And he would bat and bat and bat until the place got dark. If you had brought a gas-lamp, Rohan would have continued to bat. Batting was already his life. And he would play such beautiful strokes; he was always elegant, and you could see him trying out, experimenting, with a new shot, or polishing up an old one. Until today, I haven't seen any player with Rohan's skills, his gracefulness. Even in those early years, he gave me such joy, such life. But, to me, that sweep to the leg boundary, when he swept and fell on his backside, says it all. That came later.

C S: What Cardus called 'the triumphant fall'.

I M: Fantastic! I can't recall Rohan ever getting out playing that shot. He either got a four or a six. Beautiful stroke! A tremendous batsman! A graceful player! A dedicated player! Rohan had the dedication to cricket of Geoff Boycott, but more than Boycott, the Gods made him a genius. It was as if he always told himself, 'I am going to bat, and I must make runs; and I'm going to play some strokes that are not in the book.' And Rohan invented that sweep. Even from the early days, he knew that people came to see *him* play.

C S: What sort of a young man was he during those early days at Port Mourant?

I M: Full of confidence, but a very agitated person, eager to play all the time, to play non-stop. Give him a bat and someone to bowl to him, and he could go without food. But having come from a very humble family, and not having a job, Rohan was also very, very frustrated. He would go from job to job. He worked as a bus-conductor, as I said before; he worked on a bus doing the run to New Amsterdam. He also did labouring jobs. It was frustrating, but he was pleased to take it out on a cricket ball, even when I bowled to him. He had a temper, a fiery temper. And he took it out on the poor bowler.[19]

C S: Did he work at the Rice Marketing Board at Stanleytown, Berbice, at some point?

I M: Yes, he did. I believe that was after Rohan, Basil and I played for British Guiana against the Australians at Bourda in April 1955. We became established; respectable, I suppose. But Rohan was well on his way to stardom; he was already playing Case Cup cricket for the E.I.C.C. (East Indian Cricket Cup) in Georgetown. He played some lovely innings there. Anyway, after the Australian tour, I got a job with the Public Works Department, Basil went to Pure Water Supply, and Rohan joined the Rice Marketing Board. Sonny Moonsammy worked with his brother-in-law at his saw mill at Crabwood Creek, and Saranga Baichu worked at Skeldon Estate.

C S: It is often asked why, at this particular time, in 1954-55, so many outstanding players emerged at Port Mourant. How do you explain this?

I M: There are many reasons. I think that watching a great cricketer like Johnny Teekasingh fired us up in a way that we didn't, couldn't realise then. But, Clem, watching Uncle Johnny made us all feel that cricket came from heaven. He remains one of our unsung heroes. Let's hope that from today nobody forgets the name Johnny Teekasingh. Rohan, Basil, Joe and I can never repay him.

C S: Did you know John Trim?

I M: I heard of John Trim, we all heard of John Trim, but I had never seen the gentleman.[20] I found out later that he was from No. 11, Port Mourant. He lived near my moasie's [mother's sister's] house. So his little house was like a shrine to us, because he had played Test cricket for the West Indies in India.

C S: Yes, he toured India with the West Indies team in 1948-49, and he went to Australia in 1951-52.

I M: Yes, we heard his name all the time, and that was why, as a boy, I tried to bowl fast; we heard that John Trim bowled fast.

C S: Did he ever play for Port Mourant?

I M: Not in my time. He was much older than us. He was born in 1915, I think. And when I was a boy he went to live in Georgetown, so I never saw him in his prime. I did see him bowling for Demerara Cricket Club v. E.I.C.C., when I played for the latter. I didn't play in that particular match; I wasn't well. (We used to travel to Georgetown to play Case Cup for E.I.C.C. – Rohan, Joe, Sonny Moonsammy, Saranga Baichu and I. We would return to Berbice on Monday mornings.) Anyway, I saw John Trim bowl. He didn't impress me at all. But to be fair to him, he was well past his peak. But he was a legend to us little boys: he was the first man to leave Port Mourant to play for British Guiana and the West Indies. So in some little way, he cleared the path for us. Although John Trim was black, we saw him as our own. That was before politics and race made a mess of our way of thinking.

C S: Many have argued that while there was much natural talent at Port Mourant, had it not been for the work of Clyde Walcott[21] after 1954, you, Rohan, Basil and Joe might never have played for the West Indies.

I M: I certainly agree. Robert Christiani[22] came to Port Mourant Estate before Clyde Walcott took up his appointment as cricket coach with the Sugar Producers' Association. All I remember of Christiani was that he was there; he lived in the white people's compound, and that he was supposed to help us. I can't say that I recall what he actually did. It was Clyde Walcott who opened the door for us. He literally opened the doors and the minds of the gods of cricket and said, 'These chaps are good. I know something about cricket. Take a look at these fellas.'

I remember Clyde came one evening to Port Mourant, on his tour of Berbice sugar estates. He stopped in front of Roopmahal cinema and asked to see Rohan, Basil and I. He spoke with Raymond Boodram, who got a message to us to meet Clyde at the cinema. (Raymond was the son of the proprietor. He was a very kind man. He provided us with funds so that we could get clothes and other things.) It was the first time I was seeing Clyde Walcott, the man I had heard so much about. This was around August, 1954. We went to Roopmahal cinema; we met Clyde, and he invited us to go with him to a school bazaar at the Anglican school at Port Mourant. I said, 'Skipper, I can't go. I don't have money.' Clyde replied, 'Don't worry. Come along.' He gave me $3 and money to buy a pair of yachting shoes, trainers made out of canvas. He also gave Rohan and Butch money. And he took us in his car that evening to the bazaar, paid for us to go in, spoke with us for a while, and left us to enjoy ourselves.

I remember Clyde, this massive man with a deep, commanding voice. But I remember him as a kind, gentle man. He will have a place in my heart as long as I live. The next thing we knew was that we were playing in the trials in preparation for the Australian tour of British Guiana in 1955. Clyde was our captain, I think, against Australia. Rohan got a half century in the first innings; Butch got a forty-odd in the second. I got three wickets for one hundred and twenty something. I got the great Neil Harvey, Peter Burge and Ron Archer. This was the beginning, and we owe plenty to Clyde Walcott.

C S: Kanhai has written about this match and he mentioned that he cross-batted the great Keith Miller…

I M: That's right. That's right.

C S: …something Miller did not enjoy at all.

I M: That's right. I remember at the reception in Georgetown, given in honour of the Australians, Rohan, Basil and I were together. Miller came over to us and his remark was – I'll never forget – 'You play like this again (cross-batting; all three of us played cross-bat), I'll put a kick up your ass.' Those were his words. We admired Miller, because here was a man on the other side advising us how to play next time. I always took advice; Miller was a great person to my batting in particular. Rohan was already there – a lot of straight bat.

C S: What was Rohan's response?

I M: We didn't say anything; we were frightened: this huge whiteman talking to us. We were saying, 'Yes skipper, yes sir.'

C S: What impressed you about Richie Benaud's style as a leg-spinner?

I M: Oh! His beautiful reach, his disguise of the googly. And I tried to bowl the googly, but I just couldn't, because I was a natural wrist-spinner, bowling a lot of top-spin and the leg-break.

C S: Do you think that not having the googly in your repertoire was a setback?

I M: No. I don't think so, because my top-spin was just as good as the googly, and I used to turn the ball from the very first day of a first-class match, especially at Bourda. If anyone could turn the ball from the very first day at Bourda, that was good. I'm not being big-headed here, but I used to turn the ball; I turned it a lot. So it was not a case of my not having the googly militating against my selection in the West Indies side which toured India in 1958. I was a reasonable batsman as well. I remember in my first Test match, against Pakistan in Port of Spain, I stayed around nearly an hour to give Rohan the chance to make his hundred.

C S: He made 96.

I M: That's right. I stayed there till the end with Rohan. I would consider myself a good leg-spinner.

C S: It's almost an extinct species now, the leg-spinner. It's not often that a good one comes along; probably only Qadir is in the class of the great Australian leg-spinners of the 20s and 30s – Arthur Mailey, Clarrie Grimmett, Bill O'Reilly. But in 1953, a young leg-spinner, Subhash Gupte, toured the West Indies with the Indian team. What are your recollections of him, of the Indian team?

I M: I saw the Test match at Bourda in 1953. I was still in high school. I saw Gupte and Mankad. And when I returned to Port Mourant after the Test, I said to my family, 'One day I will play cricket on that ground.' I said it to my friends also, 'One day I will play cricket on that ground.' It was a year later, in 1954, that I played in the trials at Bourda.[23]

C S: What fired that great resolve within you? Was it the presence of the Indians?

I M: Watching the Indians – this was the first Test match I ever saw – observing Gupte as he bowled, watching the keenness, the neatness of the Indians; it was a privilege to be an Indian watching this first Indian side playing in the West Indies. Although I was born in the West Indies and I should have identified with the West Indies team, I was, at that time, in total sympathy with the Indians. I think that was true of most Indians in British Guiana in 1953. At Port Mourant, we were very proud of this Indian side, and it made cricket even more attractive to us.

C S: I have often been told that this was a great fielding side.

I M: It was a fantastic fielding side: people like Manjrekar, Polly Umrigar; Apte was like lightning in the field. They chased the ball to the boundary as if their lives depended on it; picked it up and hurled it in one motion right above the bails. Effortlessly. Cleanly. All day.

It was a feast for me; it was like eating a bowl of rice.

C S: And you love rice. Of course, you do.

I M: My stomach was filled; I was filled with joy watching the Indians play. I was filled with sadness leaving that scene of the Test match and returning home. But I became more dedicated to my cricket; I played with a new spirit. And I made that pledge to play first-class cricket on that ground. Gupte made a great impression on me. He was my idea of what a leg-spinner should be.

C S: What was his special strength as a leg-spinner?

I M: His stamina, his intelligence, and his ability to control his emotions. On a number of occasions when he was hit, he would stroll back slowly, thoughtfully, to his bowling mark, as if nothing had happened. And when you thought he was giving you the leg-break again, he would bowl his beautifully-disguised googly or he would toss it up or shift it. He would try everything in one over, a different ball each time. And rarely did he lose control: it is so easy to make mistakes when you are trying so many things. He made few.

C S: Always teasing the batsman to move down and drive?

I M: He made your mind work overtime. Always seducing the batsman, luring him to go for it. You know, Grimmett and O'Reilly had a master wicket-keeper in Bert Oldfield. I wonder what Subhash would have done if he had a 'keeper like Oldfield. A leg-spinner must never have to worry about the competence of the wicket-keeper; to be successful he needs a really great one.

C S: Rohan had many great confrontations with Subhash Gupte. He recalls an incident after Gupte had dismissed him twice in the Test at Kanpur in 1958. He whispered to Rohan, so that others nearby could hear, 'Hello, rabbit!' In the following Test, Rohan made 256.

I M: But Rohan and Subhash were very close, very close friends. It was through Rohan that I got to know Subhash very well; we became friends also. Yes, Rohan, in his long career, conquered great master bowlers – Miller and Lindwall, Tyson, Davidson, Trueman and Statham, Lock and Laker, Benaud, Gupte. These were all illustrious, brilliant bowlers. And Rohan mastered these men when there was no helmet, no padded this and padded that. Rohan would go out there without a cap and play against the chaps who hurled ferocious bouncers at him. He used to hit them all over the place, cutting, hooking, driving. Whether he played at Lord's or Calcutta or Sydney, it was like he was playing at Port Mourant – never awed by the occasion.

C S: What was it about the man that made him such a master against all types of bowling?

I M: As I said, Rohan was totally dedicated to cricket. He put every ounce of effort into his batting. His reflexes were as if God gave them to him at birth. He was also fearless. He saw each bowler as someone to be wiped out, off the face of the earth. What more can I say? He was a genius. You can't train a man to be a genius. What more can I say? As early as October 1956 when we played against Barbados in the Quadrangular Tournament at Bourda, I saw that Rohan had all these qualities already. He had the qualities to be one of the masters of all time. He made 199. I think...

C S: 195 run out.[24]

I M: 195? And that was against Frank King, bowling all his bouncers. Later, in 1964 against Barbados, against Hall and Griffith, he played as if he was batting at Port Mourant. He didn't care who you were; once you bowled against him, you were an enemy to be destroyed. In cricket only, of course.

C S: You got 4 for 61 in the first innings in the match against the great Barbadian team of 1956.

I M: Yes. And I remember Clyde enforced the follow-on against Barbados, and we were doing well when rain brought an end to the match. I got the wicket of Everton. Weekes twice in one day.

I M: It must have been a great prize.

C S: It was a great prize, but I think it was a prize that cost me my Test career. Because Lance Gibbs and I had destroyed several of the top West Indian batsmen – Allan Rae, Everton Weekes, Sobers, Goddard, Holt – the West Indian selectors' plans were shattered. The team to tour England in 1957 should have been selected after the Quadrangular Tournament in late 1956. We were told it would be. That was why all the matches were played in one territory, so that all the selectors could be there. But Lance and I shattered the selectors' minds. The team was not selected. Instead, we were told that trials were to take place in Trinidad in early 1957, and the team would be selected after the trials.

C S: An anti-climax.

I M: That's right. I hated being put on trial after I had put everything into the Quadrangular Tournament. I detested it. You see, if they had selected a team on the basis of our performance in the Tournament, then four or five established players would have been dropped, because several of us on the British Guiana side did really well: Joe got a hundred, Basil made one as well, and Rohan got two.[25] Lance bowled really well; he got many wickets, and I got four wickets against Jamaica and four against Barbados.

So we went to Trinidad to play trials. I was put in Everton Weekes's side, against Rohan, who was my wicket-keeper, and Bruce Pairaudeau, who had been my captain on several occasions. I played against them. I picked up one or two wickets for plenty. Joe didn't get much, neither did Basil. I didn't bowl well at all. I was slaughtered by Rohan and Bruce. They both understood my bowling, my tactics, my whole mental make-up. They felt sorry for me, and they tried to console me. I said, 'Thanks. Let's forget about it.' The night after the trial the team was announced; I wasn't selected for the English tour. They picked Andy Ganteaume [aged 35], Nyron Asgarali [aged 35], chaps who had faded out. I was deeply hurt. Bruce and Rohan were selected; they both got hundreds in the trials.

I was told by some prominent people that Everton Weekes held the position that leg-spinners could never do well in England; I was deeply hurt by that; I was depressed. I went back to Port Mourant, and I told my parents that I was giving up cricket. (In the two trial matches in Trinidad in January-February 1957, Madray's figures were: 28 overs, 3 maidens, 100 runs, 1 wicket.)[26]

C S: Has there always been prejudice against leg-spinners in the West Indies?

I M: Barbados had a leg-spinner and they brought him to England; I can't remember his name now. The Trinidadian leg-spinner, Willie Ferguson, was also brought to England. I was young; they put me on trial and I failed. I had never failed throughout my first-class career in British Guiana. And I was damn mad to hear that leg-spinners couldn't do well in England.

So throughout the summer of 1957, when the West Indies were in England, I played no cricket at all. I actually packed up and started to drink. I just took up drinking…[27]

C S: You think that Weekes had something to do with your non-selection?

I M: Yes. I'll tell you something that happened at the hotel where we were staying during the trials in Trinidad. After the team was announced, I bought a bottle of whisky, and Joe and I started to drink. I saw Everton Weekes and I asked, 'Skipper, would you like a drink?' He replied, 'Ivan, you drinking?' 'Yes, skip,' I said. 'I'm drowning my sorrows because I was not picked.' I could see a smile on his face, not one of sympathy – a sort of smile as if to say, 'Bloody right, too.' Not a word of consolation, not a word of encouragement. I really felt that the cricketing world had shut me out. It was a kind of death.

C S: Were you in touch with Clyde Walcott during this time?

I M: Clyde did his best for me to play. As you know, he was our captain during the Quadrangular Tournament. He had observed me closely; he had encouraged me. He thought I had a future in West Indies cricket, and he said it.

C S: You had a deep respect for the man.

I M: I will respect him as long as I live. I recall that during our match against Jamaica in October 1956, I bowled 84 overs for 168 runs and I got 4 wickets. I was dog-tired. I went to him at one stage and I said, 'Skipper, me weary.' He tapped me on the shoulder, as if to say, 'Go on son, the task will soon be over. You can do it.' That was all I needed. A new life came into me. I could have walked to the end of the earth for Clyde Walcott.

I always called him 'Skipper'. I never called him Clyde. There was no way I could call him Clyde. He was like a father, or a dear uncle. And that's how I still see him; I will always see him that way. He always brought out the best in me, and I always tried to do my best when I played under his captaincy. I never wanted to let him down.

C S: You said that for much of 1957 after your disappointment, you played no cricket.

I M: That's true. But I was a member of Port Mourant as well as City Star. And I did play a few matches for City Star in the Davson Cup; Port Mourant also played in the Davson Cup. So this caused an upheaval among the players at Port Mourant. And when I decided to appear for City Star against them in the final at the Port Mourant Ground, all hell broke loose.

On the morning of the match, when the two sides got together to prepare the pitch, we were told that the ground was not available; that it had rained, and that the ground could not be prepared; the pitch could not be rolled. I asked, 'Who sey so?' I was informed that the Welfare Officer of Port Mourant had given these instructions. I said, 'Abi a play [we will play]; nothing na wrang wid de pitch.'

We clipped the grass on the pitch, and were rolling it when the Welfare Officer, a Mr Baksh, came and ordered us to stop. Everybody dropped the roller. I persisted, 'We are playing; there's nothing wrong with the ground.' The Welfare Officer asked, 'Who are you to speak like this?' I replied, 'Who are you to tell us that we can't play? Do you know anything about cricket?' The argument between us got hotter and hotter, and I said, 'Gimme dis rolla.' And I grabbed the handle of the roller – my friend, the Hon. Welfare Officer, was standing officially between the handle-bar and the body of the roller itself – and I was dragging, I was dragging this man. I don't know where I got the strength from, as the roller was a massive, heavy bulk. Everybody was shouting that I was going to kill him, so I stopped. I lifted him bodily and said, 'Get out! We are rolling this pitch.' A message had already reached the Personnel Officer, Robert Christiani.

C S: What year was that?

I M: 1957, the latter part.

C S: Kanhai wasn't there?

I M: No, Ro wasn't there. Joe and Butcher were. I got Butcher's wicket. Anyway, the match was played; it ended in a draw. But we won on first innings, so we got the Davson Cup. But it didn't end there.

I was sent for by Christiani. He was living in the white people compound. I told him that he had to see my side of the story as well. He said that he didn't want to hear anything from me. He said, 'Get out from here.' He repeated, 'Get out from here, Ivan Madray. I don't want to hear anything from you.' He also told me that I must never enter the Port Mourant Cricket Ground again. I replied, 'You can't stop me. I am the Chairman of the Youth Council there, I will go back.'

They called a meeting – it was a big thing on the plantation; everybody was talking about it. The Administrative Manager was involved; my father was threatened with his employment; I was voted out of the Committee, and banned from the ground. I didn't accept it, but I took it. I resented them all, the big-shots, the authorities. The whole issue reminded me of my experience several years before when I was not selected to play for Port Mourant, because my father could not afford to pay my dues – a hate and a bitterness was there all along. And the whole thing started because I decided to play for the poor man's club, City Star. They took me in when the big-shots kicked me out. I wasn't going to desert them.

C S: After this incident in late 1957, did you not play any cricket in preparation for the tour by the Pakistanis in early '58?

I M: None at all. No training, no practice. As I said, I had actually given up cricket after the trials in Trinidad in early '57. I played a few Davson Cup matches in late 1957; that was all. And after this trouble at Port Mourant Ground, none whatsoever. So I was really shocked when someone told me that I was required to stand by for the second Test v. Pakistan in Trinidad in February 1958. Apparently, this announcement was made during the first Test in Barbados. I knew nothing of this. I had actually given up cricket. That was how the West Indies Cricket Board was preparing me for a long career in Test cricket.

So I asked some boys to go along with me to the Port Mourant Cricket Ground in order for me to get some practice, bowling on the concrete. It had been raining heavily; I could not use the City Star ground. Shortly after I started to bowl, the Welfare Officer, my old friend from the roller, came to me and announced, 'You are not allowed to come here.' I told him that I was required to stand by for the Test match in Trinidad, and that I needed to get some practice. He insisted that I must leave, or he would call Robert

Christiani. Imagine, I was going to my first Test with no cricket match for several months, no practice, no training. I was given a few days to organise myself, and I was not allowed to use the Port Mourant Cricket Ground.

Anyway, I flew to Trinidad, and my old buddy, Rohan Kanhai, met me at the airport. He was very kind to me, very loving. It touched me. He gave me new shirts, clean shirts to wear, and he took me to the Queen's Park Savannah to practise. He said, 'Come on, bowl.' I said, 'Ro, I haven't played any cricket in months. I've had no practice.' He encouraged me in that brotherly way he has when he speaks to me. 'Come on bowl, man. Yu ga pick it up quick. Bowl.' So Rohan tried his best for me in the circumstances.

C S: So you played in the Test?

I M: Yes, I played in the second Test. I remember my first few overs, I was just loosening up, trying to get the feel, bowling straight. And then, the first ball I decided to really turn, it was short, and it turned; I think it was hit for four. I think about the fourth over, I bowled a very short ball, I tweaked it, and Wallis Mathias went to pull it; he got a top edge. And Conrad Hunte, who was at mid-on, dropped the catch. Conrad Hunte dropped the catch. I couldn't believe it. I continued to bowl. Soon afterwards, one of the other batsmen, I can't remember who it was, went to drive me through cover. He got an edge, and the ball went between Alexander, the 'keeper, and Everton Weekes at first slip for four. That was an easy catch which Alexander should have taken. And I recall – it might have been in the second innings – Alexander missed a stumping chance off my bowling. So in my first Test match, not only was I physically and mentally unprepared, I believed I was picked just so that I would fail and be forgotten. I did try my best to hold my place, but I feel I wasn't given enough overs to settle in. A leg-break bowler needs a lot of overs, and the Pakistani batsmen were very cautious with me in the second innings.

C S: In the first innings your figures were: 6 overs, 0 maidens, 22 runs, 0 wicket. In the second innings they were: 13 overs, 5 maidens, 32 runs, 0 wicket.

I M: So, you see, I didn't fail, considering the several dropped chances. *Wisden* won't tell you so. But I recall when I was fielding by the boundary, at deep third-man, someone from the crowd shouted, 'We don't want more coolie in this side.' And then a cigarette end was flicked on my back. An over or so afterwards, a Coca-Cola bottle was hurled at me, and I complained to my captain, Gerry Alexander. At lunch time, in the dressing room, I was so dejected, so hurt, not at the words from the crowd, but from the dropped chances. It didn't seem real. It really hurt.

C S: And Gerry Alexander offered no encouragement, no consolation?

I M: Nothing at all. And he couldn't keep well to my bowling, and I think I signed my death warrant – these words will haunt me to my grave – when I said to him, 'Skipper, Rohan understands my bowling. Let Rohan keep wicket.' Without malice or anything of the sort.

C S: You were rubbing salt in his wounds: people were speaking of his weakness as a 'keeper, especially to spin.

I M: Rather naive on my part. I remember during that Test match, the only person who came to me and threw a consoling arm over my shoulder was Roy Gilchrist [1934-2001]. Roy was so kind...

C S: Contrary to the image painted of him.

I M: Right, I know the man personally; we became friends during the Quadrangular Tournament in 1956. Roy said to me, 'Man cho, nuh worry.' Those were his words. 'Cho man, nuh worry.' And that reminded me of my friend, Rupchand from Miss Sibi, who had said, 'Nuh hurry; me ga mek fu abi two.' I'll never forget Roy. At the end of play on the Saturday, he said, 'Come man, abi goh town.' We went and sat in a bar and chatted. I wasn't drinking. I had given up everything for the few days of the Test match – sleep early, drink Tono, drink milk. I wasn't having a nice time; my self-confidence wasn't there; but Gilly was trying to cheer me up. But I became more disillusioned as the match progressed. To make things worse, I was dropped for the third Test in Jamaica, the Test when Gary Sobers broke the world record [365 not out].

C S: The young player needs emotional support to build his confidence.

I M: I got none. I felt that they knew the circumstances, my lack of practice, my lack of training, etc. So I was selected so that I could fail and be written off quickly. I didn't fail, in spite of my difficulties. Holding those chances would have done a lot for my confidence. This is very important for any player.

C S: You feel that the main problem was the treatment you got from Gerry Alexander?

I M: It was.

C S: And this was related to the statement you made to him about his 'keeping?

I M: It was. I made that statement without putting any meaning to it, that it was a terrible thing to say to my captain. I was saying it because I felt that we had to play to win, and it didn't matter who batted or bowled first, it was the best combination in the circumstances that mattered.

C S: It is interesting that Clyde Walcott did not play in the Trinidad Test.

I M: If Clyde had played, I believe I would have had a lot of support, and I would have regained my confidence. He always brought out the best in me. When the Pakistanis came to British Guiana, I played under Clyde in the territorial game. I got a few wickets.

C S: You got 3 for 60.

I M: I bowled reasonably well; I can't remember how many overs I bowled. But I was starting to feel better about my bowling.

C S: In the first innings you bowled 28 overs, 2 maidens, 60 runs, 3 wickets.

I M: Jesus Christ! Isn't that good bowling?

C S: Very good.

I M: Well, the team for the fourth Test was picked; I was not selected again. So I returned to Port Mourant. On the night before the Test, Eric Atkinson fell ill or he decided that he wasn't going to play, because the bugger wasn't ill, but because of the wicket 'Badge' Menzies prepared…

C S: Good for batting?

I M: Yes. I got a message that an announcement was made on the radio for me to report to Georgetown. That's how the West Indies Cricket Board was preparing me mentally for my second Test match. Anyway, I didn't hear it. But Richard, Rohan's brother, and a very good friend, Brij Bahadur, and Dr Alli Shaw came to see me. They said, 'You're playing tomorrow.' I replied, 'That's rubbish. What are you talking about? Doctor, you know I'm not well. I've got my knee trouble.' Doc said, 'Don't worry about that.' He gave me a few injections and I played the next morning. Again in that Test I bowled and I got no wickets.

C S: You bowled 10 overs for 42 runs in the first innings, and 6 overs for 12 runs in the second.

I M: We won the match; Lance got 5 wickets in the second innings. I took a fantastic catch to dismiss Hanif off Gilly's bowling. I'm not boasting; I was very quick in the field. Hanif went to cover-drive Gilly; I was at extra cover; I walked in very fast, dived, and scooped up the ball. The team for the fifth Test was named, and I was dropped again.

C S: During the fourth Test in Georgetown, did you have any support from Alexander?

I M: Throughout my two Test matches for the West Indies while Gerry Alexander was captain, I did not get a kind word from him. He gave me no support. He was just giving me a couple of overs to pacify me. He wasn't concerned about me as a bowler; he wasn't concerned about my feelings, my welfare as a person.[28] I was going through sheer hell, sitting in the dressing room, sometimes not having lunch, feeling very sad, asking myself, 'How can I get a quick wicket? Gawd, how can I get a quick wicket?' No, Alexander did not encourage me at all. He wanted to see the back of me.[29]

C S: When did you decide to play professional cricket in England?

I M: It was just after the fifth Test in Trinidad. During the second Test, Conrad Hunte was reading a magazine [possibly *The Cricketer*] and I asked him to borrow it. That was where I saw that Penzance Cricket Club in Cornwall needed a professional. So, secretly, I wrote this address down, and I asked Conrad, who was already playing League cricket in England, 'What is professional cricket like?' He replied, 'Oh good! You can earn a lot of money, Ivan.' I didn't bother immediately. My main aim was to keep my place in the West Indies team. Although I wanted to play professional cricket, I knew that the tour to India later that year was on. So my mind was really set on going to India. But when I was dropped for the third Test, I wrote off to Penzance, and I got a prompt reply accepting me, and asking whether I could travel.

I informed Clyde of this, my offer from Penzance. His response was, 'Ivan, hold on. Ivan, hold on.' Clyde was positive that I would be selected for the tour of India. He said, 'Ivan, you will be going to India.' He was also positive that Frankie Worrell, that noble man, would captain the West Indies in India. This was during the fourth Test in Georgetown. So I took Clyde's advice and I informed Penzance that I could not take up the offer. Clyde left for the fifth Test in Trinidad, where the team to tour India was announced. My name was not there; I couldn't believe it; my eyes became dark; my mind was numb; I just didn't think it was real.[30] I asked, 'My Gawd, wha' de hell going on hay?' So I immediately cabled Penzance asking whether they were still prepared to have me. They said they were, and arrangements were made for me to travel.[31]

As soon as Clyde returned to Georgetown, he came to see me. He was very sorry; I could see it written on his face.

C S: He had nothing to do with the selection of the team?

I M: Nothing, nothing to do with it. He said, 'Ivan, I'm very sorry.'

C S: Did he give you an explanation?

C S: Clyde was more furious than I. I said, 'Skipper, it doesn't matter. Thanks very much for your help.' And he said, 'Ivan, I'm sorry.' And the way Clyde talked, his heavy voice, and the look on his face, he was hurt. He really wanted me to go to India.[32]

C S: You would obviously have liked the conditions in India.

I M: You know they ruled me out of the English tour in 1957 because they said leg-spinners couldn't do well there. In the 1958 season, in England, I took over 100 wickets; I made over 1,000 runs, although I came four games late. And I was turning the ball, whether the pitch was hard or soft. I was turning it even when it was damp. Oh yes! I really wanted to play in India. I wanted to go back and see where my grandparents came from, and to show the people there that I had made good. It would have been a great challenge. But I was never given a chance. I was only given about 40 overs in Test cricket.

C S: 35 overs.

I M: And that at a time when I was not prepared physically or mentally. If I was taken to India, I am sure I would have learnt, developed, matured and, perhaps, I would have picked up the googly as my confidence grew.

C S: Studying the great Gupte would have been a rewarding experience.

I M: An education. I know we would have hit it off, as we did in the League; like Hanif and I. I think that another thing that annoyed the selectors was that I became a close friend of Hanif. But then I got his wicket in the colony match, as well as in the match at Rose Hall, Canje – B.G. Indians v. Pakistan. I played my cricket hard. I got a few wickets in the colony match, so being friendly with Hanif had nothing to do with my not getting any wickets in my 35 overs in the two Tests.

I overheard during the fourth Test at Bourda, as I was coming down from the dressing room during the break, I heard Gerry Gomez telling Berkeley Gaskin (West Indies Board officials), 'Ivan doesn't have any future.' That was what I heard from that man as I went past, but I pretended that I heard nothing.

C S: Gerry Gomez had already made up his mind?

I M: It didn't strike me at that moment that that was so. I didn't realise that they were already selecting the team for India; the fourth Test was still in progress. It was long afterwards that I realized that Gaskin and Gomez were not prepared to give me another chance. Of course, Alexander was not on my side, and Weekes never supported me since I dismissed him twice in one day in the Quadrangular Tournament in 1956.[33]

Clyde had nothing to do with the selection of the team. Imagine a team being captained by this incompetent novice, Alexander, whilst this great man, Walcott, looked on. That says it all. The other man I admired, Frankie Worrell, was out of West Indian cricket at the time; he was studying at Manchester University. But I was told that Frankie was offered the captaincy for the Indian tour in 1958, and that he underlined that he wanted a leg-spinner in India. He didn't mention any particular leg-spinner. They refused him, and he turned down the captaincy as well as the chance to tour.[34] So at all times, Clyde Walcott tried to help me. But he wasn't exactly a darling of the West Indies Cricket Board.

And Clem, let me say this, Clyde Walcott and Frankie Worrell were two of the biggest men I ever knew. They had no time for race, pettiness, or spite. They were highly cultured men, who took a man for what he was worth. Nothing more.

I was told that Frankie also wanted me to go to Australia in 1960. He saw me in the nets around the same time they were going. I knew he wanted me to go. But he was again over-ruled. The long knives were out a long time ago for me.

C S: Why did you never return to play inter-colonial cricket in the West Indies after 1958? Would this not have improved your chances of regaining your place in the Test side?

I M: I never went back, that's true. I got married in England, I had a child. In 1960, when I saw the West Indies team on their way to Australia, Berkeley Gaskin asked me, 'Ivan, why don't you go home and play inter-colonial cricket?' He said that they would pay my passage and living expenses, but they could not provide support for my family. I said to Gaskin, 'Skipper, how come Peter Lashley and Seymour Nurse are getting allowances from the Board for their families? If the Board gives me some security for my family, I will return.'

C S: Lashley and Nurse were also playing League Cricket in England?

I M: Yes. These remarks were made in the presence of Worrell. Gaskin then suggested that I write to Kenny Wishart. I did so. But he replied saying that he was sorry that the Board could not provide any allowances for my family. I replied to Wishart stating that as the Board was prepared to give substantial help to others and little to me, I could not return; I could not leave my wife and child in England without financial support. So I wasn't going to risk destroying the little bit I had in England for an uncertain future in West Indian cricket, especially after the prejudice I experienced when I played in those two Tests in 1958.

C S: Looking back, Ivan, should you have approached things differently?

I M: Yes. I was an innocent from the country, and I didn't understand the nature of prejudice and the pettiness of supposedly big men. If I had known the nature of prejudice in West Indian cricket, I would never have made that remark to Gerry Alexander. That was like digging my own grave.

But I have no bitterness in me. I have had a full life; I am happy and comfortable. And I am so pleased that my buddies, Ro, Butch and Joe made it. I'm so glad Rohan's genius blossomed and became a gift to the world. Deep down, Rohan must have known that if he failed, he was out – as an Indian. He never told me anything, but I think that he always had this at the back of his mind, and that was why he tried to be better than all of them. And he wanted all Indians to be the same: attacking, attractive, dedicated West Indian cricketers. Rohan never let me down. He remains my living God.

C S: What do you remember of Joe Solomon?

I M: A most dependable batsman. I remember Frankie Worrell said many years ago, 'Whenever Joe goes to bat, I can afford to have a nap.' That was very true. With Joe batting, you could go in and rest for a few hours, because of his dedication, his great powers of concentration. Always safe. And Worrell, always a perceptive man, knew that Joe had a role to play at No. 6. He was the rock of West Indian batting during Worrell's time. As soon as Worrell went, Joe's career was over.

C S: And Basil Butcher?

I M: Different class, different style from Rohan. Not as graceful, but in his own way, a great batsman. He was a very strong player, he cuffed the ball; he jabbed it; he punched it. But a great player, a classical player in his own style, very determined, and like most of us from a poor family, dedicated to his work, to his batting. He was also a reasonable leg-spinner. He bowled the googly. And he was a good team man.

C S: What are your recollections of the late Sonny Moonsammy [1929-1963]?

I M: A player of outstanding class, a brilliant stroke-player. He had a great cover-drive, executed the hook, and was certainly one of the greatest cover-point fieldsmen I ever came across.

C S: Leslie Amsterdam once told me that he had seen a few great cover fielders, among them Graham Vivian of New Zealand, who went to the West Indies in 1972. But the greatest, for him, was Sonny Moonsammy.

I M: Sonny Moonsammy was the 12th man against Jamaica in the Quadrangular Tournament in October 1956. He went in to sub for someone, and I saw him pick up a ball from deep square-point, and he hurled it – you could only see one stump – he hurled it into Rohan's gloves, above the bails, to run out someone. Brilliant fieldsman, tremendous arm any part of the field. But he wasn't a close fielder; it would have been a folly to put him in the slips, or silly mid-on.

C S: Yet he never made the British Guiana team. [He did v. Barbados in Barbados in 1959.]

I M: If Moon were alive today, he would have told you that he encountered prejudice from Berkeley Gaskin. Apparently he played trials before us, sometime during the early PPP years in the early 1950s, and he made a 68 in which he hit Gaskin all over the place. During the second innings, Moon went off to the airport to receive one of the

PPP politicians from Skeldon. (I met him, but I can't remember his name), and they never forgave Moon for that. And when the time came to pick the team for British Guiana, he was not selected. So he never got another chance until Clyde came to British Guiana as coach with the Sugar Producers' Association in 1954. Clyde Walcott made up his mind, over the heads of the Georgetown bigots, to go out and find us. And for a man to go out of his way to look for people like Sonny Moonsammy and Saranga Baichu, Rohan Kanhai and Joe and Basil and myself, what can I say, he should be a national hero in Guyana, a real one this time.

C S: You mentioned Saranga Baichu.

I M: Yes, from Springlands. A tremendous, frightening bowler, similar to Eric Atkinson, a medium-pace cutter. Saranga cut it viciously: off-cutters, outers as well. In and out. He had a very short run, but he really pinned the ball down, and he bowled at the stumps.

C S: He played for Berbice on a few occasions.

I M: Yes, he played for Berbice, and he nearly played for British Guiana, but the competition was really hot then. Both Saranga and Moon should have been selected, but that would have meant dropping two more players from Georgetown. We had already replaced four of them. But the bosses in Georgetown were not prepared to do that. In the meantime, I think Victor Harnanan came on the scene. And Victor got his place for British Guiana because he was a good batsman.

C S: He only played for B.G. once, against Barbados in February 1964, with Hall and Griffith at their ferocious best.

I M: That's right. And he was never picked again. Someone with the great talent of Victor Harnanan was taken and pushed into the tiger's mouth and was then dumped. Other chaps failed, people like Colin Wiltshire. To me, they should never have played for B.G. Les Amsterdam was a far better batsman; they kept him back for years. But he also was from Berbice. Other people in Canje I knew could have made the side. And the present situation [1987] is even more prejudicial to the Indian, especially in Guyana.

C S: Any final thoughts, Ivan?

I M: Yes. I always told people when something went wrong with Rohan, keep clear. In March 1958, Rohan and I went to a function held in honour of the Pakistan team at the East Indian Cricket Club in Georgetown. All the dignitaries were there, including 'Wing' Gillette, the umpire. I remember Rohan and I went to the bar (we became good pals with Ikram Elahi, Hanif and Haseeb Ahsan); we went to get drinks. The Pakistani players took their drinks. When our turn came, there was some delay – Rohan was drinking whisky; he already had a few drinks. A man named Roopnaraine, the Secretary of the

E.I.C.C., asked Rohan to pay for his drinks. Rohan replied, 'We don't pay.' Roopnaraine said, 'The Pakistani team don't pay; you pay.' I never felt so humiliated in my whole life. We had to pay for our drinks. And Rohan said he was not paying. And Rohan went berserk. And he crashed all the glasses on the table. Nobody could control him, not even his elder brother, Richard. 'Wing' Gillette went to talk to him, and he told 'Wing' Gillette to go to hell. Rohan screamed, 'You mother-fuckas ahyu. Ah yu fuck off! Me a pay fu drinks and dem diss a get free drinks.' Me sey, 'Ro, be quiet.' And he pushed me aside and shouted, 'Shut yu fuckin' mout'.' He grabbed me to hit me as though to take out that hurt, that humiliation. Richard couldn't control him. He said, 'Ivan, you a de only maan who can control Ro.' 'Wing' Gillette came back to me and said, 'You are the only one.' I said, 'Skipper, I am not going to touch him. They told him we have to pay for our drinks.' I said, 'When he in dat pashan (same word me use), no maan can control him.'[35]

C S: Like when he was batting.

I M: Right. Exactly. Rohan's runs did not come in drops; they came like a waterfall, a fireball, all the time. People couldn't understand him; I did. And that's why I wasn't going to touch him. I allowed him to wreck the bar.

The next day Rohan was reprimanded. He told E.I.C.C. to go to hell. And I don't think he ever played cricket for E.I.C.C. again. Like what happened to me at Port Mourant. We played well; we did everything good for our village, our club. We wanted to do more; we wanted to go back; we wanted to help, but we weren't allowed to do that, because petty men always came in the way.

Yes, Rohan is my living God. Some years ago Sonny Ramadhin said something which will always stay with me. Ram was playing for Lincolnshire, Ro for Warwickshire. And Ro was dropped early in his innings. Ram was fielding at deep fine-leg on the boundary, and I was sitting, watching, along the boundary edge. When the catch went down, Ram turned to me and said, 'Lo'd boy, da coolie ga mek abi hunt ledda.' I replied, 'Da coolie a go kill ahyu.' Rohan made a century.

C S: Ivan, thanks. It's been an education.

I M: My pleasure, Clem. Time for a drink. On the house!

C S: *My* pleasure.

Notes

1. 'That Indian will make us hunt leather'. 'Hunt ledda', a colloquialism which literally means having to hunt for the [leather] ball, and is often used in describing an utterly destructive batsman. Madray attributes this remark to Sonny Ramadhin who was speaking of Rohan Kanhai.
2. It was common for young boys in the countryside to wear no pants or undergarments until they were well into their teens. Such lads were referred to as 'dem shut tail bai', boys in shirt-tails. Ivan apparently did better: he probably wore pants; the bottom, long eaten away; no buttons on the gaping crotch, with the front held together tenuously by the waist-band and the folds, suggesting an intent for modesty. So it was quite common for the willy to pop out and dangle ceremoniously as one chased after a ball or attempted a catch. That was acceptable; dropping a catch was a criminal matter.
3. Rohan Kanhai writes: 'Ivan and I were team-mates in the Port Mourant Roman Catholic school team. Joe, a little older, had been in the team before us. Basil was our arch enemy with the Anglican school.' *Blasting for Runs* (London: Souvenir Press, 1966), p. 17.
4. Schools administered by the Anglican denomination in British Guiana were called English schools; those run by the Roman Catholic denomination were known as Roman schools.
5. Kanhai writes: 'Naturally in school games lasting one afternoon the batsman had to hit the ball hard and often. This was my first kind of game and it has stuck with me ever since.' *op. cit;* p. 18.
6. Flood Cup. This was a competition played between the three counties of British Guiana – Berbice, Demerara, and Essequibo. It was named after Thomas Flood, an Indo-Guyanese businessman and founder of the British Guiana East Indian Cricket Club in 1914. The match in question was probably between Essequibo and Berbice.
7. Johnny Teekasingh, a leg-spinner, who captained Port Mourant when Madray, Kanhai, Salomon and Butcher played for that club. Johnny Uncle, as Madray calls him, is one of the legends on the Corentyne Coast, Berbice. When old men speak of their heroes in village cricket, they often invest them with Bradmanesque powers. As a leg-spinner, 'Johnny Uncle' was certainly no Grimmett or O'Reilly or Gupte, but Madray maintains, '…this old man, to me, was one of the greatest bowlers in my time; even when I played Test cricket.'
8. 'all-in-one', a popular dish in rural Guyana, which, as the name suggests, involves the boiling of rice with coconut-milk, and the addition of whatever is available. All-in-one and cricket occupy a position of kingship in the imagination of rural Indo-Guyanese men. Rum also.
9. Wata bai, the little boy who fetched water and did other errands for the cricket team. Boys vied for this position: it brought in a few cents, lunch, and the privilege to be ordered about by one of the local Bradmans. As Madray says, '…anyone who played cricket well had to be near to God.'

10. Sponge ball cricket was a celebrated activity in each village. It was played with a rubber ball, and involved under-arm bowling. Boys (and men) affected and perfected super-human contortions of their wrists so as to extract maximum pace, spin and break. The number of players per side could be limitless, and the bets hazarded induced fierce competition. A score of 10 was a mammoth one. And one could often hear mothers shouting themselves hoarse, waving a stick in despair, as they tried to get absconding lads to perform yesterday's chores.
11. Bung Yaad – bound yard, a section of Plantation Port Mourant, probably named thus from the days of East Indian indentureship, a place where the coolies bound to the estate were housed. As I recall, there are still sections of Port Mourant which are known as Portuguese Quarter and Nigger Yaad – sign-posts on the social landscape of the plantation.
12. Kanhai writes: 'Ivan Madray and I decided to join Port Mourant Cricket Club, where Joe was already playing, and Basil Butcher came along too.' *op cit;* p. 18.
13. Boys my age, growing up in the late 50s, could not have known that Kanhai worked as a bus-conductor; we heard that he did. Nevertheless, I recall that whenever his recurring knee problem threatened to keep him out of a Test match, the chaps would argue that the injury occurred when he worked on 'Superfine' or 'Honolulu' or some other popular bus. Often some smart-ass would pronounce that he saw when Kanhai fell on his knees, trying to lift a passenger's bicycle onto the tray, at the top of the bus. And he would insist that it happened in front of Globe Cinema or Harry Ganpat's, or some such place of repute. It was our way of repossessing our idol as his international reputation threatened to make him too elusive, too incomprehensible, to our simple minds.
14. In early 1961, V. S. Naipaul visited Port Mourant. He tells us how the people perceived themselves. He writes: 'Port Mourant is a sugar-cane estate of flat, hideous vastness, miles long and miles deep. The people are proud of the vastness, and believe that Port Mourant produces the finest Guianese. They are only slightly less proud of their cricketers than they are of Dr Jagan. The house of Joe Solomon, who miraculously threw down the last Australian wicket in the tied Test at Melbourne [Brisbane in December 1960], was pointed out to me more than once by people who had known Solomon ever since he was a boy.' *Middle Passage* (London: Andre Deutsch, 1962), p. 133.
15. Jagan (1898-1960), the father of Cheddi Jagan (1918-1997), lived at Port Mourant. He was born in India, and was brought to British Guiana, at the age of 2, by his parents who were indentured to Plantation Port Mourant. He was a 'driver' (head of a gang of labourers) at Port Mourant, and a rice farmer. He was also a member of the Drivers' Association. Madray's father was also a member of this quasi-union; and his difficulties with the authorities on the estate were probably connected with this.
16. The Kawall Cup was the symbol of cricket supremacy among the Indians of these three territories. It was donated by an Indo-Guyanese businessman, Francis Kawall, in 1941.

17. The East Indian Cricket Club (E.I.C.C.) was the premier Indian cricket club in British Guiana. It was founded in 1914 in Georgetown. As early as 1919, it sent a team to play the Trinidad East Indians. Francis Kawall was once President of the club.
18. Plantation Albion, four miles to the west of Port Mourant, has also produced several good cricketers. Its most celebrated player was 'Sugar Boy' Baijnauth, an effective left-arm medium pacer, who represented British Guiana in the '40s and '50s. He was often identified as a potential West Indies player. Albion is also the home of the former Guyana and West Indies all-rounder, Sew Shivnarine, who played in 8 Tests. He scored three half-centuries and toured India in 1978-79, under the captaincy of Alvin Kallicharran.
19. Kanhai has commented on his instinct for demolishing all bowlers. He writes: 'When I bat my whole make-up urges me to destroy the opposition as quickly as possible and once you are on top to never let up. I've never been one for second-best – that's why I never want fours, I want sixes. Once I've got the fielders with their tongues hanging out I aim to run them into the ground.' *op. cit.,* p. 16.
20. This is at variance with Kanhai's recollections of John Trim (1915-1960). Kanhai recalls: 'My earliest recollections are of playing cricket with my friends Basil, Joe and Ivan in the backstreets of Port Mourant, where my father worked in the sugar factory. Often 'Uncle John' would join in the game and give us a bit of advice… John Trim....lived next door to us; Basil Butcher 200 yards down the road; Ivan Madray 100 yards further on; and Joe Solomon half a mile away.' *op cit.,* pp. 16-17. John Trim played in 4 Tests. He toured India in 1948-49. His 4 for 48 in the Test at Madras was important to the West Indies' 1-0 victory in the series. He also toured Australia in 1951-52.
21. Clyde Walcott was born in Barbados in 1926. He played in 44 Tests between 1948 and 1960, scoring 3,798 runs at an average of 56.68. He made fifteen centuries. Henderson Dalrymple writes of him: 'He hit the ball around the wicket with such fierce, venomous power that many a bowler suffered injury in attempting to save his strokes going to the boundary.' *50 Great Westindian Test Cricketers* (London: Hansib Publishing Limited, 1983), p. 187. Walcott died in 2006.
22. Robert Christiani was born in 1920 in British Guiana. He played in 22 Tests between 1948 and 1954. He died in 2004.
23. Kanhai has recorded the bizarre circumstances surrounding their selection for this trial, and he has sketched the feeling of consuming awe which this big encounter, in the big city, released. He writes: 'Evidently there were three vacancies in one of the sides and the British Guiana Cricket Board asked Berbice, our county, to fill them. 'Cobra' Ramdat, a left-arm spinner who struck with the swiftness of his namesake, was an obvious choice. The other two spots were allocated to Port Mourant… The Club reckoned that three players – Basil Butcher, Ivan Madray and myself – all had equal claims. The haggling went on without ever getting nearer until eventually someone came up with a bright idea of drawing names out of a hat. You can guess who lost. That Thursday night I was nearly

in tears. To a boy of 18 a break like that takes on enormous proportions. It was like the end of the world to me... ...Next morning, Mr Duncan Stewart, the Berbice President, knocked on our door to tell me that 'Cobra' had twisted an ankle. 'Would I go to Georgetown?' he wanted to know. Would I go? I'd have walked the whole 90 miles if he had asked me to. ...after the first excitement, the rot set in. I began to feel nervous and couldn't sleep, By the time I caught the bus with Basil and Ivan at 4 o'clock on the Saturday morning my heart was pounding like a tom-tom. What a journey that was – 15 miles by bus to New Amsterdam, across the ferry, then a long, hot train ride into Georgetown, all the time clutching my old tattered cricket bag to me and trying to look calm... beneath all the nonchalant expression we were dead scared...' *op. cit.,* pp. 19-20.

24. The role of Clyde Walcott in the development of cricket in Guyana in the '50s and '60s, deserves a book on its own. To Kanhai, Butcher, Solomon and Madray, he contributed much to their technical development, erasing flaws and building confidence to experiment and advance. But it was also his knowledge of the social and psychological forces which shaped the character of these men that endeared him to them. He was compassionate, and, as Madray says, 'I could have walked to the end of the earth for Clyde Walcott... He always brought out the best in me... I never wanted to let him down.' No leader could hope for a better testimonial. The following quote from Clyde Walcott's 1958 book is largely about Kanhai. But it is also about Walcott, the leader. He writes: 'The more I saw of these youngsters, the happier I became. After their success in the first round against Jamaica they showed no signs of over-confidence – one of the most dangerous states of mind one can bring to cricket – but a quiet determination to do as well as, or better than, they had done before. During a break which came just after Rohan Kanhai had topped his century I talked to him in the dressing-room. I explained that a century was something that came sometimes to quite ordinary cricketers, but that a double century was a comparatively rare thing even for the very best player. If he reached this coveted target, I promised him, I would give him a bat... Well, Rohan was run out only a few runs short and, when he arrived back in the dressing-room he collapsed from fatigue – both mental and physical. I think he felt that, as much as anything, he had let *me* down: that I wanted two hundred runs from him and that he had failed me. I talked to him – he was in a sort of daze and my words took some time to sink in – and told him not to worry, that he had done very well indeed and would have plenty more chances to score double centuries in the future. At this he brightened up when, perhaps subconsciously, he realised that he had not let me down after all. A clever and likeable cricketer, and one of great promise, he fully deserved the bat which, of course, I gave him even though the 'conditions' had not been exactly fulfilled.' *Island Cricketers* (London: Hodder and Stoughton, 1958), p. 126. Walcott brought a scholarly circumspection and an efficiently brutal effervescence to his cricket. And he was a social psychologist. In December 1958, Kanhai made 256 at Calcutta in the third Test v. India; in March 1959, he scored 217 in the third Test

v. Pakistan at Lahore. It is necessary to compare Walcott's approach to young players with that of Gerry Alexander, the captain of the West Indies in 1958-60. See Madray's recollections of his two Tests under Alexander's captaincy. See also, note 28 for C.L.R. James's assessment of Alexander.

25. In fact, Joe Solomon got two centuries: 144 not out v. Jamaica and 108 v. Barbados. Butcher made 154 not out in the Jamaica match; and Kanhai had scores of 129 and 195 (run out) against Jamaica and Barbados respectively.
26. That this could have happened to a promising, young cricketer was tragic. And it was a sad commentary on the character, the aloofness, the social class background of the West Indian cricket czars. And, unfortunately, Clyde Walcott was away in England for several months in 1957: he stayed on for a course after the tour. Madray's impetuosity could/should have been channelled into his cricket.
27. Madray was deeply frustrated, violent and hard-drinking throughout 1957. His mind was certainly not on cricket. And Robert Christiani, the Personnel Manager at Port Mourant, himself an experienced cricketer, 'lived in the white people compound.' Madray's problems were none of his business! Madray would say that Christiani was one of his problems.
28. In early 1960, C.L.R. James initiated an unremitting critique of Alexander's captaincy, and demanded that Frank Worrell be made captain. The following incisive observations on Alexander's failure/inability to address Basil Butcher's technical problems explain the basis for Madray's despair. James argues: 'He [Butcher] was obviously mentally upset and unable (a) to wait; and (b) after waiting, to go through freely with his stroke. Butcher is a far finer player than his performances in the second Test would indicate. Here is where the knowledge and the authority of the captain come in. Frank Worrell could tell Butcher exactly what was wrong (his right foot is pointing too much to extra-cover and his elbow is out of place). Things like this happen to all batsmen at certain times, even the greatest. It was, it is Alexander's business to put Butcher right in the nets by having his fast bowlers bowl to him, standing behind and showing him what was wrong. Alexander cannot do this. He doesn't know. And even if he did, he hasn't the authority. Clyde Walcott will have to put Butcher right. That is the mess we are in.' *The Nation,* 12 February 1960.
29. One has to speculate on the circumstances surrounding Madray's precipitous inclusion in the West Indies team for the second Test against Pakistan at Port of Spain between 5 and 11 February 1958. I suspect it stemmed from Pakistan's unexpectedly robust response to the West Indies during the first Test – Hanif Mohammad made 337. Both Lance Gibbs and Ivan Madray were called up for the Trinidad Test in anticipation that the pitch there, as usual, would help spinners. And J. S. Barker wrote, 'Willie Rodriguez, scarcely the best leg-spinner in the West Indies, gave the Pakistanis a number of very uncomfortable moments last week, quite enough in fact to justify Madray's inclusion.' *(Trinidad Guardian,* 5 February 1958). Madray says that he was mentally and physically unprepared for this; he had played no major cricket since January 1957: 'I just took up drinking...' Did the West Indies selectors not know this? It was known throughout British

Guiana. Madray feels that he was selected so that he could fail and be dumped. He bowled a mere 6 overs for 22 runs in the first innings; in the second, his figures were 13 overs, 5 maidens, 32 runs, 0 wicket. In spite of the circumstances, Madray insists that he did not fail; he points out that three possible chances were missed, two by Alexander, the other by Hunte. At this point, he says, he told Alexander, 'Skipper, Rohan understands my bowling. Let Rohan keep wicket.' He is convinced that this was the signing of his own death-warrant. His selection for the fourth Test in Georgetown is even more bizarre. Madray bowled well in the British Guiana v. Pakistan match preceding the fourth Test in Georgetown: he got 3 for 60 off 28 overs in the first innings. He was not included in the Test side, so he returned to Port Mourant after the Colony match. On the morning of the Test, 13 March 1958, *The Daily Argosy* carried this caption:

W.I. WILL RELY ON SAME TEAM WHICH WON THEM THEIR THIRD TEST IN JAMAICA.

Madray argues that Eric Atkinson decided not to play, at the last moment, because he felt that the Bourda pitch would not suit him; he was not unfit. This was what *The Daily Argosy* reported on the pitch on the morning of the Test: 'The ground was in excellent shape yesterday afternoon and the wicket looked full of runs. I had a chat with Head Groundsman, 'Badge' Menzies, and he told me that the setting appeared to be one under which batsmen should revel. He did not know if and when the wicket would take spin.' So the fact that three scouts discovered an unsuspecting and unprepared Madray at Port Mourant, the night before the Test, and presented him to play at Bourda the next morning, is puzzling indeed. Why did they not select the Jamaican off-spinner, Reg Scarlett, who had been called up for this match? He would certainly have been more mentally prepared than Madray. Alexander, as in Trinidad, gave Madray a token bowl, 16 overs for 56 runs in the match, a mere 7 on the first day, almost a miserly after-thought. Pryor Jonas, with his devastatingly subtle wit and delicate sense of discernment, reflected on this absurdity in *The Daily Argosy*, 14 March 1958. He wrote: 'Eric Atkinson was declared unfit. And Eric Atkinson was your fast medium bowler used as first change with the shine on the ball. Who should be your obvious replacement? I refuse to answer this question. I have the feeling, however, that with his sparing use of an off-form Madray, Franz Alexander was the sole dissentient to the leg-spinner's selection. I respect, too, the feasible retort here – one selects one's bowler not in order that they may bowl but in case they are needed. Hence Madray's 7 overs for 30 runs, I suppose.' Whatever Alexander's views on Madray's selection were, his niggardly, intermittent use of the leg-spinner – a mere 35 overs (108 runs) in his two Tests, merely a stop-gap – was clearly not designed to boost his confidence. This, at a time when Madray himself concedes that he was physically and mentally unprepared, lends credence to his contention that his selection at that point was contrived to ensure his failure, and to prepare the way for his omission from the team to tour India in late 1958. A leg-spinner was needed, especially in view of

Gupte's mastery; and Madray, on the basis of his performance in the Quadrangular Tournament in 1956, was the first choice. But, he argues, Alexander and his friends in the West Indies Cricket Board had their own preference.

30. The West Indies team to tour India was announced at the completion of the fifth Test against Pakistan on 31 March 1958. Sixteen players were named, with Frank Worrell as captain. Kanhai, Butcher, Solomon and Lance Gibbs were the Guyanese players selected. Madray was not chosen; Willie Rodriguez, a leg-spinner from Trinidad, a novice, was preferred. Frank Worrell, shortly afterwards, turned down the offer, and declined the captaincy and the opportunity to tour.
31. *The Daily Argosy,* 10 April 1958 reported:

> MADRAY FOR THE LEAGUE.
>
> Ivan Madray, the British Guiana and West Indies leg-spinner, will be leaving for England shortly. He will be playing League Cricket for Cornwall.

32. I have seen no specific response from Clyde Walcott to the preference for Rodriguez over Madray. But the following report is highly suggestive. On the day that *The Daily Argosy* reported the news of Madray's impending departure for England, it also quoted Walcott as saying that the team '...was a bit short in bowling. That was due to the fact that only two recognised spinners were named – Sonny Ramadhin and Lance Gibbs.' A few days before, Walcott, aged 32, had announced his retirement from international cricket. On these matters, C.L.R. James's opinion could be trusted. He writes: '...at the height of his powers Clyde had put big cricket behind him. Why? I would say a general feeling that he was tired of intrigues and manoeuvres which were not based on cricket ability.' *Beyond A Boundary* (London: Stanley Paul, 1963), p. 223.
33. Weekes was dismissed twice in one day during the final of the Quadrangular Tournament in 1956. *The Daily Argosy,* 25 October 1956 reported: 'Weekes definitely looked unhappy against the slow men. We have never seen him like this before. He did everything but play the correct stroke. ...he got himself out lifting Madray to mid-on for Solomon to take a one-handed catch going backwards.'

    But Madray *did not* get Weekes's wicket in the second innings, as British Guiana enforced the follow-on. The same article continues: 'In came Weekes and he remained for 29 minutes for four runs before he was out – run out through a misunderstanding [with Sobers] and a good throw-in by substitute, Edun.' I am unable to say what impressions Weekes formed of Madray. But I can state with certainty that the great batsman would have preferred to forget his experiences in British Guiana. *The Daily Argosy,* 26 October 1956 reported:

> RAIN WASHES OUT LAST DAY OF QUADRANGULAR FINAL BUT B.G. EMERGE CHAMPIONS OF TOURNEY BY FIRST INNINGS VICTORY.

It continues: 'The Barbadians have been humiliated – and the chief architects responsible for such a state of affairs were the spin twins – Lance Gibbs and Ivan Madray, who shot out the Bimshire men for 211 in their 1st innings in reply to B.G.'s mammoth 581, and following on the islanders lost four batsmen for 67 runs at the close of play yesterday... We saw a batsman who was Everton Weekes in the physical sense of the word. He was not the same Everton Weekes, the West Indies and world class batsman we have seen and read of. Everton Weekes's batting was a comedy of errors, and a nightmare, and it is best we forget about it... The final has brought many interesting things to the fore. We have noted that this colony can depend on no less than four batsmen – Bruce Pairaudeau, Rohan Kanhai, Basil Butcher, and Joe Solomon... And that we have two spinners of top class in Gibbs and Madray – definite prospects for the English tour next year. ' The article concludes: 'British Guiana can hold her chin up and face the other Caribbean cricketing territories, square in their cricketing faces, because we have won and won handsomely, and the Barbadians cannot say that had it not been for the rain the outcome would have been different. A new era has been ushered in on the local cricketing scene.'

34. Several days after our conversation, I reminded Madray that Worrell was in fact named captain of the team to tour India, and that the Trinidadian leg-spinner, Willie Rodriguez, was selected. He replied that he was informed by a 'knowledgeable' source that one of the reasons Worrell withdrew from the tour was that the Board had chosen Rodriguez instead of him as the leg-spinner. He said that both Worrell and Walcott saw the inclusion of Rodriguez as another manifestation of the 'politics of skin' in West Indies cricket. And Madray adds, 'Everybody knew that in spite of my lack of form in 1958, I was still the best leg-spinner in the West Indies. Rodriguez was given my place because he was a local white, like Alexander, like Gomez, like Goddard. He was a novice, and we were the same age. If I were a light-skin man I would have been selected. That was why I was brought into Test cricket suddenly, through the radio so to speak, at a time when I was not physically and mentally prepared, so that I would fail and make room for Rodriguez. That was what Alexander wanted.'
35. Trevor Bailey reported: 'Originally his character, like his batting, was inclined to flashes of impetuosity...' *The Cricketer,* September 1973, p. 17.

Clem Seecharan reading from the Ivan Madray interview at Moray House Trust, Georgetown 2014

INDEX

A Bend in the River (V.S. Naipaul), 147
A House for Mr Biswas (V.S. Naipaul), 35 n. 22, 147, 152, 153, 157, 160 n. 26
Adams, Grantley, 283
Adamson, Alan, *Sugar Without Slaves*, 153
African Society for Cultural Relations with Independent Africa (ASCRIA), 266
Ahirs and cattle-raising (CS ancestral caste origins), 104-105, 129-131
Albion (Plantation), 102, 124, 321, n. 18, 229, 234
'A Leopard in the Sky' (McDonald), 17
Alexander, Gerry, 286, 309, 310, 311, 313, 314, 322, n. 28
Ali, Arif, 20
Allfrey, Phyllis, 28
Among the Hindus and Creoles of British Guiana (Bronkhurst), 73, 85 n.24
Argosy, The (B.G.), 24, 96-97, 165
Arkatis (recruiters), 114, 115, 120, 127, 135, 136
Arya Samaj, 66, 99, 122, 194, 197, 198
Aryanism, 87, 93-94, 96, 98
Asgarali, Nyron, 306
Asiatic Society of Bengal, 98
Atkinson, Eric, 311, 316
Backdam People (Monar), 112, n. 12, 249 n. 16
'Backra': the white managers and overseers, 102, 105
Baichan, Len, 123
Baichu, Saranga, 299, 300, 316
Baijnauth, 'Sugar Boy', 320, n. 18
Balgobin, Joe, 296
Bechu, 'bound coolie radical', 74, 97, 101 n. 14, 138 n. 11, 120
Benaud, Richie, 302-303
Benjamin, Joel, 24, 27
Benn, Brindley, 191, 192, 197
Bentham, Dr F.C., 60, 61
Berbice Gazette, 90
Berbice High School (for boys and girls), 70
Berbice Slave Rebellion (1763), 226
Berbice: and cricketers, 20-21, 109, 284
Beyond a Boundary (James), 116, 153, 154, 155, 158, 271, 273, 280, 281, 282, 324; Naipaul's review, 158
Bhagavad Gita, 69
Bible, influence on Guyanese language and literature, 186 n. 4
Birbalsingh, Frank, 20, 40, 247, 250 n. 41
Black Midas (Jan Carew), 84 n. 7, 227
Blasting for Runs (Kanhai), 32, 33, 158
Blunt, E.A.H., 131-132, 139 n. 23
Blyden, Edward, 266
Bogle-L'Ouverture Press, 267
Bollywood films and images of India in Guyana, 64
Bond-slavery and lowest castes in India, 133
Booker Bros, McConnell & Co, 25, 49, 53, 76, 77, 102, 103, 104, 105-106, 109, 110, 111, 179, 185, 192, 197, 204, 210, 218; dominance of Guyanese sugar plantations, 227, 228-229; Jagan's anti-Booker crusade, 229, 240, 241
Boycott, Geoffrey, 300
Brahmins, as indentured immigrants, 65, 125, 128, 129, 130, 131, 134; role of in sustaining Hinduism by inclusion of lower castes, 66; privileged role and fear of pollution in social engagement, 144-145; caste role, 146, 147, 148, 150, 151, 152, 157, 194, 196
Brathwaite, Edward Kamau, 253; *The Development of Creole Society in Jamaica*, 153, 253: creative creolisation and unequal power relations, 253-254; *Contradictory*

Omens: Cultural Diversity and Integration in the Caribbean, as a model for cultural relations, 254
Brereton, Bridget, *Race Relations in Colonial Trinidad*, 153
British Guiana Colonisation Scheme, 34, 40, 75-76; impact on Afro-Guyanese insecurities, 269
British Guiana East Indian Association, 24, 28, 34, 37, 48, 67, 74, 164, 233, 260
British Guiana East Indian Cricket Club, 49, 74, 318 n. 6
British Guiana East Indian Institute, 91
British Guiana Labour Union, 164
Bronkhurst, H.V.P., 73-74, 88-89, 90, 91, 93, 94
Burnham, Forbes, 12, 23, 51, 77, 110, 173, 180, 182, 193, 198, 200, 204, 225; split from PPP and formation of PNC, 173, 205-206, 246; electoral defeats, 1957-1964, 208; PNC violence to subvert pre-independence British Guiana, 204, 212-213; British and American support for in constitutional talks, 215-217; machiavellian triumph, 216-217; detention of PPP activists as 'terrorists', 219-220, 221; as Co-operative Socialist and nationalisation, 221-222, 241, 242
Butcher, Basil, 20, 109, 28, 235, 288, 289, 292, 294, 295, 299, 300, 304, 315
'Caged' (McDonald), 13
Campbell, Dr W.W, 99
Campbell, Jock, 18, 25, 28, 52-53, 102, 103, 104, 105, 106, 110, 111, 179, 184, 192, 210, 229, 235; on Guyana's need for foreign capital, 228
Canadian Mission (Presbyterians), proselytization among Indians and role in providing education, 28, 69-70, 73, 85 n. 17, 150
'Candlelight' (McDonald), 15
Cardus, Neville, 300
Carew, Jan, 84 n. 7, 227
Carr, Bill, 15
Carter, Jimmy, 78, 225
Carter, Keith, 178
Carter, Martin, 15, 43, 45, **162-188**: born into the 'coloured' middle class, 164-165; ethnic competition under Crown colony government in formative years, 164; literary and Bible-enriched family, 165; education, 165; employment in civil service, 166; introduction to Marxism and friendship with Jagan, 167-168; political work for PPP, 170-172; response to arrest and suspension of constitution, 171-172; early perception of danger of African-Indian divisions, 173, 174-176; communist vision, 173; political despair in 'Poems of Shape and Motion', 175-177, 178; denounced by Cheddi Jagan, 178; leaves PPP, 177, 208; joins Bookers, 179; response to riots of 1962, 182-183; on Cheddi Jagan, 233; *The Hill of Fire Glows Red*, 168: 'Looking at your Hands', 168; *The Hidden Man*, 169; *The Kind Eagle*, 170, 'All of a Man', 170; *Poems of Resistance*, 171: 'I Come from the Nigger Yard', 171, 'This is the Dark Time', 172, 'I Clench My Fist', 172, 'I am no Soldier', 172; *Selected Poems*, 45, 48: 'A Banner for the Revolution', 169, 'I Stretch My Hand', 169, 'If Today', 174, 'Conversation', 180, 'They Say I Am', 180; 'Groaning in this Wilderness', 180-181, 'So that we Build', 181; 'Jail Me Quickly', 182-184: 'Black Friday 1962', 182-183, 184, 'After One Year', 183; 'What can a Man do More', 184-185; essays: 'Sensibility and the Search', 179, 185; 'Recent Events...', 184
Carter, Victor Emmanuel (father of Martin Carter), 164

Caste origins of Indians in Guyana, myths and reality, 90, 128-131; opportunities for social mobility in British Guiana, 144; transference of untouchability to Africans, 145-146; residual caste instincts, 197; continuing significance of in Guyana, 66, 81
Castro, Fidel, 77, 123, 180, 182, 195, 198, 208, 210, 211, 212, 241
Catholic Standard, role in anti PPP agitation, 212; support for Burnham and PNC before 1964 elections, 214-215
Centenary History of the East Indians in British Guiana (Peter Ruhomon), 37, 40, 42, 138 n. 10
Centre for Caribbean Studies (University of Warwick), 45
Centre for Research in Asian Migration, 26
Chandisingh, Ranji, 200
Chase, Ashton, 167
Chaudhuri, Nirad C., 98
Christian missionaries, proselytization among Indians, 66. See Canadian Mission
Christiani, Robert, 301, 308, 309, 320 n. 22
Chronicle, The (B.G.), 24, 91, 97, 165; role in anti-PPP agitation, 212
CIA: destabilizing subversion in Guyana, 78, 212, 213-216, 223 n. 14
Cold War: Jagan and conflict with USA: 78, 180, 182, 192, 198, 204, **212-218**, 219; British and American collusion, 214
Constitutional conferences pre-Independence, 214-217
'Coolie stain', the: stereotypes of Indians in Guyana, , 87, 88, 90, 98
Cozier, Tony, 14, 44
Crawford, Hon W.C., 99
'Cricket: A Hunger in the West Indian Soul' (McDonald), 54
Cricket: creolisation of, 259; emergence of Indo-Guyanese players, 71, 109; and see entries on Ivan Madray, Rohan Kanhai and C.L.R.James
Cripps, Louise (C.L.R. James's lover in the 1930s), 278, 280
Critchlow, Hubert Nathaniel, 166, 167
Crooke, William, 135-136, 139 n. 22
Cropper, Rev. J.B., 27, 28, 69, 70
Crown Colony government in British Guiana, 163-164
Cruikshank, J.G., 30
Cuban missile crisis, 214
Curtin, Philip, *Two Jamaicas*, 153
D'Aguiar, Peter, 182, 198, 199, 204; anti-communist crusade and role of Catholic Church in British Guiana, 212-213; in constitutional talks, 215-216, 217, 218
Dabydeen, David, 18, 19, 20, 24, 26, 32, 40, 41, 43, 44, 46
Das Kapital, 239
Dayananda, Swami, 98, 194, 203 n. 5
de Caires, David, 11, 15, 25, 186
Debt burden, as motive for Indian emigration, 132
Demerara Publishers, 36, 42, 50
Demerara Slave Rebellion (1823), 169, 226
Devonshire Castle (Plantation), strike on, 65
Dingwall, Rev. J., 99
Discovery of India (Nehru), 116, 153, 154
DuBois, W.E.B., 266
Dunn, Richard, *Sugar and Slaves*, 153
East Indian Cricket Club, 299, 320 n. 17
Edinburgh Indian Association, 98
Edun, Ayube, 30, 76, 85 n. 29, 234
El Dorado, myth of in Guyanese consciousness, 61, 76, 84 n.7, 94, 110, 169, 223, 227, 247
Elections: PPP victories pre-1963, 77, 211, 225; PR elections 1964, 204, 218; rigged elections, 23, 77; free

elections, post 1992, 78-79, 225
Elvry, Ben, 'To India', 96
Engels, Friedrich, 239
Enmore (Plantation), resistance on, 65, 76; shootings on, 168, 169, 170
Epidemics of disease as motives for Indian indentured emigration, 133
Ethnic nationalism, 74-75
Etwarie (wife of Sewnath CS family), 103, 104, 124, 125, 131, 135
Family life (Indians in Guyana): joint family, 72-73; early marriage, 73; sexual relations in, 73
Famine, as motive for Indian indentured emigration, 132-133
Ferguson, Willie, 306
Fiji, Indians in, 114, 127-136; comparison with origins of Indians in British Guiana, 128
Finding the Centre: Two Narratives (V.S. Naipaul), 115, 138 n. 2, 140
Fishing (as sugar estate activity), 106
Fitzpatrick, Miles, 15
Flood Cup, 291, 319 n. 6
Friends (Plantation), resistance on, 65
Gandhi, Mohandas K., 33, 40, 75, 93, 115, 116, 122, 123, 144, 153, 156, 233, 236
Ganteaume, Andy, 306
Gaskin, Berkeley, 313, 314
Gibbs, Lance, 284, 286, 305, 311
Gibson, J.C., 231, 234-235
Gibson, Keane, *The Cycle of Racial Oppression in Guyana*, 81
Giglioli, Dr George, 70-71
Gilchrist, Roy, 310, 311
Girmitiyas (Indentured labourers), 114, 119
Girmitiyas and the Origins of the Fiji Indians (Brij Lal), 116, 126-137
Gokul, Harry, 289
Goldwater, Barry, 214
Gomez, Gerry, 313
Goodland, Arthur, 15, 29
Gorbachev, Mikhail, 242
Gott, Richard, 221
Goveia, Elsa, 153, 253, 262 n. 3; *Slave Society in the British Leeward Islands*, 153
Grace, W.G., 155, 156
Greater India, in myth and desire, 34, 40, 75-76, 93, 95; see also British Guiana Colonisation Scheme.
'Grief' (McDonald), 39-40
Grimshaw, Anna, on CLR James, 282
Guiana Review, The, 76, 85 n. 29
Gupte, Subhash, 304, 305
Guyana Agricultural Workers Union (GAWU), 202, 213, 217
Guyana United Muslim Party, 198, 202
Guyana: geography, drainage systems and African effort, 59, 60, 61, 226-227; demography, 70-71; African workers after emancipation and impact of indentured labour on wage rates, 60; food shortages in 1980s, 12; rigged elections, 23, 77; crime, corruption and the drug-based economy, 79, 81, 83; decline in educational standards, 80; mass emigration and loss of skills, 79, 80-81, 199, 222-223; loss of subsidies for sugar, 80; occupational and resource ethnic imbalances, 80; independence and British and US manoeuvrings, 204, 212-218
Hanuman Chalisa, 137, 155
Hanuman, 119, 146
Harnanan, Victor, 317
Hazlitt, William, 20
Hearne, John, 226, 249 n.2,
Hennessy, Professor Alistair, 19, 32
Hill, Robert, 281
Hinduism, in Guyana: 65-66; caste in, 66; festivals, 66-67
Hindu-Muslim relations in Guyana, improvements in, 260
Holden, David, 221
Hoyte, Desmond, 23, 31, 41, 51, 77
Hubbard, H.J.M., 167, 191
Hunte, Conrad, 285, 309, 312, 323

Huntley, Jessica and Eric, 267
Immigration Agents General, 62, 65
Indentureship: from India, 60; from Madeira, 60; funded from taxed revenues, 60; African opposition to, 60; numbers involved and origins, 61-62; recruitment and stories of deception, 114, 115, 120, 127; motivations, 129, 131-135; contractual terms, wage rates and return passages, 62; degrees of protection, 62; inequality under labour laws, 62; indentureship not a form of slavery, 63, 132; desertions and resistance, 64, 65
India, indentured labourers from, 60; geographical origins, 61-62, 128-133; hardship, land-hunger and debt-burden as motives for emigration, 63, 131-134; culture and incidence of labour migration, 133-134; gender and age distribution of migrants, 63; women as emigrants, 63; caste and occupation as factors in decision to emigrate, 134-137; as single passengers, 136; myths of India in Indo-Guyanese imagination, 64, 87-101
India: A Million Mutinies Now (V.S. Naipaul), 142, 159
India: The Progress of Her People at Home and Abroad (Joseph Ruhomon), 74, 94-96; responses to: 96-97, 138 n. 8, 259
Indian Diaspora, in Indo-Guyanese imagination, 92
Indian missionaries in Guyana, 99-100
Indian Muslims in British Guiana, 74, 129
Indian Opinion, 24, 34, 36, 41, 48, 49, 50
Indians in Guyana: myths about indenture as forced emigration and a new form of slavery, 61, 114, 115, 120, 127, 132; origins, comparisons with Fiji, 128-133; labour resistance on plantations, 64-65; rice cultivation and rise of middle class, 67; rise of business class, and role of joint family in sustaining enterprise, 69; education and rise of professional middle class, 69-70; gender balance and sexual relations, 71-72; restoration of patriarchy in villages, 72-73; the 'coolie stain', 87, 88, 98; definitions of self as 'not-African', 88; the making of a Guyanese Indian identity and the need for the African presence, 260-261
Indology, 98-99
Indo-Westindian Cricket (Birbalsingh and Seecharan), 20, 33, 40, 41
Intellectual life in Guyana, 27, 29, 73-74, 91
Island Cricketers (Clyde Walcott), 285
Jagan, Cheddi, 12, 21, 40, 44, 51, 59, 76-77, 166-168, 173, 190, 199, **225-251**: family origins, 114, 115, 225, 230-231; influence of father, 231-232, 236; humiliations of growing up on a sugar estate and anti-colonial passion, 231-232; hatred of caste, 232; independent spirit of Port Mourant workers as an inspiration, 235-236; schooling, 231, 233; 'lostness' and discomfort with Georgetown, 232-233; utilitarian attitudes to education and learning, 232, 233-234; lack of interest in literary culture, 233-234, 236; as a man without Hindu cultural moorings and sensibility, 194-195, 233, 236; lack of social involvement with Afro-Guyanese, 233, 234; absence of involvement with Indian middle class intellectuals, 233; departure to USA to study dentistry, 234; marriage to Janet Rosenberg, 237, 238, 239; interest in political science and discovery of Marxism,

167, 236-237; admiration for People's government in Czechoslovakia, 240; Marxism as total understanding, 237, 239; as a 'true believer' in 'scientific' Marxism, 195, 196-197, 210, 240; Political Affairs Committee (PAC), 167, 225; election to Legislative Council, 167-168; founding of PPP, 168, 225; British suspension of constitution and imprisonment, 205, 225; split in PPP, 173, 205-206, 246; attacks on 'left-deviationists and increasing dogmatism, 178-179; support for Castro and influence of Cuban revolution, 180, 198, 208-209, 210, 219; election victories (1957, 1961), 225; opposition to Jock Campbell's reforms and offer of partnerships with foreign capital, 110-111, 192-193, 228, 240-241; commitment to nationalisation and antagonism to joint ventures with foreign capital, 193, 228-229, 240-241; Marxist dogmatism and ethnic triumphalism, 180, 198, 211, 225; Indian loyalty to, 199, 225, 248; as local hero, 109-110; failure to recognise racial insecurity as an issue, 77, 146, 218, 244, 245-246; fatal meeting with Kennedy, 211-212; anti-PPP riots and subversion, 18, 204; tricked out of office by British and Americans, 78, 158, 199, 204, 215-217, 225; naivety at constitutional talks, 216-217; defeat in 1964 elections, 218; on true political independence, 204-205, 218, 220; boycott of independence celebrations, 219; explicit support for Soviet Union, 78-79, 195, 219, 241, 244; on critical support for Burnham's 'socialism', 221-222, 241; on converting the PPP into a Marxist-Leninist Communist party, 222, 225, 241-244; criticism of 'eclectic' Marxism of WPA, 243; on commitment to world revolution, 247; response to collapse of Soviet Union, 248; elected in 1992, 79, 83, 226, 248; as an incorruptible man of abstemiousness and unshakeable conviction but without self-knowledge, 226, 231, 232, 234, 236; capacity for El Doradian hyperbole, 236; *The West on Trial*, 115, 138 n. 3, 4, 221, 249 n.1

Jagan, Janet (nee Rosenberg), 167, 196, 197, 216, 237, 238-239, 243

Jagmohan, Sarran (CS uncle), 112 n. 5, 124-125, 139 n. 15

Jahaji/jahajins (shipmates), 119, 120

Jailall, Ivy, 235

James, C.L.R, 116, 155, 286, 322 n. 28, 324 n. 32; **271-283**: colonial education, 271-272; family background, 272, 273, 274; context of Trinidad post-emancipation, 272-273; Protestantism and lower middle-class racial consciousness in James's upbringing, 273-274; Bessie James (mother) and reading in the James' household, 274; discovery of cricket, 275, study of society through cricket, 276; Matthew Bondman and discovery of working class, 276-277; cricket as art, 277; writing about the 'yard', 277; rebellion against family and colonial values, 276, 277-278; Marxist Trotskyite, 275-276; acknowledgement of the tradition of Western European thought, 275-276; emigration to Britain, 278; as Marxist sectarian, 278-279; wives, 278-279, 282, relationship with V.S. Naipaul and portrait as Lebrun in *A Way in the World*, 281; as perpetual rebel, 280; in the USA, 280-281; CS unpersuaded by CLR's dialectics and political philosophy, 280-281;

view of Grace Lee Boggs, 281; view of Robert Hill on James' achievements, 281; view of Anna Grimshaw, 282; 'Triumph', 277; *Beyond a Boundary*, 116, 153, 154, 155, 158, 271, 273, 280, 281, 282, 324; *Black Jacobins*, 280, 281
Janjhat (Rooplall Monar) 73
Jarrell, Randall, 47
Jaundoo, F.E., 91
Jayawardena, Chandra, 66, 153
Jeffrey, Lionel, 178
Josa, Archdeacon, 99
Justice Party, 190, 198, 202
Kaila (CS maternal great-grandmother), and possible tribal origins, 118-121, 122, 125, 126-127, 128, 130, 132, 133-134, 137, 143, 155
Kala pani, 94
Kallicharran, Alvin, 20, 44, 235, 288, 297
Kanhai, Rohan, 19-20, 21, 31, 32, 71, 109, 155, 156, 157, 235, 284, 286, 288, 280-290, 292, 295, 299-300, 304-305, 309, 315, 316-317, 318, n. 3, 5, 320, n. 19,
Karran, Ram, 191, 246-247
Kawall Cup and Indo-Caribbean cricket, 298-299, 319 n. 16
Kaywal [Kilpax] (CS grandfather's brother), 122-123
Kempadoo, Fielda, 293, 294, 299
Kempadoo, Peter, *Guiana Boy*, 156, 249 n. 16
Kennedy, President John, 7, 180, 182, 192, 204, 210; meeting with Jagan, 211-212
Khan, Helen, 70
Khan, Marie, 70
Kharian (threshing floor), 119
Khilnani, Sunil, 87, 88
Klass, Morton, 153
Kowlessar, Katie, 70
Khrushchev, Nikita, 195
Kwayana, Eusi, 192, 196, 200-201, 243, 245-246, 266, 268; on attempts to forge racial unity before PPP split, 205; on need to confront racial stereotyping and insecurity, 207, 218, 268-269; critique of Jagan's lack of cultural roots and dependence on external model of Soviet Union, 196, 208; on Jagan's failure to confront racism and triumphalism in PPP, 207-208, 244-246; role in formation of WPA, 269
Kyk-over-Al, 26, 27, 36, 48, 166, 175
Lal, Brij, 63, 116, 11, 139 n. 31; *Girmitiyas and the Origins of the Fiji Indians*, 116, 126-137
Laski, Harold, 210
Lee Boggs, Grace, estimation of James, 281
Lenin, V.I., 172, 173, 178
Leonora (Plantation): resistance on, 64, 65, 76, 259
Lethem, Sir Gordon: liberal governor of British Guiana, 25, 165-166, 169
Little Lenin Library, 239, 240
London's Heart-Probe and Britain's Destiny (Edun), 76
Luckhoo, E.A., 29
Luckhoo, E.V., 29, 32
Luckhoo, Indrani, 33, 35
Luckhoo, J.A., 27, 30, 33, 36, 37, 40, 75, 76, 90
Macmillan, Harold, 77, 208, 213
Madeira, indentured labourers from, 60, 91, 257, 258, 259
Madrasis (Tamils), 62, 115, 128
Madray, Ivan Samuel, 20, 71, 235, **284-325**: context of interview, 286-287; growing up on Port Mourant, 284, 287, 288, 296-298; school cricket, 289-291; respect for elders and harsh punishments, 291; local Port Mourant cricket clubs, 292-294; becoming a leg-spinner, 292-293, 303, 304; playing for Port Mourant CC, 294-295; thiefing and survival, 296-297; playing for B.G. Indians in Kawall Cup, 298-

299; playing for Berbice in Jones Cup, 300; playing for British Guiana, 300-301; on race and class in cricket, 301-302, 307, 309, 316, 325 n. 34; on contribution of Clyde Walcott, 301-302, 312; on Rohan Kanhai, 289-291, 299-300, 304-305, 316-317; playing against Australia, 302-303; playing against India, 303-304; trials and non-selection for the Test side, 305-306, 320-321, n. 23; rebelliousness, 307-308; disillusion with cricket, 308; Test career, 284; selection for West Indies Test matches, 309-312; on dropped catches and failed stumpings, 309-310; not selected for Indian tour, 312-313; on emigration and cricket in the UK, 286, 287, 312, 324 n. 31; career in social work, 286, 297

Madray, Labrick, 299

'Magnanimity' (McDonald), 55

Mahabharata, 66, 145

Malaria, impact of eradication on Indian population growth, 60, 70-71, 77, 166, 235, 269

Malcolm X, 266

Mandle, Jay R., 71

Mandelstam, Nadezhda, *Hope Against Hope*, 43

Mangru, Basdeo, 64, 65

Mankad, Vinoo, 304

Manley, Norman, 282

Manpower Citizen's Association (MCPA), 76, 85 n. 29, 164, 213

Mao Tse-Tung, 178

Marryshow, T.A., 264

Marx, Karl, 172, 239

Marxism, 30; opponents of, within PPP, 193-194

Marxism-Leninism (Third International), 197, 208, 210, 211, 222, 225, 239, 241, 243, 245, 247

McDonald, Ian, 11-12, 13, 14, 111, 288; correspondence with Clem Seecharan, 22-53; vision of Indian contribution to Guyana, 14, 15-17; vision of humanity in midst of social dereliction, 15; *Stabroek News*, 'Viewpoint' contributions, 19; on Rohan Kanhai and Berbician cricketers, 19-20, 21-22; work for Guyana Sugar Corporation, 51; on censorship and corruption of language, 51-52; Frank Worrell Lecture, 54; on Martin Carter, 165, 168, 177

Mcleod, Iain, 77, 78, 208, 210

Mercy Ward (McDonald), 37, 43, 44, 45

Miller, Keith, 302

Mishra, Vijay, 262 n. 8,

Mittelholzer, Edgar, 84 n. 7, 91, 156, 164, 249 n 12; *Corentyne Thunder*, 165, *A Morning at the Office*, 249 n.12

Mohammad, Hanif, 311, 313

Monar, Rooplall, 73, 112 n. 12, 249 n. 16

Moonsammy, Sonny, 296, 300, 315-316

Moore, Brian L., 'Culture and Ethnicity in Post-Emancipation Guyana', 253-262: reservations about Walter Rodney's historiography on the importance of class, 253, 254, 255, 261, 262 n. 12, 269-270; on British cultural hegemony and the cultural subordination of colonised groups, 255; on material and temporal culture of subordinate groups: Africans, 255-256, Chinese, 256, Indians, 256-257, 258; brahminisation, 259; overemphasis on Hindu Indian cultural diversity, 258; inadequate treatment of economic spheres, 258-259, and of evolving culture of intellectual middle classes, 259; on Hindu-Muslim relations, 260; on importance of cricket, 259; *Race, Power and Social Segmentation in Colonial Society: Guyana after Slavery, 1838-*

1891, on the absence of a core Guyanese culture, 254
Mother India: in the Indo-Guyanese imagination, 64, **87-101**: India as a 19th century construct, 87-88; its Hindu-Muslim faultlines, 87; its role in countering the 'coolie stain', 88
Motorcycles, romance of, 109
Moyne Commission, 76, 166
Mudaliar, Veerasawmy, 91
Muller, Max, 93, 98, 99-100
Nagamootoo, Mahendra, 235
Naipaul, Seepersad, 152
Naipaul, Shiva, 149
Naipaul, V.S., 47, 59, 64, 72, 114, 115, 121, **140-160**: VSN's criticism of abstraction in academic discourse and his reliance on individual stories, 140-142; CS shared commonalities and intellectual promptings but disagreements with VSN, 143; VSN failure to see Caribbean achievements, 142, 151; differences from CS in caste background, 143-144, 145, 150; Brahmin privilege, social restrictions and way of seeing, 144-145, 147-152, 148; lack of religious sensibilities, 14, 148, 149; Brahmin arrogance, 151; VSN self-awareness, 151-152; on Guyanese fantasy, 223; on Port Mourant, 320 n. 14; on Cheddi Jagan, 196, 233, 234, 239; relationship with C.L.R James and portrait as Lebrun in *A Way in the World*, 280; *Finding the Centre: Two Narratives*, 115, 138, n2, 140; *India: A Million Mutinies Now*, 142; *The Loss of El Dorado*, 142; *A House for Mr Biswas*, 147, 152; *A Bend in the River*, 147, *The Mimic Men*, 147, 148; *A Way in the World*, 280
Naoroji, Dadabhai, 92, 93, 95
Naraine, Onkar, 291
Nath, Dwarka, 120, 138 n. 9
National Democratic Party, 192
Nationalisation of sugar estates, 110
Negro Progress Convention, 75, 85 n. 28, 164
Nehru, Jawaharlal, 114, 116, 122, 123, 144, 156, 206, 236; *Discovery of India*, 116, 153, 154
New Amsterdam, 13, 29, 34, 69, 91, 105, 112 n. 12, 156, 164, 171, 178, 300, 321
Nicole, Christopher, 28, 30
Niehoff, Arthur and Juanita, 153
Non Pareil (Plantation), resistance on, 65
Nurse, Seymour, 314
Pairaudeau, Bruce, 306
Palmyra Village, 14, 34, 44, 54, 104, 105, 106, 111, 112, 118, 121, 124, 138 n. 14, 139 n. 15
Panday, Basdeo, 44
Parmanand, Pandit Saraswat, 99-100
Patterson, Orlando, *The Sociology of Slavery*, 153
Payne, Tommy, 24
People's National Congress (PNC), 51, 78, 79, 80, 81, 82, 180, 189, 192, 200, 201, 202, 204, 208, 210, 211, 212, 213, 215, 216, 219, 220,, 241, 246, 247, 248, 263, 269
People's Progressive Party (PPP), 77, 79, 80, 82, 163, 168, 170, 171, 174, 175, 176, 178, 189, 192, 196, 197, 198, 199, 201-203, 204, 205, 213, 215, 219, 220, 221, 222, 225, 228, 234, 241, 243, 244, 245-246, 247, 248, 263, 269, 316; communists v socialists, Africans v Indians in 1955 split, 172-173, 205-207; Marxism and Indian ethnic support, 179-180, 189, 208;in power post-1992 and reluctance to share power, 79, 248-249
Persaud, Ganesh, 300
Pillai, Dewan Bahadur P. Kesava and Tivary, V.N., 90, 101 n. 5
Plumb, J.H., 142
Podgorny, Nikolai, 238
Political rivalry between Africans and Indians, 60, 71, 75, 76, 77-78, 79,

166, 175-176, 216-218; sources of African-Guyanese hostility to Indian immigration in post-slavery period, 226-227; African-Guyanese alienation, 79-80, 218, 270; failure to find constitutional means of power-sharing, 79, 81; stereotyping and abuse, 81-82, 198; failure to recognise mutual contributions, 82; need to lessen racial insecurity, 190
Port Mourant (Berbice), 16, 19, 20, 21, 31, 32, 52, 106, 109, 112 n. 13, 138 n. 4, 155, 196, 197, 225, 229, 230, 231, 232, 234-235, 236, 284, 285, 286, 287, 288-289, 290, 291, 292, 293-294, 297, 298, 299, 300, 301, 302, 303, 304, 305, 307, 308, 309, 311, 317, 318 n. 3/n.7, 319 n. 11/14/15, 320 n. 18/20/23, 322, 323; cricket and social life on, 235-236
PR (Proportional Representation) system as device to oust Jagan, 199, 215-217
Prostitution, 63, 71, 72-73, 107
Quamina, 169
Queen's College (Georgetown), 165, 166, 167, 222, 230, 231, 232, 233, 236, 253
Queen's Royal College (Trinidad), 271
Radhakrishnan, S., 100-101
Rai, Balram Singh, **189-203**: upbringing in mainly African village, 195; expelled from PPP, 190, 197; founding of Justice Party and policies, 190, 202; sees ethnicity as paramount over class, 190, 192, 195; long opposed to Marxism, 192, 193, 202; member of Jagan governments of 1959, 1962, 192; commitment to capitalist route to development, 193-194; as devotee of Arya Samaj and politics influenced by teachings of Swami Dayananda, 194; contrasts with Jagan's Marxist secularism, 195-196; awareness of cultural diversity and history, 197, 201; popularity of Rai in Indian villages until split from PPP, 197; demonization as racial traitor, 198; failure at 1964 elections, 198; exile, 199; shortcomings in political judgement, 200
Raleigh, Sir Walter, 61, 84 n.7
Ram Lila festival, 64
Ramadhin, Sonny, 317
Ramayana, 64, 76, 85 n. 11, 88, 94, 100, 105, 110, 112 n. 6, 114, 115, 136-137, 143, 144, 145, 155, 247, 258, 262 n. 8
Ramchand, Kenneth, 28, 40, 43, 44
Ramdeholl, Irene and Clara, 70
Ramdularie (CS grandmother), 112 n. 5, 118, 119, 134, 138
Ramharack, Baytoram, 189-190, 192, 194, 195; claim that Jagan was uncomfortable among Africans, 196, 198, 200-201
Ramjeet, Iris, 109
Ramphal, J.I., 82-83, 91
Ramsahoye, Fenton, 189, 191, 192-193, 200, 203 n. 11, 220
Ranjitsinhji, Prince, 156
Rastafari, 266
Reddock, Rhoda, 262 n. 10
Reid, Ptolemy, 220
Return to India of ex-indentured Indians, 115
Rice cultivation, in Guyana, 67-69
Rig Veda, 100
Robber Barons, The (Matthew Josephson), 236
Robertson Constitutional Commission, 172, 173, 187 n. 25, 188 n. 41, 205
Robinson, Andrew, 158-159
Rodney, Walter, 61, 243, 253, **263-270**: Kwayana on, 263; return to Caribbean from Africa, 263; on bringing pride in Africa to diasporic Africans, 264, 265, 267;

commitment to transcend academic orthodoxy, 267; commitment to address class and race in Guyana and build an alliance sensitive to cultural differences, 269; founding of Working People's Alliance, 269-270; attempts to overthrow Burnham dictatorship and assassination, 269; legacies, 271; *A History of the Upper Guinea Coast*, 153, 264; *A History of the Guyanese Working People*, 253, 268; *How Europe Underdeveloped Africa*, 263, 267; *Groundings With My Brothers*, 266, 268
Rodriguez, Willie, 286
Rodway, James, 30, 43, 60, 99-100
Rohlehr, Gordon, 30, 178
Roopnaraine, Rupert, 170, 171, 172, 187 n. 23, 269
Rose Hall (Plantation), 14, 17, 44, 104, 105, 106, 109, 112 n. 7, 121, 124, 313; resistance on, 65; CS ancestral beginnings on, 104, 118, 124
Roth, Walter, 30
Royal Agricultural and Commercial Society, 165
Rudder, Josh (C.L.R. James's grandfather), 273-274
Ruhomon, Joseph, 29, 40, 42, 43, 74, 76, 91, 94-97, 120, 259
Ruhomon, Peter, 29, 37, 42, 74, 91, 94, 120, 138 n. 10, 233
Ruimveldt (Plantation), resistance on, 65
Rupchand, 294, 313
Rupununi, 122
Russell, William, 27, 28, 29
Sallahuddin, 189
Samaroo, Brinsley, 119
Sanatan Dharma, 66
Sandys, Duncan, 78, 214, 215-216, 219
Schlesinger, Arthur, 213
Scholes, Dr T.E.S., 266
Scrimgeour, Rev. J.A., 69-70
Searwar, Lloyd, 15, 42
Seecharan, Clem, return to Guyana 1982 and feelings of suffocation, 13; inspired by Ian McDonald's radio broadcast on contribution of Indians, 14; search for ancestry, 17, 102-105, 114-127; begins research, 18; leaves Guyana, 1986 for University of Warwick, 18; correspondence with Ian McDonald, **22-53**: researching in London, 23-24, 36; encouragement to work on life of Jock Campbell, 25-26, 47, 52-53; reflections on role of historian, 29; evolution vs revolution, 29; marriage, 33; on spelling of name, 34-35; on lack of possibilities at Warwick, 46; completion of thesis, 49; publication of *'Tiger in the Stars': The Anatomy of Indian Achievement in British Guiana*, 52, 142, 157; publication of *'Sweetening Bitter Sugar': Jock Campbell, the Booker Reformer*, 53-54, 102; Family histories: Sewnath (father's maternal grandfather), 102, 104, 123-124, 128, 131; Etwarie (father's maternal grandmother), 104, 124, 131, 134; Sonbersi and Raghu (maternal great-aunt and uncle), 104, 123; Sohan (mother's paternal grandfather), 104, 118, 121-122, 128; Harpal, 125; Jagarnath (CS maternal great-grandfather), 125-126; Kaila (maternal great-grandmother), 118-121, 122, 126, 128, 133-134, 137, 143; Ramdularie (CS grandmother), 118, 119, 134; Sohan, Latchman ('Skipper', CS maternal grandfather), 122; Kaywal [Kilpax] (maternal grandfather's brother), 122-123; Baichan, Len, 123; Jagmohan, Sarran (CS father's brother), 124-125; 'Uncle Joe' Dhanna, 153; caste origins, 104-105, 122, 123, 126; grow-

ing up in Palmyra, 106-107; routines of sugar and rice cultivation, 107-108, 119; social life of workers, 107; play, 108; skilled workers, 109; unions, 109; India as an area of darkness to be lightened, 114-115, 121, 146; influential books, 116, 126-127, 153-154, 155, 156-158; discovery of C.L.R. James and passion for cricket, 155, 156; discovery of contemporary India and third world politics, 123; discovery of V.S. Naipaul, 156-157; identification with and differences from VS Naipaul, 145-152; freedom and enrichment of growing up within a vast network of relations without the restrictions of the joint household, 149-150; eclecticism of religious observance in family, 150-151; absence of gender constraints in upbringing, 151; a literate in a bookless family, 158

Selvon, Sam, 156

Sewnath (CS's father's maternal grandfather), 102, 104, 124, 128, 131

Seymour, A.J., 26, 47, 48, 49, 166, 186 n. 7; *Collected Poems*, 48

Shahabuddeen, M., 111

Sherlock, A.P., 43

Shinebourne, Jan, 112 n. 12

Ships' Registers, 12, 17, 114, 121, 123, 125, 138 n. 13, 230

Shortages of newsprint and books in Guyana, 12-13

Singaravelou, Professor, 44

Singh, Jainarine, 37, 38

Singh, Tulsi (friend), 19, 21

Sita (wife of Rama) and Indo-Guyanese women, 137

Slave Song (Dabydeen), 112, n. 8

Smith, Raymond T., 128, 129, 134, 139 n. 19, 258

Sobers, Garfield, 305, 310, 324

Sohan (CS's mother's paternal grandfather), 104, 118, 121-122, 128

Sohan, Latchman (CS's maternal grandfather), 122

Solomon, Joe, 20, 71, 109, 235, 284, 288, 292, 294, 295, 299, 304, 315

Sonbersi and Raghu (CS's maternal great-aunt and uncle), 104, 123

Soviet Union, 51, 59, 78, 173, 196, 198, 204, 210, 211, 212, 226, 237, 241, 243, 244, 245, 247, 248

St. Pierre, Maurice, 167, 172

Stabroek News, 11, 19, 21, 25, 48, 80, 81, 190, 248

'State of the Nation' (McDonald), 12

Stewart, Professor Thomas Grainger, 98

Stollmeyer, Jeff, 27

Strikes: African (in 1842, 1848), 60; Indians (in 1869), 64; (in 1872, 1896, 1903, 1913, 1924, 1939, 1948), 65; 80-day strike in 1963, 213-214

Suez, 210

Sugar estates: Backra and racial divide, 105; social life on, 106-110; routines, 107-108; landscape and drainage, 107

Suslov, Mikhail, 238

Swan, Michael, 59, 163; on Cheddi Jagan, 229

Swettenham Circular, 70

Tagore, Rabindranath, 43, 99, 176

Teekasingh, Johnny, 290, 291, 293, 301, 319 n. 7

'That my Son be Kept Safe' (McDonald), 38-39

The Ancestry and Origin of Our East Indian Immigrants (Bronkhurst), 73, 93-94

The Colony of British Guiana and its Labouring Population (Bronkhurst), 73

The Hill of Fire Glows Red (Carter), 168

The Hummingbird Tree (McDonald), 30-31, 41

The Last English Plantation (Shinebourne), 112 n. 12
The Loss of El Dorado (V.S. Naipaul), 142
The Middle Passage (V.S. Naipaul), 153, 157
The Mimic Men (V.S. Naipaul), 147, 148
The Origins of the Family (Engels), 239
'The Tongue Set Free' (McDonald), 51-52
The West on Trial (Jagan), 115, 138 n. 3, 158, 178, 221, 223 n.1, 249 n. 1
They Came in Ships: An Anthology of Indo-Guyanese Prose and Poetry, 41, 42
Thomas, Clive Y., 40, 83
Thunder, 168, 172, 173, 176, 180, 219, 225
'Tiger in the Stars' (McDonald), 14, 15-17
Timehri, 26, 27, 51
Tinker, Hugh, 40; *A New System of Slavery*, 153
Tri-Continental Conference, Havana (1966), 219
Trim, John, 235, 288, 301, 320 n. 20
Vaughan, Chris (wife), 18-19
Vedas, 66, 194
Veerasawmy, J.A., 49
Vivekananda, Swami, 95, 123
Voelcker, Dr., 130
Walcott, Clyde, 284, 286, 301-302, 306-307, 309, 312, 313-314, 320 n. 21, 321, 322 n. 24, 324 n. 32
Waugh, Evelyn, *Ninety-Two Days* and *A Handful of Dust*, 122
Webb, Constance (C.L.R. James's second wife), 279
Webber, A.R.F., 43, 163, *The New Daily Chronicle*, 163
Weekes, Everton, 306, 307, 310, 325 n. 33
Wesleyan East Indian Young Men's Society, 43, 74, 233, 260
Westmaas, Rory, 173, 174, 176, 178
Wharton, J.R., 91
Wharton, William Hewley, 75, 91, 94, 97-98, 99, 259
White Boy (Nicole), 28, 30
Whorehouses, 13, 18, 72, 73, 107, 108, 145, 150, 183
Wilde, Violet Eugene (mother of Martin Carter), 165
Williams, Denis, 85 n. 19
Williams, Eric, 282
Williamson, Karina, 41
Wishart, Kenny, 314
Women: as emigrants from India to Guyana, 63; as active in labour resistance, 65; access to education, 70, 73; relative sexual freedom under indenture, 71; male violence and restoration of patriarchy, 72-73; early marriage, 73; in post-independence Guyana, 73
Wood, Donald, *Trinidad in Transition*, 112 n. 10, 153
Working People's Alliance, 243, 263, 269
Worrell, Frank, 54, 285, 286, 288, 312, 313, 314, 315, 322 n. 28, 324 n. 30, 325 n. 34
Yangasammy, Sonny, 289

ABOUT THE AUTHOR

Professor Clem Seecharan is a writer and historian of the Indo-Caribbean experience, as well as a historian of West Indies cricket. He was born at Palmyra, East Canje, Berbice, Guyana, in 1950. He attended the Sheet Anchor Anglican School, Berbice Educational Institute and Queen's College. He studied at McMaster University in Canada; and taught Caribbean Studies at the University of Guyana before completing his doctorate in History at the University of Warwick in 1990. He joined the University of North London (now London Metropolitan University) in 1993 and was the Head of Caribbean Studies there for nearly 20 years. In 2002 he was awarded a Professorship in History at the London Metropolitan University where he is now Emeritus Professor of History. He has taught courses, in the UK, on the intellectual history of the Caribbean, the history of Indians in the Caribbean and the history of West Indies Cricket. In 2003 he was awarded a Certificate of Distinction by the Guyana High Commission (London) 'in recognition of his achievement in his profession in the United Kingdom'.

His main publications are (with Frank Birbalsingh) *Indo-West Indian Cricket* (Hansib,1988); *India and the Shaping of the Indo-Guyanese Imagination: 1890s-1920s* (Peepal Tree Press, 1993); *'Tiger in the Stars': The Anatomy of Indian Achievement in British Guiana, 1919-1929* (Macmillan Caribbean, 1997); *Bechu: 'Bound Coolie' Radical in British Guiana, 1894-1901* (UWI Press, 1999); *Joseph Ruhomon's India: India and the Progress of her People at Home and Abroad* (UWI Press, 2001); *Sweetening 'Bitter Sugar'. Jock Campbell, the Booker Reformer in British Guiana 1934-1966* (Ian Randle Publishers, 2005) [awarded the Elsa Goveia Prize (2005), by the Association of Caribbean Historians]; *Muscular Learning: Cricket and Education in the Making of the British West Indies at the End of the 19th Century*, (Ian Randle Publishers, 2006); *From Ranji to Rohan: Cricket and Indian Identity in Colonial Guyana 1890s-1960s* (Hansib, 2009); *Mother India's Shadow over El Dorado: Indo-Guyanese Politics and Identity, 1890s-1930s* (Ian Randle Publishers, 2011).

He has delivered several prestigious lectures, including the Walter Rodney Memorial Lecture, University of Warwick (2007); the Sir Frank Worrell Lecture, University of the West Indies, Cave Hill, Barbados (2011); the Leonard Tim Hector Memorial Lecture, Antigua and Barbuda (2011); the feature lecture to Global Organisation of People of Indian Origin (GOPIO), New York City (2011); and the 2014 Republic of Guyana Distinguished Lecture.

OTHER RELATED PEEPAL TREE TITLES

Clem Seecharan
India and the Shaping of the Indo-Guyanese Imagination
ISBN: 9780948833618; pp. 98; pub. 1993; price: £7.99

When the first East Indian intellectuals emerged in British Guiana at the end of the nineteenth century, most of their compatriots were still working as indentured or free labourers on the colony's sugar estates. Indians were conscious that they were looked down on as barbarous 'coolies' by other sections of the population. In response, the intellectual elite constructed a view of India, drawn from the writings of Max Muller and Tagore, which provided the Indo-Guyanese community with a sustaining sense of self-esteem and the sources of its resistance to colonialism.

Focusing on individuals such as Joseph and Peter Ruhomon, J.A. Luckhoo and W.H. Wharton, the study looks at the way the beginnings of the nationalist movement in India stimulated such individuals to start defining the nature of their presence in the New World. Seecharan argues that while the vision of 'Mother India' stimulated the community's cultural revival, it constrained the way it thought about Guyana.

'Dr. Seecharan's research is meticulous and his analysis penetrating. This is why, despite its specific Indian focus and slender look, *India* offers much insight into the broader history of Guyanese society as a whole.' – Frank Birbalsingh.

Dale Arlington Bisnauth
The Settlement of Indians in Guyana 1890-1930
ISBN: 9781900715164; pp. 260; pub. 2000; price: £14.99

As Guyana struggles to overcome its legacy of ethnic hostility between Indo- and Afro-Guyanese, this is a timely and unbiased study of the historical processes which led in part to these divisions.

It focuses on the crucial period when Indian indentured labourers became a permanent part of Guyanese society. It explores both the inner processes of Indian settlement and the beginnings of that community's political involvement with the wider society and relationships with the Afro-Guyanese.

It charts how, in the process, Indian peasants were transformed into industrialised wage labourers on the sugar estates, rice farmers and urban professionals. In exploring how a distinctive Indo-Guyanese culture emerged, Dale Bisnauth counters the tendency amongst some sectors of the Indo-Guyanese community to deny the humble, low-caste origins of those who were its makers. His is a history that gives full weight to the efforts of the nameless and forgotten to shape their lives.

The book also looks frankly at the ethnic considerations which shaped relationships between the Indo-Guyanese and the wider Guyanese society. In looking critically at the divide and rule policies of successive colonial governments, and situating both Africans and Indians in a common history of exploitation, Dale Bisnauth's study offers a clear and insightful basis for contemporary understanding of the role of ethnicity in a plural society and a cogent discussion of the processes of settlement and cultural change.

Simon Lee writes in Caribbean Beat: 'Dale Bisnauth has provided an exhaustive study of the Indian community during the period in which it became the most significant element in Guyanese society. This vital document on the region's largest Indian settlement and culture traces the history of ethnic hostility against a background of colonial exploitation and divide-and-rule strategy, and makes an important contribution to understanding not only the South Asian diaspora but also the complexities of Caribbean society.'

Ed. Joel Benjamin, Laxmi Kallicharan, Ian McDonald & Lloyd Searwar
They Came in Ships: an Anthology of Indo-Guyanese Writing
ISBN: 9780948833946; pp. 320; pub. 1998; price: £14.99

From 1838 until 1917, Indians arrived to work as indentured labourers in Guyana. The majority never returned to India and today over 50% of the Guyanese population is of Indian origin.

This anthology of prose and poetry shows how the Indians changed the character of Guyana and the Caribbean and how, over 150 years of settlement, Indians became Indo-Guyanese. Ranging from the earliest attempts at cultural self-definition in the 19th century (and early narrative images of the Indian presence in non-Indian writing), to the creative writing of the 1990s, this anthology provides a fascinating insight into the transformation of an ancient culture in the New World.

Extracts from novels, short stories, essays and poems explore the experience of plantation life, of relationships with other ethnic groups, issues of gender within Indo-Guyanese culture and the adjustments in cultural practices which separation from India and involvement with the new environment required.

Brief introductory essays by Jeremy Poynting set historical contexts, and there is an invaluable bibliography of Indo-Guyanese writing. This is the only anthology of its kind.

Stewart Brown
All Are Involved: The Art of Martin Carter
ISBN: 9781900715263; pp. 420; pub. 1999; price: £15.99

This book sets out to celebrate Martin Carter's life and work and to establish a context for reading his poetry. It locates the several facets of Carter's work in the historical and cultural circumstances of his time, in Guyana, in the Caribbean. It includes essays by many leading academics and scholars of Caribbean literature and history. It is distinguished particularly by a collection of responses to Carter's work by other creative writers, both his contemporaries and a younger generation for whom Carter's work and commitment has been a powerful influence on their own thinking and practice. As well as demonstrating the profound respect in which he is held as a writer, what emerges most strongly from this group of essays and poems from his fellow writers is the extent to which he was loved and admired as a man who – despite the turmoil Guyana has experienced over the last fifty years – remained true to his fundamental belief in the dignity of humankind.

Contributors include John Agard, Edward Baugh, Kamau Brathwaite, Stewart Brown, Jan Carew, David Dabydeen, Fred D'Aguiar, Kwame Dawes, Michael Gilkes, Stanley Greaves, Wilson Harris, Roy Heath, Kendel Hippolyte, Louis James, Linton Kwesi Johnson, Eusi Kwayana, George Lamming, Ian McDonald, Mark McWatt, Mervyn Morris, Grace Nichols, Ken Ramchand, Gordon Rohlehr, Rupert Roopnaraine, Andew Salkey and many others.

Visit Peepal Tree's website, www.peepaltreepress.com for further information on titles by other Guyanese authors.

Churaumanie Bissundyal
Malika Booker
Jan Carew
Brian Chan
Juanita Cox
Cyril Dabydeen
David Dabydeen
Mahadai Das
Michael Gilkes
Beryl Gilroy
Stanley Greaves
Denise Harris
Wilson Harris
Janet Jagan
Andrew Jefferson-Miles
Peter Kempadoo
Karen King-Aribisala
Harischandra Khemraj
Marc Matthews
Ian McDonald
Mark McWatt
Edgar Mittelholzer
Rooplall Monar
Moses Nagamootoo
Sasenarine Persaud
Rupert Roopnaraine
Vincent Roth
Judaman Seecoomar
Narmala Shewcharan
Jan Shinebourne
Denis Williams
Evelyn Williams
Milton Vishnu Williams
N.D. Williams